SHYNESS AND EMBARRASSMENT

SHYNESS AND EMBARRASSMENT

PERSPECTIVES FROM SOCIAL PSYCHOLOGY

Edited by
W. Ray Crozier

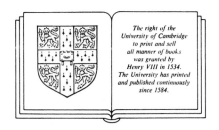

The right of the
University of Cambridge
to print and sell
all manner of books
was granted by
Henry VIII in 1534.
The University has printed
and published continuously
since 1584.

CAMBRIDGE UNIVERSITY PRESS

CAMBRIDGE

NEW YORK   PORT CHESTER   MELBOURNE   SYDNEY

Published by the Press Syndicate of the University of Cambridge
The Pitt Building, Trumpington Street, Cambridge CB2 1RP
40 West 20th Street, New York, NY 10011, USA
10 Stamford Road, Oakleigh, Melbourne 3166, Australia

First published 1990

Printed in the United States of America

Library of Congress Cataloging-in-Publication Data
Shyness and embarrassment : perspectives from social psychology/
edited by W. Ray Crozier.
p. cm.
ISBN 0-521-35529-X
1. Bashfulness. 2. Embarrassment. I. Crozier, W. Ray, 1945–   .
BF575.B3S57 1990
152.4'7–dc20 89–77376

British Library Cataloguing-in-Publication Data
Shyness and embarrassment : perspectives from social psychology.
1. Man. Shyness
I. Crozier, W. Ray
155.232
ISBN 0-521-35529-X (hardback)

To Sandra, John, and Beth

Contents

Part III   An emphasis upon shyness

Acknowledgements

Two symposia at British Psychological Society conferences provided an impetus to my own thinking on shyness and embarrassment and led me to believe that there were fundamental questions in this area that could usefully be examined at book length. I am grateful to the participants in those symposia, three of whom have contributed to this volume – Jens Asendorpf, Robert Edelmann, Peter Harris – and to Tony Manstead. I thank, too, the Research Committee and the School of Psychology of Lancashire Polytechnic for enabling me to attend those conferences and for supporting the research described in my own chapter. My thanks also go to all the contributors to this volume, to Susan Milmoe, and to Helen Wheeler, Michael Gnat, and their colleagues at Cambridge University Press for their support in the development and production of this book. I have been fortunate in having had the opportunity to study shyness and related psychological topics for several years, and I am indebted to many for their support and encouragement over that time. In particular, I owe much to my parents, Vina and the late Walter Crozier, to Sandra Crozier, and to John Archer, Tony Chapman, Michael Crowther, Paul Greenhalgh, Andrew Hill, and Robert Ranyard.

Preston, July 1989   Ray Crozier

Contributors

ROBERT M. ARKIN, Department of Psychology, Ohio State University, Columbus, OH 43210, USA

JENS ASENDORPF, Max-Planck-Institute for Psychological Research, Postfach 440109, Leopoldstrasse 24, D-8000 Munich 40, Federal Republic of Germany

STEPHEN R. BRIGGS, Department of Psychology, University of Tulsa, Tulsa, OK 74104, USA

CRISTIANO CASTELFRANCHI, Istituto di Psicologia del Consiglio Nazionale Italia, Viale Marx, 15, 00156 Roma, Italy

JONATHAN M. CHEEK, Department of Psychology, Wellesley College, Wellesley, MA 02181, USA

PATRICIA A. CLELAND, Addiction Research Foundation, 33 Russell Street, Toronto, ON M5S 2S1, Canada

W. RAY CROZIER, School of Psychology, Lancashire Polytechnic, Preston, PR1 2TQ, United Kingdom

ROBERT J. EDELMANN, Department of Psychology, University of Surrey, Guildford, GU2 5XH, United Kingdom

FREDERICK X. GIBBONS, Psychology Department, Iowa State University, Ames, IA 50010, USA

PAUL GILBERT, South Derbyshire Health Authority and University of Leicester, Kingsway-Pastures Unit, Masson House, Pastures Hospital, Mickleover, Derby, DE3 5DO, United Kingdom

ROM HARRÉ, Sub-Faculty of Philosophy, University of Oxford, 10 Merton Street, Oxford, OX1 4JJ, United Kingdom

PETER R. HARRIS, Psychology Division, School of Natural Sciences, The Hatfield Polytechnic, College Lane, Hatfield, Herts., AL10 9AB, United Kingdom

LORNE M. HARTMAN, Jackson–Smye, Yonge Corporate Centre, 4100 Yonge Street, Suite 503, Toronto, ON M2P 2B5, Canada

ISABELLA POGGI, Dipartimento di Scienza del Linguaggio, Universita di Roma "La Sapienza", Via del Castro Pretorio 20, 00195 Roma, Italy

JAMES A. SHEPPERD, Department of Psychology, College of the Holy Cross, Worcester, MA 01610, USA

PETER TROWER, Solihull Health Authority and University of Birmingham, Middlefield, Station Road, Knowle, Solihull, West Midlands, B93 0PX, United Kingdom

HENK T. VAN DER MOLEN, Department of Personality and Educational Psychology, University of Groningen, Grote Markt 31–32, 9712 HV Groningen, The Netherlands

Introduction

W. RAY CROZIER

The terms *shyness* and *embarrassment* are familiar to us all and describe experiences that are widely shared in our culture. My 6-year-old daughter can use both words in the appropriate context. Incidents can be embarrassing, or someone can appear to be embarrassed, whereas "shyness" can describe a person ("He's shy") or a reaction to a situation ("Why were you shy when we visited so-and-so?"). Some interesting descriptive research, such as that of Zimbardo, Pilkonis, and Norwood (1974) and Zimbardo (1986), has established that the experience of shyness is indeed widespread and is not restricted to any one age group, gender, or class of persons (shy people). Similarly, surveys have provided useful insights into the experience of embarrassment (see Edelmann, this volume).

Nevertheless, as is so often the case in psychology, closer scrutiny of routine social experiences shows that these are much more problematic than they at first appear, and the states of shyness and embarrassment raise fundamental and difficult questions about the social psychology of interpersonal behaviour. Indeed, as this volume demonstrates, there is scarcely an area of contemporary psychological enquiry that is not recruited in an attempt to classify and explain the experiences of shyness and embarrassment, and researchers in this field find that they have to draw upon concepts from personality theory, social psychology, psychophysiology, sociobiology, and clinical psychology, in relation to the self, the nature of emotion, social norms, group dynamics, and the study of language, to take but a sample. A major objective of this volume is to bring together for comparison and reflection a range of different perspectives upon shyness and embarrassment. We have imposed some order on the arrangement of chapters, in that part I includes chapters that tend to consider shyness and embarrassment together, whereas the remaining two parts focus on one or the other, but this is not a rigid classification, and indeed one of our principal objectives is to bring together phenomena that usually have received separate attention.

I

The meaning of shyness and embarrassment

It might be thought that it would be useful to begin to meet this objective by providing definitions of the subject matter of the volume, but here, too, we are are quickly into controversy: There is as yet no consensus as to definitions; indeed, there is dispute whether or not it is appropriate to offer definitions at all (Harris, 1984; see also Harris, this volume). Harris has argued that because "shyness" (and a similar argument could be made for "embarrassment") is in the lay vocabulary, psychologists have no business to define it and are only storing up conceptual confusion by doing so. Psychologists are free to invent and define technical terms where appropriate, but their job is to attempt to understand the lay use of personality terms, not to prescribe their use. The relationship between implicit and explicit conceptualisations of shyness and embarrassment is addressed in several contributions to this volume and remains an important issue. Ortony, Clore, and Collins (1988) have addressed a related question in their discussion of the vocabulary of emotions, in which they distinguish between emotion *types* and emotion *tokens*. There is a very large number of words that refer to emotions, but these may provide an incomplete or misleading guide to the structure of emotions:

> Thus, instead of selecting as its theoretical terms particular English emotion words (e.g., "fear"), the theory purports to be a theory about emotions themselves – what we have called "emotion types" – characterized in terms of their cognitive eliciting conditions. Having characterized emotions in this way, it then becomes possible, as a separate enterprise, to investigate the degree to which and the way in which the emotion words in any particular language map onto the hypothesized emotion types. (Ortony et al., 1988, p. 173)

Inspection of a thesaurus or dictionary of synonyms reveals a large number of "tokens" of shyness and embarrassment – bashfulness, humiliation, mortification, shame, self-consciousness, timidity, wariness, and so on – and we can pose the question of what emotion types might underlie this diversity. Crozier (chapter 1) has approached this empirically in an analysis of similarity relationships among these words and has proposed that there are four discernible clusters in overlap in meaning, as operationalised in terms of shared synonyms and antonyms in a dictionary: guilty, penitent, and repentant; ashamed, embarrassed, and humiliated; afraid and anxious; bashful, self-conscious, shy, and timid.

Although such exploratory studies will have their place, it is apparent that progress must be made on many fronts, including conceptual analysis of the kind recommended by Harré in his chapter on embarrassment (chapter 6) and the development of a theoretical framework that can underpin empirical enquiry. We can identify several enduring influences upon the development of theory and methodology in this area: personality trait theory, social skills theory, approaches to the classification of human emotions, and the study of social encounters. We may also identify more recent perspectives from the social psychology of the self, drawing in particular upon the burgeoning interest in self-awareness and impression management.

Theoretical approaches to shyness and embarrassment

The personality trait approach

Although the trait approach, in association with multivariate statistical techniques, has achieved some ascendancy in the study of personality, there is dispute as to its productivity in the investigation of shyness and embarrassment; for many years it led to the neglect of shyness (Crozier, 1979), and more recently it has encouraged a proliferation of trait labels and ultimately scepticism among many psychologists as to the value of studying shyness. Nevertheless, psychologists are understandably reluctant to relinquish this approach: It can have useful classification and clarification functions on the one hand, and on the other hand there is considerable support from everyday understanding and from surveys that people are willing to attribute a disposition towards shyness to themselves and to others. Several questionnaires purporting to measure shyness have been constructed, and a considerable body of findings about individual differences is now emerging (Jones, Cheek, & Briggs, 1986). Cheek and Briggs (chapter 11) argue that there is now considerable evidence to support the status of shyness as a personality trait and that criticisms of this approach have been targeted at a very impoverished version of trait theory. They review a large number of studies on the development of shyness and on its correlates, proposing that a clear picture of shyness is emerging. Although a trait of embarrassability has been posited (Edelmann, 1987), it has not attracted as much attention, and its relationship to shyness is unclear: Shyness may *be* embarrassability. There has been some dispute whether or not the underlying trait is social anxiety, and that is examined in a number of chapters in this volume. Leary (1986, pp. 28–31) has defined shyness as a syndrome of social anxiety and inhibited social behaviour, or, rather, he has suggested that it would be less ambiguous and of greater heuristic value to distinguish these two components. Cheek and Briggs counter that it is necessary to distinguish three components of shyness: somatic anxiety, cognitive symptoms, and awkward or inhibited social behaviour. Many of our contributors share the assumption that individual differences in the potential to be shy can be accounted for in terms of differences in social anxiety, but problems do arise when we flesh out what is meant by this term and in particular if we assume, as does Leary, that the affective experience of shyness is anxiety or nervousness. Crozier (chapter 1) and Harris (chapter 2) propose that this assumption is at the very least controversial and is in need of further investigation. Harris suggests that the balance of available evidence is against the proposition that "the affective experience underlying all states of social anxiety is anxiety". A further set of problems arises if the concept of social anxiety is extended to the experience of embarrassment (see Edelmann, chapter 7, for a review of studies guided by such an approach); it has proved possible to provide meaningful accounts of embarrassment without recourse to the notion of anxiety (Babcock, 1988; see also Harris, this volume; and Harré, this volume), and this notion may be inappropriate in the explanation of vicarious embarrassment. Harris also points out that whereas embarrassment is essentially reactive, anxiety is generally believed to be anticipatory. The nature of the relationships among anxiety, shyness, and embarrassment is problematic and is examined from varied perspectives in this volume.

Social skills and intervention

Equally perplexing is the relationship between overt behaviour and shyness and embarrassment. It is integral, I think, to our common-sense understanding of shyness (and embarrassment) that overt behaviour is inhibited (or interrupted) and that this is accompanied by feelings of not knowing what to do or say, of awkwardness, of foolishness, or of being flustered. There is an immediate problem in identifying shyness or embarrassment with any behavioural display: Mr. Jones might plausibly report that he is shy or that he has been embarrassed when to an observer his appearance is one of poise and composure. That is why theorists like Cheek and Briggs have felt it necessary to postulate different components of shyness. Nevertheless, Asendorpf's thorough review of the literature on dispositional shyness (chapter 3) concludes that studies do show that "shy people appear to show less initiative during conversations; they speak less, let more and longer silences develop, and are less effective at steering the conversation through successful interruptions of the partner". For many psychologists, the notion that findings such as these are due to an inadequate repertoire of social skills has been a compelling one, as has the belief that such inadequacies may be remediated by teaching social skills. Two chapters discuss this question of intervention. Van der Molen (chapter 9) argues that shyness is multi-determined, and he proposes that the belief that one cannot cope with social situations, anticipatory fear, negative affect and unwanted symptoms, unskilled behaviour, and avoidance of situations can together form a vicious circle from which it is difficult to escape. Consequently, therapy has to involve all these components of shyness, and the explicit teaching and practice of overt behaviours form only a part of the programme and need to be augmented by techniques aimed at reducing anxiety symptoms, altering self-defeating cognitions, and so on. Even where the focus is upon a more traditional notion of social skills, van der Molen distinguishes between behaviours that are not in the individual's repertoire and those that would be available were they not inhibited through lack of confidence. The first half of his chapter is devoted to developing a "working definition" of shyness, and this serves to demonstrate that definitions are not merely academic matters, because they can have a profound influence upon the design of therapeutic techniques. Hartman and Cleland (chapter 12) approach the question of intervention within the framework of social anxiety rather than of shyness, taking as their starting point the definition of the avoidant personality pattern as "hypersensitivity to potential rejection, humiliation, or shame; an unwillingness to enter into relationships unless given unusually strong guarantees of uncritical acceptance; social withdrawal in spite of a desire for affection and acceptance; and low self-esteem" (American Psychiatric Association, 1979). Again, these authors stress the need to break a vicious circle, this time a "closed loop of self-centred meta-cognition", and their approach utilises techniques designed to reduce such excessive self-focus by encouraging the practice of other-centred awareness.

The expression of shyness and embarrassment

An alternative approach to the link between overt behaviour and shyness and embarrassment is to consider that there may be behaviours that are *expressive* of these states of mind. Edelmann (chapter 7) cites three functional classes of non-verbal behaviour in embarrassment – nervous responses, disaffiliative behaviours, and attempts at impression management – and he reports survey data on the incidence of blushing, smiling and laughing, and gaze avoidance, among other physiological symptoms and behaviours. Each of these was reported by a significant number of respondents as characteristic of their responses to embarrassing incidents. The Stanford Shyness Survey (Zimbardo, 1986; Zimbardo et al., 1974) similarly identified non-verbal behaviours characteristic of shyness. It can, of course, be misleading to rely upon information gleaned from surveys; as Asendorpf (chapter 3) points out, there may be subtle cues of which we are not aware. He provides a review of published studies on the expression of shyness and embarrassment, avoiding those that relied largely upon role-playing methods. Studies of adults who were videotaped while they were being asked potentially embarrassing questions converged on three reliable indicators: less looking while talking, more body motion, and more speech disturbances. Although little blushing or smiling was reported, Asendorpf's own experiments found evidence of both and demonstrated that these phenomena can be elusive and require very systematic investigation. Observations of behaviours in different social tasks revealed that blushing did occur, but in a situation intended to produce embarrassment, not one that was designed to elicit "stranger anxiety". Close scrutiny of the videotapes allowed a distinction to be drawn between embarrassed and non-embarrassed smiling; the timing of gaze aversion during the smile proved to be the discriminant factor. Such careful examination may provide answers to long-standing questions about the nature of the relationship between shyness and embarrassment and the functions of displays associated with them: Are they expressive and characteristic of a particular emotion (as many emotion theorists would argue), are they signs of a more generalised state like arousal or nervousness, or do they serve communicative functions?

Expression or communication?

This last explanation is stressed by Castelfranchi and Poggi (chapter 8), who dispute the Darwinian proposition that blushing is merely expressive. They analyse shame in terms of the assumptions that are made about the self and others, in order to produce a model that specifies the necessary and sufficient conditions for the experience of shame. Their account makes a distinction between feeling ashamed in one's own eyes and feeling ashamed in the eyes of others. Castelfranchi and Poggi argue that blushing occurs only in the latter case and has a specific communicative function; the person who blushes is indicating both sensitivity to the judgements of others and also adherence to others' values, and this signal has value both for the individual (in protecting him or her from aggression or rejection) and for the group. A blush is superior to a functionally similar signal such as an apology in that its involuntary nature attests to the ashamed person's sincerity.

Castelfranchi and Poggi also regard blushing as being linked to shyness and modesty, both involving, in their view, fear of falling short of some value. Blushing is also, as we have seen, associated with embarrassment (itself, of course, linked with shame by many theorists; see Crozier, chapter 1), and this model raises interesting questions about the survey data presented by Edelmann (chapter 7). There seem to be cross-cultural differences in several indicators of embarrassment, and

British respondents in particular were more likely to report responding to embarrassing incidents with blushing (55%, compared with a range of 21–34% for other European and Japanese respondents). Do these apparent cultural differences reflect linguistic considerations, in that words for embarrassment in different languages may not translate exactly? (Harré, in chapter 6, notes that French and Spanish do not mark a distinction between blushing and embarrassment; Castelfranchi and Poggi, in chapter 8, offer a similar comparison of the English and Italian words for embarrassment.) Or do responses reveal cultural stereotypes about the nature of embarrassment or about national personality "types"? Perhaps, as Harré suggests, there are cultural differences in embarrassability. Alternatively, there may be cultural variations in display rules (Ekman, 1972) guiding the expression of embarrassment. Castelfranchi and Poggi's model implies that it might be fruitful to consider cultural variations in the communicative significance of blushing and in the use and meaning of blushing relative to alternative kinds of signals of apology and of public adherence to group norms and values; indeed, it might be thought a strength of their approach that it sensitises us to such variation, as opposed to seeing it as a problem (being embarrassed about it). Similarly, it suggests an alternative approach to the understanding and reduction of individuals' anxieties over chronic blushing.

The cultural context of embarrassment

Comparison of these different approaches to blushing does highlight one of the polarities in shyness and embarrassment research – we can focus upon the individual and consider his or her experience and behaviour, or we can think more about the social significance of these phenomena and their communicative function. Certainly there has been a tendency among psychologists to study shyness in individualistic terms, while attending more to the social dimensions of embarrassment. This does reflect our everyday English use of these words, as may be demonstrated in the following example. What would be our reaction to hearing about someone who could never experience shyness, embarrassment, or shame? I suspect that whereas we might be prepared to attribute to the person who is never shy admirable qualities (being poised, confident, at ease with people) or even believe that never being shy is the norm, we might think that a person who is never embarrassed or ashamed is lacking some important human quality, is insensitive, thoughtless, or uncaring, a "brazen hussy" or an "arrogant son of a bitch". A person's shyness is in a sense his or her own concern, but a lack of embarrassment is of more social concern: It is Castelfranchi and Poggi's point that offering evidence of embarrassment rescues the individual from the hostility of the group, and many writers on shame and embarrassment have stressed the social control function of these emotions (see Crozier, chapter 1, Gibbons, chapter 4, and Harré, chapter 6: "not to display shame at a fault is also a fault, just as not to be embarrassed at an infraction of conventions is also an infraction of conventions"). It is clear that there is a moral dimension to embarrassment, and attention to this aspect of psychology, together with a denunciation of its putative individualistic bias, has characterised the approach of Harré (1983; see also chapter 6).

Harré is concerned with distinguishing shame and embarrassment, and he locates them at different points on a two-dimensional representation or "map" whose dimensions refer respectively to the seriousness of the transgression and to the extent of one's fault for it. His analysis suggests that in writing about behaviour we have erroneously lumped together appearance and conduct. One source of the distinction between embarrassment and shame might be that one is embarrassed over one's appearance but ashamed of one's conduct, but Harré argues that while this would be a useful starting point, it would be an oversimplification in that, for example, one would be ashamed of one's appearance if it could be taken as a sign of defective moral character. Harré argues further that the force and functions of these emotions are not fixed or universal but are subject to change in conjunction with variation in cultural context; he proposes that shame is being replaced by embarrassment as the major form of social control and that bodily exposure is becoming less a source of embarrassment than is one's conduct, both of which trends are to be understood within the context of an alleged blurring of the distinction between manners and morality and of the changing place of women in society. In support of this thesis, Harré draws our attention to an *Oxford English Dictionary* gloss on "modesty" (clearly related to both shyness and embarrassment, but little studied by psychologists in its own right) as "womanly propriety of behaviour": Modesty may be becoming a matter of convention rather than of virtue.

The evolutionary context

If the chapters by Castelfranchi and Poggi, Edelmann, and Harré stress the culturally variable and historically contingent, that of Gilbert and Trower (chapter 5) concerns cultural universals and is a necessarily speculative piece on the evolutionary significance of social anxiety. Just why should shyness and embarrassment be widespread? Why should embarrassment be so feared as to provide such a powerful constraint on behaviour? Darwin (1872/1965, p. 350) had indicated something of the paradoxical nature of sensitivity to the opinions of others in his example of the person bold in battle but timid in the presence of strangers. The first part of their chapter locates the evolution of social anxiety within the process of sexual selection, particularly its influence upon the display behaviours of organisms. They propose that evolutionary processes have shaped both the social organisation of groups and the display behaviours of individuals and that social anxiety is related to the appraisal of threat, particularly a threat to one's display. A distinction is offered between two modes of social behaviour, the agonic, with an emphasis upon hierarchies of power and threat, and the hedonic, characterised by reassurance and mutual reinforcement. It is argued that social contexts that are appraised as agonic can trigger defensive reactions such as submissiveness in those individuals who evaluate themselves as having little power or status in the hierarchy. However, anxiety can also arise in the hedonic mode, when the individual is unable to feel secure even in the absence of threat, and appraisal of threat and elicitation of a defensive mode result in failure to capitalise on the situation's possibilities for social reinforcement. Gilbert and Trower stress that these are evolved, innate appraisal and response tendencies, and hence to a large extent they may be outside the individual's conscious control. This emphasis upon the individual's concern with display – with projecting an acceptable self and with hiding undesirable features – and with his or her status in the group leads Gilbert and Trower to consider relationships between social anxiety and shame and embarrassment on the one hand and impression management on the other, and this serves to integrate their psychobiological perspective with predominant themes of this volume.

The self in shyness and embarrassment

Recent years have witnessed an enormous revival of interest among psychologists in the study of the self and particularly in the application of "mainstream" empirical methods to what had hitherto been regarded as too problematic, subjective, or private for scientific investigation. Two paradigms have attracted intensive examination – self-awareness theory and impression management theory – and both of these have provided an impetus for research into shyness and embarrassment. This impetus is not surprising in that it is hardly possible to discuss these emotions without recourse to the self. If these emotions constitute the inhibition or interruption of the flow of behaviour, then what disrupts this flow is the intrusion of self into consciousness. Dispositional shyness has invariably been linked either with low self-esteem, poor self-image, and lack of self-efficacy or with excessive preoccupation with the self, as in egocentrism or narcissism. Two theoretical statements have been particularly influential. The first is Schlenker and Leary's (1982) conceptualisation of social anxiety in impression management terms: Social anxiety arises when the individual is motivated to create a positive impression in others but his or her subjective probability of attaining this is low (see Harris, chapter 2, for an account of this approach). The second is the explicit link made between the experience of self-consciousness and the theoretical construct of self-awareness, for example, the account of the individual whose attention is focused upon himself or herself and who has a low subjective probability that he or she can reduce the discrepancy between current attainments and personal standards that has been made salient by this self-attention (Carver & Scheier, 1986): The resemblance between this account and the phenomenology of shyness and embarrassment has been compelling.

Impression management

The connections among creating a desired impression in others, achieving success in social encounters, and experiencing shyness and embarrassment were made by Erving Goffman (1972), and his work is having increasing influence upon more empirical social psychological approaches. Although he wrote specifically upon (and saw the importance of) embarrassment and, to a lesser extent, shyness (his influence is reflected in this volume in the chapters by Castelfranchi and Poggi and by Harré), his impact has largely been mediated by the observation that routine social behaviour serves impression management goals, with the implication that social difficulties are the results of failure to attain these goals. Crozier (chapter 1) offers a brief overview of some of the research into shyness and embarrassment within this framework; in comparison with Goffman's approach, there has been a shift of emphasis away from the participants' management of the social encounter to the individual's sense of satisfaction with his or her performance. Within this latter emphasis, an alternative to the notion that social anxiety (or embarrassment or shyness) is a consequence of a failure to attain impression management goals is Arkin's conceptualisation of shyness as a defensive strategy motivated to forestall threat and thereby protect one's self-image; Shepperd and Arkin (chapter 10) review research findings compatible with this conceptualisation and compare this approach with the Schlenker–Leary model and with the concept of self-handicapping (i.e., one's attempt to influence the attributions that others will make for one's performance by fabricating impediments to success). Of course, social anxiety may or may not produce self-handicapping behaviours, and Shepperd and Arkin suggest that insight into this question can be gained by classifying handicaps along two orthogonal dimensions: internal versus external attributions, and pre-existing versus situationally constructed handicaps. Empirical evidence suggests that the availability of pre-existing sources of self-handicap interacts with the internal–external dimension in that while the socially anxious person can recruit internal handicaps to influence others' attributions of his or her anticipated failure, the presence of external sources of handicap can have the effect of reducing anxiety and defensive behaviour. In contrast to the tendency to recruit pre-existing handicaps, there seems little evidence that socially anxious individuals actively engage in constructing impediments to their success. Shepperd and Arkin propose that this pattern of findings can be interpreted in terms of the individual's evaluation of the risks or costs associated with the choice of different strategies. Throughout their chapter, these authors stress that social anxiety is not just a reactive process but is an active, coping process in which the individual attempts to manage his or her feelings of anxiety within some appraisal of the affordances of the social environment.

Self-awareness theory

Research has shown that self-consciousness is at the core of the experience of shyness and embarrassment, and not surprisingly many psychologists have turned to the rapidly developing field of self-awareness theory for an explanation of this. There has been discussion in that field as to whether focusing attention on the self is inherently aversive or whether negative affect is a consequence of self-focused attention combined with an appraisal of some discrepancy between one's attainments and one's personal standards or normative expectations. This second position has been adopted by Carver and Scheier (1986) in their model of shyness and by Edelmann (chapter 7) in his account of embarrassment. A further distinction in the literature is that between the public self and the private self. This was originally intended to contrast aspects of the self that were the focus of attention. Private self-awareness is being attentive to one's thoughts and feelings, and public self-awareness is focusing upon those aspects of the self that may be perceived and evaluated by others, with the latter being regarded as more relevant for shyness and embarrassment. This distinction has been interpreted in rather different ways. Gilbert and Trower (chapter 5) contrast three sets of *schemata*, referring to an ideal self, a private self that draws upon internal sources of information about the self, and a public or interpersonal self that incorporates knowledge about the person's habitual display behaviour. In their view, social anxiety is associated with difficulties in constructing appropriate schemata and with conflict among them, such as, for example, experiencing problems in reconciling the public self with the ideal self, or being motivated to conceal aspects of the private self that would attract censure. This notion of these self-aspects as schemata in the sense of organisations of knowledge is compatible with current thinking about self-knowledge (e.g., Greenwald & Pratkanis, 1984) but goes beyond, I think, the original distinction.

Gibbons (chapter 4) distinguishes two sources of *motivation* for social behaviour: the desire to please the self, which involves self-focused attention, and the desire to create an appropriate impression in others. The former is concerned with personal standards, and the latter with social norms and expectations, and failure involves guilt or disappointment in the first case and embarrassment and shame in the second. Which of these emotions is experienced is thus held to depend on whether attention is focused on the self or on others. Gibbons reviews a substantial number of studies that have demonstrated the differential effects of self-focused versus other-focused attention. Although public self-focus and private self-focus typically have both been regarded as forms of self-awareness (as opposed to other-awareness), Gibbons restricts the concept of self-awareness to the former case: "In contrast, the attention of a person in a group is typically on that group and what its members may think. That may very well include concern about what the group thinks *about the self*. However, the perspective (on the self) that is assumed is external – it is that of other persons.... But it is not the same as self-awareness". Crozier (chapter 1), in a similar vein, argues that the notion of attention being directed towards the self does not capture the experience of self-consciousness as reflected in people's accounts and fails to distinguish between shyness, shame, and embarrassment on the one hand and disappointment and depression on the other. What needs to be considered is the observation made by Darwin (1872/1965, p. 325) that "it is not the simple act of reflecting on our own appearance, but the thinking of what others think of us, which excites the blush". The idea that one takes another's perspective upon the self is at the heart of Sartre's analysis of shame (see Harré, chapter 6, for further discussion of the implications of this analysis). Thus, what is important may be the perspective that is taken rather than the aspect of the self that is the object of attention. Taylor (1985) introduces a further qualification, suggesting that it is not the perspective of a particular other that counts but a "higher order point of view" whereby the individual realises how his or her behaviour could be seen. These discussions of the nature of self-consciousness have been solely in terms of shame and embarrassment; shyness researchers have been more interested in the *consequences* of self-focused attention, influenced by analogies between social anxiety and test anxiety. Hartman and Cleland (chapter 12), for example, characterise the socially anxious person as trapped in "a closed loop of self-centred meta-cognition", with resulting failure to participate appropriately in the social encounter. The concept of meta-cognition does, however, capture something of the nature of taking a detached observer's stance on one's self that seems central to these experiences.

Harris (chapter 2) argues that we can bring order to the confusing picture of relationships among shyness, embarrassment, and social anxiety by defining an affective state of "acute negative public self-attention" (ANPS-A) that relates to our common-sense notion of self-consciousness and that underlies the reactive experiences of shame and embarrassment. This state is unpleasant and is accompanied by an awareness of negative discrepancy between desired self-image and projected self-image; however, despite its superficial similarity to Schlenker and Leary's model, it is not to be equated with anxiety (social or otherwise). It is Harris's proposition that ordinary language uses terms like "shame", "embarrassment", "shyness", and so forth, to label these two states of social discomfort (anxiety and ANPS-A) and that psychologists should examine the rules of employment of these terms. The similarity between "shame" and "embarrassment" arises because both refer to the same affective state: ANPS-A. "Shyness" is a label that can refer either to anxiety or to ANPS-A, depending on whether it is used in an anticipatory or reactive way. How, then, does reactive shyness differ from embarrassment if both are drawing upon the same affective state? Harris argues that the difference resides in the perceived appropriateness or legitimacy of the reaction to its eliciting circumstances, with ("foolish") shyness being regarded as inappropriate. This analysis can be brought to bear on our earlier example of the hypothetical individual incapable of experiencing shyness, shame, or embarrassment: It is one thing never to respond inappropriately, quite another never to encounter or recognise a situation that calls for an appropriate response.

Conclusions

Although we have organised this overview of the contributions according to the perspectives that are being taken upon shyness and embarrassment, the major themes that have emerged from these different approaches should also be apparent. One is the demand for closer scrutiny of the ordinary language terms "shyness" and "embarrassment". A second is a call for careful conceptual analysis of the theoretical terms we are using. Third, although researchers still find it useful to draw upon the traditional distinction between trait and state, there is growing realisation of the dangers of the tendency for this to polarise towards the study of shyness on the one hand and embarrassment on the other. There are pointers to the future in the questions about shyness and embarrassment that have been posed. Although shy people are characterised as having a predisposition towards responding in a shy or anxious way, we are still unclear about the nature of this affective experience, and there is a need for the study of individual differences to become integrated with the analysis of emotional reactions. We now have some insights into the kinds of events and circumstances that elicit shyness and embarrassment, but as yet we have little grasp of the psychological processes that mediate reactions to these eliciting events. For example, several chapters in this volume have worthwhile (and novel) points to make about blushing, but this only highlights how little we understand this central phenomenon. There has, as yet, been too little recognition of other possibilities in the study of personality. To take one example, the emergence of alternative approaches to psychology inspired by feminist critiques (e.g., Holloway, 1989) has as yet had no impact on research in this area, despite the clear relevance of this area for questions having to do with relationships between the social construction of shyness, embarrassment, and modesty and the location of women in society (see Baines, 1988, for further discussion of this question; see also Harré, this volume).

We hope that readers will be impressed by a sense of the vigour with which questions about shyness and embarrassment are currently being pursued and also by the reluctance of many contributors to leave central assumptions unexamined. Schlenker and Leary's self-presentational account of social anxiety, in conjunction with the notion that self-consciousness is a form of public self-awareness, has attained some dominance in this area, but our contributors, while recognising that the legacy of Goffman has been of great heuristic value and that there is considerable evidence that the focus of attention is an important influence upon behaviour, have challenged the central assumption that anxiety is the affective component of shyness and embarrassment and have been prepared to explore alternative conceptualisations of self-consciousness. It is not yet possible to offer simple definitions or explanations of shyness or embarrassment, and techniques for helping people with problems of shyness, anxiety, or chronic blushing are still at an early stage of development. We do hope that this volume will make a useful contribution to these important issues; when we have achieved a grasp of these phenomena we will have gained considerable insight into ourselves and our social world.

REFERENCES

American Psychiatric Association. (1979). *Diagnostic and statistical manual of mental disorders – III*. Washington. DC: APA.
Babcock, M. K. (1988). Embarrassment: A window on the self. *Journal for the Theory of Social Behaviour, 18*, 459–483.

Baines, A. (1988). *Success and satisfaction: Reconciling women's public and private selves.* London: Paladin.

Carver, C. S., & Scheier, M. F. (1986). Analyzing shyness: A specific application of broader self-regularity principles. In W. H. Jones, J. M. Cheek, & S. R. Briggs (Eds.), *Shyness: Perspectives on research and treatment* (pp. 173–185). New York: Plenum.

Crozier, W. R. (1979). Shyness as a dimension of personality. *British Journal of Social and Clinical Psychology, 18,* 121–128.

Darwin, C. (1965). *The expression of the emotions in man and animals.* University of Chicago Press. (Original work published 1872)

Edelmann, R. J. (1987) *The psychology of embarrassment.* Chichester, Sussex: Wiley.

Ekman, P. (1972). Universal and cultural differences in facial expression of emotion. In J. R. Cole (Ed.), *Nebraska Symposium on Motivation* (pp. 207–283). Lincoln: University of Nebraska Press.

Goffman, E. (1972). *Interaction ritual.* Harmondsworth, Middlesex: Penguin.

Greenwald, A. G., & Pratkanis, A. R. (1984). The self. In R. S. Wyer & T. K. Srull (Eds.), *Handbook of social cognition* (Vol. 3, pp. 129–178). Hillsdale, NJ: Erlbaum.

Harré, R. (1983). *Personal being.* Oxford: Blackwell.

Harris, P. R. (1984). Shyness and psychological imperialism: On the dangers of ignoring the ordinary language roots of the terms we deal with. *European Journal of Social Psychology 14,* 169–181.

Holloway, W. (1989). *Subjectivity and method in psychology: Gender, meaning and science.* London: Sage.

Jones, W. H., Cheek, J. M., & Briggs, S. R. (1986). *Shyness: Perspectives on research and treatment.* New York: Plenum.

Leary, M. R. (1986). Affective and behavioral components of shyness: Implications for theory, measurement and research. In W. H. Jones, J. M. Cheek, & S. R. Briggs (Eds.), *Shyness: Perspectives on research and treatment* (pp. 27–38). New York: Plenum.

Ortony, A., Clore, G. L., & Collins, A. (1988). *The cognitive structure of emotions.* Cambridge University Press.

Schlenker, B. R., & Leary, M. R. (1982). Social anxiety and self-presentation: A conceptualization and model. *Psychological Bulletin, 92,* 641–669.

Taylor, G. (1985). *Pride, shame and guilt: Emotions of self-assessment.* Oxford: Clarendon Press.

Zimbardo, P. G. (1986). The Stanford Shyness Project. In W. H. Jones, J. M. Cheek, & S. R. Briggs (Eds.), *Shyness: Perspectives on research and treatment* (pp. 17–25). New York: Plenum.

Zimbardo, P. G., Pilkonis, P. A., & Norwood, R. (1974). *The silent prison of shyness* (Office of Naval Research Technical Report Z–17). Stanford, CA: Stanford University.

PART I

Theoretical issues in the study of
shyness and embarrassment

1

Social psychological perspectives on shyness, embarrassment, and shame

W. RAY CROZIER

Shyness and embarrassment are frequently encountered in everyday life, and expressions such as "he's come over all shy" or "I was so embarrassed I didn't know where to look" can readily conjure up for us the image of a person in some difficulty in a social encounter. In everyday talk we do not always make a sharp distinction between the two words, and sometimes they refer to much the same thing, so that to call someone shy is to say that he or she is easily embarrassed. Despite their ubiquity, it is only recently that these phenomena have received any detailed consideration by psychologists. Shyness and embarrassment have been studied in isolation from each other and often have been regarded as separate phenomena. In particular, shyness has tended to be viewed as characterising a person, whereas embarrassment has been seen as a property of social interactions. Whenever the focus in research into embarrassment has been on the individual, it has been on the person's role, with the implication that embarrassment is a temporary phenomenon that can be experienced by anyone. On the other hand, the trend has been to regard shyness as a personal dispositional attribute, a potential that the individual brings to the interaction.

Consideration of the earlier literature on shyness and embarrassment reinforces this impression of separate topics. References to shyness are found in the personality and clinical literature (i.e., those fields of psychology that study the individual), whereas references to embarrassment appear in the sociological literature. Ironically, shyness itself was rather "shy", obscured in the personality literature by the domination of the traits of introversion–extraversion and anxiety that had been revealed in the large-scale factor analytical studies that had characterised much personality research since the 1950s. Although that research did regularly identify a shyness factor that correlated with, but was separable from, both introversion and anxiety (Crozier, 1979a), the thrust of investigation was into exploration of the two independent traits. In clinical studies of social difficulties the emphasis was largely behavioural, and the concern was with identifying those observable behaviours that could serve to distinguish people with social problems from their peers

and with deriving strategies for reducing those differences. The notion
that social problems like shyness were produced by deficits in "social
skills" has been a very powerful one. One consequence has been that the
identification of a number of specific deficits and problems has obscured
any consideration of a broad and generalised notion of shyness.

An upsurge of interest in these questions can be understood in the
context of broader changes within the field of social psychology, as well
as in the contribution of one seminal study. Before discussing this wider
context we shall describe the investigation of shyness that was carried
out by Philip G. Zimbardo and his colleagues at Stanford University.
Rather than proceeding with the traditional approach of constructing a
questionnaire measure of shyness and identifying its correlates, Zimbardo, Pilkonis, and Norwood (1974) allowed their respondents simply to
characterise themselves as shy or not shy and then asked them about the
experiences and behaviours that were associated with their shyness: the
situations and kinds of people that elicited it and its consequences for
their personal and social life. That survey, which was replicated with
several large samples of respondents, confirmed that the experience of
shyness was widespread, that it was unpleasant and to be avoided if
possible, and that it could, for a sizeable minority of people, amount to
a considerable personal handicap. A second, more traditional form of
report followed (Pilkonis, 1977), correlating the Stanford survey measure
of shyness with a number of personality questionnaires. Pilkonis suggested that it might be useful to think in terms of two kinds of shyness:
public and private. The former reflected a concern with shortcomings in
one's social behaviour, and the latter a concern with the feelings of
anxiety and self-consciousness that could be triggered by social situations. These two investigations ushered in what is now a substantial
series of empirical investigations into the correlates of self-reported shyness. They also foreshadowed a concern with the nature of shyness:
whether it is unidimensional or multidimensional and how it might be
distinguished from other related constructs. These are questions that are
discussed in several chapters in this volume.

The Stanford research was essentially empirical and correlational,
starting with a word from everyday language that described an aspect of
social behaviour and examining what it was that people had in mind
when they used the word to describe themselves. Subsequent research
began to use "shyness" as a technical term to identify an underlying
personality trait. Harris (1984, also this volume) has argued forcefully
that this development brought with it severe conceptual problems that
would only promote confusion. These studies were still essentially exploratory in nature and were not guided by any explicit theory. The view
from Stanford seemed to be that an individual's sense of shyness was a

personal construction, an interpretation of behaviour influenced by one's past socialisation experiences, rather than a reflection of any social skills deficits. Thus, Pilkonis and Zimbardo (1979, p. 141) concluded that attributional processes might produce differences between those who characterised themselves as shy and those for whom shyness was a transitory reaction to some kinds of social situations: "The difference between the dispositionally and those situationally shy people is primarily a difference in labelling and the tendency to blame oneself for one's social anxiety or to look to the external situation for the causes of one's own distress." Research into shyness was stimulated, and links with embarrassment research began to be forged, when psychologists could draw upon a theoretical framework. Such a framework was offered by some new directions in experimental psychology, in particular the rediscovery of the self (Hales, 1985), and it is to this phenomenon that we now turn.

It is clear from personal accounts of shyness and embarrassment and evident in subjects' responses to questionnaires that self-consciousness is at the core of these experiences. Harré (1983) has described self-consciousness as arising when "the normal intentionality of actions in which they are thought of as ends or outcomes is suspended and the self-conscious actor focuses on the actions he or she is performing, bringing on that characteristic incapacity in performance we call 'stage fright'." We can surely be confident that self-consciousness is an essential feature. It has been stressed by many writers on shyness and embarrassment (Darwin, 1872/1904; Edelmann, 1987; Goffman, 1956; Lewinsky, 1941). It was alluded to by 85% of shy respondents in the Stanford Shyness Survey (Zimbardo et al., 1974). In one of our studies (Crozier, 1985), a sample of college students was presented with a list of adjectives and asked which, if any, of these would be implied if they knew that someone was a shy person. There was widespread belief (defined as at least 85% agreement among respondents) that being self-conscious, not self-assured, and not self-confident were all implied by shyness.

These feelings of self-consciousness needed to be interpreted within some theory of the self, and the 1970s witnessed a development of interest in the self among social psychologists. This development was piecemeal, with different researchers working on discrete problems. To some extent it was inadvertent, as Hales (1985) has argued, in that several traditional areas of research in experimental psychology, such as altruism, cognitive dissonance, and conformity, pointed to the significance of impression management concerns. As Hales (1985) and Tetlock and Manstead (1985) have pointed out, a whole set of explanations of these phenomena has been rivalled by a theory, or class of mini-theories, that asserts the influence upon behaviour of people's desires to create a good impression in the eyes of others, or, to put it another way, to create an acceptable social identity.

As was suggested earlier, the clinical literature on shyness had a behavioural focus, but many workers in this area found it useful to introduce the concept of *social anxiety*, because whatever the causes of an individual's social difficulties, they were commonly associated with anxiety (Hall & Goldberg, 1977; Watson & Friend, 1969). Social psychologists related this concept of social anxiety either to emerging theories of self-consciousness or to theories of impression management, to yield a framework that has encouraged research on shyness and has also forced consideration of the relations among shyness, embarrassment, and shame. In this way the separate strands of research have begun to converge. One problem that this trend has highlighted is a lack of clarity about the relations among these "social emotions". For some theorists (Harré, this volume; Harris, 1984, also this volume; Silver, Sabini, & Parrott, 1987) this problem is primarily a conceptual one. For others (Buss, 1980; Izard & Hyson, 1986; Plutchik, 1980) it is a problem amenable to empirical investigation. This growing concern with shyness, embarrassment, shame, and the self has also resulted in a revival of interest in the classic study of the emotions of "self-attention", as in Darwin's *Expression of the Emotions in Man and Animals* (1872/1904).

One outcome of these critical examinations of these emotions is a questioning of the assumption that shyness and embarrassment are (or, alternatively, are best understood as) forms of social anxiety. We would argue that theories of social anxiety have produced a much needed impetus to research in this area, but that further developments will benefit from a closer look at the assumptions of these theories. This is one of the principal objectives of this volume; this chapter provides a brief critical overview of these theories, considers questions raised by this overview, including making reference to lacunae in our understanding of shyness and embarrassment, and discusses the relations among the social emotions.

Social anxiety and self-consciousness

The propositions by Duval and Wicklund (1972) that attention could be directed either towards the environment or towards the self, that this latter state of "objective self-awareness" was essentially aversive, and that this state could be induced by manipulating the presence or absence of mirrors and television cameras seemed to provide an ideal opportunity for a study of self-consciousness that could transcend phenomenological reports. Equally productive were further theoretical developments in this area. Carver (1979) provided a cognitive explanation of the circumstances that produce the state of self-awareness and argued that this state is not necessarily aversive nor does it invariably motivate the individual to avoid it.

According to Carver, self-attention would involve an assessment phase in which one would compare one's ongoing behaviour with one's personal standards, and the normal outcome of that comparison process would be an increased effort to reduce any discrepancy between the two. However, the combination of a failure to reduce this discrepancy, an inability to withdraw from the situation, and a low expectancy that one would be able to match one's standards for behaviour would produce an interruption of behaviour that would be accompanied by a state of mind in which people would be "frozen in the self-assessment phase of the sequence, where they repeatedly reconfront the evidence of their inadequacy" (Carver, 1979, p. 1266). The correspondence between that description and phenomenological accounts of shyness is, of course, striking, and subsequently Carver and Scheier (1986) have made more explicit the relevance of this model of self-attention for shyness.

A second development was the demonstration that there were individual differences in propensity towards self-awareness. Fenigstein, Scheier, and Buss (1975) produced a questionnaire measure that tapped differences along three dimensions: Private Self-consciousness, the tendency to focus attention upon one's private thoughts and feelings; Public Self-consciousness, the tendency to focus upon oneself as a social object; and Social Anxiety, where the test items refer to experiences of shyness and embarrassment. Subsequent research (Carver & Scheier, 1987) has supported these distinctions (although few studies have used the short Social Anxiety scale) and has demonstrated a parallel relationship between these individual difference dimensions and also the states of private and public self-awareness (i.e., at any time, attention can be directed to either private or public aspects of the self).

The integration of these developments with the dimension of social anxiety was provided by Buss (1980), who offered an ambitious theory of shyness, shame, embarrassment, and audience anxiety. These were all conceptualised as different forms of social anxiety, which was defined in terms of "discomfort in the presence of others ... being upset or disturbed by others' scrutiny or remarks, or merely because others are present" (Buss, 1980, p. 204, italics omitted). All four states shared an origin in the experience of acute public self-awareness. There were features that differentiated these forms of social anxiety, and these tended to pair embarrassment with shame and shyness with audience anxiety. Buss also proposed psychophysiological differences among them, with the first pair involving heightened parasympathetic nervous system reaction, and the latter pair heightened sympathetic reaction.

Although the details of this formulation attracted criticism (e.g., Crozier, 1982; Harris, this volume), and Buss's subsequent research has not emphasised these particular distinctions, the assertions that shyness and embarrassment are both forms of social anxiety and that both involve a state of public self-awareness have been influential. So, too, has been the notion that self-awareness entails some assessment of a discrepancy between one's behaviour and standards. For example, Edelmann (1985a, 1987, also this volume) has developed a model of embarrassment as a process with two important stages in which "awareness of a discrepancy between present state and standard leads to the focus of attention on the self.... The presence of an audience, whether real or imagined, directs attention to the public rather than the private self" (Edelmann, 1987, p. 104).

It cannot be denied that this approach has had considerable heuristic merit, but it does raise at least two important questions. The first is whether or not whatever shyness and embarrassment share is best construed as a form of social anxiety. Not all psychologists take this view, and we shall not discuss this further here, because we return to it later in the chapter, and it is discussed at length by Harris in his chapter.

Our second question concerns the state of self-awareness and the notion of a discrepancy between one's behaviour and standards. We need to consider the nature of self-consciousness as it has been described in accounts of shyness and embarrassment and ask if this can be captured by the theoretical concept of self-awareness. We argue that an approach that conceptualises shyness as a discrepancy between behaviour and standards focuses too much on the shy individual's appraisal of his or her performance and insufficiently on the role or the projected role of the other person(s) in the situation. It does not make sense to talk of experiencing shyness in the absence of other people. In shyness, it is not that we fall short of standards in our own judgement, but that we fear that we may be judged by others to fall short. Our preoccupation is with ourselves as we fear that we may be viewed by others. If our analysis is valid, then of course it will also have implications for embarrassment and shame.

The relevance of this shift in perspective in self-consciousness might be brought out by considering a recent influential conceptualisation of test anxiety, and the analogy that some psychologists have drawn between shyness and test anxiety, in the light of an analysis of shame and embarrassment provided by Taylor (1985). The tendency to be highly anxious about the prospect of taking a test is commonly associated with poor performance on tests, and it has been proposed by Wine (1971) and Sarason (1975, 1984) that this poor performance results because one focuses attention on one's own worries rather than on the test itself.

Anxious self-preoccupation (Sarason, 1975) interferes with appropriate task involvement. Crozier (1979b) suggested that this theory might provide a useful framework for the study of shyness, because it seemed to show how anxiety, self-consciousness, and reticence might be related, and it could be elaborated to accommodate the common finding that shyness was correlated with low self-esteem and also Zimbardo's observation that shy persons were prone to attribute their problems to their own shortcomings. Some subsequent studies have confirmed that there is some value in relating shyness to the distribution of attention; for example, Arnold and Cheek (1986) have used the Stroop color test to demonstrate significant correlations among shyness, test-irrelevant thinking, and task performance. Sarason and Sarason (1986) have begun to adapt their questionnaire measure of anxious reactions to tests to the investigation of social anxiety and shyness.

Note that there is nothing *social* in this hypothetical person's worries; the comparisons between one's current state of affairs and one's ideals can be entirely private. To say, however, that one is embarrassed or ashamed of one's condition is to say that one is viewing one's performance as it is or could be seen by an audience; one believes that one will be judged as inadequate by another. Taylor (1985) argues that shame and embarrassment entail just this kind of self-consciousness; she proposes that there is a critical distinction to be made between the person who is conscious of himself or herself as an actor and the person who is conscious of being seen as an actor. Now, a theorist of shame or embarrassment would not want to be restricted to the claim that one can experience these feelings only when one is actually in the company of others. Taylor contends that this can be overcome by assuming that only a shift of perspective need be involved. In the case of shame, she writes that "there is, then, this point to the metaphors of an audience and of being seen: they reflect the structural features of the agent's becoming aware of the discrepancy between her own assumption about her state or action and a *possible detached observer-description* of this state or action, and of her further being aware that she ought not to be in a position where she could be so seen, where such a description at least appears to fit" (1985, p. 66, emphasis added). In the case of embarrassment, this detached observer is more palpable. Embarrassment is the inability to respond in such a way as to maintain a satisfactory image in the eyes of some audience. It involves taking another's perspective upon oneself, the awareness that one's behaviour could be judged as untoward, and an uncertainty about how to correct that impression.

A person who is completely absorbed in some activity cannot be embarrassed; therefore, some form of self-consciousness is necessary. It is our claim, however, that having one's attention drawn to aspects of one's social self and being aware of discrepancies between one's social self and one's standards are not sufficient for embarrassment to ensue.

To take an example, imagine that I am in some public place, perhaps even with someone I do not know very well, when I begin to think about myself, stimulated perhaps by catching sight of my reflection in a mirror. I contemplate my appearance, my "social self", and become aware of discrepancies between my social self and my standards. Perhaps I seem to appear overweight, or my clothes are unfashionable. I go on to think about my inability to say the right thing and my tendency to become flustered in company. Now, this self-reflection may well induce feelings of depression, but I would argue that I would not describe this experience as one of shyness, and I believe that the reason for this is that although in one sense I may be in a state of acute self-consciousness, it is still my perspective that I am adopting, not the perspective of another. That the actual presence of another person may be necessary for shyness is suggested by the intuition that one could become ashamed and perhaps embarrassed in this situation.

To what extent can these claims and this example be accommodated by self-awareness theory, which asserts that embarrassment is due to the combination of a state of public self-attention and an inability to produce a match between behaviour and standards? The arguments might proceed as follows:

1. There is a substantial literature on the construct validity of the state of public self-attention, in which one directs attention to one's social self, to "how one is viewed by others" (Carver & Scheier, 1987, p. 533). Attention to public aspects of the self is in fact "an increased concern with how one is perceived by others" (Fenigstein, 1979, p. 83). Fenigstein (1987, p. 549) makes this point explicitly:

As an example, consider the feelings of observability or conspicuousness that often underlie embarrassment or social anxiety. It has been argued that these experiential states are likely to proceed from an awareness of oneself as an object of the observation of others, and have little to do with attention to aspects of the self that are private and unobservable.

2. There is also a substantial literature that validates the individual difference trait of public self-consciousness. There are parallel sets of findings obtained by manipulating self-attention and by selecting subjects on the basis of their self-consciousness scores. The Public Self-consciousness Scale correlates moderately but significantly with social anxiety (Fenigstein et al., 1975), shyness (Pilkonis, 1977), and embarrassability (Edelmann, 1985b).

3. Some experiments seem to show that manipulating public self-attention does lead people to take an external perspective. For example, Hass (1984) asked subjects to trace the letter E on their foreheads. In the public self-attention condition (tracing the letter while apparently being filmed with a TV camera) subjects were more likely to orient the letter to an observer's perspective than were subjects in a control (no camera) condition, who were more likely to orient the letter to their own perspective.

In response to these arguments, we would, however, refer again to the preceding example to reiterate that it is not just the focus of attention that is relevant, but also the perspective that is taken. It is only when one reflects upon oneself from the imagined viewpoint of a detached observer, whom Sartre (1969) has termed "the Other", that shyness and embarrassment can ensue. Some researchers into embarrassment have explicitly recognised the need to take into account the individual's perspective on the perspectives of others actually or potentially present. Semin and Manstead (1981), for example, distinguish the self-image from the subjective public image. An emotional reaction is elicited by a discrepancy between these images occasioned by the recognition that some action unfairly reflects poorly on one's subjective public image. It is this recognition that differentiates embarrassment and other possible emotional reactions to the situation. Buss and Briggs (1984) have emphasised the role of the audience in their account of shyness as a form of stage-fright, but this aspect of shyness has not yet been explored.

To take the second point of the argument, there is nothing in this analysis that is incompatible with the notion that people who have a greater tendency to reflect on what others think of them, who are self-conscious about the way they look, and who worry about making a good impression (to paraphrase three of the seven items of the Public Self-consciousness Scale) should be more prone to shyness or embarrassment. Indeed, it would be surprising if they were not. People who are prone to worry about what others think of them are more likely to take an observer's perspective upon the social self. What we are asserting is that it is not yet clear that the process of self-attention is sufficient to generate the "self-consciousness" that characterises shyness and embarrassment.

The third point, that public self-attention induces one to take another perspective upon the self, has recently been challenged by one of the leading self-consciousness theorists. Fenigstein (1988) has argued that on logical, theoretical, and empirical grounds, heightened self-attention should produce egocentrism, not the perspective of another. In doing so, he has offered methodological criticisms and alternative interpretations of the study by Hass summarised earlier, as well as others that have been claimed to demonstrate that the state of public self-attention elicits a greater tendency to take the perspective of another. If Fenigstein is correct – and we find his arguments convincing – then it becomes more difficult to show how self-attention processes in themselves can produce embarrassment, especially that form in which the embarrassed person is not the perpetrator of the act that triggers the experience. We should make it clear that we are *not* disputing the validity of research into self-attention processes nor the distinctions that have been drawn by theorists; rather, we argue that this theory will need elaboration before it can account for the "social emotions".

Shyness, embarrassment, and self-presentation

Goffman's theory of embarrassment

The influence of impression management research upon the study of shyness and embarrassment has been twofold. First, it has brought to psychologists' attention the seminal work of Erving Goffman (1956, 1972) and other sociologists who have analysed social interaction processes. Second, impression management concerns have been incorporated directly into explanations of social anxiety.

The focus of much of Goffman's writing has been the management of everyday face-to-face encounters. Embarrassment represents a breakdown in such an encounter, and Goffman has argued that understanding embarrassment will provide insight into the processes that maintain the normal, uninterrupted flow of interaction. Embarrassment occurs when the definition of a situation that participants have constructed (and such a construction is a necessary condition for interaction to take place at all) cannot be sustained. In Goffman's words,

> Embarrassment has to do with unfulfilled expectations ... the elements of a social encounter consist of effectively projected claims to an acceptable self and the confirmation of like claims on the part of the others. When an event throws doubt upon or discredits these claims, then the encounter finds itself lodged in assumptions which no longer hold. (1972, p. 105)

The individual's experience of embarrassment is an unpleasant one related to loss of self-esteem or feeling ashamed, and it can involve mental confusion, blushing, perspiration, and other physiological reactions. According to Goffman, embarrassment is always a potential threat to a social situation. Because it is such an unpleasant experience, individuals will make use of "preventive practices" to try to pre-empt events that would be embarrassing. These practices can be either protective (designed to enable others to maintain their identity) or defensive (aimed at protecting the actor's identity). Because an embarrassing incident will bring an encounter to a stop, it will have to be reconstructed if it is to continue, and participants will make use of "corrective practices" to bring about this reconstruction. Thus, to take an example of a protective corrective practice from an observational study influenced by Goffman, Emerson (1970) showed how the medical staff at a gynaecological examination would ignore or redefine reactions of a patient that threatened the consensus definition of the situation.

Schudson (1984, p. 636) has related this distinction between defensive and protective strategies to a classification of two types of disruptive events in Goffman's theory: "inconsistency of character and discontinuity of interaction". Consistency of character requires poise, whereas the maintenance of continuous interaction requires tact.

Many authors have drawn attention to the requirement of poise for social interaction. For example, Gross and Stone (1964) classified people's recollections of embarrassing incidents and identified loss of poise as a major category. Goffman's own emphasis was on the maintenance of interaction, but he did consider the possibility that some people might have a predisposition to lack poise, and he appeared to think of shyness in those terms: Shyness is the sense that one is "disqualified" in some way from claiming an appropriate identity. Although such perceived disqualifications might be situation-specific (one might become shy at parading one's pretensions to expertise on shyness before a group of distinguished shyness researchers), they also might characterise an individual across a whole range of encounters. As Goffman wrote,

An individual who firmly believes that he has little poise, perhaps even exaggerating his failing, is shy and bashful; dreading all encounters, he seeks always to shorten them or avoid them altogether. (1972, p. 104)

Furthermore,

Various kinds of recurrent encounters in a given society may share the assumption that participants have attained certain moral, mental, and physiognomic standards. The person who falls short may everywhere find himself inadvertently trapped into making implicit identity-claims which he cannot fulfil. Compromised in every encounter which he enters, he truly wears the leper's bell. (1972, p. 107)

There has been some research specifically into individual differences in the tendency to be embarrassed, sometimes labelled embarrassability (Modigliani, 1968), and a review of such studies has recently been provided by Edelmann (1987, pp. 108–131). Those psychologists who approach embarrassment from the perspective of social anxiety, whether related to self-consciousness or to self-presentation, seem to concur with Goffman in identifying shyness with a readiness to become embarrassed.

Rather than concentrating on the actor, one can take the encounter itself as the object of study, and one advantage of this is that one can do justice to the inherently social nature of embarrassment (Schudson, 1984; Silver et al., 1987). Such an approach also recognises the common observation that it is not necessarily the individual whose loss of poise may have triggered the incident who will feel embarrassed; indeed, that person may remain oblivious, while others present during the encounter may experience intense embarrassment. And, of course, embarrassment may prove contagious, spreading throughout a group and affecting people who bear no direct responsibility for any faux pas or loss of poise. Silver et al. (1987) have argued that the essence of embarrassment is being flustered and unable to react appropriately to an incident, and therefore an incident may be expected to embarrass others present to the extent that it makes them uncertain how to behave. Frequently it will be the person who is "to blame" who will be most uncertain how to rescue the situation and hence most embarrassed. However, there is, it is claimed, no particular problem in explaining contagious or vicarious embarrassment. An alternative account of this phenomenon has been provided by Miller (1986, 1987), who has proposed that observers may experience embarrassment through empathy: They can imagine what it feels like to be in the position of the embarrassed person.

Contagious embarrassment has attracted scarcely any empirical attention. An exception is the recent study by Miller (1987) of the embarrassment experienced by observers of people who have been persuaded by the experimenter to engage in potentially embarrassing activities like singing an anthem or imitating a child's temper tantrum. By trying to induce either an empathic or a more objective stance towards the person performing the embarrassing task (the "actor"), Miller attempted to demonstrate that any vicarious embarrassment experienced was due to empathy. Observers who were instructed to imagine the feelings of the actor ("how it feels to be him [or her] performing the task", p. 1063) apparently were more embarrassed than observers who were simply encouraged to concentrate on the actor's behaviour. This empathic embarrassment was also related to the nature of the prior relationship established between actor and observer and to subject differences in sex and embarrassability. Persuasive as these results are, it is not possible to rule out the alternative explanation in terms of the observer's own uncertainty about how to behave. They may well have been embarrassed at witnessing these performances in these experimental conditions, and perhaps they experienced less embarrassment when they adopted an objective stance because the instruction to concentrate on the actor's behaviour may have reduced their uncertainty both by giving them something specific to do and by providing a rationale for the rather strange situation in which they found themselves. Miller's clever experiment is a welcome attempt to look more closely at this distinctive feature of embarrassment, but clearly it requires further attention.

There have been criticisms of the details of Goffman's account of embarrassment (Miller, 1986; Schudson, 1984), extensions of it (as in the recommendation by Silver et al., 1987, that more attention be paid to the element of surprise in embarrassment), and rival explanations (e.g., Semin & Manstead, 1981). Perhaps the greatest influence upon social psychology has been the concept of "face work", which embraces the preventive and corrective practices discussed earlier. There has been substantial research into behaviours designed to create a desired impression in others (Jones & Pittman, 1982) and into the possibility of influencing others' attitudes and behaviour by providing apologies, excuses, and justifications for one's own actions (Semin & Manstead, 1983; Snyder, Higgins, & Stucky, 1983). Theories of embarrassment and shyness have been developed by an integration of notions of self-presentation and face work, on the one hand, and social anxiety, on the other, and it is to these developments that we now turn.

Self-presentation and social anxiety

Central to the self-presentation approach is the belief that "people are highly sensitive to the social significance of their conduct and are motivated to create desired identities in interpersonal encounters" (Tetlock & Manstead, 1985, p. 60). One can think in terms of the goals that people try to attain in this way and also of strategies that may be adopted in their pursuit. Several motives have been proposed for self-presentation; for example, creating a good impression can increase one's power over others (Jones & Pittman, 1982) and can gain material rewards (Jellison, 1981). Harré (1983) is opposed to this kind of explanation, arguing that for most people most of the time, the pursuit of reputation is itself the overriding preoccupation of human life, and therefore it should not be thought of as serving other practical goals. There have also been proposed differences in the kinds of immediate goals that self-presentation behaviours are intended to achieve. Arkin (1981) has distinguished two classes of motives for self-presentation: People may be motivated either to create a favourable impression or to avoid creating a poor impression. A similar point is made by Jones and Pittman (1982), who contrast behaviours intended to establish a particular identity with defensive behaviours intended to protect a threatened identity. Jones and Pittman provide examples of strategies that can be adopted in pursuit of these goals; for example, defensive strategies include offering apologies, excuses, and justifications.

The most influential approach to social anxiety from a self-presentation framework has contended that anxiety arises when people are motivated to create a good impression but are not confident that they can do so (Schlenker & Leary, 1982). This theory is discussed in detail in the chapters in this volume by Harris and Shepperd and Arkin; thus, we shall not pursue it at length here. This conceptualisation of social anxiety has several strengths. First, it proposes that the combination of motivation and lack of self-confidence is necessary for shyness, and this both captures the conflict inherent in shyness and helps to distinguish it from introversion or lack of interest in socialising. Second, Schlenker and Leary avoid the problem of defining shyness in behavioural terms because they allow the possibility that it can be expressed in different ways. Finally, the theory provides an interactionist account of individual differences, and we shall now consider further the merits of such an account.

The conceptualisation of shyness as a unitary personality trait runs the risk of failing to take into account the impact that situational differences can have on a person's behaviour. A person who is extremely shy in one situation may be at ease and confident in another. Apparently slight differences in a social encounter (such as having a new person join a group of people with whom one is already familiar) can markedly alter one's shyness. Psychologists can identify individual differences in one situation, such as conversing with a stranger, as in the experiment by Cheek and Buss (1981), and yet they cannot be confident that they can predict how these same people will respond in another situation: The rank order of individuals' shyness established in one place may not be maintained in another. An interactionist approach to personality attempts to incorporate both dispositional factors and situational influences. It also holds that people's cognitive representations of situations must be taken into account. Schlenker and Leary's theory proposes that individual differences pertinent to self-presentation motives and to self-confidence will contribute jointly with situational demands to any individual's level of shyness. Hence, people who are equally shy in one particular setting may be shy for very different reasons, and one should not expect that this equality would be maintained in different social settings.

To take a specific hypothetical example, one can imagine professors A and B, who have similar total scores on a social anxiety questionnaire, in two typical academic situations: making a conference presentation and interacting at a social function (in Schlenker and Leary's terms, respectively a non-contingent encounter and a contingent encounter). Professor A lacks self-confidence because a rather sheltered home life has failed to develop her social skills, whereas professor B's overambitious parents have caused him to have low academic self-esteem. Professor A tackles the presentation with poise, whereas professor B is highly anxious, but these anxiety "scores" are reversed in the informal gathering. There are many routes to shyness.

Shyness as stage-fright

Buss and Briggs (1984, p. 1316) criticise the self-presentational model of Schlenker and Leary and argue that it places too much emphasis upon impression management strategies consciously adopted by the individual. Although they agree that the dramaturgical metaphor underlying the self-presentational approach is useful, they claim that it has not been sufficiently explored. In their scheme, shyness is compared to an actor's stage-fright. Buss and Briggs distinguish between on-stage and off-stage behaviour: Off stage, a person is natural and at ease, a condition that is characterised as expressiveness. One cannot be shy "off stage". However, when one is "on stage" and a performance is required, then one may suffer from shyness:

... here the behavior analogous to stage fright is shyness. Although the interaction involves only one other person or just a few others, the experience is roughly equivalent: anxiety or embarrassment, a feeling of awkwardness, a tendency to say nothing, and an intense desire to escape (1984, p. 1317)

We have doubts about the usefulness of drawing too close an analogy between shyness and stage-fright. It is not altogether clear that the experiences described earlier characterise either shyness or stage-fright, and this is not helped by the vagueness of the description. Nor is it clear why stage-fright should induce a tendency to say nothing, nor why, as Buss and Briggs propose elsewhere in their paper, it should follow that the stutterer should be the prototypical shy person. Most writers on shyness see it as anticipatory rather than reactive (Harris, this volume), whereas stage-fright, as Buss and Briggs construe it, seems clearly to be a reaction to a disruption in performance. In stage-fright, the actor is forced out of his role and is unable to get back into it; this failure is due to the presence of the audience (forgetting one's lines would possibly be mildly embarrassing in a rehearsal, but it would scarcely be said to elicit stage-fright). Actors and performers frequently admit to nervousness before a performance (i.e., when they are still off stage) but suggest that they lose it when they go on stage and assume their roles. These pre-performance anxieties would seem analogous to shyness, but it does not seem to be these that Buss and Briggs have in mind (1984, p. 1316).

The broader theme of Buss and Briggs's argument is that a complete

34   W. RAY CROZIER

account of social interaction requires consideration of a person's individuality, as well as consideration of people's roles or situated identities, and that self-presentational theories do not pay sufficient attention to individual differences in the motivation or ability to convey a suitable impression. This criticism is perhaps overstated in that, as they themselves recognise (1984, p. 1314), at least some self-presentation theories have attended to relevant traits such as self-monitoring (Snyder, 1987), and Schlenker and Leary (1982) have specifically addressed individual differences in social anxiety. Even if there is some substance to their claim, the argument of Buss and Briggs is not helped by the stage-fright analogy, because, prototypically, stage-fright is highly situation-specific, a reaction to a particular incident that can disrupt the performance of the most experienced of actors. Nevertheless, their paper brings into the limelight the difficulty of locating shyness within individual difference schemes. Buss and Briggs distinguish two general biases in a person's identity that can accentuate either that person's social roles or idiosyncratic traits. An emphasis within one's identity upon social roles is associated, it is claimed, with a high level of public self-consciousness, whereas emphasis on more personal aspects of identity is associated with a high level of private self-consciousness (Buss & Briggs, 1984, p.1322). Unfortunately, shyness does not fit neatly within this scheme; although dispositional shyness is certainly correlated with acute public self-consciousness (Buss & Finn, 1987), other evidence suggests that the shy person is narcissistic and self-absorbed (Zimbardo, 1977). There is a conflict in shyness, a point that has often been made, but bears repeating. Shy people have aspirations beyond keeping in the background.

Shyness as a ploy

Both theories that we have discussed have concentrated on people's anxiety about their ability to present a satisfactory identity. Other self-presentational approaches have emphasised the shy role as a strategy that people may adopt. Arkin (1981) has argued that one may appear modest and unassuming and may be reluctant to express one's true opinions, appearing to concur with others, all in an attempt to protect one's precarious sense of identity. The preoccupation is with avoiding disapproval. We find this a plausible account of shyness, although, as he admits (Arkin, Lake, & Baumgardner, 1986, p. 199; Shepperd and Arkin, this volume), the difference between his account and that of Schlenker and Leary is one of emphasis, because the latter authors also propose something akin to a protective self-presentation style. Asendorpf (1984) has made the point that shyness and embarrassment in themselves create further self-presentation problems in that a lack of poise is not normally compatible with creating an effective impression.

Snyder, Smith, Augelli, and Ingram (1985) have characterised shyness as a self-handicapping strategy: By claiming a handicap, one can provide a ready excuse for potential failure, and one can mitigate the consequences of any failure for one's self-esteem. In the case of shyness, the handicap one claims is still self-relevant and hence must have some negative implications for self-esteem; thus, it will be an appropriate self-presentation strategy only to the extent that it offers a less damaging explanation of failure than do available alternatives. Snyder et al. (1985) manipulated the descriptions of evaluative tests to demonstrate that for male subjects, but not for female subjects, high scorers on a social anxiety scale were somewhat less likely to characterise themselves as anxious when shyness was discounted as an explanation of failure. This perspective on the self-serving function of shyness needs further empirical investigation.

Although the accounts of Arkin and Snyder and associates both emphasise *strategic* dimensions of shyness, one must not lose sight of important differences between them. For Snyder, the use of the label "shyness" is or can be a ploy that allows people to justify to themselves and to others certain anticipated shortcomings in their performance. Arkin, however, emphasises the individual's attempt to cope with a situation that induces shyness: The shyness is genuine, not a ploy, but the individual's behaviour serves protective impression management goals. There has been a long tradition in shyness research of construing the prototypical shyness reaction as reticence or "non-behaviour" (Crozier, 1979a), although definitions of shyness in terms of a distinctive pattern of behaviour have been criticised by Harris (1984). The tendency has been to regard reticence, whenever it occurs, as being due to lack of social skills or due to inhibition brought about by anxiety. Drawing attention to the goals that people might be trying to achieve is welcome in that it helps forge links with embarrassment research, where there has been an emphasis upon face-work practices and attempts to rescue social situations. It is also welcome in that it respects the dynamic nature of social encounters: Researchers' narratives of shyness too often end with the person "frozen in self-assessment", but that is surely an unrealistic portrait of the shy person, except perhaps for those for whom withdrawal from social interaction is their only coping style.

Shyness and embarrassment

We have been stressing the impression management perspective on shyness, but several authors have taken this approach to embarrassment as well. Asendorpf (1984) has argued that embarrassment is a consequence of a perceived discrepancy between one's "public image" and a standard for that image. Edelmann (1985a) has incorporated a similar process in his model. What, then, is the difference between shyness and embarrassment, according to this perspective? In Asendorpf's account, shyness is the anticipation of a discrepancy between self-presentation and one's standards, whereas embarrassment arises when an actual discrepancy has been perceived. A similar distinction between anxiety brought about by a specific social predicament and that caused by the anticipation of such an event has been made by Schlenker and Leary (Leary, 1983, pp. 23–28). Other self-presentation accounts have had little to say about embarrassment. That the difference between these states is essentially a temporal one largely reflects theorists' emphasis upon anxiety as central to the experience of both shyness and embarrassment. Similarly, accounts of the manifestation of these states stress the disruptive effects upon performance of emotional arousal, with little attention being paid to, say, blushing. Leary (1983) has discussed three categories of behaviours concomitant with social anxiety: arousal-related responses, disaffiliation, and self-presentational or strategic behaviours. The research that he reviews in terms of these categories mostly concerns studies of behaviours that are correlated with individual differences on shyness and social anxiety questionnaires and hence does not address differences between shyness and embarrassment. Thus, whereas the self-presentation approach to shyness has the merit of introducing the consideration of face-saving behaviours, this approach has not yet fostered research into possible differences in face-work practices in shyness and embarrassment.

Shyness and embarrassment as aspects of shame

Shyness as a fundamental emotion

The principal alternative to the social anxiety theory of shyness and embarrassment is that these are both aspects of a single primary emotion: shame. This theory, which has been explicitly proposed by Tomkins (1963) and Izard (1977), can be traced back to Darwin (1872/1904), and we begin this section with a brief outline of the latter's account.

Darwin devoted one chapter of *The Expression of the Emotions in Man and Animals* to an examination of blushing and of "The Nature of the Mental States which induce Blushing – These consist of shyness, shame, and modesty; the essential element in all being self-attention" (1872/1904, p. 345). With hindsight, we see that there are several distinctive features in his account. The first is the central position that he assigns to blushing: This is the only chapter in the book in which the title is oriented to expression rather than to the emotion being expressed, and the chapter itself makes it clear that blushing is the defining characteristic of these states of mind. Blushing is also associated with gaze aversion and with attempts to conceal the face; it may also be accompanied by mental confusion and changes in breathing and heart rate, but Darwin regards blushing, rather than these other bodily changes, as the direct cause of mental confusion; indeed, blushing is the precursor, not the consequence, of feelings of foolishness or an inability to say the right thing.

A second distinctive feature is that the chapter makes no mention of emotion as such: Blushing is excited by different states of mind, and it is one of Darwin's goals to show what these different states of mind have in common that might explain their tendency to induce blushing. As is perhaps well known, Darwin emphasises self-attention and, in particular, our attention to what others think of our appearance. This reflected appraisal need not be deprecatory, because consciousness of being the object of admiration or sexual interest is also a common source of blushing. By extension, according to Darwin, blushing and gaze aversion may also be consequent upon shame or guilt, which reflect moral shortcomings rather than sensitivity to one's appearance. It is noteworthy that the chapter makes no mention of embarrassment.

There is discussion of shyness: "Shyness seems to depend on sensitiveness to the opinion, whether good, or bad, of others, more especially with respect to external appearance" (1872/1904, p. 349). Accordingly, shyness will be more likely the more that attention may be drawn to our appearance, whether because of some real or imagined conspicuous feature or because we are in the presence of strangers who may tend to appraise us on our appearance rather than on our accomplishments. Furthermore, we will be more shy in the presence of those who may be more disposed to evaluate us, such as our superiors, and less shy when evaluation is less salient, as with friends and colleagues. These predictions have been confirmed in contemporary questionnaire studies (Zimbardo et al., 1974).

Finally, Darwin touches upon two questions that are addressed at several points in this volume. First, what is the relationship of shyness to shame, on the one hand, and to fear, on the other? He refers to synonyms for shyness, such as shamefacedness, false shame, or *mauvaise honte*, and he makes explicit connections between shyness and shame. Subsequently he alludes to the etymological relationships between shyness and fear and to such states as stage-fright and timidity, but he makes an important distinction: "A shy man no doubt dreads the notice of strangers, but can hardly be said to be afraid of them; he may be as bold as a hero in battle, and yet have no self-confidence about trifles in the presence of strangers" (1872/1904, p. 350). The second question is linked to Darwin's approach, which was to begin with blushing and gaze aversion and work back to their causes. Blushing is a consequence of one of several states of mind, including shyness, but does shyness, or any of these other states of mind, necessarily produce a distinctive bodily display? Can one be shy without blushing? This is not a question addressed by Darwin, but it has dogged more recent accounts of both shyness and embarrassment.

One strand of research since Darwin has attempted to identify a small set of fundamental emotions that could underlie the diversity of emotional experience. How have the states of mind that Darwin associated with self-attention been classified within that tradition?

Izard (1971) has argued that there is a small set of fundamental emotions each of which is characterised by a neurophysiological level, a neuromuscular expressive pattern, and a phenomenological quality. Shyness-shame was identified as one of this set, and his early research tended to treat this as a unitary emotion. Izard distinguished between shyness and anxiety, with the latter being classed as a complex emotion composed of a mixture of primary emotions. The theory as a whole has received considerable empirical support. Izard stressed the role played by the facial muscles in the differentiation and communication of emotions, and cross-cultural studies of the recognition of facial expressions have lent some support to his classification. In another series of investigations, the different emotions in the basic set also attract distinct patterns of ratings when subjects are asked to imagine and rate situations in which they have experienced those emotions.

However, the status of shame as one of this set seems less secure than is the case for the other emotions. In facial recognition studies, shame expressions received much lower recognition rates in Izard's own studies and in an investigation by Crozier (1981a) that attempted to rule out some confounding factors in the design of rating experiments. One rationale for this lower rate, provided by Izard, is that shame may be experienced less frequently than the other basic emotions, but that theory is not supported by research into shyness showing that shyness is in fact a common experience (Zimbardo et al., 1974). Also, the large and systematic research programme into the facial expression of emotion organised by Ekman and associates (e.g., Ekman, Friesen, & Ellsworth, 1972) has not identified shame as a universal.

Ratings studies suggest that shame-shyness may not be unitary. Izard (1972) has reported findings from factor analytical studies that two distinct factors – shame and shyness – can be isolated. Mosher and White (1981) have utilised Izard's measure of emotional experience, the Differential Emotions scale, to show that shame and shyness have different patterns of reactions. Izard (1971) has presented findings from a study in which subjects were asked to recall and rate on a number of dimensions a situation that had elicited shyness; that situation was rated as higher in both interest and enjoyment than any other "negative"-emotion-eliciting situation. Yet, elsewhere in the same report, Izard concluded that "shame is greatly dreaded and is either most dreaded or second only to fear-terror" (1971, p. 315). Shyness appears to involve an approach–avoidance conflict that is not present in shame – a conflict that we have already noted in our discussion of social anxiety, and one that has been recognised by Izard and Hyson (1986).

Notwithstanding the uncertainties concerning the relations between shyness and shame, Izard and Hyson (1986, p. 157) have concluded that shyness clearly can be classed as an emotion. Although that position has the merit of treating shyness as a phenomenon in its own right, rather than as an aspect of a different emotion, anxiety, it does not clarify the relations between shyness and embarrassment. Nor is it clear what criteria should be adopted to decide whether or not shyness is distinct from shame, embarrassment, guilt, or humiliation, which formerly were treated as aspects of a single basic emotion.

Shame and the classification of emotions

The difficulty of distinguishing emotions in terms of physiological reactions and the influential research conducted by Schachter and Singer (1962) into the effects of the labelling of situations upon the experience of emotion have led psychologists to alternative methods of classification. Roseman (1984), Scherer (1984), and Higgins (1987) have all proposed sets of dimensions or attributes that can be used to categorise emotions, and they have outlined conditions that must be fulfilled for shame to be experienced. We shall concentrate here on the theory of Higgins, because it explicitly discusses shame, embarrassment, and social anxiety.

Higgins (1987) has argued that emotions are influenced by the nature of discrepancies between the self-concept and some standard for behaviour, or *self-guides*, as he has termed these. The notion that such discrepancies are psychologically significant is long-standing, and we have already discussed it for theories of social anxiety and self-presentation. Higgins has proposed that one can distinguish emotions by considering the kinds of discrepancies between self-concept and self-guides. These discrepancies can be classified in terms of (1) the domain of the self involved – the actual self, the ideal self, and the self that one ought to be – and (2) the perspective or *standpoint* being taken upon the self. We shall limit our discussion of the complex set of predictions made by Higgins to his treatment of shame, embarrassment, and social anxiety.

Shame and embarrassment are conceived of as dejection-related emotions contingent upon a discrepancy between one's actual self and the ideal state that some significant other person hopes that one will attain: "shame, embarrassment . . . are associated with people believing that they have lost standing or esteem in the opinion of others" (Higgins, 1987, p. 322). That is, shame reflects an actual-own/ideal-other discrepancy. Shame is distinguished from both anxiety and guilt, which are considered agitation-related emotions. Guilt is contingent upon an actual-own/ought-own discrepancy, where one's current state fails to match the state one feels that one ought to have attained. Anxiety and fear are also associated with agitation and reflect an actual-own/ought-other discrepancy.

Higgins thus follows Izard in making a clear distinction between shame and anxiety and in regarding embarrassment as associated with shame rather than with anxiety; indeed, like Izard, shame is not separated from embarrassment. However, a closer examination shows that the position of embarrassment within this scheme is somewhat ambiguous. For example, Strauman and Higgins, as described by Higgins (1987), analysed relationships between their measure of self-discrepancies, the Selves questionnaire (Higgins, Klein, & Strauman, 1985), and measures of social anxiety, including the Social Avoidance and Distress scale and Fear of Negative Evaluation scale of Watson and Friend (1969). Social anxiety was significantly correlated with the actual-own/ought-other discrepancy score, but was independent of the actual-own/ideal-own discrepancy score. Thus, scores on a social anxiety measure that have been shown to correlate with shyness and embarrassability would seem to be closer to anxiety than to shame, although the underlying theory would locate embarrassment closer to shame. Because the Selves questionnaire does not explicitly refer to anxiety, this correlation between an agitation-related emotion and social anxiety is not spurious. Higgins also discussed possible similarities between public and private self-consciousness and these discrepancies, and he made the point that "both 'own' and 'other standpoints' are personal, covert aspects of one's internally represented self-guides, and thus *both* of these standpoints would be associated with *private* self-consciousness" (Higgins, 1987, p. 333, emphasis in original). Whether or not one considers that his interpretation of public self-consciousness as involving an external perspective is accurate, it is clear that the covert discrepancy proposed by Higgins cannot accommodate embarrassment, where, as we have seen, an audience's point of view is essential.

These theoretical developments in the classification of emotions have instigated a number of empirical studies of relationships among the emotions. Typically these studies ask people directly to indicate the degree of similarity among emotion words, or else similarity is estimated from content analyses of descriptions of emotion-eliciting situations. These measures then provide the basis for multivariate analysis techniques such as multidimensional scaling and cluster analysis, which provide some indication of people's mental representations of relations among emotions. This research seems to support Higgins's proposition that shame is related to dejection rather than to agitation or anxiety. Confirmation for this comes from studies by Higgins et al. (1985), Roseman (1984), and Shaver, Schwartz, Kirson, and O'Connor (1987). This last study identified fear and sadness as separate clusters, with shame, embarrassment, and humiliation belonging to sadness. However, there are also findings that cast doubt on the separation of social anxiety from shame. Scherer (1984) carried out a cluster analysis of similarity judgements of emotion words and found a less sharp division between anxiousness and embarrassment. Scherer identified a cluster of emotions that were elicited by some unpleasant event in which the individual was unable to cope because of lack of self-confidence. Guilt and shame would arise after some action of the self, whereas anxiousness and embarrassment would precede taking action whenever the event created uncertainty about how to behave. Even closer associations among shame, shyness, and anxiety were obtained in a similar kind of study by Conte in 1975, as described by Plutchik (1980, pp. 167–172). Conte produced a circumplex model of the emotions in which the proximity of emotion words on a circle modelled similarities in ratings. The words *afraid, shy, embarrassed, anxious, self-conscious*, and *ashamed* were all close together, extending across a range of angular locations of only 13 degrees on the circle.

An empirical study of similarity among emotion words

One starting point for the clarification of these relations is the observation that over and above their status as theoretical terms, emotion words exist within the lay vocabulary, and indeed theories do not hesitate to draw upon this lay vocabulary. A fruitful method of enquiry would be to understand these words as they are used in ordinary language and to explore regularities in their usage. One could then point to similarities and differences among these descriptions of emotional experiences that could suggest hypotheses about underlying patterns and about relations among eliciting circumstances, cognitions, physiological reactions, facial expressions, and behaviours. We present brief details of some studies that have examined the patterns of similarities among a selection of emotion words. The selection was made to reflect the emotions that we have been discussing and, in particular, those terms that have been taken by Izard (1971) as indicative of shame-shyness.

Studies of similarity among words have tended to rely upon multivariate analysis of judgements of similarity that either were provided directly by respondents or were derived from sorting techniques. The findings reviewed earlier imply that such judgements may underestimate the differences among emotion words that can be inferred from other kinds of studies. Hence, our preference was, at least initially, to avoid such direct estimates of similarity. Semin (1985) has devised a procedure for determining the degree of similarity among words in a dictionary of synonyms and has used this technique to explore relations between personality traits as they are organised in a dictionary and traits as they have been identified in psychological theories.

We applied this procedure to analyse relations among these emotion words: *afraid, anxious, ashamed, bashful, embarrassed, guilty, humiliated, penitent, repentant, self-conscious, shy,* and *timid.* This list comprises the nine words acceptable to Izard (1971) as correct identifications of shame–shyness in a facial recognition task, together with the words *afraid* (to reflect fearful shyness), *anxious,* and *self-conscious.*

Each word was looked up in the *New Nuttall Dictionary of English Synonyms and Antonyms* (1986), and its synonyms and antonyms were recorded. Each antonym was subsequently looked up, and its synonyms and antonyms were also recorded. An index of similarity was then calculated for each pair of words using the formula provided by Semin (1985), which provides an index of similarity that can take the range of values -1.0 to 1.0. Thus, the more synonyms that were shared by any pair of words, the more similar those words were judged to be. A score of 1.0 was obtained when all the synonyms of one word were shared with another, and a score of -1.0 was obtained when all the synonyms of one word were the antonyms of another. A 12×12 matrix of similarity indices was drawn up, with unities in the diagonal. The obtained indices ranged from 0 to 0.818, with a mean of 0.417. In the first stage, the 12×12 matrix was subjected to "agglomerative hierarchical cluster analysis" using the method of average linkage between groups for forming clusters. Figure 1.1 presents the resulting dendrogram for the 12 words, together with re-scaled distances between them. Four clusters were identified. The first linked *penitent, repentant,* and *guilty;* the second linked *ashamed, embarrassed,* and *humiliated;* the third combined *anxious* and *afraid;* the fourth linked *bashful, timid, shy,* and *self-conscious.* The first and second clusters, and the third and fourth, are closer to each other. Confirmation of these four clusters was obtained by submitting the matrix to principal components analysis, followed by varimax rotation. Four factors were extracted with eigenvalues greater than unity, accounting for 70.6% of the variance. Table 1.1 presents the four rotated factors together with the 12 words and all factor loadings greater than 0.30. Clearly this analysis replicates the pattern of four discernible clusters obtained in the first analysis.

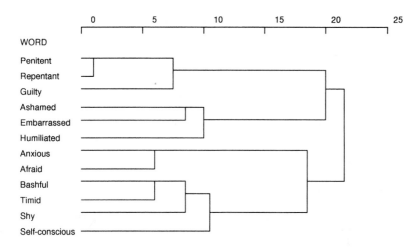

Figure 1.1. Cluster analysis of shame–shyness words: dendrogram showing clusters and re-scaled distance values.

Differences among emotions along cognitive dimensions

Our second study is an attempt to study empirically some possible dimensions upon which these emotions may differ. We were influenced by the approach by Roseman (1984), who attempted to identify a set of cognitive dimensions that would be sufficient to specify which of a small set of basic discrete emotions would be experienced. He identified five dimensions related to the following:

1. the consistency or inconsistency of an event with motives;
2. two kinds of motives, corresponding to rewards and punishments;
3. power, characterising the individual as weak or strong in the situation;
4. agency, whether oneself, another person, or circumstances were responsible for the event;
5. probability, distinguishing events that might possibly happen from those that are psychologically certain to occur.

Using these dimensions, Roseman characterised shame as a negative emotion that is inconsistent with one's motives when one is weak and when the event is caused by oneself. The scheme distinguishes between shame and regret but does not separate shame from guilt, nor does it distinguish among shame, shyness, and embarrassment. What dimensions could be utilised to make these distinctions? Crozier (1987) devised a questionnaire that asked respondents to consider five emotion-eliciting situations in which one felt shy, embarrassed, ashamed, anxious, or angry. Anger was included as a control and to avoid having the situations seem

Table 1.1. *Factor analysis of similarity indices of emotion words: Factors and factor loadings*

	Factors			
Word	I	II	III	IV
Penitent		893		
Repentant		913		
Guilty		795		
Ashamed		370	714	
Embarrassed			852	
Humiliated			793	
Anxious				895
Afraid				880
Bashful	857			
Timid	784			
Shy	755			
Self-conscious	700			

Note: Decimal points omitted. This table includes all loadings greater than 0.30.

too similar. Twenty-eight respondents completed the questionnaire, each answering a series of questions about all five emotion-eliciting situations. These questions were chosen to reflect Roseman's set of dimensions and also some of the issues already raised in this chapter.

The questionnaire. The items are listed in Table 1.2. Seven items were related to the Roseman dimensions: uncertainty ("uncertain what to expect"); power ("active versus passive", "unable to cope with the situation", "that you could have acted differently"); and agency ("that you were responsible for bringing about the situation", "that other people were responsible for bringing about the situation", "that you were the central figure in the episode"). One item related to the pleasantness of the situation, because pleasantness seemed to distinguish between shyness and shame in Izard's research. One item asked whether the emotion could be experienced alone, prompted by consideration that shyness and perhaps embarrassment are experienced only in social situations. One item explored the notion that embarrassment and shame are reactions to a specific incident, whereas shyness and anxiety are anticipatory. Further items explored Taylor's assertion (1985) that the thought of being seen is at the core of shame and embarrassment: "See yourself through the eyes of others", "that other people present would think badly of you".

Table 1.2. *Study Two questionnaire items*

You are in a position where you feel.... Please attempt to answer all the following questions about that situation and your experience of it, using the following scale:

+3   Almost certainly
+2   Probably
+1   Likely
 0   Don't know
−1   Likely not
−2   Probably not
−3   Almost certainly not

See yourself through the eyes of others ...
Feel unworthy ...
Self-confident ...
Uncertain what to do or say ...
Unable to cope with the situation ...
That you were responsible for bringing about the situation ...
That other people were responsible for bringing about the situation ...
Uncertain what to expect ...
That these feelings were a response to some specific incident ...
That you were the central figure in the episode ...
That you could have acted differently ...
That other people present would think badly of you ...
That you deserve to be in this situation ...

Would you say that these feelings were
  (a) very pleasant
  (b) pleasant
  (c) unpleasant
  (d) very unpleasant
  (e) a mixture of both

Could you have these feelings alone, or is it necessary that other people are present?

Would you say that in that situation you were:
  Very active/Active/Neither/Passive/Very passive

The concept of self-esteem has been found to be close to that of shyness (Crozier, 1981b). Shott (1979) has proposed that shame is distinct from embarrassment in that the former, but not the latter, entails a loss of self-esteem. Thus, one item probed feelings of unworthiness. Taylor (1985) and Parrott, Sabini, and Silver (1988) have argued that embarrassment is characterised by the individual's inability to respond appropriately to the demands of the situation, and accordingly one item concerned being uncertain what to do or say. All items were presented for each of the five emotions. Each respondent was contacted individually and completed the questionnaire alone.

Table 1.3. *Mean ratings of pleasantness and level of*
activity associated with five types of emotions

	Mean ratings	
Emotion	Pleasant	Active
Shy	−0.778	−0.571
Embarrassed	−1.444	0.071
Shame	−1.593	0.143
Anxious	−1.111	0.250
Angry	−0.963	0.536

Note: Rating scales ranged from −2 (very unpleasant or
passive) to 2 (very pleasant or active).

The format of the questionnaire was as follows. The first question
asked respondents to rate the situation on 13 dimensions using a 7-point
scale ranging from +3 ("Almost certainly would feel the following") to
−3 ("Almost certainly would not"). Respondents also rated on two
5-point scales how active or passive they would be in the situation and
how pleasant or unpleasant they would find it. Finally, they were asked
to respond to the question whether they could have these feelings alone
or whether other people needed to be present. The different response
formats meant that these various questions needed to be analysed separately, and the results will be discussed for the different kinds of items in
turn.

Ratings of the pleasantness of the feelings were subject to a repeated
measures ANOVA: Emotions × Subjects. There was a significant main
effect for Emotions [$F(4, 104) = 5.44, p < 0.001$]. From Table 1.3 it can
be seen that shyness (mean −0.778 on a scale from −2 to +2) was the
least unpleasant, and shame was the most unpleasant; comparisons
among the individual means confirmed this. These results replicate those
of Izard. Ratings on the active–passive dimension were analysed in a
similar way, and again there was a significant main effect for Emotions
($F = 3.702, p < 0.01$). Shyness was rated as significantly more passive
than the other four emotions, which did not differ from each other.

Respondents were quite clear that shyness and embarrassment could
occur only in the presence other people, as only 11% thought that
shyness could be experienced while alone, and 18% thought that embarrassment could be experienced alone. The concept of shame elicited a
mixed response, in that 52% of respondents believed that it could be
experienced alone. Most subjects (85%) responded that anxiety could be

experienced when alone, and a substantial majority thought that anger could be experienced while alone.

The four emotions of shame, shyness, embarrassment, and anxiety attracted different patterns of ratings on the 13 dimensions of question 1. In general terms, feeling ashamed attracted the most extreme ratings, and anxiety attracted the least extreme ratings, reflecting the fact that the dimensions were designed with the emotions of self-assessment in mind. These global impressions were subjected to a series of statistical tests, the most relevant of which will now be briefly summarised. To determine if any particular pair of emotions elicited different patterns of ratings, the differences between ratings on the 13 dimensions were calculated for each respondent, and these difference scores were subjected to a repeated measures ANOVA: Dimensions × Subjects. We now discuss four of these comparisons.

Shyness and embarrassment. These emotions did elicit different patterns of ratings in that there was a significant main effect for Dimensions [$F(12, 324) = 3.736, p < 0.001$]. Inspection of the mean difference scores suggested that shyness was characterised by the belief that other people were responsible, whereas embarrassment tended to be characterised by beliefs that the respondent was responsible, that these feelings were responses to a specific incident, and that the respondent could have acted differently.

The Shy–Ashamed comparison also produced a significant main effect for Dimensions ($F = 7.274, p < 0.001$). Again, inspection of the mean difference scores suggested the principal differences: Shyness was associated with believing that other people were responsible, whereas feeling ashamed was associated with feeling unworthy and with beliefs that these feelings were responses to a specific incident, that the respondent was the central figure in the episode, that the respondent could have acted differently, and that other people present would think badly of the respondent.

The Shy–Anxious comparison was significant ($F = 2.566, p < 0.01$). In comparison with anxiety, shyness was more likely to elicit responses of seeing oneself through the eyes of others, of being uncertain what to do or say, of being unable to cope with the situation, of feeling unworthy, and of feeling that other people would think badly of the respondent.

The final comparison to be presented found a significant difference in the pattern of ratings between Embarrassed and Ashamed ($F = 2.922, p < 0.001$). The belief that other people were responsible for the situation characterised embarrassment, whereas feeling ashamed was more likely to be characterised by feeling unworthy and by the judgement that one deserved to be in the situation.

We now summarise the pattern found in these results. Feelings of being shy, ashamed, and embarrassed do share common features, in that all entail seeing oneself through the eyes of others, being uncertain what to do or say, and lacking self-confidence. One feels that one is the central figure in an episode, that this is in response to a specific incident, and that other people will think badly of one. There are also differences in agency, self-esteem, and uncertainty about how to behave. First, we consider agency: Oneself, not others, is responsible in shame and embarrassment, but not to the same extent in shyness. That one could have acted differently characterises shame and embarrassment, but not shyness. Interpretation of differences in agency is not straightforward, in that the concept itself needs further clarification; for example, Shaver and Drown (1986) point to the need to distinguish carefully notions of causality, responsibility, and blameworthiness, and further research is needed to consider differences among shyness, shame, and embarrassment in the light of these distinctions. In terms of self-esteem, feeling unworthy does characterise shyness and embarrassment, but it is elevated in shame. Uncertainty about what to expect is higher in shyness than in either shame or embarrassment.

Conclusions from empirical studies

We have outlined the principal findings from two preliminary studies into possible relations among shame, shyness, embarrassment, and anxiety. Although these findings must be approached with caution, they do have some implications for our understanding of these relations. The first is that both studies show that distinctions *can* be made among them, and thus it is not satisfactory to talk of shyness and anxiety or shame and embarrassment as if these terms are interchangeable. We need to explore these relations further, and the methods adopted here may prove useful in teasing out subtle differences among these emotions. This approach is more searching than previous research along these lines, which had been restricted to asking subjects to rate shyness and shame situations only in terms of a small set of emotion words (Mosher & White, 1981). Our second study suggests that we can identify dimensions that do distinguish shyness from shame, anxiety, and embarrassment. These dimensions include, but are not restricted to, those proposed by Roseman.

Furthermore, both studies suggest that both shyness and embarrassment can be distinguished from anxiety, and hence we would argue that it is not sufficient for theories to make the assumption that these are but forms of social anxiety; these relations must be demonstrated. Although shyness has some associations with anxiety, it equally has associations with shame. One recent theory does seem sensitive to this. Buss (1983, 1986) has proposed that there are two kinds of shyness: fearful shyness and self-conscious shyness. Whereas the first form leads to fear and distress, the second results in public self-consciousness. At our current state of knowledge, this is speculative, and we certainly do not wish to make excessive claims about these small studies, particularly in light of the possible criticism that "anxiety" may have a narrower meaning for our respondents than for shyness researchers. Nevertheless, we would suggest that future research should address shyness and embarrassment in their complexity.

We conclude this chapter with brief consideration of two neglected aspects of shyness and embarrassment that are suggested by our discussion of these two emotions as components of shame. The first concerns blushing, and the second concerns the reasons why shyness might be so widespread in contemporary society.

Blushing

Darwin regarded blushing as central to an understanding of the emotions of self-attention, and although later writers (e.g., Buss, 1980; Edelmann, 1987) have concurred with this in their discussions of social anxiety and embarrassment, none of the perspectives that we have been reviewing has been able to provide a satisfactory explanation of this phenomenon. Because blushing does not seem to be associated with any other form of anxiety, this would suggest that social anxiety may provide a less useful account of shyness and embarrassment than do those approaches that suggest their relationship with self-consciousness and shame. The lack of research into blushing is particularly regrettable as it must surely provide clues as to the nature of self-attention.

Even at the physiological level blushing remains obscure (Folklow & Neil, 1971, p. 455; Rushmer, 1976, p. 169). Frijda (1986, pp. 167–168) provides a short summary of relevant research, suggesting that blushing is caused by "inhibition of sympathetically controlled vasoconstriction and the release, by the sweat glands, of a substance called bradykinin, which has strong vasodilatory effects". Edelmann (1987, p. 70) relates blushing to increases in blood temperature, but concludes that little is known about the causal links between embarrassment and increases in blood temperature. Frijda considers that blushing may be an appeasement or "endearment" signal, and Castelfranchi and Poggi (this volume) pursue the notion that blushing has a subtle communicative significance. Certainly this helps to explain why the desire to conceal oneself that can often characterise shyness and embarrassment should be associated with such a conspicuous bodily display. Yet for some people, blushing is the cause of their anxiety. Darwin argued that shyness may be a consequence of some conspicuous feature of the individual's appearance, and for some, that feature is their apparently uncontrollable blushing. Again, we can note that there are social norms about blushing, which may be more acceptable in women and children, and this possible correlation with social power relationships may be a matter of appeasement. The psychoanalytical view, at least as represented by Chasseguet-Smirgel (1985, p. 158), is that blushing is linked to homosexual phantasies:

The person who feels ashamed hides his face. Thus not only does he attempt to disguise the signs of the re-sexualization of his homosexual instincts (his blushing) but also the displacement, from the rear to the front, of which he is the object. He has *lost face*, and his face has become his rear (cf. the equation cheeks = buttocks). (Emphasis in original)

Perhaps our lack of knowledge in this area encourages such speculation. The phenomenon of blushing highlights an enormous weakness in all our theories of shyness and embarrassment, and its neglect by psychologists interested in social interaction is a disgrace: We should blush to think of it.

Public and private dimensions of shyness

Our second question is raised by the findings from survey data of the widespread nature of shyness. These prompt us to ask not what makes any individual shy but what social conditions foster shyness in the community. When considering individual cases, the concept of social anxiety may provide a plausible explanation for social difficulties, but when one is faced with evidence of the very high incidence of self-reported social difficulties, then one should seek an explanation in the society in which these social encounters take place.

The incidence of self-labelled shyness was significantly higher in an American sample (44%) than in an Israeli sample (31%), and self-consciousness was emphasised as a central feature in shyness by 79% of American respondents, as compared with only 30% of Israelis (Pines & Zimbardo, 1978). There is also some anecdotal evidence of cross-cultural differences in shyness (Zimbardo, 1977), and the anthropologist Howell (1981) has described a society, the Chewong of Malaysia, in which shyness appears to be the norm. The explanation offered by Pines and Zimbardo (1978) for the high incidence in American findings is that

the American culture promotes and emphasizes the ego, with its narcissistic introspection, self-absorption, and excessive preoccupation with the self ... where group and not ego is central, shyness should be less likely.

It is clear that individualism and the tendency to regard self-acceptance as contingent upon uncertain standards are at the heart of Zimbardo's conceptualisation of cross-cultural differences. His observation that a preoccupation with individualism puts people "under the spotlight" is interesting, but it lacks theoretical grounding, and it fails to make clear what level of self-preoccupation should be regarded as excessive.

Our approach to this issue is guided by the observation that writers on shame have given thought to the broader social significance of this emotion, a significance captured in the notion of the "shame culture". This notion has two aspects. The first is that shame is a form of social control, that people internalise the standards of society and hence monitor their own behaviour; the second is that cultures may differ in their use of this mechanism.

Shott (1979) expresses this first aspect:

Role taking emotions like embarrassment and shame are the foundation for the large part of social control, that is self-control . . . so central to social control that society as we know it could not function without them. . . . In the final analysis no one except ourselves can make us ashamed, guilty or embarrassed and without our capacity to experience these sentiments society as we know it would surely be impossible.

Izard makes much the same point in disagreeing with those psychologists who conceive of emotions as essentially disruptive. He counters that emotions are *adaptive* and that they both motivate and organise behaviour: Shame and shyness provide the motivation for self-control, for the regulation of emotional expression, and thus for more effective social interaction. Semin and Manstead (1983) locate self-presentation strategies within the context of the monitoring and regulation of everyday activities and the maintenance of social order. Orderly social interaction is possible only if people monitor and control their own behaviour. Finally, within the self-awareness paradigm, Wicklund (1982) argues that self-awareness is a civilising agent that brings individuals under the control of social norms by forcing them to attend to the self and in so doing to attend to the point of view of others. From all these different perspectives the emotions of self-attention are related to mechanisms of internalised social control.

Although the notion of shyness as excessive internalised self-control is suggestive, it still leaves important questions unanswered, such as When does self-control become excessive for a society, and indeed why should everyday social encounters trigger self-evaluation? It is instructive to note here that our ordinary use of the word *shy* does not necessarily emphasise self-evaluation. Inspection of dictionary definitions reveals meanings relating to wariness, caution, reluctance, and reserve that need not entail critical self-evaluation. For example, consider this sentence from Dickens, as quoted in the *Oxford English Dictionary*: "Since the catastrophe recorded in the last chapter, Mrs. Tibbs had been very shy of young-lady boarders".

Crozier (1984) tackled these problems by considering the distinction between the public self and the private self within a broader cultural context. Social encounters of a public kind, which make salient a presentation of the public self, create widespread unease. And it seems natural to us that they should do so. They also seem threatening to the self, and again that seems only natural. Rather than accept these as natural phenomena, we should try to understand the social conditions that produce these assumptions. In his historical analysis of changes in public life, Sennett (1976) has discussed the notion of a balance between public and private life, and this concept may allow us to understand why certain kinds of social encounters do seem to create unease.

When private and public areas of life are in balance, there are patterns of social interaction that are appropriate either for public encounters or for home life. Both of these are in equilibrium in the sense that both afford emotional gratification – neither is regarded as inherently superior to the other. Sennett describes such forms of social relationships in the eighteenth century, when, he argues, in public, man was an *actor*, and civility was the standard for behaviour, which was governed by convention and hence was not revealing of personality. These conventions were apparent, for example, in dress; there were strict rules governing public appearance. It was illegal to wear in public clothes that were inappropriate to one's station in life, whereas in domestic life all social classes wore rather simple, uniform garments.

But according to Sennett, that balance was eroded by the enormous social and economic changes of the nineteenth century. The balance was upset, the public realm became treated as inferior to the private, and the private became the yardstick for judging the public. It was no longer *authentic* to be an actor, and appearance became a self-presentation. Two consequences of this trend are of particular interest here. The first Sennett describes as the evaluation of public life in terms of *intimacy:* Unreasonably, one expects intimacy throughout all social encounters, and social relationships are judged as authentic the closer they approach the inner psychological concerns of each person. Intimacy in this sense leads to narcissism or self-absorption, where one is unable to conceive of social encounters as not involving the self. People attempt to authenticate their public identities by means of their personal qualities, and this involves processes of self-evaluation.

Although Sennett does not broach the question of shyness, his analysis does allow us to tackle some of the problems that confront those accounts of shyness that have focused on the individual at the expense of the social context. It suggests why shyness might involve an excessive preoccupation with the self and why there should be such widespread unease at the prospect of many routine social encounters. When public and private realms of life are in balance, routine social encounters outside the family are governed by convention and are not revealing of self. The social skills required will relate to knowledge of the rules governing appropriate forms of behaviour, and a breakdown in inter-action will result in embarrassment. There will be no necessary impli-cations for self-esteem, because only one's situated identity will be involved. Contrast this with Sennett's case of the society in which intimacy is the standard for behaviour, and appearance is a self-presentation. Here greater demands are placed upon one's social skills, and a breakdown in an encounter will be shaming and will have implica-tions for self-esteem. In the first case, shyness will be wariness or uncer-tainty how to behave; in the latter it will be a matter of narcissism or self-absorption.

Our point is not that this analysis is necessarily correct; rather, it identifies questions that must be tackled by a social psychological theory of shyness and embarrassment. Why should so many routine encounters apparently produce such unease among so many people, and why should the breakdowns, mismatches, and "false notes" that must accompany any social interaction that is not entirely scripted have such implications for an individual's sense of worth? The answers to these questions will not be found in investigation of individuals alone, but in consideration of relations that hold between individuals and their society.

Summary

Recent research into shyness and embarrassment has largely adopted one of two frameworks. Either these phenomena are seen as forms of social anxiety or they are regarded as aspects of the underlying fun-damental emotion of shame. The social anxiety perspective has drawn upon the resurgence of interest among social psychologists in the self, and in particular, models of self-awareness and of impression manage-ment have been elaborated to provide accounts of both shyness and embarrassment. These theoretical developments have provided a wel-come impetus to research in a previously neglected area, but they face several problems. It is not clear that the assumption that shyness and embarrassment are forms of anxiety is warranted. We have also argued that the treatment of the experience of self-consciousness within the self-awareness paradigm has not been satisfactory, that the issue of blushing has been ignored, and that appeal to a notion of anxiety makes it difficult to see why shyness in particular should be so widespread in contemporary North American and European society. Conceptualising shyness and embarrassment as aspects of shame does permit a grasp of some of these issues: Blushing and feelings of self-consciousness have long been regarded as characteristic of shame, and the notion of the "shame culture" at least makes some reference to the societal dimension. Yet empirical research has failed to locate shyness or embarrassment convincingly within the emotion of shame, and detailed discussion of psychological processes has been the province of adherents to the social anxiety and self-awareness perspectives, rather than those who have postulated fundamental emotions. It may be that Buss is correct in postulating different kinds of shyness. Our conclusions are that the affinities between shyness and embarrassment are such that these should be considered together and that progress requires both conceptual analyses and empirical investigations of all the "emotions of self-attention".

REFERENCES

Arkin, R. M. (1981). Self-presentation styles. In J. T. Tedeschi (Ed.), *Impression management theory and social psychological research* (pp. 311–333). New York: Academic Press.

Arkin, R. M., Lake, E. A., & Baumgardner, A. H. (1986). Shyness and self-presentation. In W. H. Jones, J. M. Cheek, & S. R. Briggs (Eds.), *Shyness: Perspectives on research and treatment* (pp. 189–203). New York: Plenum Press.

Arnold, A. P., & Cheek, J. M. (1986). Shyness, self-preoccupation and the Stroop Color and Word Test. *Personality and Individual Differences, 7*, 571–573.

Asendorpf, J. (1984). Shyness, embarrassment and self-presentation: A control theory approach. In R. Schwarzer (Ed.), *The self in anxiety, stress, and depression* (pp. 109–114). Amsterdam: North Holland.

Buss, A. H. (1980). *Self-consciousness and social anxiety.* San Francisco: Freeman.

Buss, A. H. (1983). *Two kinds of shyness.* Paper presented at the Roundtable Conference on Anxiety and Self-Related Cognitions, Berlin.

Buss, A. H. (1986). A theory of shyness. In W. H. Jones, J. M. Cheek, & S. R. Briggs (Eds.), *Shyness: Perspectives on research and treatment* (pp. 39–46). New York: Plenum Press.

Buss, A. H., & Briggs, S. R. (1984). Drama and the self in social interaction. *Journal of Personality and Social Psychology, 47*, 1310–1324.

Buss, A. H., & Finn, S. E. (1987). Classification of personality traits. *Journal of Personality and Social Psychology, 52*, 432–444.

Carver, C. S. (1979). A cybernetic model of self-attention processes. *Journal of Personality and Social Psychology, 37*, 1251–1281.

Carver, C. S., & Scheier, M. F. (1986). Analyzing shyness: A specific application of broader self-regulatory principles. In W. H. Jones, J. M. Cheek, & S. R. Briggs (Eds.), *Shyness: Perspectives on research and treatment* (pp. 173–185). New York: Plenum Press.

Carver, C. S., & Scheier, M. F. (1987). The blind men and the elephant: Selective examination of the public–private literature gives rise to a faulty perception. *Journal of Personality, 55*, 525–540.

Chasseguet-Smirgel, J. (1985). *The ego ideal. A psychoanalytic essay on the malady of the ideal.* London: Free Association Books.

Cheek, J. M., & Buss, A. H. (1981). Shyness and sociability. *Journal of Personality and Social Psychology, 41*, 330–339.

Crozier, W. R. (1979a). Shyness as a dimension of personality. *British Journal of Social and Clinical Psychology, 18*, 121–128.

Crozier, W. R. (1979b). Shyness as anxious self-preoccupation. *Psychological Reports, 44*, 959–962.

Crozier, W. R. (1981a). Do photographs of facial displays provide a sound basis for classifying the primary emotions? *Current Psychological Research, 1*, 199–202.

Crozier, W. R. (1981b). Shyness and self-esteem. *British Journal of Social Psychology, 20*, 220–222.

Crozier, W. R. (1982). Explanations of social shyness. *Current Psychological Reviews, 2*, 47–60.

Crozier, W. R. (1984). *Public and private dimensions of shyness.* Paper presented at the British Psychological Society annual London conference, City University, London.

Crozier, W. R. (1985). *Shyness as self-standards discrepancy.* Paper presented at the British Psychological Society annual conference, University College, Swansea.

Crozier, W. R. (1987). *Shyness as a basic emotion.* Paper presented at the British Psychological Society International Conference on Skilled Behaviour, University of Sussex.

Darwin, C. (1904). *The expression of the emotions in man and animals* (2nd ed.). London: John Murray. (Original work published 1872)

Duval, S., & Wicklund, R. A. (1972). *A theory of objective self-awareness.* New York: Academic Press.

Edelmann, R. J. (1985a). Social embarrassment: An analysis of the process. *Journal of Social and Personal Relationships, 2*, 195–213.

Edelmann, R. J. (1985b). Individual differences in embarrassment: Self-consciousness, self-monitoring, and embarrassability. *Personality and Individual Differences, 6*, 223–230.

Edelmann, R. J. (1987). *The psychology of embarrassment.* New York: Wiley.

Ekman, P., Friesen, W. V., & Ellsworth, P. (1972). *Emotion in the human face: Guidelines for research and a review of findings.* New York: Pergamon.

Emerson, J. P. (1970). Behavior in private places: Sustaining definitions of reality in gynecological examinations. In H. P. Dreitzel (Ed.), *Recent sociology. Number 2: Patterns of communication behavior* (pp. 74–97). New York: Macmillan.

Fenigstein, A. (1979). Self-consciousness, self-attention, and social interaction. *Journal of Personality and Social Psychology, 37,* 75–86.

Fenigstein, A. (1987). On the nature of public and private self-consciousness. *Journal of Personality, 55,* 1–12.

Fenigstein, A. (1988). *Self-attention and egocentrism.* Unpublished manuscript, Kenyon College, Gambier, OH.

Fenigstein, A., Scheier, M. F., & Buss, A. H. (1975). Public and private self-consciousness: Assessment and theory. *Journal of Clinical and Consulting Psychology, 43,* 522–527.

Folklow, N., & Neil, E. (1971). *Circulation.* Oxford University Press.

Frijda, N. H. (1986). *The emotions.* Cambridge University Press.

Goffman, E. (1956). Embarrassment and social organization. *American Journal of Sociology, 62,* 264–274.

Goffman, E. (1972). *Interaction ritual.* Harmondsworth, Middlesex: Penguin.

Gross, E., & Stone, S. P. (1964). Embarrassment and the analysis of role requirements. *American Journal of Sociology, 70,* 1–15.

Hales, S. (1985). The inadvertent rediscovery of self in social psychology. *Journal for the Theory of Social Behaviour, 15,* 237–282.

Hall, R., & Goldberg, D. (1977). The role of social anxiety in social interaction difficulties. *British Journal of Psychiatry, 131,* 610–615.

Harré, R. (1983). *Personal being.* Oxford: Blackwell.

Harris, P. R. (1984). Shyness and psychological imperialism: On the dangers of ignoring the ordinary language roots of the terms we deal with. *European Journal of Social Psychology, 14,* 169–181.

Hass, R. G. (1984). Perspective taking and self-awareness: Drawing an E on your forehead. *Journal of Personality and Social Psychology, 46,* 788–798.

Higgins, E. T. (1987). Self-discrepancy: A theory relating self and affect. *Psychological Review, 94,* 319–340.

Higgins, E. T., Klein, R., & Strauman, T. (1985). Self-concept discrepancy theory: A psychological model for distinguishing among different aspects of depression and anxiety. *Social Cognition, 3,* 51–76.

Howell, S. (1981). Rules not words. In P. Heelas & A. Lock (Eds.), *Indigenous psychologies: The anthropology of the self* (pp. 133–143). London: Academic Press.

Izard, C. E. (1971). *The face of emotion.* New York: Appleton-Century-Crofts.

Izard, C. E. (1972). *Patterns of emotions.* New York: Academic Press.

Izard, C. E. (1977). *Human emotions.* New York: Plenum Press.

Izard, C. E., & Hyson, M. C. (1986). Shyness as a discrete emotion. In W. H. Jones, J. M. Cheek, & S. R. Briggs (Eds.), *Shyness: Perspectives on research and treatment* (pp. 147–160). New York: Plenum Press.

Jellison, J. M. (1981). Reconsidering the attitude concept: A behavioristic self-presentation formulation. In J. T. Tedeschi (Ed.), *Impression management theory and social psychological research* (pp. 107–126). New York: Academic Press.

Jones, E. E., & Pittman, T. S. (1982). Toward a general theory of strategic self-presentation. In J. Suls (Ed.), *Psychological perspectives on the self* (Vol. 1, pp. 231–262). Hillsdale, NJ: Lawrence Erlbaum.

Leary, M. R. (1983). *Understanding social anxiety.* London: Sage.

Lewinsky, H. (1941). The nature of shyness. *British Journal of Psychology, 32,* 105–113.

Miller, R. S. (1986). Embarrassment: Causes and consequences. In W. H. Jones, J. M. Cheek, & S. R. Briggs (Eds.), *Shyness: Perspectives on research and treatment* (pp. 295–311). New York: Plenum Press.

Miller, R. S. (1987). Empathic embarrassment: Situational and personal determinants of reactions to the embarrassment of another. *Journal of Personality and Social Psychology, 53,* 1061–1069.

Modigliani, A. (1968). Embarrassment and embarrassability. *Sociometry, 31,* 313–326.

Mosher, D. L., & White, B. B. (1981). On differentiating shame and shyness. *Motivation and Emotion, 5,* 61–74.

Parrott, W. G., Sabini, J., & Silver, M. (1988). The roles of self-esteem and social interaction in embarrassment. *Personality and Social Psychology Bulletin, 14,* 191–202.

Pilkonis, P. A. (1977). Shyness, public and private, and its relationship to other measures of social behavior. *Journal of Personality, 45,* 585–595.

Pilkonis, P. A., & Zimbardo, P. G. (1979). The personal and social dynamics of shyness. In C. E. Izard (Ed.), *Emotions in personality and psychopathology* (pp. 133–160). New York: Plenum Press.

Pines, A., & Zimbardo, P. G. (1978). The personal and cultural dynamics of shyness: A comparison between Israelis, American Jews and Americans. *Journal of Psychology and Judaism, 3,* 81–101.

Plutchik, R. (1980). *Emotion: A psychoevolutionary synthesis.* New York: Harper & Row.

Roseman, I. J. (1984). Cognitive determinants of emotion: A structural theory. In P. Shaver (Ed.), *Review of personality and social psychology* (Vol. 5, pp. 11–36). Beverly Hills: Sage.

Rushmer, R. F. (1976). *Cardiovascular dynamics* (4th ed.). Philadelphia: Saunders.

Sarason, I. G. (1975). Anxiety and self-preoccupation. In I. G. Sarason & C. D. Spielberger (Eds.), *Stress and anxiety* (Vol. 2, pp. 27–44). Washington, DC: Hemisphere.

Sarason, I. G. (1984). Stress, anxiety, and cognitive interference: Reactions to tests. *Journal of Personality and Social Psychology, 46,* 929–938.

Sarason, I. G., & Sarason, B. R. (1986). Anxiety and interfering thoughts: Their effect on social interaction. In W. H. Jones, J. M. Cheek, & S. R. Briggs (Eds.), *Shyness: Perspectives on research and treatment* (pp. 253–264). New York: Plenum Press.

Sartre, J.-P. (1969). *Being and nothingness* (trans. H. E. Barnes). London: Methuen.

Schachter, S., & Singer, J. (1962). Cognitive, social and physiological determinants of emotional state. *Psychological Review, 63,* 379–399.

Scherer, K. R. (1984). Emotion as a multicomponent process: A model and some cross-cultural data. In P. Shaver (Ed.), *Review of personality and social psychology* (Vol. 5, pp. 37–63). Beverly Hills: Sage.

Schlenker, B. R., & Leary, M. R. (1982). Social anxiety and self-presentation: A conceptualization and model. *Psychological Bulletin, 92,* 641–669.

Schudson, M. (1984). Embarrassment and Erving Goffman's idea of human nature. *Theory and Society, 13*, 633–648.

Semin, G. R. (1985, December). *Towards a systematic reconstruction of studying the person in social psychology and personality: A plea for empirical studies with N = 0.* Paper presented at the British Psychological Society annual London conference, City University, London.

Semin, G. R., & Manstead, A. S. R. (1981). The beholder beheld: A study of social emotionality. *European Journal of Social Psychology, 11*, 253–265.

Semin, G. R., & Manstead, A. S. R. (1983). *The accountability of conduct: A social psychological analysis.* London: Academic Press.

Sennett, R. (1976). *The fall of public man.* Cambridge University Press.

Shaver, K. G., & Drown, D. (1986). On causality, responsibility, and self-blame: A theoretical note. *Journal of Personality and Social Psychology, 50*, 697–702.

Shaver, P., Schwartz, J., Kirson, D., & O'Connor, C. (1987). Emotion knowledge: Further exploration of a prototype approach. *Journal of Personality and Social Psychology, 52*, 1061–1086.

Shott, S. (1979). Emotion and social life: A symbolic interactionist analysis. *American Journal of Sociology, 84*, 1317–1334.

Silver, M., Sabini, S., & Parrott, W. G. (1987). Embarrassment: A dramaturgic account. *Journal for the Theory of Social Behaviour, 17*, 47–61.

Snyder, C. R., Higgins, R. L., & Stucky, R. J. (1983). *Excuses: Masquerades in search of grace.* New York: Wiley Interscience.

Snyder, C. R., Smith, T. W., Augelli, R. W., & Ingram, R. E. (1985). On the self-serving function of social anxiety: Shyness as a self-handicapping strategy. *Journal of Personality and Social Psychology, 48*, 970–980.

Snyder, M. (1987). *Public appearances/private realities: The psychology of self-monitoring.* San Francisco: Freeman.

Taylor, G. (1985). *Pride, shame, and guilt: Emotions of self-assessment.* Oxford: Clarendon Press.

Tetlock, P. E., & Manstead, A. S. R. (1985). Impression management versus intrapsychic explanations in social psychology: A useful dichotomy? *Psychological Review, 92*, 59–77.

Tomkins, S. S. (1963). *Affect, imagery, consciousness. Vol. Two: The negative affects.* New York: Springer-Verlag.

Watson, D., & Friend, R. (1969). Measurement of social-evaluative anxiety. *Journal of Consulting and Clinical Psychology, 43*, 448–457.

Wicklund, R. A. (1982). Orientation to the environment versus preoccupation with human potential. In R. M. Sorrentino & E. T. Higgins (Eds.), *The handbook of motivation and cognition: Foundations of social behavior* (pp. 64–95). New York: Guilford.

Wine, J. D. (1971). Test anxiety and direction of attention. *Psychological Bulletin, 76*, 92–104.

Zimbardo, P. G. (1977). *Shyness: What it is, what to do about it.* Reading, MA: Addison-Wesley.

Zimbardo, P. G., Pilkonis, P. A., & Norwood, R. M. (1974). *The silent prison of shyness* (Office of Naval Research Technical Report Z-17). Stanford, CA: Stanford University.

2

Shyness and embarrassment in psychological theory and ordinary language

PETER R. HARRIS

Introduction

The purpose of this chapter is to focus on shyness and embarrassment as aspects of an integrated and dynamic social psychological process that passes – erroneously – under the rubric of social anxiety. The belief underpinning this approach is that (1) the time is ripe for such conceptual integration and that (2) conceptual, theoretical, and empirical progress will be stimulated by the articulation of such a framework. The intention is to work towards this framework by building upon and refining an approach that is already available in the literature: the self-presentational theory of social anxiety developed and elaborated by Schlenker and Leary (1982). Indeed, it is suggested that many of the propositions to be outlined in this chapter are currently tacit within the existing literature on social discomfort, and it is time that they were made explicit.

It is contended that the proposed framework accounts for many of the outstanding features of social anxiety – in particular, why it is that a predisposition to shyness and inhibition is linked to a proneness to embarrassment. It also parallels in certain respects Wine's model (1971, 1980, 1982) of test anxiety and Buss's approach (1980) to audience anxiety.

Schlenker and Leary's self-presentational model of social anxiety

Schlenker and Leary's model (1982) is one of the few attempts that have been made to develop an integrated account of the experience of social anxiety. Although the theoretical model they elaborate is quite broad, and not all of it is strictly relevant to the current discussion, the essence of the argument is entailed in the notion that "social anxiety arises whenever people are motivated to make particular impressions on others, but doubt that they will be successful in doing so" (Leary, 1986,

p. 122). According to this viewpoint, experiences such as shyness and embarrassment arise in response to perceived or anticipated self-presentational failures. The individual experiences anxiety because such failures receive the negative evaluation of others and can affect adversely how the individual is defined and responded to. Ultimately, therefore, such failures can have profound implications for the individual's *identity*, defined as "a theory constructed by oneself or others about how one is defined and regarded in social life" (Schlenker & Leary, 1982, p. 643).

The theory is a cognitive one: The self-presentational failures are perceived, and thus may not be actual (and, likewise, actual self-presentational failures may not be perceived), and the negatively evaluating audience may be imagined rather than present.

According to the model, the individual engages in an assessment process with regard to the likely self-presentational outcome whenever the self-presentational goal is important or the individual's social performance is impeded. If the outcome of the assessment leads to the expectation that the individual cannot achieve the desired impression, then the response will be to withdraw, either by avoiding the situation or by physically withdrawing from it. If such physical withdrawal is not possible, then the response will be to withdraw "cognitively" by "mentally dissociating [oneself] from the task ... of creating a preferred impression on the audience" (Schlenker & Leary, 1982, p. 657). Such a response will be accompanied by negative affect.

In Schlenker and Leary's terms, individuals who cannot physically withdraw from the situation become "trapped in the assessment stage", "re-examining themselves and the situation and replaying the problems they confront" (1982, p. 657). This, in turn, can lead to a marked decline in the quality of the individual's social performance. One response to this can be the abandonment of the original self-presentational goal and its replacement with a less preferred, but more viable, alternative (i.e., one with a higher perceived probability of success).

In contemporary approaches to self-presentation such a response has become known as "protective" self-presentation (Arkin, 1981). The motive underlying such self-presentation is said to be that of avoiding disapproval, rather than that of gaining approval presumed to underlie much of what is called "acquisitive" self-presentation. Thus, one of the responses to a low perceived outcome expectancy for a self-presentation may involve a shift from acquisitive self-presentation to protective self-presentation (Arkin, Lake, & Baumgardner, 1986; Shepperd & Arkin, this volume).

In a subsequent refinement of the model, Leary and Atherton (1986) differentiate two separate sets of self-presentational expectancies: "Self-presentational efficacy expectancies" concern the presumed likelihood of executing behaviour intended to convey a particular impression; "self-presentational outcome expectancies" concern the estimated probability that the behaviour so executed will indeed have the desired self-presentational effect. According to Leary and Atherton (1986), social anxiety arises when either or both expectancies are low. However, they suggest that the two sets of probabilities have different implications for the situational and dispositional antecedents of social anxiety.

The forms of social anxiety

The term *social anxiety* is employed in the literature as an umbrella term for a plethora of labels denoting the experience of discomfort in relation to social interaction. What is not clear, however, is how many disparate experiences are covered by this term, even though most of these labels have their own separate traditions of research and, until recently, invariably their own isolated literature. Rationalisation of this list is long overdue and can be one of the principal contributions of theory in this area.

Schlenker and Leary (1982) occupy one of the extremer positions on this issue, arguing that there is simply one affective experience to be had and that differences between the terms used in this area reflect either theorists' preferences for a particular word or phrase or the specific situation in which the social anxiety is manifested (Leary, 1983; Schlenker & Leary, 1982). According to them, all these terms denote the experience of anxiety in response to the "prospect or presence of personal evaluation in real or imagined social situations", where anxiety is defined as "a cognitive and affective response characterized by apprehension about an impending, potentially negative outcome that one thinks one is unable to avert" (Schlenker & Leary, 1982, p. 642).

They do, however, propose two heuristic dimensions for differentiating these experiences. The first involves a proposed analytical distinction between interactions that are *contingent* (in which the responses of the actor depend upon the prior responses of others) and those that are *non-contingent* (in which the individual's actions are guided primarily by internal plans and only minimally by the responses of others). Employing this distinction as a dichotomy, Schlenker and Leary (1982) differentiate between *interaction anxiety* (anxiety precipitated by contingent interactions) and *audience anxiety* (anxiety experienced in response to non-contingent settings). Examples they give of the former are shyness, dating anxiety, and heterosexual social anxiety. As examples of the latter, they suggest audience anxiety, stage-fright, and speech anxiety. It is not clear where embarrassment fits into this structure.

Cross-cutting this dimension, they argue, is a distinction between situations in which a self-presentational failure is anticipated and situations in which a self-presentational failure is perceived as having already occurred. In relation to the labelling of social anxiety, they suggest that anxiety experienced in response to perceived self-presentational failures (or "predicaments") "has been termed embarrassment or shame" (Schlenker & Leary, 1982, p. 663). It is, however, not completely clear from this whether it is being suggested that these are the only labels available for application to the experience of anxiety under these circumstances nor whether it is being suggested that embarrassment and shame are, or should be, employed only under these circumstances.

It is contended that there is in this framework the kernel of an integrated account of what will be termed *social discomfort*, but that such an account requires modification, extension, and the formal elaboration of certain propositions that are implicit rather than explicit in the model as it currently stands if it is to be adequate.

Anxiety and embarrassment

Although the term *social anxiety* is widely employed in psychology to refer to the kinds of experiences covered by terms such as *shyness* and *embarrassment*, there is some evidence that the affective reaction underlying terms such as these is not invariably anxiety. Admittedly, this evidence tends to be rather more subjective and circumstantial than we generally desire. However, there is a case for arguing that, such as it is, there is rather more evidence for this proposition than there is for the notion that the affective experience underlying all states of social anxiety is anxiety, and this evidence is all the more suggestive because no one has really looked very hard for it in the first place. In particular, it appears that embarrassment and shame are sometimes differentiated from the other states of social discomfort on grounds that include the proposition that they are not anxiety states.

For instance, Ashworth (1979) argues that embarrassment should not be considered a form of social anxiety because "embarrassment occurs when it is only too clear what has happened *and that it is a shaming experience* whereas social anxiety is surely the awareness that the situation is *likely* to give rise to shame" (Ashworth, 1979, p. 129, first emphasis added). Of interest here are (1) the proposition that embarrassment cannot be an anxiety experience because it is inherently *reactive* (whereas, by implication, anxiety is not) and (2) the contrasting of shame with anxiety (i.e., that shame and therefore embarrassment are not anxious experiences). Indeed, to anticipate some of the arguments to come, it is interesting to note that Ashworth adds that "anticipated embarrassment may relate to social anxiety, but to draw the parallel further leads to confusion" (1979, p. 129).

Moreover, Ashworth (1979) is not alone in arguing this. For example, although he still refers to embarrassment as one of the social anxieties, it is clear from other aspects of his analysis that Arnold Buss (1980, 1983, 1984, 1986) also differentiates embarrassment from anxiety in this way. Indeed, he is explicit about the difference between embarrassment (and shame) and anxiety: Whereas the latter is characterised by the dominance of the sympathetic division of the autonomic nervous system (ANS), the former (according to Buss) are characterised by the dominance of the parasympathetic division of the ANS (e.g., Buss, 1980). Similar arguments were advanced by MacCurdy (1930). Others who perceive embarrassment and shame as reactive experiences include Edelmann (1987) and Miller (1986), as well as Schlenker and Leary (1982, p. 664; Leary, 1983, p. 128).

Buss's assertion is based primarily on data from one study (Buck, Parke, & Buck, 1970). In this study, male subjects were monitored for their heart rate and skin conductance responses either to the prospect of electric shocks or to that of sucking on objects, such as a baby bottle, dummy [rubber nipple], or other form of baby pacifier. The authors labelled the former condition "fear" and the latter "embarrassment." The principal findings were that the level of skin conductance rose higher in the fear condition, and there was a significant heart rate deceleration in the embarrassment condition. The latter is a feature of parasympathetic reactivity (Buss, 1980).

Unfortunately, however, there are grounds for doubting that embarrassment actually was elicited in the so-called embarrassment condition, for no actual sucking of the baby pacifiers took place. Consequently, the reactions being assessed were anticipatory in both conditions. Given the suggestion that embarrassment and shame involve responses to predicaments that have already occurred, this would imply that individuals in the "embarrassment" condition were not *experiencing* embarrassment, for the predicament had yet to arise. (However, they might well have been *anticipating* the experience of embarrassment.)

It is possible, therefore, that the differences in physiological response to the two conditions reflect differences other than those between embarrassment and fear, such as differences in the anticipatory reactions to physical and social stressors. Indeed, heart rate deceleration and skin conductance decreases have been found to be typical responses to tasks that involve paying attention to environmental stimuli (Lacey, Kagan,

Lacey, & Moss, 1963). One of the additional differences between the conditions is that being shocked is passive, whereas sucking is active. It is entirely possible, therefore, that the differences in physiological reactions in the two conditions reflect (1) greater anxiety at the prospect of physical stress and/or (2) a preparation for action in the so-called embarrassment condition. (It is interesting to note that there were no differences in self-ratings of embarrassment in the two conditions.)

One study in which there is less equivocal evidence of the arousal of embarrassment is that of Strom and Buck (1979). In this study, embarrassment was induced by being stared at, and this was indeed reflected in higher self-ratings of embarrassment relative to a non-staring condition. However, although this was accompanied by greater changes in skin conductance, whether or not these deflections were predominantly in one direction is not reported. Moreover, there were no differences between base-line values and manipulation values for mean skin conductance, and, unfortunately, heart rate was not assessed.

There have been several other studies that have investigated changes in physiological indices over time. Events assessed have included unstructured interactions with opposite-sex confederates (Beidel, Turner, & Dancu, 1985; Fremouw, Gross, Monroe, & Rapp, 1982; Turner, Beidel, & Larkin, 1986) or same-sex confederates (Beidel et al., 1985; Turner et al., 1986), the giving of an impromptu speech or other public speaking tasks (Beidel et al., 1985; Fremouw et al., 1982; Knight & Borden, 1979; Turner & Beidel, 1985; Turner et al., 1986), role-playing in response to filmed vignettes (Lehrer & Leiblum, 1981), motor performance tasks in front of an audience (Hrycaiko & Hrycaiko, 1980), and analogues of testing situations (Holroyd & Appel, 1980). The results of these studies tend to be somewhat confused, although there is a certain amount of evidence that there is a general reduction in physiological reaction as time passes. However, as with the Buck et al. study (1970), it is difficult to tell quite what this means, for it is difficult to tell from these studies whether or not the tasks subjects were required to perform induced embarrassment. The likeliest possibility is that these data reflect habituation to the setting and events, with there being some evidence that this response is attenuated in those rated as being more prone to social anxiety (Beidel et al., 1985) or less assertive (Lehrer & Leiblum, 1981).

Clearly, more studies are required on the physiology of embarrassment. In particular, studies employing the time scale implicit in the framework emerging from this analysis and using manipulations that unequivocally induce embarrassment would be desirable. In order to clarify the question of the relationship between anxiety and embarrassment we need to monitor physiological changes in settings in which there is a clear manipulation of embarrassment during the anticipatory and reactive phases, together with those occurring at the time of the manipulation itself.

At present, therefore, and in relation to the literature on psychophysiology, the notion that embarrassment is not an anxiety state remains as unproven as the proposition that it is. However, in relation to the broader psychological literature, there appear to be certain features of embarrassment that are *not* generally attributed to anxiety.

It has already been suggested that embarrassment is inherently reactive. Analyses of anxiety, on the other hand, tend to stress its *anticipatory* nature – that it is a response to potential dangers, rather than a reaction to events that have already occurred. For instance, Mischel (1976) has argued that one of the central characteristics of anxiety that emerges from an analysis of a wide variety of perspectives on the topic is that it involves a conscious feeling of fear and *anticipated* danger. Indeed, Epstein (1972) has argued that anxiety is essentially an anticipatory condition that serves to protect the individual against dangers that will produce unacceptably high levels of arousal. Similarly, and from a very different theoretical perspective, Kelly (1955) suggests that anxiety revolves around concerns with the unknown and their implications for the individual's psychological and physical welfare.

This emphasis on the anticipatory nature of anxiety also seems to be implicit in less formal references to anxiety. Indeed, closer examination of the definition of anxiety employed by Schlenker and Leary (1982), as given earlier, reveals that it contains several key words – such as "apprehension", "impending", "potentially", and "avert" – that have anticipatory, rather than reactive, connotations. Such emphasis on the *anticipation* of threat would appear to militate against the notion that embarrassment is an anxiety state.

There also appears to be some evidence that, subjectively at least, individuals do not equate embarrassment and anxiety. For instance, MacCurdy (1930) argued that "the unhappy wretch who blushes, averts his eyes, hangs his head, and 'wishes he might sink through the floor', is hardly the picture of fear" (p. 177). Similarly, when Mosher and White (1981) looked for differences in response to items on a revised version of the Differential Emotions Scale (Izard, Dougherty, Bloxom, & Kotsch, 1974) in subjects instructed to visualise certain emotional experiences, those items they designed to tap embarrassment were endorsed more in embarrassment, shame, guilt, and shyness situations than in an anxiety one.

Finally, two of the features that are generally attributed to embarrassment appear *not* to be so attributed to anxiety. In the first place, *blushing* is often taken to be one of the characteristic features of the embarrassment reaction. It has even been described as its "hallmark" (Buss, 1980). At the same time, embarrassment is also said to be characterised by the acute negative awareness of self embodied in the reaction known colloquially as "self-consciousness". Indeed, it is interesting to note that the items that Mosher and White (1981) took to be indicative of embarrassment for the purposes of their study were "embarrassed", "self-conscious", and "blushing".

Although the evidence is currently slim – largely, of course, because no one has looked at the problem from this perspective – what little evidence there is does not appear to contradict the following set of propositions:

1. *Embarrassment is not an anxiety state*, though – and this will become important later – *anticipating* embarrassment is anxiety-provoking. (Hence the use here of the umbrella term social *discomfort*, rather than the more widely used social *anxiety*. On the basis of the arguments being advanced here, only some of the states of social discomfort are states of social anxiety.)

2. There is, in fact, a group of states of social discomfort that are inherently anticipatory – in that the source of the discomfort has yet to occur – and another group of states that are inherently reactive – in that they are responses to events that are perceived as having already occurred.

3. Those states that are anticipatory are characterised by anxiety, whereas those that are reactive are characterised by a non-anxiety arousal state.

4. The principal exception to this is *shyness*, which can be either anticipatory or reactive. (The logical consequence of this, of course, within the current framework, is that shyness is a label that can be applied to *either* arousal state. The implications of and justification for this assertion will be discussed later.)

In terms of the model developed by Schlenker and Leary (1982), therefore, exception is being taken to the proposition that all states of social discomfort involve the affective experience of anxiety.

Acute negative public self-attention

If it is being postulated that embarrassment – together with the other reactive states of social discomfort – is a state of non-anxious arousal, then what exactly are the characteristic features of this reaction?

If Buss is correct in assuming that the parasympathetic division of the ANS is dominant in embarrassment, then the characteristic features of the reaction should include a lowering of heart rate, together with facial flushing or blushing. However, somewhat surprisingly, no one appears to have looked at the experience of blushing in embarrassment from a physiological viewpoint, even though this is frequently reported to be one of its most characteristic features (Edelmann, 1987, also this volume). At the same time, the notion of lowered heart rate is not entirely consistent with subjective reports of the condition, in which references frequently are made to *increases* in heart rate. However, this could be because of the problems endemic to the subjective reporting of aspects of physiological arousal.

Nevertheless, two features of embarrassment on which there appears to be reasonably widespread agreement are that it is accompanied by blushing and by feelings of acute self-awareness. This self-awareness is of the form that has become known as *public* self-awareness: awareness of those aspects of the self that may be perceived and evaluated by others (Buss, 1980; Fenigstein, 1979; Leary, 1983).

It is argued here that these two aspects of embarrassment – blushing and acute public self-awareness – are two sides of the same coin, integral features of a single experience. This is the experience entailed in the common-sense notion of "self-consciousness" (as in "*feeling* self-conscious"). It is this experience that is postulated to be the non-anxious arousal state underlying embarrassment and shame. Consequently, it is being proposed that self-consciousness is inherently affective.

Interestingly, in addition to being echoed in the remarks of MacCurdy (1930) cited earlier, the notion that self-consciousness is different from anxiety is implicit in the work of Buss (1980, 1983, 1984, 1986). Moreover, he makes the same link between this experience and that of embarrassment: "Embarrassment implies the presence of public self-consciousness, whereas anxiety suggests the presence of fear" (Buss, 1986, p. 128).

Although it has been neglected by academic psychologists (at least in recent years), the experience of self-consciousness appears to be a well-known feature of common-sense psychological explanation: "The disintegrating effect of self-consciousness produced by the seeming exposure of oneself to the perception of another is familiar to naive psychology" (Heider, 1958, p. 74). The word "disintegrating" is telling here; the emphasis in the references to this experience in the psychological literature is largely on self-consciousness as a disruptive and psychologically painful experience:

This "sense of other persons" may break up all the mental processes. The present writer cannot think the same thoughts, nor follow the same plan of action, nor control the muscles with the same sufficiency, nor concentrate the attention with the same directness, nor, in fact, do any blessed thing as well, when this sense of the presence of others is upon him. (Baldwin, 1902, pp. 213–214)

The subjective experience itself is described by Campbell (1896, p. 806) as "the soul shuddering to feel itself naked":

> The "ego" feels itself isolated, laid bare to inspection, no longer comfortably, and, according to its wont, merged in its environment, and but half-conscious of itself, but by the attention centred on it ... brought vividly forward and made to realise the gulf that separates the Me from the Not-me. (1896, p. 806)

However, self-consciousness is deployed already in academic psychology to denote the *disposition* to become self-aware (Fenigstein, Scheier, & Buss, 1975). As this marks something of a departure from its usage in ordinary language, it seems that we need to coin a new label for academic reference to the experience denoted by the everyday notion of self-consciousness.

The principal feature of self-consciousness as understood in common-sense psychology appears to correspond to what psychologists might describe as an acute awareness of a negative discrepancy between a presumed or desired self-image and that projected. On the basis of this it appears that a reasonable label for this experience would be acute negative public self-attention (ANPS-A): acute, because it is sudden and sharp (even those who may be chronically predisposed to this experience are not continuously self-conscious, but simply experience this acute reaction more frequently than is usual); negative, because it is affectively unpleasant and aversive and is accompanied by an awareness of a negative discrepancy between presumed or desired self-image and that projected; public self-attention, because it is characterised by a painful sense of how one appears in the eyes of others.

One of the advantages of demarking this experience with a precise label is that it helps us to keep in perspective the limitations on what is being proposed: It is *not* being argued that the experience of self-attention is necessarily affective, let alone aversive. It is simply being asserted that one type of self-attention – that characterised by acute public self-awareness – under certain conditions is. The positing of a state of ANPS-A is in no way a *general* statement of the properties of the experience of self-attention.

Hence, the call made earlier for the social psychophysiological investigation of embarrassment is in fact a call for the social psychopysiological investigation of the experience of ANPS-A. It is just that this experience has been investigated by psychologists under the rubric it receives socially (i.e., embarrassment) when certain labelling conventions are satisfied, as described later. Effectively, therefore, in comparing embarrassment and anxiety we have been comparing two phenomena that, it is to be argued, operate at different levels of analysis. Similarly, Buss's claim (1980) that blushing is the hallmark of embarrassment is wrong: It is, in fact, the hallmark of ANPS-A. (That is why it is also a feature of shame and, in some circumstances, shyness; these are also labels that may be applied to ANPS-A.)

It is being proposed, therefore, that there are two basic affective reactions underlying the experience of social discomfort: anxiety and ANPS-A. Additionally, it has been proposed that those states of social discomfort typified by anxiety are reactions to events that have yet to take place, whereas those that are typified by ANPS-A are reactions to events that have already taken place. The questions then become: What are people anticipating, and why do they get anxious about it? What are the events that precipitate ANPS-A?

The dynamics of social discomfort

The answer proposed here is that these events are one and the same; that is, the events that are feared when anticipated – and that therefore elicit anxiety – are those that, if they occur, one reacts to with ANPS-A. Thus, social anxiety arises when individuals anticipate events in which they may experience ANPS-A. But why are these events feared? It is proposed that they are feared because the experience of ANPS-A is affectively unpleasant. That is, individuals become socially anxious because ANPS-A is an unpleasant, aversive experience. It is this property of ANPS-A that is, therefore, the linchpin of the experience of social discomfort.

There are several propositions here that require justification. The first is that ANPS-A is affectively negative. On this point there appears to be much agreement between common-sense and academic psychology; certainly, as discussed earlier, the few references to the experience of self-consciousness in the psychological literature comment on it as an unpleasant and psychologically disruptive experience. In terms of formal psychological theory, there is also a precedent for assuming that the experience of self-attention can be affectively negative; indeed, this property was a pivotal feature of the first attempt at developing a comprehensive theory of self-attention in social psychology (Duval & Wicklund, 1972). Moreover, subsequent theorising (e.g., Carver, 1979; Carver & Scheier, 1981; Scheier & Carver, 1982) has never ruled out the place of negative affect, but only reduced its role in the broad field of self-attention – a proposition that is entirely consistent with what is being argued here. There are also clear precedents in psychology for presuming that experiences can be intrinsically negative; indeed, anxiety is just such a case.

The second proposition is that this negativity is aversive. The problem with establishing this notion in relation to the academic literature is that comparatively few direct references to the experience of self-consciousness are available. However, there are several references to the role of the threat or fear of embarrassment in the experience of social discomfort. In terms of the arguments being elaborated here, this is tantamount to the same thing – embarrassment is essentially a label applied to the experience of ANPS-A when certain labelling conditions are satisfied.

For instance, empirical evidence appears to suggest that individuals are strongly motivated to avoid embarrassment; subjects appear to be prepared even to forgo financial rewards in order to avoid experiencing embarrassment in front of others (Brown, 1970; Brown & Garland, 1971; Garland & Brown, 1972). Indeed, the motive to avoid embarrassment is central to Goffman's classic analysis of the experience (1955, 1956, 1959, 1963, 1971), and two recent analyses of embarrassment have both separately emphasised its aversive nature. Miller (1986), for example, in his review of the literature on embarrassment, argues that the evidence suggests that it "is an aversive state of both physiological and psychological arousal that is avoided if possible" (p. 305). Similarly, Edelmann (1987) emphasises the fact that individuals typically attempt to avoid behaviours that are potentially embarrassing, and he even acknowledges the possibility that the fear of embarrassment might play a central role in the experience of social anxiety. Indeed, his analysis of the findings of the copious research into help-giving and help-seeking emphasises heavily the role that potential embarrassment plays in the inhibition of these activities. Moreover, Modigliani (1971) has even suggested that the findings from Milgram's provocative studies (1965) on obedience to authority, together with those of Asch (1956) on conformity, can be understood in terms of the inhibition brought about by the fear of embarrassment.

In fact, the intrinsic aversiveness of embarrassment is attested to quite powerfully by the existence of a form of behaviour therapy – shame-aversion therapy – that has been used in the treatment of behaviours such as exhibitionism and voyeurism (Reitz & Keil, 1971; Schaefer, 1976; Serber, 1970; Wardlaw & Miller, 1978). This treatment requires the client to engage in the deviant behaviour in front of real or imagined audiences. Subjects typically report experiencing strong feelings of guilt, shame, and embarrassment under these circumstances, and this experience appears to lead to marked reductions in the frequency of the undesirable behaviour (Edelmann, 1987).

The third proposition is that the events that precipitate ANPS-A are of the same nature as those that one anticipates. Effectively, this amounts to the proposition that those factors that induce or increase social anxiety are the same as those that precipitate or increase the likelihood of becoming embarrassed.

Schlenker and Leary (1982) outline a number of factors that, they argue, increase the likelihood of experiencing social anxiety. Factors they perceive as increasing the *motivation to impress others* include the following: the characteristics of those others, such as status and attractiveness; the evaluative implications of the performance, such as the number of co-performers present and the size of the audience; the centrality to the individual's identity of the image being presented; self-attention; and personality variables, such as the motivation to gain approval/avoid disapproval or the fear of negative evaluation. Factors they see as inducing *low outcome expectancies* include uncertainty, particularly regarding factors likely to influence the perception of the individual's performance by relevant others, and self-doubts about the individual's capacity to achieve his or her desired self-presentational goals. These are, indeed, precisely the sorts of factors seen as being likely to increase the probability of experiencing embarrassment (e.g., Edelmann, 1987; Miller, 1986).

Finally, examination of the cognitive features of ANPS-A suggests that these are very close to what logically must be the cognitive consequences of the processes being postulated to underlie social anxiety by Schlenker and Leary (1982), particularly during the proposed assessment phase, and especially if the reaction is to a predicament that has already occurred. Cognitively, at the heart of such an experience would appear to be an acute awareness of a negative discrepancy between some desired self-presentation and that achieved. Implicit in the self-presentational approach, therefore, appears to be a set of propositions regarding what cognitively amounts to a state of self-attention.

It is being proposed, therefore, that the anticipation of a predicament arouses anxiety precisely because the occurrence of a predicament entails the experience *automatically* of ANPS-A. That is, ANPS-A is the cognitive and affective experience that accompanies – or, more properly, is intrinsic to – the experience of the type of self-presentational failure that is embodied in the notion of a predicament.

Implications of the emphasis on ANPS-A

In order to show why the experience of self-presentational failures should be unpleasant and therefore feared when anticipated, Schlenker and Leary's model (1982) stresses the negative social consequences that such failures can have for the individual. This is entirely consistent with the framework being elaborated here. The current emphasis on the aversive nature of ANPS-A is simply the other side of the same coin. The principal difference is one merely of emphasis.

However, there is evidence to suggest that the overall identity implications of the sorts of self-presentational failures that underlie embarrassment, at least, may not always be all that profound. For instance, Manstead and Semin (1981) examined subjects' ratings of filmed vignettes of social transgressions. In so doing they distinguished conceptually among the actor's self-image (SI), public image (PI) (the observer's impression of the actor), subjective public image (SPI) (the actor's perception of how he or she is perceived by the observer), and inferred subjective public image (ISPI) (the observer's perception of the SPI). Although the differences between ratings were not large, they were significant and suggested that whereas actors rated their SPIs more negatively following the transgression, this did not in fact carry over to their SIs, and in any case observers did not evaluate the actor's PI more negatively (although they were aware of the actor's belief that they would – the ISPI was more negative). This confirmed the findings from a previous study (Semin & Manstead, 1981) and those of Modigliani (1968, 1971), who anticipated, but failed to find, that embarrassment was accompanied by a loss of self-esteem.

Such findings appear to be easier to reconcile with an approach that emphasises the immediate and intrinsic aversiveness of the experience of self-presentational failures than with an approach that locates the negativity of this set of occurrences in the remoter social and identity consequences that stem from them. However, still to be accounted for is the reason why the experience of ANPS-A should be intrinsically aversive (given that it is not being assumed that self-attention is aversive per se). One possibility for this is quite clearly the individual's cumulative experience of the social problems that can arise when his or her identity claims fail. The distinction is ultimately one between proximate and distal causation.

Emphasis on the self-attentional aspects of a self-presentational failure, however, alerts us to the possibility that there might in fact be two distinct paths to the induction of ANPS-A, and therefore two separate sets of causes of social anxiety: a direct route, involving self-presentational difficulties, which *automatically* arouse a state of negative public self-attention, and an indirect route involving factors that lead initially to the induction of public self-attention. These latter factors would induce anxiety when anticipated because they increase the possibility that the individual might be "tripped" into negative public self-attention (i.e., they raise the base-line probability of experiencing ANPS-A). Moreover, having to perform while publicly self-attentive will reduce the attention that can be devoted to the task at hand, and this will constitute a performance handicap (thereby increasing the dangers of a self-presentational failure). In fact, closer examination of the factors postulated by Schlenker and Leary (1982) to increase the likelihood of social anxiety reveals several – such as audience size and the presence of co-performers – that appear to work primarily by raising the probability of ANPS-A indirectly rather than directly.

Although Schlenker and Leary's model (1982) indicates that acts that are perceived as having low self-presentational efficacy and low outcome expectancies are implicated in social anxiety, the current model also implicates acts that increase the base-line likelihood of experiencing public self-attention, and the more susceptible such acts are to interference from reduced attentional input, the greater is the likelihood of the public self-attention becoming ANPS-A. Thus, the worst kind of act from the viewpoint of someone with a performance to make is one that is demonstrative (i.e., that draws public attention to the self) and that entails self-presentational claims for which the individual has low expectancies. It is no accident, therefore, that the act of public speaking is widely used in experimental investigations of social anxiety and is one of the most widespread and powerful of the social fears. Because we can hear ourselves speak, the very act of giving a speech is one that automatically induces public self-attention; it is not simply the words that have to be spoken (and the identity consequences of these) but the very act of speaking itself that is feared. Indeed, the types of act typically inhibited in socially anxious individuals appear to be demonstrative in nature and frequently involve speaking (Buss, 1980, 1984; Harris, 1984a; Zimbardo, 1977). By the same token, acts that come under the auspices of protective self-presentation appear to achieve both ends simultaneously: In responding protectively, the individual engages in acts that simultaneously make reduced identity claims and that are less demonstrative in nature.

Finally, an emphasis on ANPS-A as an intrinsically aversive experience has interesting implications. For instance, it might be predicted that anything that reduces arousal should have a disinhibiting effect on actions that have negative self-presentational consequences, even though the cognitive and social consequences remain the same (i.e., are negative). Drugs such as alcohol and the β-adrenoceptor blockers (Granville-Grossman & Turner, 1966; James, Pearson, Griffith, & Newbury, 1977; Tyrer & Lader, 1973), therefore, may work not only by reducing the individual's awareness of the negative consequences of his or her actions (i.e., a *cognitive* effect) but also – or, indeed, instead – by reducing the negative affect that accompanies ANPS-A and, therefore, the inhibitory force (i.e., an *affective* effect).

Anxiety and ANPS-A in contingent and
non-contingent interactions

Whereas the anticipating/reacting distinction is a clear dichotomy and appears to fit the available data well, some reservations might be expressed regarding the contingent/non-contingent distinction introduced by Schlenker and Leary (1982).

The principal usefulness of this distinction appears to be that – in the notion of non-contingent interactions – it alerts us to a group of situations with which most individuals are less experienced, which tend also to be more formal, conducted in front of larger audiences, and in which evaluation tends to be more salient, than is the case with the contingent interactions that comprise the more usual form of interaction in everyday life. For these, and other reasons, these situations tend by and large to induce greater anxiety and desire for avoidance in the majority of those confronted by them; less experienced individuals, especially, approach these events with apprehension. Indeed, for the most part, this apprehension is sufficiently high that they will be prepared to avoid the setting altogether or, if this is not possible, to reduce the likelihood of experiencing ANPS-A by rehearsing their lines.

The critical feature of these situations, however, appears to be not so much the contingency or otherwise of the interaction but the fact that non-contingent interactions are invariably *performances* (i.e., acts with explicit identity implications performed knowingly in front of audiences). Performances raise the likelihood of ANPS-A: With the exception of the greater structure inherent in non-contingent interactions, all the factors that differentiate the two types of situation appear to increase the probability of encountering a self-presentational failure (e.g., lack of experience) and the social costs of such a failure (e.g., importance of performance) or of experiencing public self-attention from the outset (e.g., audience presence and size). All these factors should increase the perceived likelihood of experiencing ANPS-A. Moreover, identity claims on the part of the performer tend to be salient in such settings, and often these claims are not under the control of the actor but are thrust upon him or her by virtue of the role he or she is expected to occupy. Indeed, one of the difficulties with non-contingent performances is that often it is harder to make the reduced identity claims typical of protective self-presentational practices (i.e., to engage in one of Schlenker and Leary's principal responses to a perceived predicament).

The weakness of the distinction, therefore, lies in the fact that not all performances are non-contingent (such as those to be undertaken at interviews or when meeting prospective employers, in-laws, etc.). Indeed, it is proposed here that as far as the individual is concerned, *all* instances of social anxiety involve the anticipation of a *performance*, regardless of the contingency or otherwise of the forthcoming interaction.

Nevertheless, one of the interesting features of performances, for current purposes, is that individuals confronted by them, and unable to avoid them, tend to actively prepare for them (by rehearsing lines, anticipating questions, preparing speeches, etc.). This, in turn, can be seen as a means of actively reducing the likelihood of experiencing ANPS-A by anticipating and attempting to develop strategies to cope with those aspects of the forthcoming situation that are perceived as being likely to induce this state. In some respects, however, individuals are handicapped in this process: Firstly, the presence of an audience means that almost inevitably they will be pushed into the domain of public self-attention; secondly, often many crucial aspects of the forthcoming situation will remain unknown to them in advance, therefore making preparation difficult.

With regard to the distinction introduced by Schlenker and Leary (1982), however, the key question is really whether or not the contingency of the situation has any systematic impact on the individual's coping behaviour – prior to or during the situation itself, or in response to ANPS-A. If not, then the distinction appears to be of limited usefulness for our purposes.

The nature of outcome assessment

According to the model being elaborated here, therefore, the acts that are inhibited in an attack of social anxiety are those that are most likely to give rise to ANPS-A. By virtue of the two paths to ANPS-A, these can be either acts that are seen as being likely to lead to a predicament or acts perceived as being likely to induce public self-attention. Consequently, in the case of the latter route to ANPS-A there appear to be two aspects to the process of outcome assessment: awareness of the likelihood of experiencing public self-attention and a subsequent assessment of the likelihood of this transmuting into ANPS-A. Where the individual believes that events are likely to induce ANPS-A, then anxiety will arise if these events or their consequences cannot be avoided.

In the case of an anticipated predicament, the elaboration introduced by Leary and Atherton (1986) suggests that there are also two sets of outcome assessments: those concerning the likelihood of executing the desired behaviour, and the likelihood of that behaviour achieving the desired self-presentational effect. (Indeed, interestingly enough, these appear to differ in perceived locus of causality for low outcome expectancies. Low self-presentational efficacy expectancies appear to implicate the actor, and low self-presentational outcome expectancies, the observer.)

At the heart of social discomfort, therefore, are acts. It is saying or doing something within a particular context that is feared. During the anticipatory phase the nature of the act that is feared may be vague, and effort will be expended in anticipating and developing strategies to cope with those acts that may arise in the forthcoming situation. Nevertheless, the individual has no guarantee that such strategies will be successful in warding off ANPS-A. During the reactive phase, however, the nature of the unfortunate act will be acutely known, and any coping strategies will be concerned with damage limitation. Equally, however, ANPS-A may arise *without* anticipation; the individual may fail to anticipate self-presentational difficulties and be caught unawares by the events that take place. In such a case, although there would be ANPS-A, according to the model being proposed here there would be no social anxiety.

Individuals will vary both in their assessments of a given situation and in their tendencies to anticipate experiencing ANPS-A per se. This, in turn, will affect their propensity to experience social anxiety. In addition to such individual differences, however, there will be differences in the social norms governing the experience of social discomfort in relation to these situations. This will, in turn, affect the labelling of what is essentially the same experience. Sometimes this experience will be seen as normative, and therefore legitimate. At other times it will be seen as being non-normative, and therefore not legitimate. For example, at all times the ideal probably is *not* to react with anxiety, although there will be occasions when this reaction (to some degree) will be acceptable. The polished performer, however, probably does not *appear* to experience anxiety (which is why betrayal of the individual's genuine state through, for instance, uncontrollable voice or hand tremors can have its own undesirable image consequences). However, clearly there will be occasions when it will be *expected* that the individual will react with ANPS-A. Here the failure to react with ANPS-A will be perceived as inappropriate, and the individual potentially will be subject to the negative attributions of others – which, in the extreme absence of, for example, embarrassment, may even amount to attributions of psychopathology (McDougall, 1926, 1948).

Anxiety and ANPS-A in ordinary language

The framework as it stands is that of a basic and dynamic psychological process stripped of its social context. Embarrassment and shyness make sense only when this context is added. They are labels applied to the experience of anxiety and ANPS-A in a social environment. In order to understand and analyse these experiences, we need to know the rules appropriate for their employment as labels. The rules are, therefore, those of ordinary language.

Analyses of embarrassment often address the relation between this state and that of shame. From the point of view of this chapter that is not surprising, as they are both states of ANPS-A and therefore have a common affective basis. As Leary (1983) points out, the difference between the use of the terms appears to lie in the nature of the infraction that causes the predicament. In particular, shame appears to be reserved for those predicaments involving moral transgressions, especially those perceived as having been intentional and avoidable (Leary, 1983; Schlenker & Leary, 1982). Harré (this volume) provides a fuller discussion of the differences between shame and embarrassment in terms of the responsibility for and severity of the infraction.

Obviously, the actual dimensions that differentiate these experiences will emerge only from an appropriate empirical investigation. But the important point is that whatever dimensions are suggested, these are effectively statements about the conditions that have to be satisfied in our ordinary language community for the correct (or agreed) employment of these terms. The point is, therefore, that differences between states of social discomfort need not simply arise in the pattern of reactions that accompany them, but may also arise in the rules governing their usage as terms (i.e., language rules). That is, the difference between embarrassment and shyness, say, may simply lie in the rules governing their employment as terms, rather than in the characteristics of the basic affective reaction that underlies them.

This dimension is completely absent from the *formal* structure of Schlenker and Leary's theory, although there are occasions when it appears to be tacitly invoked. Indeed, the anticipated/reactive dimension is essentially a proposition about (or the "discovery" of) just such an ordinary language rule; the contingent/non-contingent distinction is in part a similar proposition (in so far as it makes a statement about the conditions of employment of ordinary language terms such as *shyness* and *stage-fright*). However, in proposing something about the conditions that should govern the use of professional terms such as *heterosexual social anxiety* and *audience anxiety*, it is also an attempt to establish an academic language rule.

In fact, whenever recourse is made to the eliciting object or circumstance as the principal feature differentiating experiences of social discomfort, tacit use is being made of a linguistic rule for this purpose. Indeed, just such a means of distinguishing the experience of social anxiety is implicit in many of the labels that have been coined professionally (such as audience anxiety, heterosexual social anxiety, speech anxiety, etc.). Here, tacit reference is being made to the linguistic rule that "if the object of the fear is ... then employ the term...". For example, if the object of the fear is appearing before an audience, then employ the term *audience anxiety*; if, on the other hand, it is meeting a member of the opposite sex, then employ the term *heterosexual social anxiety*, and so on. There is clear acknowledgement here that the affective reaction underlying these experiences is the same regardless of the label.

However, though this tends to be recognised for those terms that psychologists have coined themselves, it remains a possibility also for those that we have *borrowed* from ordinary, everyday language – terms such as *shyness, embarrassment, nervousness*, and *shame* (Harris, 1984a). That is, it is entirely possible that the difference between shyness and embarrassment or shyness and nervousness lies simply in the rules of employment of these terms, not in anything intrinsically different about these experiences as experiences. (This is not to argue that the connotations of labelling one's experience as shyness rather than as nervousness, say, are the same. That is, the consequences of the labelling choice can be profound.) How would this look in relation to embarrassment and shyness?

Embarrassment and shyness

In the first place, of course, there need not be a difference. That is, it is quite possible for these terms to be synonyms, referring to the same experience *in toto*. However, it is proposed here that this is not in fact the case.

Earlier on it was suggested that "shyness" was a label that could be applied to either ANPS-A or anxiety (Harris, 1982, 1985). Additional support for this proposition comes from the work of Arnold Buss. In a series of papers (1980, 1983, 1984, 1986), Buss has developed the notion that a distinction can be made between two types of shyness. In one of his more recent statements of this position (Buss, 1986), this takes the form of a distinction between *fearful* shyness and *self-conscious* shyness. This distinction appears to parallel that between anxious shyness and ANPS-A shyness posited here (and, of course, lends further credence to the proposition that there is a distinction to be made between anxiety and self-consciousness).

Ultimately, however, Buss employs this distinction to suggest that different types of individual are prone to the different types of shy reaction, and he even posits differences in aetiology and age of onset for these different types of shyness (Buss, 1984, 1986). In the current analysis, however, the distinction is between anxiety and ANPS-A as two phases of a social process. Here the propensity to become socially anxious hinges upon the capacity to experience ANPS-A. Consequently, there is no implication of dispositional differences in the propensity to experience these two basic reactions, although there may, of course, be differences between individuals in the tendency to anticipate ANPS-A (and, therefore, to become socially anxious).

In the case of anxious shyness and embarrassment, therefore, the experience of anxiety in anticipation of an event that has yet to take place is a distinguishing feature (ultimately linguistic in its implication) of shyness and embarrassment (though not, say, of shyness and nervousness). In the case of embarrassment and non-anxious shyness, however, it has been argued that the arousal state – ANPS-A – is the same. For these not to function as synonyms, therefore, we have to point to at least one linguistic rule that indicates a difference in usage for these terms. A hint as to where such a difference might lie comes, interestingly enough, from a consideration of differences in the *academic* approach to these phenomena.

Academic approaches to shyness and embarrassment

Academic analyses of embarrassment have tended to focus on its social function. For example, in Goffman's classic analysis (1955, 1956, 1959, 1963, 1971), embarrassment is seen as being a legitimate and acceptable, indeed prescribed, response to certain types of social events. In a similar vein, Manstead and Semin (1981) have argued that embarrassment works essentially as a non-verbal apology for the violation of a social norm (Castelfranchi & Poggi, this volume). Such analyses have tended to emphasise the role that embarrassment plays in offering restitution for certain types of social transgression. It is seen largely as a sort of "bottom-line" option for restoring lost face. Implicit in such notions is the appropriateness of the embarrassment reaction to the events that precipitated it.

Accordingly, the focus of interest of embarrassment researchers has been predominantly on the characteristics of the social events that precipitate it and the responses of those in interaction to it. That of shyness researchers, however, has been on the characteristics of those who are prone to experience it (Harris, 1984a). In contrast to the literature on embarrassment, the emphasis in the research literature on shyness has traditionally been on shyness as a trait or disposition. Indeed, it is interesting to note that it is only when embarrassment is seen as being unduly extreme or frequent that the analysis becomes an analysis of the trait of *embarrassability* (Edelmann, 1987; Modigliani, 1968).

The essence of the difference in approach, it is contended, is that embarrassment is conceived of as being a normative social experience (i.e., one that is potentially experienceable by anyone), whereas in most instances shyness is perceived as being peculiar to a sub-group of individuals or a stage of psychosocial development.

It is contended here that this presents us with a dimension that enables us to tease apart embarrassment and non-anxious or ANPS-A

shyness. This is that shyness is seen as being an illegitimate or inappropriate response to the eliciting circumstances, whereas embarrassment is seen as being legitimate or appropriate. In attributional terms,
where the response is seen as being appropriate to the context, then the
attribution is *situational*, and the analysis is of the state. Where the
response is seen as being *inappropriate*, then the attribution is *personal*, and
the analysis is dispositional.

It is proposed here, therefore, that one of the dimensions distinguishing the employment of shyness and embarrassment in what we rather
condescendingly call ordinary language is that shyness is seen as being
inappropriate to the setting or event that precipitates it, whereas embarrassment is seen as being appropriate to the events that have taken place.
This is true also of shyness as anxiety. Thus, it is also being proposed
that "shyness" is a label applied to social anxiety in ordinary language
when this reaction is perceived as being inappropriate to the precipitat-
ing setting or event.

There are two aspects to this appropriateness. Firstly, the experience
may be perceived as being inappropriate to the eliciting event or context
per se; that is, the experience of anxiety or ANPS-A may be perceived by
the labelling individual as being out of context. Secondly, the intensity
of the experience may be deemed inappropriate to the eliciting event or
context. Thus, there may be occasions when the anxiety or ANPS-A
reaction, though not wholly inappropriate to the setting, may be perceived by the labelling individual as being unduly extreme. These possibilities are, of course, not mutually exclusive.

Here, of course, we have to remind ourselves that there is a distinction
to be made between *social* and *statistical* norms. It may, for instance, be
normative statistically to react to a first date with apprehension, but for
the prescribed social ideal to suggest that one should be calm, relaxed,
and confident. Indeed, this reminds us of the possibility that appro-
piateness as a criterion lies in the eye of the beholder. That, in turn, may
be why certain people who do not appear to have particular social
difficulties nevertheless come to label themselves as shy (Zimbardo,
1977). Such individuals will tend to label more of their social experiences
as shyness and hence will be likelier to label themselves as shy. Moreover, they should perceive more of those around them as being shy, too –
contrary to the current explanations for this effect, which are predicated
on the assumption that such individuals *underestimate* the extent to which
their perceived social difficulties are shared by others (Harris, 1984b;
Leary, 1983; Smail, 1984). When Harris and Wilshire (1988) investigated this issue empirically, they found evidence consistent with the
former, rather than the latter, argument.

It is being proposed, therefore, that relationships between terms employed to denote states or experiences of social discomfort – whether professional or lay – may be of the following kind:

1. There may be no difference between them (i.e., they can be synonyms).
2. They may be used to denote the same experience (i.e., either anxiety or ANPS-A), but be differentiated from each other by some linguistic rule (e.g., concerning the conditions of elicitation, or, in the case of shyness, whether or not the affective experience is perceived as being appropriate to the setting).
3. They may be denoting different affective experiences (i.e., either anxiety or ANPS-A). (Of course, ultimately *all* differences between these terms are linguistic. It is simply that in certain cases such rules make reference to differences in underlying affective reaction.)

Implications of the proposed model

It is hoped that the framework developed in this chapter will function heuristically: that at the very least it alerts us to the points where critical conceptual and empirical attention should be focused. Some of these have already been pointed out.

Because this is a cognitive model, attention needs to be focused on those factors that affect cognition. In particular, it seems that empirical attention should be addressed to the factors that influence the induction and course of outcome assessment. Moreover, attention should also be directed to an examination of the characteristics and eliciting features of the postulated state of ANPS-A.

There are also clear dispositional implications to the model. Opportunities for individual differences arise throughout. There may be individual differences in outcome assessments, in the propensity to anticipate or experience ANPS-A, in the propensity to engage in the process of outcome assessment at all, in coping strategies to ward off ANPS-A or to cope with it once it has arisen, and in assessments of the appropriateness of coping and/or the anxiety reaction. Thus, individuals may come to label themselves as shy or not for a variety of reasons, and this may have clear implications for therapeutic approaches to this area.

Finally, although some consideration has been given in this chapter to the means by which the experiences of anxiety and ANPS-A are differentiated in ordinary language, as research psychologists we are by no means obliged to address this question. Our concerns are principally with the dynamics of the underlying social psychological process. Although an understanding of the means by which this process is translated socially into experiences of shyness, embarrassment, shame, nervousness, stage-fright, and so forth, is a necessary part of any full analysis of these experiences themselves – and thus academic analyses of these experiences that currently lack this dimension are necessarily inadequate – there is no obligation upon us to treat such ordinary language translations of this process as sacrosanct. Of course, these terms provide us with important insights into the nature of this underlying process, but there is in fact no reason why, in principle, we should concern ourselves with analyses of embarrassment or analyses of shyness per se; ultimately, we are concerned with the psychological dynamics of social discomfort, not with arriving at a comprehensive analysis of how this experience is understood in everyday life. (This is not, of course, to argue that such an understanding would be uninteresting and of little usefulness, but simply that it is a separate research question.)

One practical consequence of this is that we would be well advised to be more cautious in our mixing of ordinary language and professional terms. Currently these are used interchangeably, even though in regard to their status these terms are quite different (Harris, 1984a). Moreover, it is clear that we need to rationalise the list of terms currently available in the professional vocabulary for referring to social discomfort and arrive at an agreed set of uses for the terms that remain. At the moment, too many of these terms are redundant, and there is too great a tendency to introduce unique interpretations of the terms that are shared. These issues have been discussed in greater depth elsewhere (Harris, 1984a).

REFERENCES

Arkin, R. M. (1981). Self-presentation styles. In J. T. Tedeschi (Ed.), *Impression management theory and social psychological research* (pp. 311–333). New York: Academic Press.

Arkin, R. M., Lake, E. A., & Baumgardner, A. H. (1986). Shyness and self-presentation. In W. H. Jones, J. M. Cheek, & S. R. Briggs (Eds.), *Shyness: Perspectives on research and treatment* (pp. 189–203). New York: Plenum Press.

Asch, S. E. (1956). Studies of independence and conformity. 1: A minority of one against a unanimous majority. *Psychological Monographs, 70* (9, Whole No. 416).

Ashworth, P. D. (1979). *Social interaction and consciousness.* Chichester, Sussex: Wiley.

Baldwin, J. M. (1902). *Social and Ethical interpretations in mental development* (3rd ed.). London: Macmillan.

Beidel, D. C., Turner, S. M., & Dancu, C. V. (1985). Physiological, cognitive, and behavioural aspects of social anxiety. *Behaviour Research and Therapy, 23,* (2), 109–117.

Brown, B. R. (1970). Face-saving following experimentally induced embarrassment. *Journal of Experimental Social Psychology, 6*, 255–271.

Brown, B. R., & Garland, H. (1971). The effect of incompetency, audience acquaintanceship, and anticipated evaluative feedback on face-saving behavior. *Journal of Experimental Social Psychology, 7*, 490–502.

Buck, R. W., Parke, R. D., & Buck, M. (1970). Skin conductance, heart rate, and attention to the environment in two stressful situations. *Psychonomic Science, 18*, 95–96.

Buss, A. H. (1980). *Self-consciousness and social anxiety.* San Francisco: Freeman.

Buss, A. H. (1983). *Two kinds of shyness.* Paper presented at the Roundtable Conference on Anxiety and Self-Related Cognitions, Berlin.

Buss, A. H. (1984). A conception of shyness. In J. A. Daly & J. C. McCroskey (Eds.), *Avoiding communication: Shyness, reticence, and communication apprehension* (pp. 39–49). London: Sage.

Buss, A. H. (1986). *Social behavior and personality.* Hillsdale, NJ: Lawrence Erlbaum.

Campbell, H. (1896). Morbid shyness. *British Medical Journal, 2*, 805–807.

Carver, C. S. (1979). A cybernetic model of self-attention processes. *Journal of Personality and Social Psychology, 37*, 1251–1281.

Carver, C. S., & Scheier, M. F. (1981). *Attention and self-regulation: A control-theory approach to human behavior.* New York: Springer-Verlag.

Duval, S., & Wicklund, R. A. (1972). *A theory of objective self-awareness.* New York: Academic Press.

Edelmann, R. J. (1987). *The psychology of embarrassment.* Chichester, Sussex: Wiley.

Epstein, S. (1972). The nature of anxiety with emphasis upon its relationship to expectancy. In C. Spielberger (Ed.), *Anxiety: Current trends in theory and research* (pp. 291–342). New York: Academic Press.

Fenigstein, A. (1979). Self-consciousness, self-attention, and social interaction. *Journal of Personality and Social Psychology, 37*, 75–86.

Fenigstein, A., Scheier, M. F., & Buss, A. H. (1975). Public and private self-consciousness: Assessment and theory. *Journal of Consulting and Clinical Psychology, 43*, 522–527.

Fremouw, W. J., Gross, R., Monroe, J., & Rapp, S. (1982). Empirical sub-types of performance anxiety. *Behavioral Assessment, 4*, 179–193.

Garland, H., & Brown, B. R. (1972). Face-saving as affected by subjects' sex, audience's sex, and audience expertise. *Sociometry, 35*, 280–289.

Goffman, E. (1955). On face-work. *Psychiatry, 18*, 213–231.

Goffman, E. (1956). Embarrassment and social organisation. *American Journal of Sociology, 62*, 264–271.

Goffman, E. (1959). *The presentation of self in everyday life.* New York: Doubleday.

Goffman, E. (1963). *Stigma.* Englewood Cliffs, NJ: Prentice-Hall.

Goffman, E. (1971). *Relations in public.* New York: Basic Books.

Granville-Grossman, K., & Turner, P. (1966). The effect of propanolol on anxiety. *Lancet, 1*, 788–790.

Harris, P. R. (1982). *The psychology of shyness: Towards a new approach.* Paper presented at the annual conference of the Social Psychology Section of the British Psychological Society, Edinburgh.

Harris, P. R. (1984a). Shyness and psychological imperialism: On the dangers of ignoring the ordinary language roots of the terms we deal with. *European Journal of Social Psychology, 14*, 169–181.

Harris, P. R. (1984b). The hidden face of shyness: A message from the shy for researchers and practitioners. *Human Relations, 37*, 1079–1093.

Harris, P. R. (1985). *Shyness and embarrassment: Towards an integrated theory.* Paper presented at the Symposium on the Social Psychology of Shyness and Embarrassment, at the annual conference of the British Psychological Society, Swansea, Wales.

Harris, P. R., & Wilshire, P. (1988). Estimating the prevalence of shyness in the "Global Village": Pluralistic ignorance or false consensus? *Journal of Personality, 56*, 405–415.

Heider, F. (1958). *The psychology of interpersonal relations.* New York: Wiley.

Holroyd, K. A., & Appel, M. A. (1980). Test anxiety and physiological responding. In I. G. Sarason (Ed.), *Test anxiety: Theory, research, and application* (pp. 129–151). Hillsdale, NJ: Lawrence Erlbaum.

Hrycaiko, D. W., & Hrycaiko, R. B. (1980). Palmar sweating in an evaluative audience situation. *Journal of Social Psychology, 111*, 269–280.

Izard, C. E., Dougherty, F. E., Bloxom, B. M., & Kotsch, W. E. (1974). *The differential emotions scale: A method of measuring the subjective experience of discrete emotions.* Unpublished manuscript, Vanderbilt University.

James, I. M., Pearson, R. M., Griffith, D. N. W., & Newbury, P. (1977). Effect of oxprenolol on stage-fright in musicians. *Lancet, 2*, 952–954.

Kelly, G. A. (1955). *The psychology of personal constructs.* New York: Norton.

Knight, M. L., & Borden, R. J. (1979). Autonomic and affective reactions of high and low socially-anxious individuals awaiting public performance. *Psychophysiology, 16*(3), 209–213.

Lacey, J. I., Kagan, J., Lacey, B. C., & Moss, H. A. (1963). The visceral level: Situational determinants and behavioral correlates of autonomic response. In P. Knapp (Ed.), *Expressions of emotion in man* (pp. 160–208). New York: International Universities Press.

Leary, M. R. (1983). *Understanding social anxiety.* Beverly Hills: Sage.

Leary, M. R. (1986). The impact of interactional impediments on social anxiety and self presentation. *Journal of Experimental Social Psychology, 22*, 122–135.

Leary, M. R., & Atherton, S. C. (1986). Self-efficacy, social anxiety, and inhibition in interpersonal encounters. *Journal of Social and Clinical Psychology, 4*(3), 256–267.

Lehrer, P. M., & Leiblum, S. R. (1981). Physiological, behavioral, and cognitive measures of assertiveness and assertion anxiety. *Behavioral Counselling Quarterly, 1*(4), 261–274.

McDougall, W. (1926). *An outline of abnormal psychology.* New York: Scribner's.

McDougall, W. (1948). *An introduction to social psychology* (29th ed.). London: Methuen.

MacCurdy, J. T. (1930). The biological significance of blushing and shame. *British Journal of Psychology, 21*, 174–182.

Manstead, A. S. R., & Semin, G. R. (1981). Social transgressions, social perspectives, and social emotionality. *Motivation and Emotion*, *5*(3), 249–261.

Milgram, S. (1965). Some conditions of obedience and disobedience to authority. *Human Relations*, *18*, 57–76.

Miller, R. S. (1986). Embarrassment: Causes and consequences. In W. H. Jones, J. M. Cheek, & S. R. Briggs (Eds.), *Shyness: Perspectives on research and treatment* (pp. 295–311). New York: Plenum Press.

Mischel, W. (1976). *Introduction to personality* (2nd ed.). New York: Holt, Rinehart & Winston.

Modigliani, A. (1968). Embarrassment and embarrassability. *Sociometry*, *31*, 313–326.

Modigliani, A. (1971). Embarrassment, facework, and eye contact: Testing a theory of embarrassment. *Journal of Personality and Social Psychology*, *17*, 15–24.

Mosher, D. L., & White, B. B. (1981). On differentiating shame and shyness. *Motivation and Emotion*, *5*(1), 61–74.

Reitz, W. E., & Keil, W. E. (1971). Behavioral treatment of an exhibitionist. *Journal of Behavior Therapy and Experimental Psychiatry*, *2*, 67–69.

Schaefer, H. H. (1976). Stimulus generalization treatment for exhibitionism. In J. D. Krumboltz & C. E. Thoresen (Eds.), *Behavioral counselling: Cases and techniques* (2nd ed.) New York: Holt, Rinehart & Winston.

Scheier, M. F., & Carver, C. S. (1982). Cognition, affect, and self-regulation. In M. S. Clark & S. T. Fiske (Eds.), *Affect and cognition* (pp. 157–183). Hillsdale, NJ: Lawrence Erlbaum.

Schlenker, B. R., & Leary, M. R. (1982). Social anxiety and self-presentation: A conceptualization and model. *Psychological Bulletin*, *92*, 641–669.

Semin, G. R., & Manstead, A. S. R. (1981). The beholder beheld: A study of social emotionality. *European Journal of Social Psychology*, *11*, 253–265.

Serber, M. (1970). Shame aversion therapy. *Journal of Behavior Therapy and Experimental Psychiatry*, *1*, 213–215.

Smail, D. (1984). *Illusion and reality: The meaning of anxiety*. London: Dent.

Strom, J. C., & Buck, R. W. (1979). Staring and participants' sex: Physiology and subjective reactions. *Personality and Social Psychology Bulletin*, *5*, 114–117.

Turner, S. M., & Beidel, D. C. (1985). Empirically derived subtypes of social anxiety. *Behaviour Research and Therapy*, *16*, 384–392.

Turner, S. M., Beidel, D. C., & Larkin, K. T. (1986). Situational determinants of social anxiety in clinic and non-clinic samples: Physiological and cognitive correlates. *Journal of Consulting and Clinical Psychology*, *54*(4), 523–527.

Tyrer, P. J., & Lader, M. H. (1973). Effects of beta adrenergic blockade with Sotalol in chronic anxiety. *Clinical Pharmacology and Therapeutics*, *14*, 418–426.

Wardlaw, G. R., & Miller, P. J. (1978). A controlled exposure technique in the elimination of exhibitionism. *Journal of Behavior Therapy and Experimental Psychiatry*, *9*, 27–32.

Wine, J. D. (1971). Test anxiety and direction of attention. *Psychological Bulletin*, *76*, 92–104.

Wine, J. D. (1980). Cognitive-attentional theory of test anxiety. In I. G. Sarason

(Ed.), *Test anxiety: Theory, research, and application* (pp. 349–385). Hillsdale, NJ: Lawrence Erlbaum.

Wine, J. D. (1982). Evaluation anxiety: A cognitive-attentional construct. In H. W. Krohne & L. C. Laux (Eds.), *Achievement, stress, and anxiety* (pp. 207–219). Washington, DC: Hemisphere.

Zimbardo, P. G. (1977). *Shyness: What it is; what to do about it.* Reading, MA: Addison-Wesley.

3

The expression of shyness and embarrassment

JENS ASENDORPF

Expression and impression

Shyness and embarrassment arise only in real or imagined social situations: They occur in public. Therefore, they have not only social antecedents but also social *consequences*. When I feel shy, I behave in a certain way; if you notice this behaviour, you may infer that I am shy and adjust your behaviour accordingly. Behaviours that lawfully accompany a certain state or trait and are used by most people to infer that state or trait are commonly called the *expressions* of that state or trait. Thus, the social consequences of shyness and embarrassment depend upon its expression: If you are able to control your shyness perfectly, I will not notice it, and it will have no consequences for our future interaction so far as I am concerned.

The definition of "expression" given earlier reflects its meaning in common sense, but closer inspection reveals that this is an unduly narrow concept. First, there may exist behaviours that lawfully accompany a state or trait but are not perceived as indicators of that state or trait by most people. For example, shyness may be accompanied by more subtle behavioural cues of which most of us are not aware, or of which no one can be aware during the normal course of social interaction, although these cues can be revealed by a detailed behavioural analysis.

Second, people may consider certain behaviours as expressions of a state or trait, even though they are not. Such misperceptions can be widely shared because of semantic similarities between the naming of the behaviour and the wording of concepts related to the state/trait. For example, a "soft" facial expression may be considered to be an indication of a "soft character", and angular body movements to be expressions of an "erratic character". The older pre-experimental literature about the non-verbal expression of emotion and personality is dominated by this "seduction of language" (Asendorpf & Wallbott, 1982).

Third, there may exist substantial individual differences in the externalisation of states or traits; different people may externalise the same

87

state or trait by different responses. Although these differences have rarely been investigated, two recent studies suggest that they do exist and that they are substantial. Ellgring (1986) analysed non-verbal indicators of depression over a period of several weeks in depressive patients who passed at least one depressive phase during the course of observation. He found that the sample as a whole showed the full repertoire of classical non-verbal indicators of depression when actually depressed (downward gaze, lack of smiling, and restricted facial and gestural movements); but on the individual level, most patients displayed only one or two of these indicators of depression.

Asendorpf (1988) found similar individual differences in the patterning of responses for dispositional shyness in a non-clinical sample. Each of 66 subjects was observed in nine social situations that involved two different interaction partners. The sample as a whole showed five responses that significantly correlated either with self-ratings or with global other-ratings of shyness in these situations. The five indicators of shyness showed a mean intercorrelation of only $r = .23$. This low mean correlation was due to substantial individual differences in the externalisation of shyness: The majority of the subjects showed response profiles that were significantly stable across the nine situations. For example, one subject responded consistently more with gaze aversion than with long silences, whereas another showed the opposite pattern.

Such differences become particularly obvious when different cultures or sub-groups within a culture are compared. The cross-cultural study of Edelmann, Asendorpf, Contarello, Georgas, Villanueva, and Zammuner (1987, 1989) on self-reported expressions of embarrassment (Edelmann, this volume) suggests that these differences may be substantial, although data on cross-cultural differences in real embarrassed behaviour are lacking.

Finally, people may differ not only in the externalisation of states and traits but also in their *impression formation* about others. Some may be very accurate in their perceptions, and others not; some may base their judgements on a certain set of behaviours, but others may ignore many of these behaviours and use other cues instead. People may also differ in the *inference rules* they use – implicitly or explicitly – for inferring a particular state or trait from the same set of behaviours.

These four complications suggest extending the concept of expression to the broader concept of "any behavioural indicator of a state/trait". This concept of expression does not imply that the expression is shared by most people, can be perceived by most people in regular social interaction, and is actually used by most people in the same way for impression formation. Instead, it is assumed only that the expression

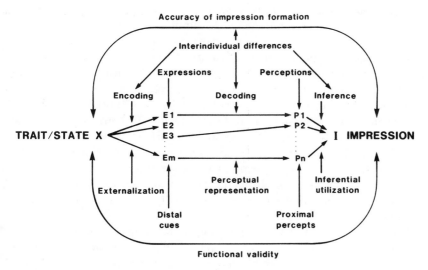

Figure 3.1. A Brunswikian lens model of expression and impression.

bears a lawful relation to a state or trait for *some* people and that therefore it could be used by *some* people to accurately infer the underlying state or trait.

The only difference between "expression" and "behaviour", then, is the lawful relation between an expression and the underlying state or trait. The close relation between expression and impression formation that is assumed in lay psychology is lost. But this relation can easily be re-established when expression and impression are treated as independent concepts within a unifying framework. One such conceptual framework is the lens model of Brunswik (1956; see Scherer, 1978, for a similar approach). Figure 3.1 shows this model. The terms in the lower part are the original ones used by Brunswik (1956); those in the upper part are common terms in the psychological literature on the expression of emotion and on person perception.

The remaining discussion focuses on the *expression* of shyness or embarrassment; studies on impression formation about shyness or embarrassment are discussed only when they also shed some light on the encoding process.

Spontaneous and controlled expression

Common-sense popular psychology and most of the older literature on the expression of emotion and personality implicitly assume that there is a fixed, one-to-one relation between each of certain emotional states and its expression. Neither of these two assumptions withstands closer analysis. Different states may be expressed very similarly; for example, both slight anger and high concentration are displayed by most people with heightened muscle tension and frowning, and it is nearly impossible to distinguish these two states only by their expressions. Also, adults are able to control their expression within limits; they can inhibit, amplify, or feign many expressions according to their actual intentions. On the other hand, it is also true that expressions are not arbitrarily encoded, neither at the level of cultures nor at the level of individuals. For the facial expression of many emotions, for example, cross-cultural consistency as well as cultural differences that are consistent across members of the same culture have been repeatedly demonstrated (Ekman & Oster, 1979; Izard, 1971).

A simple model that accounts for both findings was proposed by Ekman and Friesen (1969). According to this model, genetically fixed programs guide the expression of various fundamental emotions such as happiness, anger, and fear. These *pancultural expressions* are modified, however, by socially learned *display rules* that prescribe modifications of the pancultural expressions, such as amplification, inhibition, neutralisation, or masking with another expression. In each culture, social *norms* are well established concerning which display rule is appropriate for each emotion when it is experienced by a certain individual in a certain social situation with certain interaction partners. These norms may take into account the status (role, age, and gender) of the person experiencing the emotion and the status of the interaction partners, as well as general characteristics of the situation (private, public, a specific social routine, or ritual).

This model, like other approaches that stress the interaction of genetically pre-programmed and socially learned encoding processes, bridges the long-standing and rather unproductive dichotomy between innate and learned expressions; see Zivin (1985) for an excellent sourcebook on this question. The model can be easily extended to dissolve another, related dichotomy: *spontaneous* versus intentional expression. Whereas the innate, pancultural expression programs and their modifications by (over)learned display rules function with minimal awareness, older children and adults are able to voluntarily control some of the expressions by modifying the display rules within limits (Malatesta & Haviland, 1985). Figure 3.2 presents a simple model that takes volitional modification of display rules into account.

The model also allows for feedback effects at all intermediate stages between situation and expression of the emotional state – an important aspect of the encoding of expression that is sometimes neglected in the

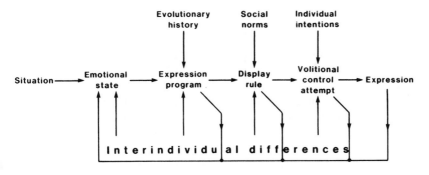

Figure 3.2. The encoding of expressions.

literature on expressive behaviour. The existence of these feedback effects is not easy to prove in a straightforward, experimental manner because often it is not possible to systematically vary the intermediate stages independently of each other. But in recent years, evidence of a more indirect nature is accumulating to show that the execution of expression programs, display rules, and volitional control attempts feed back to the emotional state under certain conditions (Ekman, Levenson, & Friesen, 1983; Leventhal, 1980).

More obvious is the possibility that one's self-perceived expression influences the emotional state from which it originated. People monitor their expressions very closely in situations where they are motivated to convey a certain image to the public. Here, interesting paradoxical control effects can occur that highlight the complex interaction of emotion and volition. Two examples of such paradoxical control effects may suffice here to illustrate the point (see Asendorpf, 1984, for a more detailed discussion and a model that accounts for these control effects).

Blushing is a common expression of embarrassment that cannot be directly controlled (Castelfranchi & Poggi, this volume; Harré, this volume). When a person holds the standard not to appear embarrassed in a certain type of situation, but still blushes, this reaction contradicts the image the person wants to convey, and in so doing it constitutes an additional source of embarrassment, according to the self-presentational approach to embarrassment of Leary and Schlenker (1981); see also Shepperd and Arkin (this volume). Thus, a vicious circle is established that intensifies the original source of embarrassment: The person begins with being embarrassed about some unintended mistake, for example, and ends up being embarrassed about this mistake *and* about blushing, which he or she perceives as embarrassing.

A similar vicious circle often emerges in shyness. Consider a young adolescent going on his first date with a girl he secretly admires. He most likely will lack the social skills to handle the situation gracefully, and that will make him even more shy. The more he wants to convey the image that he is a cool hand at dates, the more his shyness will interfere with his self-presentation: Shyness will promote itself via a positive feedback loop.

Thus, the encoding of expressions of shyness or embarrassment is a multi-stage process that may contain feedback loops that will prevent any simple one-to-one relation between emotion and expression. Furthermore, individual differences influence each stage of the externalisation process (Figure 3.2): Genetic differences lead to variations in expression programs; people differ in the degree to which they have learned display rules and are able to execute them with minimal awareness, and they differ in their tendencies and in their abilities to control their expressions on purpose.

Shyness and embarrassment as states and traits

Before a review of the existing studies on the expression of shyness and embarrassment can be attempted, a common confusion in the literature must be clarified. In lay psychology, "shyness" denotes both an emotional state, which everybody may experience in certain situations, and a trait (i.e., the tendency to experience state shyness with an above average intensity consistently over time and across a wide variety of social situations). State shyness and trait shyness are related, though quite different concepts; results obtained for one of them cannot be generalised to the other.

"State shyness" refers to *intra*individual differences. These differences can be studied in a within-subject design in which the behaviours of a given person are compared in at least two situations that elicit state shyness to different degrees (e.g., a "shyness situation" versus a "control situation"). State shyness can also be studied in a between-subjects design in which in each such situation another group of subjects is observed, and in which these groups of subjects are otherwise completely comparable (most important, they should not differ in the degree of mean trait shyness).

"Trait shyness" refers to *inter*individual differences; they are studied in a between-subjects design in which the persons to be compared are observed in the same situations. The same applies to intraindividual differences in the state of embarrassment, and interindividual differences in the trait of embarrassability (Edelmann, this volume).

Behaviours or feelings that covary interindividually with trait shyness need not show a similar covariation with intraindividual differences in state shyness, and vice versa. Sometimes, even the direction of the covariation is reversed. For example, in a study of 192 students who rated their likely reactions to different social situations that varied considerably in the degree to which they would induce state shynesss, Asendorpf (1985a) found that intraindividually, reports of a "happy mood" correlated *positively* with state shyness, whereas interindividually, a *negative* correlation between "happy mood" and trait shyness was found for each situation as well as for the aggregate of all situations. The positive intraindividual correlation indicates that people experience mixed feelings when they become shy (see Izard & Hyson, 1986, for comparable findings); the negative interindividual correlations suggest that the relative contributions of shy and happy feelings to these mixed feelings vary with trait shyness: The higher is trait shyness, the more dominant is state shyness relative to state happiness (see Epstein, 1982, for similar data for the relation between anger and happiness, and a more detailed discussion of the distinction between intra- and inter-individual analyses).

Probably the most widespread error in the literature on shyness is to confuse state shyness and trait shyness. Very often, interindividual correlations are interpreted as if they would tell us something about the processes that give rise to the emotional state of shyness in everybody. They do not. This argument also applies to the expression of shyness and embarrassment. Behaviours that covary with state shyness need not differentiate between people high and low in trait shyness, and vice versa; behaviours that regularly accompany embarrassment need not be typical for high embarrassability, and vice versa.

State shyness and embarrassment

A short note on the distinction between state shyness and embarrassment appears necessary, too. The self-presentational approach of Leary and Schlenker (1981) allows for a first distinction (Shepperd & Arkin, this volume). According to this approach, state shyness arises when people are motivated to make a favourable impression on others, but doubt that they will do so, whereas embarrassment arises when an event occurs that appears to repudiate one's intended self-presentation. Thus, "state shyness" refers to an anticipatory embarrassment to a reactive emotional state. In some sense, then, shyness is the anticipation of embarrassment.

A major problem of this self-presentational approach is that state shyness is restricted to situations that induce fear of social evaluation. There are other social situations that also can induce state shyness. One important class of these situations concerns meeting a stranger. In a recent study in our laboratory, fear of strangers and fear of social evaluation were systematically varied independently of each other in a between-groups design with adults. The results clearly show that both types of fear induce state shyness according to self-ratings and other-ratings and do not interact with each other (Asendorpf, 1989a).

Thus, it seems to be more appropriate to extend the definition of state shyness proposed by the self-presentational approach to include fear of strangers. This extension still preserves the fundamental difference between state shyness as an anticipatory state and embarrassment as a reactive emotional state.

Expressions of shyness and embarrassment

The following review of studies on expressions of shyness and embarrassment is organised around three distinctions: state versus trait, shyness versus embarrassment, and the ages of the subjects observed (infants, children, and adults). Studies that appear to have been methodologically unsound or that presented results that could not be generalised at all, because of small numbers or peculiar selection of subjects, are not discussed. The vast numbers of studies employing role-play situations, which dominated the research on social anxiety and social skills in the 1970s, are excluded from this review because it is difficult to determine to what extent their results can be generalised to real interaction.

State shyness

A peculiar asymmetry pervades the research on state shyness when it is classified by the ages of the subjects observed: There are many studies on infants' wariness towards strangers, a few on children's wariness towards strangers, but very few on adults' wariness towards strangers. Also, all studies on the expression of state shyness appear to have been restricted to stranger anxiety; I could not find a single study that (1) had investigated people's behaviours when they had become shy for other reasons and (2) had employed a control situation that made it possible to evaluate the effect of state shyness (cf. Asendorpf, 1989a). Some studies, however, tried to induce embarrassment by asking very personal questions. Those studies are discussed in the section on the expression of embarrassment, but their results also shed some light on the expression of state shyness, because those personal interviews very likely evoked both embarrassment and state shyness at different points during their courses.

Wariness towards strangers is a well-investigated, classical research theme in developmental psychology (see Sroufe, 1977, for a review). In

Table 3.1. *Expressions of infants' wariness towards strangers*

Intensity	Description of reaction
1	*Wary brow*: As the infant is looking at the stranger, the eyebrows are drawn closer together and are raised at the centre; the mouth is either closed (and may be turned down at the corners) or open, and the lower lip may protrude. In older infants, wrinkles may be seen on the forehead.
2	*Wary averted gaze*: From either a wary brow expression or a relaxed, neutral facial expression, the eyelids begin to close smoothly over the eyes as the face is turned down and away. This can be distinguished from simply looking elsewhere by the initial partial closing of the eyes, the absence of a blink or shift of the eyes to either side, and the downward turn of the head.
3	*Avoid*: The infant stiffens as the stranger reaches, draws the hands to the body away from contact with the stranger, or uses the hands to push the stranger's hands away. The infant may fret, show a wary brow, stick lower lip out, and/or turn or look to the mother.
4	*Cry face*: The infant's eyes are narrowed, the eyebrows are lowered and flattened, the mouth is puckered, the lower lip is out, and the mouth may turn down laterally.
5	*Cry*: The infant cries audibly.

Source: Adapted from Waters et al. (1975), which is © The Society for Research in Child Development, Inc.

the typical observational procedure, an adult stranger approaches an infant when the mother is present. Studies varying the situational circumstances of the approach have consistently shown that (1) nearly all infants pass through a (rather short) phase in which they react with wariness or even clear avoidance towards adult strangers, (2) the reaction is the stronger the faster the stranger approaches, and (3) infants differ greatly both in the age at which this reaction can be observed and in the intensity of the reaction.

The *expression* of wariness towards strangers among infants varies on a continuum from slight wariness to intense crying. A detailed description yielding a high interobserver reliability was provided by Waters, Matas, and Sroufe (1975); see Table 3.1.

This description highlights two important points in the study of expressive behaviour. First, the expressions are already rather *complex* in infancy. Various non-verbal "channels" (facial expression, gazing, body position, voice) contribute to the whole expression, and the behaviour is rather *specific* within each channel (note, for example, that "gaze aversion" is not a sufficient description of the "wary averted gaze"). Second, although those authors used rather static expressions as prototypes for the levels of intensity, it becomes quite clear from the descriptions that the expression of wariness is essentially a *stream of behaviour* that represents the infant's adaptation to the behaviour of the stranger. When the stranger enters the room, the infant's behaviour may change from a sober face, progressing all along the continuum of wariness until its most extreme, depending on how fast the stranger intrudes.

In infancy, wariness towards strangers is easily recognised because most infants' reactions vary on one continuum from positive-sociable to negative-avoidant. Later, during early childhood, a clear-cut negative response becomes less and less likely. Instead, children then often show a mixture of sociable behaviour (smiling and gazing) and wary behaviour (e.g., lengthy *coy expressions* of smiling accompanied by gaze aversion). This ambivalent behaviour has been observed as early as 12 months (Bretherton & Ainsworth, 1974), but it reaches its peak among those 3 to 4 years old; in a study by Greenberg and Marvin (1982), the *majority* of the children of that age showed a coy expression at least for a short time. This ambivalent behaviour suggests simultaneous activation of at least two behavioural systems: an affiliative system that promotes sociability and a wariness system that serves a protective function (Bischof, 1975; Greenberg & Marvin, 1982; Sroufe, 1977).

Whereas the older literature on stranger anxiety focused exclusively on the reactions of infants and children, Kaltenbach, Weinraub, and Fullard (1980) reported the puzzling observation that the mothers who accompanied their children also displayed wariness towards the stranger. In fact, wary behaviour was more frequently observed among mothers than among their 8-month-old infants, particularly as the proximity of the stranger increased. Although these authors did not report data on ambivalent behaviours, the percentages of the single behaviours suggest frequent mixtures of sociable and wary behaviours among the mothers (e.g., 54% smiling and 83% wary averted gaze in one condition). Thus, wariness towards strangers is not unique to infants and young children, but appears to be a common human reaction towards a stranger when the stranger behaves intrusively (Asendorpf, 1989a).

Embarrassment

Although the research on stranger anxiety has been dominated by developmental studies, little is known about the development of embarrassment and embarrassment displays. According to the hypothesis of Buss (1986), "late developing shyness" and embarrassment emerge around the age of 5 years, when children learn to become aware of themselves as social objects. In fact, Buss, Iscoe, and Buss (1979) found that 5 years was the earliest age at which a majority of children showed embarrassment displays, such as blushing, according to reports of their mothers. In our own longitudinal study on the development of shyness, evidence for state shyness and embarrassment was derived from assessment of the children when they were 5 to 6 years old (Asendorpf, 1989c).

Ninety-two children were asked nine questions that were selected to increasingly induce public self-awareness; in order to further this effect, the interviewer looked increasingly at the child during the course of the interview. The first block of three questions tapped aspects of cognitive and motoric abilities, the second concerned aspects of the outer appearance (e.g., good-looking), and the third involved aspects of popularity and morale (e.g., "Do you often argue with other children?"). The children's answers were videotaped, the order of the three blocks was counterbalanced on the tapes, and four judges blind to the types of questions were presented these tapes without audio. The judges rated each child's answers for evidence of shyness-embarrassment. These ratings were highly consistent across raters and showed a highly significant increase of rated shyness-embarrassment from the first block of questions to the third block. Thus, the more self-related the questions were, the more shy-embarrassed the children behaved. It is not clear whether or not the increase noted by the observers was due to an increase in state shyness and/or embarrassment; a detailed analysis of the tapes will help to clarify this question.

In most studies of the expression of embarrassment among adults, similar interview techniques have been applied (Table 3.2). Three indicators of embarrassment have been replicated at least once: less looking while talking, more body motion (unspecified), and more speech disturbances. This is a meagre result when it is compared with the detailed knowledge about the expression of wariness in infants and children. The results are not specific enough (e.g., the specific kind of gaze aversion) and clearly are not exhaustive. Blushing, the most prominent expression during embarrassment, has not been studied at all.

The data of Edelmann and Hampson (1981a,b) on the role of smiling during embarrassment – although not replicated – are interesting because they touch upon the problem that some behaviours that accompany felt embarrassment may indicate display rules or volitional control attempts rather than genuine expression of embarrassment (Figure 3.2). When students were asked in a cross-cultural study on embarrassment how they had reacted in a recent embarrassing situation, about 30% within each culture reported smiling or laughing; also, when the subjects were asked what they did in order to cover or hide their embarrassment, again about 30% mentioned smiling (Edelmann et al., 1987, 1989; Edelmann, this volume). Thus, people may have learned to smile *in*

Table 3.2. *Expression of embarrassment*

Study	Subjects	Induction of embarrassment	Results
Exline et al. (1965)	40 female, 40 male students	Interview, with personal vs. control questions	For personal questions, subjects showed more silence, less looking while talking (no difference for looking while listening or during silence)
Modigliani (1971)	60 male students	Subjects were made to succeed vs. to fail at a task in a 4-person-sit.	Subjects failing reported higher embarrassment; looked less at partners after failure, no difference after success
Edelmann & Hampson (1979)	22 psychology students	Embarrassing question embedded in interview	Subjects who found the target question embarrassing showed during their answers to that question more body motion and speech disturbances; looked less at interviewer
Edelmann & Hampson (1981a)	18 female, 18 male adults	Question–answer game in dyads; increasing intimacy of topic vs. neutral topic	With increasing intimacy of topic, subjects reported more embarrassment, smiled more and looked less at partner, and showed more body motion and speech disturbances
Edelmann & Hampson (1981b) Exp. 1	21 female, 12 male students	Subjects watched responses of 9 subjects in 1979 study to critical question, 3 self-rated embarrassed, 3 mixed, 3 amused	Embarrassment was more accurately identified for face + body; for face alone, embarrassment was often identified as amusement
Exp. 2	10 female, 5 male students	As in Exp. 1, but only face + body; subjects should indicate which part of body they used for judgement	Accurate judgements of embarrassment used eyes, hands, mouth, and lower legs; accurate judgement of amusement used only mouth

Note: All differences reported in the Results column were statistically significant.

response to embarrassment in order to comment on it ("Sorry, I didn't want to do what I did"), or they may – automatically or deliberately – want to cover their expression of embarrassment. The study of Edelmann and Hampson (1981b) showed that smiles could be rather successfully used for covering embarrassment, because observers who saw only the faces of embarrassed subjects often confused embarrassment with expressions of amusement. Their study does not show that the smiles really were instances of coping attempts or that they would have been indistinguishable from smiles of amusement if they could have been studied in more detail.

Results from one of my own experiments shed some light on the role of smiling during embarrassment; they also confirm the notion that blushing is an indicator of embarrassment. Seventy subjects were brought into four social situations designed to induce shyness and embarrassment to different degrees (see Asendorpf, 1987a, 1988, for details about the situations). First, stranger anxiety was evoked by having the subjects wait together with a confederate of the experimenter for the "real experiment". Second, social-evaluative anxiety was induced by instructing the subjects to get to know each other in front of a camera so that later they could evaluate each other via a personality questionnaire. Third, each subject was embarrassed twice by being asked for some evaluative statements about the partner in the presence of the partner, and by having the confederate praise the subject afterwards. Fourth, the subjects conversed with the experimenter, who pretended that the experiment was already over; this situation served as a base-line condition.

The confederate or the experimenter observed the frequency of subjects' blushing in each situation. Figure 3.3 indicates that the social-evaluative get-to-know situation and the two embarrassing situations each induced more blushing in the subjects than did the base-line situation and the stranger situation (each of the four comparisons was significant, $p < .001$). Thus, blushing appears to be related to social-evaluative situations, but not to stranger anxiety. This is an interesting finding because it supports the notion that stranger anxiety and social-evaluative anxiety are quite different states, although both are commonly regarded as just two instances of the same state of shyness.

The videotapes of the subjects' behaviours in the four situations were also used for a closer analysis of the subjects' smiling during embarrassment. First, one observer with some training in behavioural analysis rated all smiles in the get-to-know situation on a six-point scale for a leakage of embarrassment. Second, another judge selected from the smiles with low or high scores 60 smiles that looked "clearly embarrassed". Third, three judges who had never evaluated video recordings

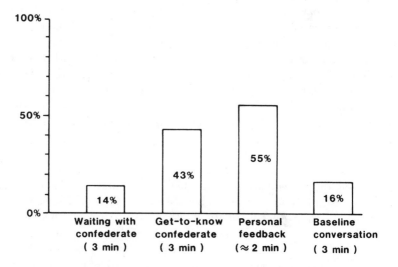

Figure 3.3. Incidence of blushing in four situations.

before rated these 106 smiles for embarrassment in a yes–no format. The three naive judges showed significant (but low) agreement (κ values between .20 and .35). Thus, lay observers appear to share some conception of what a genuine smile is and what an embarrassed smile is, but it is a fuzzy conception.

Fourth, a highly experienced observer explored the 64 smiles for which there was agreement between the expert judges and at least two of the three lay judges for behavioural indicators that may help to distinguish between embarrassed and non-embarrassed smiles; gaze, facial expression, and speech were all considered. By this procedure, we discovered one highly discriminative indicator of embarrassed smiles: gaze aversion before the apex of the smile ends.

The apex of a smile is the phase of smiling in which the corners of the mouth are maximally pulled up; the end of this phase, the so-called apex offset, can be coded reliably according to the criteria outlined by Ekman and Friesen (1978). This time criterion proved to be essential, because nearly all subjects averted their gaze during or shortly after smiling. Two coders independently coded the 64 smiles selected for exploration for the occurrence of gaze aversion between the beginning of the smile and its apex offset (90% agreement, $\kappa = .81$). A cross-classification between this coding and the consensual judgement of embarrassment showed 84% agreement.

To analyse the role of gaze aversion in more detail, the distribution of gaze aversion during the time interval from 2 sec before to 2 sec after the

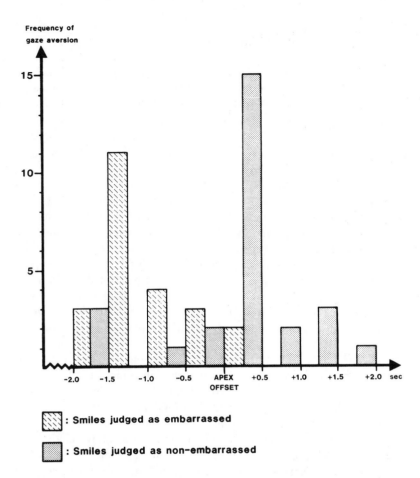

Figure 3.4. Local distribution of gaze aversion around smiles' apex offset for smiles judged as either embarrassed or non-embarrassed.

apex offset of the smiles was determined. To prevent a potential coding bias, we compared the data for apex offset from one coder with the data for gaze aversion from the other coder. Figure 3.4 shows the result. The distribution of gaze aversion shows two clear peaks: one immediately after apex offset for the smiles judged as non-embarrassed, and another 1.0 to 1.5 sec before apex offset for the smiles judged as embarrassed. A χ^2 test indicated that gaze aversion was not evenly distributed in the whole 4-sec interval ($p < .001$).

Finally, the hypothesis that embarrassed smiles are accompanied by gaze aversion before the smile's apex offset was cross-validated by comparing the frequencies of smiles coded as embarrassed or non-embarrassed between the embarrassing personal feedback situation and the base-line conversation (Figure 3.3). All smiles with a duration of at least 2 sec shown in these two situations were coded for gaze aversion. As expected, the proportion of smiles coded as embarrassed was higher during the personal feedback situation (60%) than during the base-line conversation (35%, $p < .05$ for the difference).

These results are reported here at some length because they are interesting in regard to both the methodology used and the results achieved. People apparently avert their gaze during embarrassed smiles at the most communicative part of smiling: shortly before the apex of the smile ends (i.e., when the smile reaches its peak intensity). This seems to be the reason why embarrassed smiles carry the flavor of ambivalence: approach (smiling) and avoidance (gaze aversion) at the same time. The timing of gaze aversion suggests that gaze aversion during smiling in an embarrassing situation is a *response to smiling*. A possible reason for this response is that smiling increases the intimacy of the situation. Therefore, an attempt is made to reduce the level of intimacy by averting one's gaze when the smile reaches its apex. See Argyle and Dean (1965) for an equilibrium model of intimacy regulation that can be applied here.

The results are also interesting from a methodological point of view, because they demonstrate the manner in which unreliable lay judgements can be both used and transcended by detailed analyses of expression. The description of infants' expressions of wariness (Table 3.1) has made it clear that expressions of emotion can be rather complex processes, with a certain time course encompassing many "channels" of nonverbal behaviour that often are viewed in isolation. The same applies to embarrassed smiles. Their definition includes two responses from quite different non-verbal channels and their timing relative to each other. Such unexpected, complex properties were discovered by a systematic exploratory procedure combining lay judgement, expert knowledge, and simple statistics. Such a procedure appears to be quite helpful in transcending our present poor understanding of the expression of state shyness and embarrassment.

Dispositional shyness

Infancy and early childhood. Research on the expression of dispositional shyness has been dominated by studies of adults; in all other studies, infants or young children were observed. All studies of infants' wariness toward strangers have reported high interindividual variances of the observed behaviours; but very little information is available on the stability of these interindividual differences over time and across different strangers. Smith and Sloboda (1986) found a significant stability of the observed differences among eight young children (ages 13–15 months) who were confronted with eight different strangers during four visits to their laboratory within a 3-week period. Bronson and Pankey (1977) repeatedly studied 40 young children throughout their second year and once again at the age of 3½ years in structured, mildly challenging situations. They found no evidence that the interindividual differences in shy behaviours towards peers observed at the beginning of the second year would persist for more than a few months. Instead, their data suggest a clear increase in the stability of dispositional shyness during the second year; shyness during the second and third trimesters of that year predicted shyness when meeting an adult stranger at home at age 3½ (r = .44 and r = .49, respectively), but not shyness during the first trimester (r = .08). Thus, interindividual differences in shyness demonstrate some short-term stability, but not long-term stability until the middle of the second year; then they appear to consolidate quickly.

Evidence for a moderate long-term stability of dispositional shyness beyond 22 months comes from two ongoing longitudinal studies, one at Harvard (Garcia-Coll, Kagan, & Reznick, 1984; Kagan, Reznick, Clarke, Snidman, & Garcia-Coll, 1984; Reznick, Kagan, Snidman, Gersten, Baak, & Rosenberg, 1986) and one at the Max Planck Institute for Psychological Research in Munich (Asendorpf, 1987b, 1988c, in press). In the Harvard study, a stability of r = .46 for shy-inhibited behaviour was found for 43 children between 22 and 48 months of age; however, this correlation is inflated because the children were selected for high or low shy-inhibited behaviour at 22 months. In the Max Planck study, a stability of dispositional shyness of r = .62 between 3½ and 5½ years was found for an unselected sample of 100 children for a highly aggregated index of shyness comprising a parent judgement, a teacher judgement, and two different behavioural measures. Thus, dispositional shyness appears to be a moderately stable dimension of personality after the end of the second year.

All these stability data rest upon global ratings of shyness or highly aggregated indices of shy behaviour that embrace many different behavioural indicators. Which specific behaviours differentiate between children high and low in dispositional shyness? For infants' wariness towards strangers, it seems that intra- and interindividual differences in wariness are indicated by the same behaviours (Table 3.1). For young children, the Harvard and Max Planck studies appear to be the only ones that provide more specific information about the behaviours related to dispositional shyness. Unfortunately, the Harvard data are not well documented in respect to this question because the published reports focused more on the stability issue and on physiological differences. The Max Planck data have not yet been fully analysed. Table 3.3 presents an overview of expressive behaviours that showed significant relations with dispositional shyness in these two studies.

The most obvious difference between shy and non-shy children is that shy children speak less – regardless whether the testing partner is an adult or a peer. In the Max Planck study, children's latency until they initiated verbal contact with an adult stranger and their duration and mean length of silence all correlated around $r = .40$ with parents' reports of shyness at the ages of 3½ and 5½. The interindividual differences in verbal activity were so impressive in the Max Planck study that they accounted for nearly all of the systematic variance in observers' ratings of shyness; these ratings correlated $r = -.75$ (age 3½) and $r = -.72$ (age 5½) with children's percentages of time speaking in interaction with a stranger.

Whereas the speech data are completely consistent and straightforward in interpretation, the data on children's gazing are more complex. First, we have to distinguish carefully between looking at somebody from a distance *without* social interaction and looking at an interaction partner *within* social interaction. The Harvard and the Max Planck data clearly show that shy children often are engaged in watching peers from a distance. Interestingly, shy children are engaged in extensive watching even when they try to approach others. Asendorpf (1985b) developed an observational system for coding children's contact initiation behaviours. The category most closely related to dispositional shyness was the percentage of observed "wait-and-hover" among all initiations, defined as "the child approaches the physical proximity of a partner, stops, and observes the activity of the partner for at least 3 sec without speaking". Here, watching occurs within a self-interrupted approach.

The data on gazing *within* interactions are less easy to interpret. Shy children were found to glance more at an experimenter during testing and to look less at a peer during play, and shy boys, but not shy girls, looked less at a female adult stranger before and during interaction. The problem with these data is that gazing during social interaction serves quite different functions at the same time: regulating speaker turns, expressing intimacy, exercising social control, seeking information, and regulating one's arousal, among others (see Kleinke, 1986, and Rutter, 1984, for reviews). Global measures of gazing, such as those reported in Table 3.3, confound all of these different functions. A possible solution to

Table 3.3. *Expression of dispositional shyness in early childhood*

Study/situation/age	Indicators of dispositional shyness found
Harvard study	
Testing by experimenter, age 4	Stiff posture, frequent small finger and hand movements, frequent glances at experimenter
Play with an unfamiliar peer, age 4	Staring at peer from a distance, less speaking with peer
First day in kindergarten	Staring at peer from a distance
Testing by experimenter, age 5½	Stiff posture, less speaking with experimenter
Regular kindergarten group, age 5½	More looking at peers from a distance, less looking at peers in social interaction
Max Planck study	
Meeting an adult stranger before interaction, age 3½	Long latency of first verbal utterance, high duration and high mean length of gaze aversion (only boys), no difference for self-manipulations
Same at age 5½	Long latency of first verbal utterance
Interaction with an adult stranger, age 3½	Long latency of first spontaneous utterance, high duration and high mean length of silences, high duration and high mean length of gaze aversion (only boys), no difference for self-manipulations
Same at age 5½	Long latency of first spontaneous utterance, high duration and high mean length of silences, short utterances
Interaction with unknown peer, age 4½	Long latency of first spontaneous utterance, less social interaction
Regular free play in pre-school,[a] age 3½	Greater percent age of wait-and-hover in own contact initiations
Same, age 4½	Same
Same, age 5½	Same

Note: All indicators showed significant relations with dispositional shyness, as measured by an aggregated behavioral index.
[a] In Germany, there is no difference between pre-school and kindergarten (i.e., groups consist of children of ages 3–7).

this problem is to distinguish between different categories of gazing and gaze aversion that may be differentially related to different functions, such as short glances versus frank looks versus stares, or looking away for the visual inspection of an object versus "wary averted gaze" (Table 3.1). It takes video recordings of very good quality to draw these distinctions, and they may be difficult to achieve reliably (What is a "frank" look?); but perhaps only in this way can a clear relation between dispositional shyness and certain patterns of gazing be discovered.

Popular psychology and some ethologists assume that self-stimulation increases during intrapsychic conflict as an instance of "displacement activity" (Eibl-Eibesfeldt, 1984; Tinbergen, 1952) or that self-stimulation of the face may increase as an instance of an "intentional movement" of covering the face (Eibl-Eibesfeldt, 1984; Hinde, 1970) when people would like to hide from the view of others but cannot do so. Dispositional shyness could be related to both effects. Therefore, in the Max Planck study, the frequency, duration, and mean length of self-stimulation of the face and neck were coded; no relation with dispositional shyness was found. In the Harvard study, shy children reportedly showed stiff posture and small, nervous movements of the hands and fingers; however, it is not clear if these were just ratings by observers (which often are reliable but invalid because they are heavily influenced by the overall impression of how shy a child is) or if these data were based on detailed codings. Thus, there is no clear evidence for a relation between children's dispositional shyness and certain body postures or movements.

Adulthood. Studies on the expression of adults' dispositional shyness are summarised in Table 3.4. Table 3.5 provides relevant data from our own study (Asendorpf, 1987a, 1988), which was described earlier in the section on embarrassment. Subjects' self-ratings of shyness and the mean rating by three judges who watched the subjects' videotaped behaviours were aggregated over two situations that induced state shyness (waiting with a stranger of the same gender, and getting to know each other in order to evaluate each other's personality); then, for each gender, the aggregated self- and other-ratings of shyness were correlated with various measures of the subjects' non-verbal behaviours (detailed codings with high intercoder reliability; see Asendorpf, 1988, for details of the coding procedures).

In many respects, the data of Tables 3.4 and 3.5 are consistent with the findings concerning young children's expressions of shyness reported in Table 3.3. First, shy males were again found to speak less and to let more and longer silences develop; again, their speaking behaviours strongly determined observers' judgements of shyness (the puzzling results for females' verbal behaviours will be discussed later). Second, the data on gazing were again not consistent across different studies. The only difference that emerged was that shy subjects averted their gaze more or longer than did non-shy subjects. But Pilkonis (1977) found this effect only for males, whereas in our study it occurred predominantly for

Table 3.4. *Expression of dispositional shyness in adulthood*

Study	Subjects	Definition of shyness	Situation	Results
Patterson (1973)	36 female, 36 male students	Social Avoidance and Distress (SAD) scale of Watson & Friend (1969)	Interview where subjects freely chose distance to the interviewer	Bimodal distribution of distance chosen; distant subjects had higher SAD scores ($p < .10$); correlation SAD–distance .21 ($p. < .10$)
Pilkonis (1977)	23 female, 23 male psychology students	Extreme group selection of 22 shy, 24 non-shy subjects based on various self-ratings	Subjects waited 5 min with a confederate of opposite gender for the "real experiment"	Shy subjects spoke less frequently, had more silences (> 10 sec), broke silences less often; no difference for mean length of utterances, frequency or time of looking, nodding, smiling, gesturing, self-manipulation; shy males looked less often & smaller percentage time than non-shy males; shy females nodded & smiled more than non-shy females
Daly (1978)	18 female, 18 male students	12 subjects high, 12 medium, 12 low on SAD selected from 213 subjects	Interview (not further specified)	Correlation between SAD & subjects' unsolicited talking −.47, eye contact during speech −28; no correlation for eye contact while listening, mean length of eye contact bouts, frequency of arm movements, & self-manipulation

Table 3.4. (cont.)

Study	Subjects	Definition of shyness	Situation	Results
Carducci & Webber (1979)	42 female, 31 male students	Median split on a shyness index based on five self-ratings	Subjects were asked to walk to experimenter from about 5 m until they found comfortable distance	Shy subjects chose a more distant position regardless of gender of experimenter (which was balanced within gender of subjects)
Natale et al. (1979)	36 female, 36 male students	SAD & Fear of Negative Evaluation (FNE) scale of Watson & Friend (1969)	Subjects talked freely for 30 min with an unacquainted partner (12 female, 12 male, 12 mixed dyads)	Multiple regression, with variables of partner as covariates, showed relations between SAD and less successful interruptions, short interruptions, and between FNE and the number of back-channel responses
Mandel & Shrauger (1980)	37 male students	Subjects selected from 180 subjects by high or low scores on a scale tapping hetero-sexual anxiety	Subects met female confederate who behaved pleasantly without carrying conversation	Shy subjects were rated as showing less eye contact, smiling, facial expressions, & gestures illustrating their speech; no difference for seating distance, stiffness, & motor movements
Cheek & Buss (1981)	40 female students	Subjects selected for extreme scores in shyness and/or sociability scale from a large sample (10 subjects in each of the 4 groups)	Each subject talked 5 min with an unacquainted subject of the same type (in terms of extreme scores)	Shy-sociable subjects talked & looked less at partner and showed more self-manipulations than did the other three groups (i.e., shy-unsociable & the two non-shy groups)

N (= All differences and correlations reported in the Results section were statistically significant unless indicated otherwise.

Table 3.5. *Behavioural indicators of self-rated and other-rated shyness by gender in the study of Asendorpf (1987a, 1988)*

	Self-rated		Other-rated	
Measure	Male	Female	Male	Female
% speaking	−.57***	−.06*	.81***	−.45**
% listening	−.11	−.05	.07	−.09
% silent	.58***	.08	.66***	.49**
% double-talk	−.51***	.04	−.58***	−.15
Mean length of speaking	−.19	.05	−.31	−.27
Mean length of listening	−.03	.06	.06	−.19
Mean length of silences	.46**	.17	.59***	.42**
Mean length of double-talk	−.26	.03	−.28	.06
No. successful interruptions[a]	−.51***	−.12	−.52***	−.10
No. unsuccessful interruptions[a]	−.13	−.31	−.13	.04
% gaze aversion	.25	.34*	.12	.19
Mean length of gaze aversion	.24	.16	.11	.08
% gaze aversion during speaking	.00	.16	−.07	.03
% gaze aversion during listening	.33*	.41*	.13	.23
% gaze aversion during silences	.23	.36*	.10	.20
% illustrators	−.36*	−.04	−.41*	.33
Mean length of illustrators[b]	−.22	.07	−.33	.21
% self-manipulations	−.07	−.09	.01	−.13
Mean length of self-manipulations	−.29	−.06	−.26	−.11

[a] Corrected for partner's speaking.
[b] Corrected for subject's speaking.
*p < .05; **p < .01; ***p < .001.

females, and Daly (1978) found more gaze aversion among the shy only during speech, whereas in our study, both shy males and shy females gazed less during listening or silences, but not during speaking. The results of Mandel and Shrauger (1980) are difficult to interpret because the subjects' behaviours were rated on scales but not coded in detail (as was pointed out earlier, these ratings often are strongly influenced by the overall impression of the rater, which can be based on quite different behavioural indicators than the ones rated; see Martin & Rovira, 1982, for such biases in the perception of gazing). Finally, Cheek and Buss (1981) found less looking only for a sub-group of shy sociable females. Thus, there may be a tendency for shy people to look less at their partners, but gazing is influenced by so many different factors that vary from one study to the next, depending on the exact nature of the situation, that global measures of gazing do not seem to be reliable indicators of dispositional shyness.

Third, consistent with the data for children, self-manipulations appear to be unrelated to dispositional shyness; in three studies, no relation emerged, and in the Cheek and Buss study it was found only for shy-sociable females. Our data, rather, suggest a negative relation between shyness and the use of gestures that illustrate one's speech (see Ekman & Friesen, 1972, for a definition). This relation has withstood correction for the amount of speaking, which is important because shy people are less likely to show illustratory gestures simply because they speak less; but the relation was found only for males in our study and in the rating study of Mandel and Shrauger (1980).

Three possible indicators of dispositional shyness that were not studied in children were replicated for adults, at least for one gender: greater interpersonal distance, fewer successful interruptions during a conversation, and more responses that would ensure the partner's speaking. The results for the interpersonal distance were weak (Patterson, 1973) or stemmed from a rather artificial setting (Carducci & Webber, 1979). This measure cannot be applied to most conversational situations, where the distance between the partners is fairly standardised by the furniture beforehand. It may prove to be informative, however, in situations where people are less restricted in their movements, such as in playgrounds, in school yards, or at cocktail parties.

Our study and the well-controlled study of Natale, Entin, and Jaffe (1979) converged in finding less successful interruptions among the shy (although we found clear evidence only for males). In both studies, the number of speech interruptions was corrected for the amount of the partner's speaking; that was necessary because the partners of shy subjects spoke more, and hence the shy subjects had more opportunity to interrupt them. This result suggests that shy people are less assertive in steering the flow of conversation.

Natale et al. (1979) also found "back channel responses", such as saying "hmm" or "yeah", to be related to shyness. These brief utterances ensure that the partner who holds the conversational floor will continue to do so (Duncan, 1975); they also signal that the listener is attending to the content of the partner's speech or that the listener agrees with certain opinions of the partner. Nodding and sometimes also smiling serve the same function; shy women (but not shy men) showed these behaviours more often than did non-shy subjects in the study of Pilkonis (1977). These reinforcing responses tended to be particularly related to fear of negative social evaluation in the study of Natale et al. (1979). This finding suggests that these responses may serve to protect the vulnerable self-esteem of shy people. See Arkin (1981) and Shepperd and Arkin (this volume) for the protective self-presentational style of shy people.

To summarise the findings for dispositional shyness, the most consistent results were obtained for measures of verbal activity. Shy people appear to show less initiative during conversations; they speak less, let more and longer silences develop, and are less effective at steering the conversation through successful interruptions of the partner. Also, they seem to use more reinforcing responses. As a whole, these behaviours indicate a cautious, protective attitute towards conversations that is easily perceived by others and strongly influences their impression about those who display these behaviours.

Note, however, that each of these verbal measures can be related to other characteristics of the person as well. People may talk less because they find casual conversations such as those that are arranged in psychological laboratories not particularly exciting; non-shy introverts, for example, are not likely to be very talkative in these situations. Furthermore, people may appear to be more protective simply because they are more polite. If at all, only the combination of restricted verbal activity and protective style allows inferences about speakers' shyness.

Although these inferences may be valid in the majority of cases, they should not be trusted blindly, for two reasons: First, dispositional shyness is not an ever-persistent attribute of a person, but rather a modal tendency of behaviour; in certain situations the person may react contrary to this modal tendency. In a study by Brodt and Zimbardo (1981), for example, shy women were compared with non-shy women in a conversation with a male confederate. In the misattribution condition, the conversation took place after a 3-min noise bombardment, and the subjects were led to believe that that procedure would lead to physiological symptoms, such as heart pounding, that in fact had been reported by the subjects prior to the experiment as typical reactions when they felt shy; in the control condition, the subjects were led to believe that the noise would lead to symptoms, such as a dry mouth, that had not been associated with shyness by the subjects. Both groups were told that the symptoms would last for some minutes after the noise was over; during that time, the conversation took place. These two shy groups were compared with a group of non-shy women who received the control condition. Measures of the subjects' verbal behaviours and a shyness rating by the confederate revealed that the shy women in the misattribution condition could not be distinguished from the non-shy women; as expected, the shy women in the control condition acted more shy than did the non-shy women. Thus, when the shy women were given an alternative explanation for their shyness in the presence of the unknown male confederate, they did not behave at all shyly. In a sense, we all construct our social personalities anew in each social situation, and our modal tendencies do not prevent us from reacting differently under unusual conditions. Dispositional shyness does not always imply above-average state shyness.

Finally, there can exist substantial interindividual differences or differences between sub-groups in the externalisation of dispositional shyness that also will complicate the inference of shyness from behaviour. Asendorpf (1988) showed that the majority of the subjects in a study of students' shyness showed an individual patterning of their responses that was cross-situationally stable. Furthermore, the data from that study, presented in Table 3.5, indicate a puzzling gender difference: The verbal measures that were clearly related to males' shyness appeared not to be related to females' self-rated shyness and less clearly related to the observers' judgements of females' shyness.

Because the mean levels of self-rated and other-rated shyness did not differ between males and females, this gender difference cannot be attributed to a less successful induction of females' shyness in this study. Similarly, no gender difference emerged in any other study (Table 3.4); it is therefore unlikely that this finding reflects a gender difference. An alternative explanation would be that the female confederate unwittingly made all subjects talkative regardless of their shyness. Because all female subjects met the same confederate, this hypothesis cannot be evaluated any further. If the specific choice of a confederate really had such a profound moderating effect on the relation between dispositional shyness and measures of verbal behaviour, despite the fact that the confederate was trained to act in a fairly standardised way, that would point to a high sensitivity of these measures to slight situational variation.

Embarrassability

Embarrassability, defined as the disposition to be particularly susceptible to experience embarrassment, has seldom been studied; however, see Edelmann and McCusker (1986) and Edelmann (this volume). In fact, there does not appear to have been a single study on interindividual differences in the expression of embarrassment. When embarrassability is conceptualised within the self-presentational approach to shyness and embarrassment (Leary & Schlenker, 1981; Shepperd & Arkin, this volume), people who are sensitive to the opinions of others should be prone both to state shyness and to embarrassment; thus, one would expect that dispositional shyness and embarrassability would coincide. Even if that is true, it still does not answer the question whether or not and how dispositionally shy people differ from dispositionally non-shy people when they become embarrassed. Do shy people display their embarrassment in the same way, and do they cope with it similarly? Contrary to our expectation, the shy and the non-shy subjects in our study on students' shyness and embarrassment did not blush more often in any of the four situations analysed (Figure 3.3), nor did they show a higher proportion of embarrassed smiles during the embarrassing feed-back situation or during the base-line conversation. Thus, aside from self-reports, there is no evidence that shy people are particularly prone to embarrassment.

Conclusions

The best evidence for a specific relation between certain expressions and shyness or embarrassment stems from studies of infants' wariness and adults' embarrassment. A wary brow and a wary averted gaze (Table 3.1) appear to be rather specific indicators of stranger wariness, and blushing and perhaps gaze aversion during smiling seem to be rather specific indicators of embarrassment (Figures 3.3 and 3.4). These are complex responses that are not easy to observe or to record (i.e., blushing). But because these behaviours seem to bear a *specific* relation to state shyness or embarrassment, more research should be devoted to them, despite the fact that it will be a laborious endeavour.

Do adults also tend to display a wary brow or wary averted gaze in encounters with strangers? When do children start to blush, and in which situations? Is the embarrassed smile of adults identical with the coy smile of young children when they meet a stranger? Are all these behaviours really specific for state shyness or embarrassment, or are there other situations in which they are shown? What is their evolution-ary history? Do all people display these expressions when they feel shy or become embarrassed, or do substantial interindividual differences exist for their occurrence (e.g., for blushing)? These are some questions for future research on the expression of shyness and embarrassment. Work along these lines would not only help to better identify the states of shyness and embarrassment but also illuminate the nature of these states.

More global measures of behaviour, such as the frequency, duration, or mean length of speaking, gazing, certain body movements, and so forth, show some relations to state shyness or embarrassment, but these relations are less specific. All these measures also covary with other features of the situation; therefore, it can be misleading to interpret them as indicators of shyness or embarrassment. At best, they can be consid-ered to be necessary but not sufficient conditions for these states.

This also applies to the relation of these measures to dispositional shyness. When they can be aggregated over many different social situations, reliable behavioural indices of dispositional shyness may result that will converge with judgements of informants who have known the subjects of a particular study for a long time, and who perform such aggregation intuitively (see Moskowitz & Schwartz, 1982, for the effects of aggregation on the validity of behavioural measures). Because measures of verbal activity seem to show the most consistent relations to dispositional shyness, such aggregation may be profitably done by small, portable devices that automatically record and store subjects' speaking over a whole day (see Krüger, 1989, regarding such a device). This new technique will open new avenues for naturalistic research on intra- and interindividual differences in verbal behaviour and may prove to be a powerful tool for research on dispositional shyness (cf. Asendorpf & Meier, in press, for a first application of this technique to shyness).

Much more difficult is the use of global behavioural measures for assessment of dispositional shyness in a few situations or even a single situation. The Harvard and the Max Planck studies on shyness in young children provide some evidence that it is possible to tailor situations that maximise the differences between shy and non-shy children and that allow us to distinguish them by simple behavioural measures such as response latencies. However, those studies were concerned with young children who did not use self-presentation strategies as frequently and as skilfully as do adults. The older the subjects, the more susceptible their behaviour will be to slight variations in the situational procedure; the inconsistent findings regarding gaze among shy subjects, or the clever experiment of Brodt and Zimbardo (1981), or the gender differences in our study of students should be caution enough against believing that dispositional shyness among adults can be easily captured by simple, global measures of expression in one standard situation.

To summarise, for a behavioural assessment of dispositional shyness, global measures of verbal activity may suffice if they are aggregated over many social situations. For the study of state shyness and embarrassment, these measures can be misleading; here, it seems necessary to study the expressive behaviour in more detail, and much work awaits us before we can be sure which indicators are the best for inferring shyness or embarrassment from behaviour.

REFERENCES

Argyle, M., & Dean, J. (1965). Eye-contact, distance and affiliation. *Sociometry*, *28*, 289–304.
Arkin, R. M. (1981). Self-presentation styles. In J. T. Tedeschi (Ed.), *Impression management theory and social psychological research* (pp. 311–333). New York: Academic Press.

Asendorpf, J. (1984). Shyness, embarrassment, and self-presentation: A control theory approach. In R. Schwarzer (Ed.), *The self in anxiety, stress, and depression* (pp. 109–114). Amsterdam: North Holland.

Asendorpf, J. (1985a). *Studien zur Schüchternheit. Nr. 2: Situationale Schüchternheit im Selbstbild von Studenten* (Studies on shyness. No. 2: Self-perceived state shyness among students). Research Report 9/85, Max Planck Institute for Psychological Research, Munich.

Asendorpf, J. (1985b). *Manual for coding the behavior of young children during contact initiation episodes.* Paper 7/85, Max Planck Institute for Psychological Research, Munich.

Asendorpf, J. (1987a). Videotape reconstruction of emotions and cognitions related to shyness. *Journal of Personality and Social Psychology, 53,* 542–549.

Asendorpf, J. (1987b). Social competence. In F. E. Weinert & W. Schneider (Eds.), *LOGIC – Report No. 3: Results of Wave One.* Research report, Max Planck Institute for Psychological Research, Munich.

Asendorpf, J. (1988). Individual response profiles in the behavioral assessment of personality. *European Journal of Personality, 2,* 155–167.

Asendorpf, J. (1989a). Shyness as a final common pathway for two different kinds of inhibition. *Journal of Personality and Social Psychology, 57,* 481–492.

Asendorpf, J. (1989b). Shyness, unsociability, and peer avoidance. *Human Development, 32.*

Asendorpf, J. (1989c). Social competence, In F. E. Weinert & W. Schneider (Eds.), *LOGIC – Report no.5: Results of Wave Three.* Research report, Max Planck Institute for Psychological Research, Munich.

Asendorpf, J., & Meier, G. (in press). Toward a study of shyness in daily life by continual, automatic recording of speech and physiology. *Journal of Anxiety.*

Asendorpf, J., & Wallbott, H. G. (1982). Contributions of the German "expression psychology" to nonverbal communication research. Part I: Theories and concepts. *Journal of Nonverbal Behavior, 6,* 135–147.

Bischof, N. (1975). A systems approach toward the functional connections of attachment and fear. *Child Development, 46,* 801–817.

Bretherton, I., & Ainsworth, M. D. S. (1974). Responses of one-year-olds to a stranger in a strange situation. In M. Lewis & L. A. Rosenblum (Eds.), *The origin of fear* (pp. 131–164). New York: Wiley.

Brodt, S. E., & Zimbardo, P. G. (1981). Modifying shyness-related social behavior through symptom misattribution. *Journal of Personality and Social Psychology, 41,* 437–449.

Bronson, G. W., & Pankey, W. B. (1977). On the distinction between fear and wariness. *Child Developement, 48,* 1167–1183.

Brunswik, E. (1956). *Perception and the representative design of psychological experiments* (2nd ed.). Berkeley: University of California Press.

Buss, A. H. (1986). A theory of shyness. In W. H. Jones, J. M. Cheek, & S. R. Briggs (Eds.), *Shyness: Perspectives on research and treatment* (pp. 39–46). New York: Plenum Press.

Buss, A. H., Iscoe, I., & Buss, E. H. (1979). The development of embarrassment. *Journal of Psychology, 103,* 227–230.

Carducci, B. J., & Webber, A. W. (1979). Shyness as a determinant of inter-personal distance. *Psychological Reports*, *44*, 1075–1078.

Cheek, J. M., & Buss, A. H. (1981). Shyness and sociability. *Journal of Personality and Social Psychology*, *41*, 330–339.

Daly, S. (1978). Behavioural correlates of social anxiety. *British Journal of Social and Clinical Psychology*, *17*, 117–120.

Duncan, S. (1975). On the structure of speaker–auditor interaction during speaking turns. *Language in Society*, *2*, 161–180.

Edelmann, R. J., Asendorpf, J., Contarello, A., Georgas, J., Villanueva, C., & Zammuner, V. (1987). Self-reported verbal and non-verbal strategies for coping with embarrassment in five European cultures. *Social Science Information*, *26*, 869–883.

Edelmann, R. J., Asendorpf, J., Contarello, A., Georgas, J., Villanueva, C., & Zammuner, V. (1989). Self-reported expression of embarrassment in five European cultures. *Journal of Cross-Cultural Psychology*, *20*, 357–371.

Edelmann, R. J., & Hampson, S. E. (1979). Changes in non-verbal behavior during embarrassment. *British Journal of Social and Clinical Psychology*, *18*, 385–390.

Edelmann, R. J., & Hampson, S. E. (1981a). Embarrassment in dyadic interaction. *Social Behavior and Personality*, *9*, 171–177.

Edelmann, R. J., & Hampson, S. E. (1981b). The recognition of embarrassment. *Personality and Social Psychology Bulletin*, *7*, 109–116.

Edelmann, R. J., & McCusker, G. (1986). Introversion, neuroticism, empathy, and embarrassability. *Personality and Individual Differences*, *7*, 133–140.

Eibl-Eibesfeldt, I. (1984). *Die Biologie des menschlichen Verhaltens* (The biology of human behavior). München: Piper.

Ekman, P., & Friesen, W. V. (1969). The repertoire of nonverbal behavior: Categories, origin, usage, and coding. *Semiotica*, *1*, 49–98.

Ekman, P., & Friesen, W. V. (1972). Hand movements. *Journal of Communication*, *22*, 353–374.

Ekman, P., & Friesen, W. V. (1978). *The facial action coding system*. Palo Alto, CA: Consulting Psychologists Press.

Ekman, P., Levenson, R. W., & Friesen, W. V. (1983). Autonomic nervous system activity distinguishes among emotions. *Science*, *221*, 1208–1210.

Ekman, P., & Oster, H. (1979). Facial expressions of emotion. *Annual Review of Psychology*, *30*, 527–554.

Ellgring, H. (1986). Nonverbal expression of psychological states in psychiatric patients. *European Archives of Psychiatry and Neurological Sciences*, *236*, 31–34.

Epstein, S. (1982). A research paradigm for the study of personality and emotions. In M. M. Page (Ed.), *Personality: Current theory and research. Nebraska Symposium on Motivation* (pp. 91–154). Lincoln: University of Nebraska Press.

Exline, R., Gray, D., & Schuette, D. (1965). Visual behavior in a dyad as affected by interview content and sex of respondent. *Journal of Personality and Social Psychology*, *1*, 201–209.

Garcia-Coll, C., Kagan, J., & Reznick, J. S. (1984). Behavioral inhibition in young children. *Child Development*, *55*, 1005–1019.

Greenberg, M. T., & Marvin, R. S. (1982). Reactions of preschool children to an adult stranger: A behavioral systems approach. *Child Development, 53*, 481–490.

Hinde, R. A. (1970). *Animal behavior* (2nd ed.). New York: McGraw-Hill.

Izard, C. E. (1971). *The face of emotion.* New York: Appleton-Century-Crofts.

Izard, C. E., & Hyson, M. C. (1986). Shyness as a discrete emotion. In W. H. Jones, J. M. Cheek, & S. R. Briggs (Eds.), *Shyness: Perspectives on research and treatment* (pp. 147–160). New York: Plenum Press.

Kagan, J., Reznick, J. S., Clarke, C., Snidman, N., & Garcia-Coll, C. (1984). Behavioral inhibition to the unfamiliar. *Child Development, 55*, 2212–2225.

Kaltenbach, K., Weinraub, M., & Fullard, W. (1980). Infant wariness toward strangers reconsidered: Infants' and mothers' reactions to unfamiliar persons. *Child Development, 51*, 1197–1202.

Kleinke, C. L. (1986). Gaze and eye contact: A research review. *Psychological Bulletin, 100*, 78–100.

Krüger, H.-P. (1989). Speech chronemics: A hidden dimension of speech. Theoretical background, measurement, and clinical validity. *Pharmacopsychiatry [Supplement], 22*, 5–12.

Leary, M. R., & Schlenker, B. R. (1981). The social psychology of shyness: A self-presentation model. In J. T. Tedeschi (Ed.), *Impression management theory and social psychological research* (pp. 335–358). New York: Academic Press.

Leventhal, H. (1980). Toward a comprehensive theory of emotion. In L. Berkowitz (Ed.), *Advances in experimental social psychology* (Vol. 13, pp. 139–207). New York: Academic Press.

Malatesta, C. Z., & Haviland, J. M. (1985). Signals, symbols, and socialization: The modification of emotional expression in human development. In M. Lewis & C. Saarni (Eds.), *The socialization of emotions* (pp. 89–116). New York: Plenum Press.

Mandel, N. M., & Shrauger, J. S. (1980). The effects of self-evaluative statements on heterosocial approach in shy and nonshy males. *Cognitive Therapy and Research, 4*, 369–381.

Martin, W., & Rovira, M. (1982). Response biases in eye-gaze perception. *Journal of Psychology, 110*, 203–209.

Modigliani, A. (1971). Embarrassment, facework, and eye contact: Testing a theory of embarrassment. *Journal of Personality and Social Psychology, 17*, 15–24.

Moskowitz, D. S., & Schwartz, J. C. (1982). Validity comparison of behavior counts and ratings by knowledgeable informants. *Journal of Personality and Social Psychology, 42*, 518–528.

Natale, M., Entin, E., & Jaffe, J. (1979). Vocal interruptions in dyadic communication as a function of speech and social anxiety. *Journal of Personality and Social Psychology, 37*, 865–878.

Patterson, M. L. (1973). Stability of nonverbal immediacy behaviors. *Journal of Experimental Social Psychology, 9*, 97–109.

Pilkonis, P. A. (1977). The behavioral consequences of shyness. *Journal of Personality, 45*, 595–611.

Reznick, J. S., Kagan, J., Snidman, N., Gersten, M., Baak, K., & Rosenberg, A. (1986). Inhibited and uninhibited children: A follow-up study. *Child Development*, *57*, 660–680.

Rutter, D. R. (1984). *Looking and seeing: The role of visual communication in social interaction*. Chichester: Wiley.

Scherer, K. R. (1978). Personality inference from voice quality: The loud voice of extroversion. *European Journal of Social Psychology*, *8*, 467–487.

Smith, P. K., & Sloboda, J. (1986). Individual consistency in infant–stranger encounters. *British Journal of Developmental Psychology*, *4*, 83–91.

Sroufe, L. A. (1977). Wariness of strangers and the study of infant development. *Child Development*, *48*, 731–746.

Tinbergen, N. (1952). "Derived" activities: Their causation, biological significance, origin, and emancipation during evolution. *Quarterly Review of Biology*, *27*, 1–32.

Waters, E., Matas, L., & Sroufe, L. A. (1975). Infants' reactions to an approaching stranger: Description, validation, and functional significance of wariness. *Child Development*, *46*, 348–356.

Watson, D., & Friend, R. (1969). Measurement of social-evaluative anxiety. *Journal of Consulting and Clinical Psychology*, *33*, 448–457.

Zivin, G. (Ed.). (1985). *The development of expressive behavior*. Orlando, FL: Academic Press.

4

The impact of focus of attention and affect on social behaviour

FREDERICK X. GIBBONS

This chapter concerns focus of attention and its impact on social behaviour. I shall make the argument that there are two different sources of motivation behind social behaviour. One reflects a desire to please the *self* and involves self-focused attention. The other reflects an orientation toward *others* and their opinions and expectations. The former state, called self-awareness, involves standards and values that are unique to the individual. The latter state involves social norms and is manifested in impression management behaviour. Each state is associated with certain behavioural expectations or standards. When these standards are violated, transgressed, or failed, different forms of negative affect are produced, depending on whether attention is focused on the self or on others at the time the transgression occurs. Transgression or violation of personal standards results in *guilt* or *disappointment* for the self-focused person. Violations of social norms or transgressions of normative expectations produce feelings of *embarrassment* or *shame* for a person who is in the presence of others. In addition, fear of the negative affect that could be associated with transgression can itself have a significant inhibitory effect on behaviour. Although there are many commonalities in the two motivations and reactions to their transgressions, they are not identical. In fact, in many instances they produce very different types of behaviours. Each, however, serves an important and "civilising" function in a societal context.

This argument will be presented in three main sections. The first presents an overview of the impact of self-focused attention on behaviour, with particular emphasis on the mediating role that affect plays in this process. Dispositional and situational determinants of attention are also discussed. The second section focuses on a particular type of affect – embarrassment – and its relation to attention and behaviour. Finally, the third section presents a summary of the first two in the form of a discussion of how attention and related affect influence behaviour in a societal context.

Self-focused attention and social behaviour

The theoretical framework for this chapter is provided by the Duval and Wicklund (1972) theory of objective self-awareness. This theory is based on one very important assumption, which has now been verified by more than 15 years of research and over 100 empirical studies. The assumption is that people behave quite differently when their attention is focused on themselves than when they are concentrating on the environment or external stimuli. A brief review of the theory and supporting research will help illustrate.

According to Duval and Wicklund (1972), attention can be focused either internally on the self or externally on some aspect of the environment, such as a current task or another person or a group of people. Although attention may oscillate back and forth between the two "focal points", they are, for the most part, mutually exclusive; one cannot be self-aware and non-self-aware at the same time. The theory is concerned primarily with behaviour during periods of self-focus. When one's attention is directed back to the self, by means of a mirror, a photograph, or simple introspection – actually any stimulus that reminds one of oneself is theoretically sufficient to produce self-awareness – it tends to focus on the aspect of the self that happens to be most salient at the time. Any aspect of the self is a potential focal point: the physical (e.g., appearance), the emotional, the cognitive. One immediate consequence of directing attention to the self, almost by definition, is that the individual is likely to become more in touch with or more aware of the particular dimension of the self that is salient. Thus, self-reports about attitudes and previous behaviours are likely to be more accurate when attention is self-focused (Baldwin & Holmes, 1987; Gibbons, Smith, Ingram, Pearce, Brehm, & Schroeder, 1985; Pryor, Gibbons, Wicklund, Fazio, & Hood, 1977). In addition, awareness of previous behaviour apparently increases (Kassin, 1985), as does awareness of current emotional reactions (Scheier, 1976; Scheier & Carver, 1977). In general, observable behaviour that occurs when attention is focused on the self is likely to be more reflective of the "inner" self.

A second, almost immediate consequence of directing attention internally, according to Duval and Wicklund, is that it initiates a self-evaluation process in which the current self is compared with the ideal or "standard" that is maintained for the particular dimension in question; it might be ideal behaviour, ideal appearance, ideal performance, and so forth. Simply put, it is the way the individual thinks he or she *should* be. Because most of us seldom live up to our own ideals, this self-scrutiny is likely to reveal either a *shortcoming* of some sort or else the poential for a shortcoming, in other words, a discrepancy between the way the self or the dimension of self actually is and the way it could or should be. At this point the theory becomes motivational. Awareness of the discrepancy is said to be aversive, and the negative affect that it produces acts as a "drive state". Like other drive states, it motivates the person to do something that will have the effect of eliminating or reducing the discomfort. Duval and Wicklund suggested two likely outcomes or methods of reducing the discomfort. The first is simply to avoid the state of self-focus. This can be accomplished by distracting attention, leaving the situation, taking up some other task, and so forth. Anything that will divert attention from the self will suffice. The second method is more complex, but much more interesting from a theoretical standpoint – that is, to change one's behaviour somehow in order to bring it more in line with the ideal or standard, in other words, to reduce the "real/ideal discrepancy".

Standards of behaviour

The standard or value structure that Duval and Wicklund described in many respects resembles Mead's concept (1934) of the "generalized other". Duval and Wicklund viewed standards as prescripts for behaviour, in other words, what the self would do, ideally, if given the chance. Once again, because the ideal self typically exceeds the current or perceived real self, the state of self-awareness usually is eventually experienced as aversive (Wicklund, 1975). As long as an individual's attention is focused on the self, assuming that simple avoidance of the state of self-focus is not possible, the individual will invest energy in attempting to bring behaviour in line with the appropriate standard. That may entail attempts to improve current behaviour (i.e., "discrepancy reduction") or else inhibit behaviour that might create a discrepancy (i.e., "discrepancy avoidance"). Thus, people may try harder at what they are doing, may be more careful in reporting on previous behaviours (Pryor et al., 1977), may help others when the situation calls for it (Mayer, Duval, Holtz, & Bowman, 1985), or, as in one study, simply resist the temptation to steal Halloween candy (Beaman, Klentz, Diener, & Svanum, 1979). Of course, it is never guaranteed that such increased efforts will actually reduce the perceived discrepancy. In fact, in some situations, self-focus can exacerbate feelings of frustration or disappointment to a point that they can actually interfere with goal-directed behaviour (Carver & Blaney, 1977). Negative effects of self-focus, such as these, will be discussed later in the chapter.

Origin of standards

An obvious and important question in this area, one that has received some attention from self-awareness researchers, concerns where these personal standards originate and how they develop. In fact, that issue was one of the focal points of a recent debate concerning focus of attention and private versus public standards of behaviour (Carver & Scheier, 1987; Wicklund & Gollwitzer, 1987). Duval and Wicklund suggest that the standards that guide behaviour (during self-focus) are learned through years of socialisation experience. Thus, others are influential in the *development* of this value structure, much as Mead would suggest that socialisation experience is crucial in the development of the generalised other. In this sense, personal standards are *reflections* of societal or universal values.

Duval and Wicklund are quick to point out, however, that there is an important distinction between their approach and that of Mead. Mead described the generalised other as a direct internalisation of external influences (i.e., viewing the self as one imagines others would). From his perspective, then, the self-concept is itself a reflection of how the individual thinks others see him or her. Consequently, development of the concept of self is contingent on one's ability to adopt the perspective of another toward oneself. In contrast with Mead, Duval and Wicklund (1972) suggest that the value structure that guides behaviour is unique to the individual. Although the perspective of others is important in the development of the self-concept, self-definition ultimately comes from within, and it is not dependent on the presence, physical or otherwise, of other people: "In no way do we assume that the individual is dependent upon the point of view of the other in the sense that Mead intends" (Duval & Wicklund, 1972, p. 31).

In a review and update of the existing literature in the area of self-awareness (Gibbons, 1990), I elaborated on the issue of the development of standards of behaviour (i.e., those that govern the behaviour of self-focused persons) and carried Duval and Wicklund's argument one step further. For Mead, the generalised other, being a reflection of societal values, acts as an external monitor of behaviour that is incorporated in the self. In contrast, the value structure envisioned by myself (and by Wicklund & Gollwitzer, 1987) is unique to the individual and is not reliant on external influence. Others are instrumental in its development, and this value structure certainly changes over time as a result of social experience. Once developed, however, it is not dependent on other persons. Thus, the influence on behaviour that is associated with self-focused attention is *endogenous* in nature.

This is not to suggest that the self-aware individual is somehow immune to external influence. In fact, the presence of other people can and often does act as an instigation to self-focus (Mullen, 1984). And other persons (some more so than others) are obviously used quite frequently through social comparison as sources of information concerning one's own behaviour. What it does mean, however, is that the defining characteristic of self-awareness, which is the comparison of the self with personal standards, is inhibited in group situations or, for that matter, in any situation in which the person is primarily concerned about what others may think about him or her. Although individuals in the presence of others may, for a variety of reasons, become very much aware of their own presence in the group, as long as they are primarily concerned about what others think of them, their self-awareness will be reduced. In short, one cannot be self-focused and other-focused at the same time (Duval & Wicklund, 1972). Theoretically, then, behaviour in group settings usually will be more influenced by perceptions of others' opinions and expectations than by one's own personal standards. If those external opinions and internal standards are not congruent, the link between attitude and (observable) behaviour will be weaker. In contrast, for the person whose attention is self-aware, the ultimate judge of behaviour is the self, not others; thus, actions *are* direct reflections of inner values and standards.

Standards and values

One final point on the topic of standards should be made here. Over the years, Duval and Wicklund's concept of standards has been clarified and also expanded a number of times, the most notable example being Carver and Scheier's 1981 book on self-attention and self-regulation[1] (but see also Wicklund, 1979, 1980). Carver and Scheier (1981) suggest that standards are points of comparison – more specifically, behaviour as it was or could be. They do not limit the concept to values, but suggest that any kind of behaviour can serve as a comparison point. An example would be current versus previous level of aggression. The nature of the concept as they present it is different, in many respects broader than that outlined by Duval and Wicklund, and there is a fair amount of research available to support their claims. In general, more recent discussions are in agreement that the standards of behaviour which guide the actions of self-aware persons are not always of a moralistic nature. Standards include aspirations, levels of performance, and a variety of other "goals" that are not necessarily value-laden. Once again, they are representations of the self as it could or should be. Moreover, the nature of the salient or relevant standard determines, to a large extent, the type of affective response that self-focus will elicit.

Affect and self-attention

One of the more interesting aspects of self-awareness theory, one that has proved valuable from a heuristic standpoint, involves affective reactions to the self-evaluation process that forms the core of the self-focus "sequence". As mentioned earlier, Duval and Wicklund (1972) claim that an inevitable consequence of this evaluation is a recognition of a real-self/ideal-self discrepancy and a corresponding increase in negative affect. The research is moderately supportive of this prediction, but suggests that the process is more complex than they thought. Again, research by Carver and Scheier (e.g., Carver & Blaney, 1977; Carver, Blaney, & Scheier, 1979a,b) has been most influential in clarifying this notion. They have demonstrated that an important factor that often mediates the self-focus/affect causal link is the individual's *expectation* regarding the likelihood that the perceived discrepancy or potential discrepancy will be reduced. When that expectancy is negative or pessimistic, self-focus will exacerbate negative affect (and pessimism), typically leading to avoidance of the state. The nature of this affective reaction can be characterised most accurately as *disappointment* or frustration. On the other hand, when expectations are high or optimistic, the negative affect reaction typically engendered by self-awareness is reduced or replaced, apparently with feelings of resolve and determination.

Guilt

Carver and Scheier's reasoning is most appropriate for situations in which *performance* of some kind happens to comprise the salient self-dimension, and the relevant standard or comparison point is some level of achievement. Their reasoning is less applicable in situations that promote the salience of personal values, such as sexual standards (Gibbons, 1978), cheating (Beaman et al., 1979), and telling the truth (Wojciszke, 1987). Under these circumstances the question becomes not "Can I do it?" but rather "Should I do it?" Hence, failure to live up to a prescribed standard of behaviour will definitely produce negative affect, but of a different nature, more accurately characterised as *guilt*. This type of affective reaction, which, of course, is also negative, will lead to attempts at avoidance of self-focus. Alternatively, as long as attention remains focused on the self, it would be expected that a similar form of determination or resolve would be evoked, namely, a determination not to transgress against the standard in the future.

To summarise, negative affective reactions to self-focus are likely to involve some form of guilt and/or disappointment, both of which would be considered private or personal responses. Once again, this reflects the fact that the comparison point that forms the basis of the self-evaluation – the value structure – is endogenous in nature and not adopted from external sources. The desire to reduce this negative affect, or avoid it, is the motivating force behind behavioural change associated with self-focused attention.

Self-consciousness: public and private

In 1975, Fenigstein, Scheier, and Buss published their Self-consciousness Scale, which was intended to measure individual differences in the tendency to self-focus. According to Fenigstein and associates, there are three distinct types of self-attention that are reflected in the three factors of their scale: private self-consciousness, public self-consciousness, and social anxiety. An examination of the individual items included in the *private* sub-scale indicates fairly clearly that it was intended as a dispositional correlate of the state of self-focus (e.g., "I'm generally attentive to my inner feelings", "I'm alert to changes in my mood", "I'm always trying to figure myself out"). Theoretically, then, people who are high in the trait of private self-consciousness (PvSC), or "chronically self-focused", should behave in a manner that resembles the actions of people who are situationally self-aware. This does appear to be the case. For example, people high in PvSC tend to be more accurate in their reports of their own behaviours (Scheier, Buss, & Buss, 1978); they are also less suggestible than are people who are low in this dimension (Scheier, Carver, & Gibbons, 1981). All of these are behavioural effects that had been demonstrated in previous research among persons whose attention had been temporarily focused on themselves. In short, both "high privates" and people who are situationally self-aware appear to be especially concerned with what can be considered the "inner" self.

Public self-consciousness. Perusal of the questions loading on the other two factors or sub-scales of the Self-consciousness Scale reveals a very different kind of attentional orientation. Persons who are rated high in public self-consciousness (PbSC) are said to be especially concerned with themselves as "social objects" (Buss, 1980), and the items on the scale are certainly consistent with this outlook (e.g., "I'm concerned about the way I present myself", "I usually worry about making a good impression"). "High publics" have been shown to *conform* more on certain tasks (Diener & Srull, 1979; Froming, Walker, & Lopyan, 1982), to be more cognizant of and concerned about their physical appearance (Turner, Gilliland, & Klein, 1981), and to be more sensitive to acceptance and rejection by others (Fenigstein, 1979). Experimentally, PbSC is enhanced by means of "public" manipulations, such as cameras or evaluative audience (Carver & Scheier, 1981). In general, the behaviour of PbSC people suggests a sense of being "on stage" (Goffman, 1959). Clearly, the *primary* concerns of people who have this trait are the opinions of other persons and, more specifically, the impressions that others have of them.

Although not redundant with the concept of impression management (Goffman, 1959; Schlenker, 1980) or self-monitoring (Snyder, 1974), as Fenigstein and others have suggested, increased concern with self-presentation is certainly a trademark of people with the trait of PbSC (Hass, 1984). Moreover, the public scale has been shown to correlate with a variety of other constructs that are indicative of increased concern with the (self-relevant) impressions of others; those include audience anxiousness (Leary, 1983), passivity and lack of autonomy (John, 1983), shyness (Pilkonis, 1977), social sensitivity (Fenigstein, 1979), and embarrassability (Edelmann, 1985). Perhaps most important, according to Cheek (1982), the scale also correlates very highly (i.e., .53) with the "other-directedness" factor (Briggs, Cheek, & Buss, 1980) of the Snyder (1974) self-monitoring scale.

PvSC versus PbSC. Several studies have contrasted the behaviours of persons high in PvSC with those of persons high in PbSC, and those studies have found some interesting and often marked distinctions between the two groups (in spite of the fact that the two sub-scales tend to correlate fairly highly, as discussed later). For example, whereas "privates" tend to conform less in public settings, "publics," as might be expected, tend to conform more (Froming & Carver, 1981; Froming et al., 1982). When confronted publicly with dissonance-producing inconsistency induced via forced compliance, privates are more likely to try to reduce the dissonance by ignoring their public behaviour and following their previous attitudes (Scheier & Carver, 1980). Publics, on the other hand, respond in the more typical pattern by changing their personal attitudes to bring them in line with their public behaviour. The theoretical and empirical evidence indicates that PbSC and impression management are definitely overlapping constructs involving similar if not identical underlying motives – namely, a desire to protect and to foster one's public image (Schlenker, 1980). In short, the trait of PbSC does reflect a basic concern with the impressions of others; the link to the self exists primarily through an interest in self-presentation.

Self-awareness and impression management

Several authors have suggested that the state of self-awareness, like the trait of PbSC, is associated with increased concern with one's public image and with the opinions of others (Edelmann, 1981, 1985; Schlenker & Leary, 1982). In fact, this notion is generally consistent with Duval and Wicklund's discussion of conformity in the original (1972) statement of the theory. There they suggested that self-focus increases the desire to bring behaviour in line with the norms established by a reference group, even if those norms happen to conflict with one's personal standards. Contrary to this general opinion, however, in the last 4 or 5 years several studies have indicated that self-focused attention (1) often does not lead to increased conformity (Froming et al., 1982) and (2) tends to be associated with *less* concern about self-presentation and, correspondingly, less concern with the opinions of others. This research is revealing about the nature of self-attention and is worthy of some discussion.

In most of these studies, subjects were put in a situation in which they could "save face" or present a more positive image to an observer (usually the experimenter) through either exaggerated or embellished self-report. For example, in the first of these studies (Pryor et al., 1977, Exp. 2), subjects were simply asked to report their college entrance examination (SAT) scores, along with a number of other unrelated self-dimensions. They did this while their attention either was or was not self-focused by means of a large mirror that had been placed in front of them in the experimental cubicle (mirrors are by far the most common method of increasing self-attention) (Wicklund, 1978). Unaware that the experimenter actually had access to (or even would be interested in) their actual test scores, the subjects found themselves in a situation that we thought was ripe for impression management. For the most part the results confirmed our suspicions, as almost all of the subjects chose to add some points to their scores when reporting them. The mean exaggeration was 34 points on an overall total mean score of about 1,000 points. Moreover, this tendency was much more pronounced among those students who had done relatively poorly on the SAT exam. The self-focused subjects, however, did not take advantage of this opportunity to present a more favorable image to the experimenter, or at least did so to a much lesser extent. The amount of their exaggeration was significantly smaller ($M = 16$ points) than that of the non-self-aware subjects ($M = 51$).

The standard of truth-telling. In two subsequent studies of a similar nature, subjects were asked to provide descriptions of their own behaviours in situations that inherently increased the temptation to self-present. In the first study (Gibbons et al., 1985), psychiatric patients (i.e., people hospitalised because of alcoholism and/or affective disorders) were asked to provide *objective* information about their psychiatric problems (e.g., how long they had had those problems, and how many times they had been hospitalised for them), as well as *subjective* estimates of the seriousness of those problems and the extent to which they had participated in their treatment. They also reported on their levels of education. In the second study (Gibbons & Gerrard, 1986), female prisoners were asked to report on a variety of self-dimensions, including how sociable they were, how serious their crimes were, and how much they had participated in their own rehabilitation processes. In both studies, half of the subjects were made self-aware during the self-report. In neither case were subjects aware that the experimenter would be able to check the accuracy of their self-reports, which we did by comparing them with the hospital records and the behavioural evaluations of the prisoners provided by the staff psychologists. Thus, the situation once again provided the subjects with a good opportunity for impression management in the form of both exaggerated and understated self-reports. It also provided us with an opportunity to check on subjects' self-presentational behaviours. As expected, when compared with the hospital and staff records, the responses of the non-self-focused subjects showed evidence of positive alterations to a much greater extent than was the case for the self-aware subjects. As a consequence, the latter group ended up being significantly more accurate in their self-reports than did the former group. To some extent this accuracy came at the expense of the images they could have portrayed to the experimenter.

Further evidence supporting the hypothesis that self-focused attention inhibits, or at least reduces, impression management can be seen in studies by Gibbons and Gaeddert (1984) and Hormuth (1982). In our study, subjects were asked to work on a mathematics test, which was said to be a good measure of general scholastic ability. The purpose of this manipulation was simply to increase subjects' evaluation apprehension and their desire to do well on the task. Prior to working on the test, each subject was given a "drug", which was actually a placebo. One-half of the subjects were told that the drug would have the effect of "facilitating" their performances on the math task, and the other half were told it would tend to interfere. After they worked on the task, we asked our subjects how active the drug had been. Assuming they had an implicit understanding of the Kelley (1967) augmentation principle, as well as a desire to present the most favourable image possible to the experimenter, we expected that our subjects would tend to deny that the facilitating drug had much effect on their math performances, but would overestimate the activity of the inhibiting drug. This type of self-serving attribution pattern describes the responses of the non-self-aware group fairly closely. However, the reports of the self-focused subjects, which were essentially the same in both drug conditions, appeared to provide an accurate description of their actual internal states at the time.

In the final example, Hormuth (1982) had subjects "overlearn" a particular response pattern in order to create a dominant response (Hull, 1952). For half of these subjects, the dominant response was inconsistent with a personal standard that they had previously indicated that they maintained (i.e., originality). Later on, some of the subjects were asked to run in place, in order to increase their physiological arousal. Borrowing from the work of Hull (1952) and Spence (1956), Hormuth predicted that when the subjects were aroused, they would be more likely to emit the response that they had previously overlearned, even though it might be discrepant from their personal standard. By now, the pattern of results should be familiar: The responses of the non-self-aware subjects reflected a distinct self-presentational motive, whereas those of the self-aware subjects did not, or else did to a lesser extent. More specifically, the non-self-aware subjects' behaviours tended to be consistent with the dominant, facile response. The self-aware subjects, on the other hand, chose to respond in a manner that was consistent with their personal standards, even though that involved behaviour that was less well learned.

Defensive and assertive impression management. The studies reported here presented an opportunity for one or both of the two types of impression management behaviours identified by recent theorists in that area (e.g., Schlenker, 1980; Schlenker & Leary, 1982; Tetlock & Manstead, 1985). The two types are defensive and assertive impression management. The first type is more reactive and is reflective of a desire to *protect* one's social image. It is triggered by negative affective states such as shame and embarrassment (Tetlock & Manstead, 1985). The second type is more active and is intended to improve one's social image. It is motivated by a desire to self-enhance. In each of the studies reported earlier, most of the non-self-aware subjects responded in a manner that was consistent with one or both types of motivation. For example, the embellished or exaggerated reports of test scores for the non-self-focused subjects in the Pryor et al. (1977) study were most likely a reflection of assertive impression management. These subjects were attempting to enhance the images they presented on paper to the experimenter; their self-focused counterparts were not. Evidence of defensive impression management can be seen in the descriptions of their psychiatric problems provided by the non-self-focused psychiatric subjects in the Gibbons et al. (1985) study and by the non-self-focused incarcerated women in the Gibbons and Gerrard (1986) study. In both cases these subjects were reluctant to admit the extent of their problems or their own involvement in them. Once again, such was not the case among those subjects whose attention was directed on themselves while they answered

the questions.[2] The point is not so much that self-focus reduces concern
with the image that one presents to others. In fact, it may sometimes
increase that concern, especially if the others include people whose
standards happen to have been internalised – in other words, people
whose values are themselves valued (Baldwin & Holmes, 1987). Rather,
the point is that self-focused attention increases people's concern with
the images that they present to *themselves*. Lying about one's attributes or
exaggerating one's public image may help to present the self in a more
favorable light, but such behaviour is also likely to create an internal
discrepancy with personal standards (Gibbons, 1983). Such a discrepancy would be especially upsetting for a person whose attention is self-
focused.

Summary: Self-attention versus other-attention

Differences. Differences between the behaviours of publicly self-conscious
persons and, more generally, people in group settings, on the one hand,
and those who are self-aware, on the other, often reflect very different
motives. Self-focus changes certain behaviours and inhibits others, and it
does so in the absence of immediate external influence (Gibbons, 1990).
Its motivation is *endogenous*. In contrast, the attention of a person in a
group is typically on that group and what its members may think. That
may very well include concern about what the group thinks *about the self*.
However, the perspective (on the self) that is assumed is external – it is
that of other persons. The reasoning, here, once again, sounds similar to
Mead's ideas (1934) on the self-concept or the Cooley (1902/1964)
"looking glass self", and in fact it is very similar to those constructs. But
it is not the same as self-awareness, at least not in the sense that Duval
and Wicklund (1972) described awareness of the self. The distinction,
which is the same as that between PbSC and self-awareness (or what
some have termed "private self-awareness"), is one that numerous researchers and theorists have discussed (Buss, 1980; Carver & Scheier,
1981, 1987; Wicklund & Gollwitzer, 1987), but it is perhaps articulated
most succinctly by Wegner and Giuliano (1982). They suggested that an
individual who is engaging in self-presentational behaviour (and the
argument can very easily be extended to include people who are publicly
self-conscious) has a "tacit awareness" of other people. What this means
is that they assume the perspective of others when considering the self.
In these instances the motivation behind behaviour is exogenous, and
actions are reflections of what the PbSC person thinks observers expect
or might find impressive. Failure to live up to those standards will elicit
a negative affective reaction (Buss, 1980), the nature of which will

depend on the self-conscious person's perceptions of the audience involved and of the expectations they happen to maintain.

Similarities. Two additional points of clarification with regard to the distinction between the public and private self are important and should be pointed out. First of all, it has been stated that there is no *theoretical* reason why the behaviour of PbSC persons should reflect personal values or standards. Instead, it reflects the person's interpretation of what others expect, or what he or she would like to present to them. By the same token, there is no reason to assume that an individual's personal values or standards would not resemble those of specific others or society at large. After all, others were instrumental in the development of the value structure and, to a large extent, are responsible for changes that occur in it. To the extent that personal standards reflect societal norms, the behaviour of self-aware persons will resemble that of the reference group or society at large. In short, although the motivations behind the actions of self-focused and other-focused persons may have very different origins, the resulting behaviours often turn out to be quite similar.

Finally, it might be expected that people who are particularly responsive to their personal standards and, in general, are prone to be self-focused might also be especially interested in presenting a favorable image to others. In other words, the *dispositional tendencies* to be self-focused and other-focused are not mutually exclusive. In fact, the two sub-scales of the Self-consciousness Scale that measure these tendencies, PvSC and PbSC, typically correlate significantly with one another. In our own sample of more than 6,000 undergraduates, collected over a period of 4 years, we found that the two sub-scales correlated .38; others have found similar relationships (Carver & Scheier, 1981). These results suggest that people who are prone to experience embarrassment in public may also be especially susceptible to feelings of guilt or remorse in private; they will not typically experience both emotions at the same time, however.

Embarrassment and attention

Behaviour in a group setting, including, but not limited to, conformity behaviour, is often motivated by a desire to reduce or avoid negative affect. Specifically, it is the desire to avoid the affect that would result from failure to live up to social standards or expectations. In this sense, the impacts that other-focused attention and self-focused attention have on behaviour work in similar manners. However, that group-induced affect, which is in essence a form of embarrassment, is primarily external in origin. In fact, I would suggest that whereas PbSC promotes the experience of embarrassment, self-awareness in some sense actually tends to interfere with it. As with any other heightened emotion, the physical experience associated with embarrassment, namely, blushing and feelings of discomfort, will attract attention to the self *after* a person becomes embarrassed. When that happens, the negative affect is likely to be exacerbated by the self-focus (Scheier & Carver, 1977). However, the orientation towards others – which is necessary for the experience to take place – does not happen when attention is focused exclusively on the self. A perusal of the literature in the area of embarrassment offers some support for this argument.

Audiences and embarrassment

The first person to present a theoretical discussion of embarrassment was Charles Darwin (1872/1955). He suggested that embarrassment occurs when an individual becomes concerned about what others think of him or her; specifically, it is concern about the "depreciation of others". A similar approach was taken by Erving Goffman (1955, 1956), often considered to be the first scientific investigator in this area. In his extensive and classic dramaturgical work, he described embarrassment as the consequence of a public "discrediting" of a person's "face" (i.e., public image) and/or the assumptions and characteristics upon which that face or image is based. A summary of more recent work by major researchers in the area (e.g., Buss, 1980; Modigliani, 1968, 1971; Sattler, 1965) suggests a taxonomy of four major categories of embarrassment: public display of bodily functions, social faux pas (e.g., transgressing rules of etiquette), sub-par performance in a public setting, and "leak-age" (inappropriate self-disclosure or physical intimacy). Each of these four categories, however, probably could be subsumed under the general rubric of "loss of face", as described by Goffman (1956). As such, each of them requires an audience of some kind (Apsler, 1975; Buss, 1980; Modigliani, 1968, 1971) and, just as important, some external focusing of attention. In the absence of either, embarrassment will not be experienced. In fact, in most cases the incident itself will be effectively meaningless if other people are not around to witness its occurrence. In addition, a closer examination of each of these categories indicates that in three of the four instances the degree of discomfort is determined almost entirely by the *nature* of the audience (i.e., their expectations and standards), as well as the audience's relationship with the individual. One is, for example, much less likely to experience embarrassment in front of one's spouse or immediate family than, say, in front of a colleague or neighbour. In the case of self-awareness, however, the nature of the audience is always the same.

Attention and performance

The type of embarrassment that has the most obvious overlap with self-focus is that associated with sub-par performance, in other words, failing in public to live up to a standard that one holds personally. For example, a politician (or any public figure) who espouses conservative sexual or social values will experience discomfort when reminded of previous more "liberal" behaviour, whether the politician is alone and his or her attention is self-focused or is in public and attention is directed towards others. In either case, the politician's reactions are likely to be similar. The first step is to direct attention (one's own and that of others) away from the self, and then perhaps increase one's resolve to avoid the mistake in the future. If the behaviour is not discrepant from the person's own values, however, then the resolve most likely will include the determination not to get caught again. Nonetheless, even if personal standards have not been offended, blatant inconsistency of any kind, including attitude/behaviour discrepancy (Innes & Young, 1975) or, as in this case, discrepancy among behaviours (i.e., current expression/ previous actions), is especially aversive when attention is self-focused (Wicklund, 1975).

By the same token, there are many types of standards – performance standards would be one category – that will generate very little discomfort when failed in private, but will cause considerable loss of face or embarrassment when the failure occurs in front of others. Specific examples might include culinary efforts, many recreational sports, and fashion (e.g., clothing co-ordination). One reason for this is the fact that when one is alone, attention can fairly easily be distracted from the self and therefore from the performance and the associated error. In contrast, in a group setting there is less control over the attention that is focused on the self, simply because it happens to be the attention of others.

The primary distinguishing feature in terms of the type of affect elicited by errors of one kind or another is the extent to which the dimension in question is an important part of the *self-concept*. Those dimensions that are central to the self-concept, if transgressed, will cause discomfort when attention is self-focused, *and* they will cause embarrassment – sometimes considerable embarrassment – when the transgression occurs publicly. Dimensions that are peripheral to the self-concept will cause momentary discomfort if transgressed in the presence of others, but will have virtually no impact when attention is focused on the self. My father-in-law, for example, delights in the attention that his one bright red sock and one bright green sock attract around the house on Saturday afternoon. Like most of us, he could not care less about the colour of the fabric that envelops his feet, as long as it keeps his toes warm. By Monday morning, however, each sock has its appropriate mate long before he leaves for work, not so much because of a commitment to the rules of fashion, but simply to avoid the ridicule of his colleagues. In short, errors of this nature, which are not central to the self, often produce embarrassment, but seldom much guilt.

Behaviour encouraged by guilt avoidance and by embarrassment

Perhaps a better illustration of the similarities and contrasts between the motivational potentials of internal and external foci of attention, as well as fear of guilt and fear of embarrassment, is presented by a comparison of two relevant and very similar studies. Both sets of experiments produced evidence of socially desirable behaviour, but the motivations behind that behaviour were quite different in the two situations, and that difference is informative.

Other-focus and helping. In the first study, Apsler (1975) examined the effects of embarrassment and other-focused attention on helping behaviour. He had each subject perform a series of tasks that were intended to be either embarrassing (e.g., imitate a 5-year-old having a temper tantrum) or not embarrassing (listen to a record), while someone watched the subject through a one-way mirror. When the tasks were finished, a confederate asked the subject for a favour. As the author expected, the subjects who had previously been embarrassed volunteered to help more than did those who had not been embarrassed. Apsler suggested that the embarrassed subjects may have suffered a loss of "social self-esteem" and therefore offered help in an effort to regain some of what they had lost. Interestingly, the helping behaviour occurred whether or not its recipient was the witness of the embarrassing incident. In other words, what was lost socially had to be restored socially, and whoever happened to compose the audience did not make much difference. Although the study did not include a no-observation/ embarrassment condition, in which subjects acted silly completely in private, the argument offered here (cf. also Buss, 1980; Modigliani, 1971) would suggest that there would have been much less helping behaviour in such a situation. The reason is that the helping that was demonstrated apparently was done primarily for self-presentational reasons; personal standards did not play much of a part. Thus, although the behaviour was definitely pro-social in orientation, it certainly could not be considered altruistic or value-driven.

Self-focus and helping. A series of studies by myself and Robert Wicklund (Gibbons & Wicklund, 1982) examined the same behaviour from a different perspective. Specifically, we looked at the effect of self-focused attention on helping. Subjects were made self-aware in one of several different ways (e.g., self-reflection, tape recordings of their own voices), and then they were confronted by a request for help that varied in the legitimacy of the solicitor's need. The results indicated that the self-aware subjects helped less when the request was not salient or the need not valid. There was a significant reversal of this pattern, however, when the request was clear and the need legitimate (Mayer et al., 1985). Our explanation of the results was that self-focus exacerbates self-concern (Berkowitz, 1987), and that tends to interfere with the ability to empathise with others (cf. Vallacher & Solodky, 1979). When self-concern is not elevated, however, and the request happens to be appropriate, then self-focus increases the desire to bring behaviour in line with the universal value of helping others. This type of helping behaviour occurs, then, because it is value-consistent and because ignoring the value would create a sense of guilt.

It is worth noting that in one of the four experiments in the Gibbons and Wicklund study (Exp. 4), this helping occurred in a situation that was designed to be as devoid of self-presentational concerns as we could make it. Subjects were run anonymously and alone in an experimental procedure that was presented to them entirely on tape. They had no contact with an experimenter or anyone else throughout the duration of the experiment. Consequently, whether or not they personally chose to help, the only ones who would know would be themselves. Clearly, subjects' concerns about the images they were presenting to an external audience, or what might be called "assertive impression management", had relatively little to do with their behaviour.

Motives versus outcome. Presumably, subjects in the Apsler (1975) study would not have helped if there had not been someone witnessing their loss of face *and* someone to observe the face-restoring behaviour. The specific reason for helping was to reduce some of the embarrassment they had experienced (or perhaps replace it with a more comfortable affective state). Thus, the motive for the behaviour was exogenous, and subjects' concerns focused on what others, in general, were thinking of them. In contrast, subjects in the Gibbons and Wicklund (1982) study did not help unless their attention was focused on themselves. When they did help, their motives were endogenous, and their concerns centred around what they thought of themselves. In both of the studies, however, the resulting behaviour was the same; subjects did choose to help other people who were in need. And though the origins of the motives and the orientations were different, at a behavioural level, the immediate reasons for the helping were similar. That is, both groups of helpers were trying to prevent or reduce the discomfort of negative affect – guilt in one case, embarrassment in the other. From a psychological perspective, then, self-focus and other-focus involve very different processes. From a societal perspective, however, the outcomes often are effectively the same.

Societal functions of self-focus

The Gibbons and Wicklund (1982) study helps illustrate what Wicklund (1978) suggested to be the "civilising" effect that self-awareness has on behaviour. He claimed that self-focused attention encourages persons to bring behaviour in line with ideals that they maintain personally. Logically, many of these ideals happen to be shared by other people, which means that self-focus *typically* promotes behaviour that is congruent with social values. Self-focus also works in a preventive manner (Gibbons, 1990) by inhibiting actions that, if performed, would *create* a discrepancy with personal standards. One again, although these standards are shared with many others, and in many cases would be considered universals, they originate from within, and they are adhered to in order to please the self, not others. This is an important distinction, one that is fundamental to the state of self-awareness. Self-focus causes people to act in the way they think they *should*, not necessarily the way they perceive others would want them to. Thus, self-awareness can promote independence and autonomy and achievement motivation, all of which are values that are embraced by many civilised cultures. But, paradoxically, they are also values that specific groups can and often do *inhibit* individuals. It is in this sense that self-focus (and fear of associated negative affect) is the influencing factor that promotes socially valued behaviour, even when social pressure may encourage uncivilised actions.

The civilising effect of self-focus is not without costs, however. For example, in the studies discussed earlier that involved female prisoners and psychiatric patients, self-reports of affect were also obtained. Those reports indicated that the self-focused subjects, who reported more accurately on their particular problems, also felt worse when they did. In general, one of the consequences of more careful consideration of the self vis-à-vis personal standards is the realisation that one has not lived up to the standards established for one's own behaviour (Wicklund, 1978). In most cases one would expect that realisation to be accompanied by increased determination to achieve the standard, or at least to improve behaviour. That is certainly not always the case, however, which once again presents an interesting paradox.

Disappointment

The paradox is the fact that in some instances, self-focus can actually *interfere* with the same standard-seeking or standard-consistent behaviour that it typically promotes. The earliest empirical evidence of this came from research on test anxiety (e.g., Sarason, 1975; Wine, 1971), which indicated that too much self-focus during (test) evaluations could disrupt performance. Thoughts about failing (i.e., sub-par performance) consume the anxious person's attention to such an extent that there is simply an insufficient amount left over for the task itself. Similar results have been reported more recently in a series of studies by Carver and Scheier and some of their colleagues (Carver & Scheier, 1981). This research has indicated that when individuals do not expect to be able to live up to performance standards, then self-focus will discourage efforts to do so (Carver & Blaney, 1977; Carver et al., 1979a,b). Often this leads to attempts to distract attention from the self, or simply give up the task. Thus, disappointment in one's level of performance can be a type of negative affect that is just as debilitating as the guilt associated with moral transgression, provided that attention is focused on the self.

Summary

Self-focus. Through a process mediated by negative affect (i.e., guilt, disappointment) or anticipation of such affect, self-focused attention has a profound impact on behaviour. Specifically, it enhances the motivation to bring behaviour in line with standards and values or, in some instances, to keep current behaviour in line with such standards. These standards are formed through years of social experience and thus are reflections of societal values. Which values are deemed important and therefore are internalised, however, varies greatly across individuals. Thus, the value structure becomes part of the individual's personality – an enduring but dynamic set of traits that people bring with them to different behavioural contexts. In short, self-focus is the "remote control" that a society has on its members. It has the effect of promoting civilised behaviour in those situations in which direct societal control is missing (i.e., in the absence of others), or when social influences may encourage behaviour that is discrepant with a higher societal value. This remote control is mediated by affect. Specifically, it is the desire to reduce the discomfort that accompanies the realisation that one has not done what one should, or to avoid discomfort in the future, that prompts behavioural change when attention is focused on the self.

Other-focused attention. Other-focused attention is also associated with behavioural change. Specifically, self-consciousness, which is an awareness of oneself from the perspective of others, enhances the motivation to bring behaviour in line with the assumed standards and expectations of those who happen to compose the audience. Through a process once again mediated by negative affect or anticipation of negative affect – embarrassment – it encourages behaviour that will maintain or enhance the image that an individual wishes to present to an immediate audience. Thus, other-focus is the *direct* control that groups have on their individual members. This type of control is exogenous in nature.

Although the source of the negative affect happens to be different, in many respects fear of embarrassment has effects on behaviour that are directly analogous to those associated with the fear of guilt that is often a product of self-focus. Both states are phenomenologically aversive, of course, and in both cases persons experiencing the negative affect will attempt to avoid the current state of focus by diverting attention (either their own or that of others) away from the self. In each instance the discomfort results from a perception that behaviour has not lived up to standards – one's own or those of others. And providing that the affect is not too severe, it encourages attempts to bring behaviour in line with those standards.

Conclusion. As previous research has noted, self-focus and other-focus can encourage very different behaviours (e.g., conformity vs. independence, suggestibility vs. resistance to persuasion, impression management vs. decreased concern for self-presentation); the ultimate impacts of both, however, tend to be quite comparable in many respects. In the case of other-focused attention, fear of embarrassment helps bring behaviour in line with certain accepted social rules (i.e., the dos and don'ts of social etiquette). In this sense it gives some structure to social interaction and keeps behaviour in line with prescribed guidelines. Without its impact, there would be social anarchy, and social discourse, as it exists, would be virtually impossible. At a higher level, self-focused attention encourages civilised behaviour within individuals; without it, society itself could not exist. Thus, in both cases, focus of attention acts as a source of control of the behaviour of individuals in a social setting. The rules, though sometimes quite distinct, are learned through years of socialisation experience, and they are internalised in such a manner that even fear of violation or anticipated violation can have very strong inhibitory effects on behaviour.

NOTES

1. Carver and Scheier present an elaborate model of the effects of attention on behaviour that is based on the concept of self-regulation and reflects a cybernetic orientation. However, though their model extends and modifies the original self-awareness theory, they still rely on many of the same assumptions about focus of attention and behaviour as did Duval and Wicklund (1972).
2. Under some circumstances, self-focused subjects have been shown to under-estimate responsibility for behaviour that was, in fact, attributable to them (Cohen, Dowling, Bishop, & Manley, 1985). What this research suggests is that self-awareness can promote a form of defensive impression management when the negative implications of a particular behaviour and its public acknowledgement are severe and more aversive than those associated with a recognition of misrepresentation of the self. This behaviour, however, is likely to cause considerable subsequent discomfort when the individual once again becomes self-focused.

REFERENCES

Apsler, R. (1975). Effects of embarrassment on behavior towards others. *Journal of Personality and Social Psychology, 32*, 145–153.

Baldwin, M. W., & Holmes, J. G. (1987). Salient private audiences and aware-ness of the self. *Journal of Personality and Social Psychology, 52*, 1087–1098.

Beaman, A. L., Klentz, B., Diener, E., & Svanum, S. (1979). Objective self-awareness and transgression in children. *Journal of Personality and Social Psychology, 37*, 1835–1846.

Berkowitz, L. (1987). Mood, self-awareness, and willingness to help. *Journal of Personality and Social Psychology, 52*, 721–729.

Briggs, S. R., Cheek, J. M., & Buss, A. H. (1980). An analysis of the self-monitoring scale. *Journal of Personality and Social Psychology, 38*, 679–686.

Buss, A. H. (1980). *Self-consciousness and social anxiety.* San Francisco: Freeman.

Carver, C. S., & Blaney, P. H. (1977). Perceived arousal, focus of attention, and avoidance behavior. *Journal of Applied Psychology, 86*, 154–162.

Carver, C. S., Blaney, P. H., & Scheier, M. F. (1979a). Focus of attention, chronic expectancy, and responses to a feared stimulus. *Journal of Personality and Social Psychology, 37*, 1186–1195.

Carver, C. S., Blaney, P. H., & Scheier, M. F. (1979b). Reassertion and giving up: The interactive role of self-directed attention and outcome expectancy. *Journal of Personality and Social Psychology, 37*, 1859–1870.

Carver, C. S., & Scheier, M. F. (1981). *Attention and self-regulation: A control theory approach to human behavior.* New York: Springer-Verlag.

Carver, C. S., & Scheier, M. F. (1987). The blind men and the elephant: Selective examination of the public–private literature gives rise to a faulty perception. *Journal of Personality, 55*, 417–429.

Cheek, J. M. (1982). Aggression, moderator variables, and the validity of personality tests: A peer-rating study. *Journal of Personality and Social Psychology,* *43,* 1254–1269.

Cohen, J. L., Dowling, N., Bishop, B., & Manley, W. (1985). Causal attributions: Effects of self-focused attention and self-esteem feedback. *Personality and Social Psychology Bulletin, 11,* 369–378.

Cooley, C. H., (1969). *Human nature and the social order.* New York: Scribner's. (Original work published 1902)

Darwin, C. R. (1955). *The expression of the emotions in man and animals.* New York: Appleton. (Original work published 1872)

Diener, E., & Srull, T. K. (1979). Self-awareness, psychological perspective, and self-reinforcement in relation to personal and social standards. *Journal of Personality and Social Psychology, 37,* 413–423.

Duval, S., & Wicklund, R. A. (1972). *A theory of objective self-awareness.* New York: Academic Press.

Edelmann, R. J. (1981). Embarrassment: The state of research. *Current Psychological Reviews, 1,* 125–138.

Edelmann, R. J. (1985). Individual differences in embarrassment, self-consciousness, self-monitoring and embarrassability. *Personality and Individual Differences, 6,* 223–230.

Fenigstein, A. (1979). Self-consciousness, self-attention, and social interaction. *Journal of Personality and Social Psychology, 37,* 75–86.

Fenigstein, A., Scheier, M. F., & Buss, A. H. (1975). Public and private self-consciousness: Assessment and theory. *Journal of Consulting and Clinical Psychology, 43,* 522–527.

Froming, W. J., & Carver, C. S. (1981). Divergent influences of private and public self-consciousness in a compliance paradigm. *Journal of Research in Personality, 15,* 159–171.

Froming, W. J., Walker, G. R., & Lopyan, K. J. (1982). Public and private self-awareness: When personal attitudes conflict with societal expectations. *Journal of Experimental Social Psychology, 18,* 476–487.

Gibbons, F. X. (1978). Sexual standards and reactions to pornography: Enhancing behavioral consistency through self-focused attention. *Journal of Personality and Social Psychology, 36,* 976–987.

Gibbons, F. X. (1983). Self-attention and self-report: The "veridicality" hypothesis. *Journal of Personality, 51,* 517–542.

Gibbons, F. X. (1990). Self-attention and behavior: A review and update. In M. Zanna (Ed.), *Advances in experimental social psychology* (Vol. 23; pp. 249–303). San Diego: Academic Press.

Gibbons, F. X., & Gaeddert, W. P. (1984). Focus of attention and placebo utility. *Journal of Experimental Social Psychology, 20,* 159–176.

Gibbons, F. X., & Gerrard, M. (1986). *Self-awareness and the truth-as-standard hypothesis.* Paper presented at American Psychological Association convention, Washington, DC.

Gibbons, F. X., Smith, T. W., Ingram, R. E., Pearce, K., Brehm, S. S., & Schroeder, D. J. (1985). Self-awareness and self-confrontation: Effects of self-focused attention on members of a clinical population. *Journal of Personality and Social Psychology, 48,* 662–675.

Gibbons, F. X., & Wicklund, R. A. (1982). Self-focused attention and helping behavior. *Journal of Personality and Social Psychology, 43,* 462–474.

Goffman, E. (1955). On face-work. *Psychiatry, 18,* 213–231.

Goffman, E. (1956). Embarrassment and social organization. *American Journal of Sociology, 62,* 264–271.

Goffman, E. (1959). *The presentation of self in everyday life.* Garden City, NY: Doubleday.

Hass, R. G. (1984). Perspective taking and self-awareness: Drawing an E on your forehead. *Journal of Personality and Social Psychology, 46,* 788–798.

Hormuth, S. E. (1982). Self-awareness and drive theory: Comparing internal standards and dominant responses. *European Journal of Social Psychology, 12,* 31–45.

Hull, C. L. (1952). *A behavior system.* New Haven, CT: Yale University Press.

Innes, J. M., & Young, R. F. (1975). The effects of presence of an audience, evaluation apprehension, and objective self-awareness on learning. *Journal of Experimental Social Psychology, 11,* 35–42.

John, O. (1983). *Selbstaufmerksamkeit und Selbstprasentation: Moderatorvariablen in der Persönlichkeitserfassung?* (Self-consciousness and self-monitoring: Moderator variables in personality assessment?). Unpublished dissertation, Universität Bielefeld.

Kassin, S. M. (1985). Eyewitness identification: Retrospective self-awareness and the accuracy–confidence correlation. *Journal of Personality and Social Psychology, 44,* 878–893.

Kelley, H. H. (1967). Attribution theory in social psychology. *Nebraska Symposium on Motivation, 15,* 192–240.

Leary, M. R. (1983). Social anxiousness: The construct and its measurement. *Journal of Personality Assessment, 47,* 66–75.

Mayer, F. S., Duval, S., Holtz, N., & Bowman, C. (1985). Self-focus, helping request salience, felt responsibility, and helping behavior. *Personality and Social Psychology Bulletin, 11,* 133–144.

Mead, G. H. (1934). *Mind, self, and society.* University of Chicago Press.

Modigliani, A. (1968). Embarrassment and embarrassability. *Sociometry, 31,* 313–326.

Modigliani, A. (1971). Embarrassment, facework, and eye contact: Testing a theory of embarrassment. *Journal of Personality and Social Psychology, 17,* 15–24.

Mullen, B. (1984). Participation in religious groups as a function of group composition: A self-attention perspective. *Journal of Applied Social Psychology, 14,* 509–518.

Pilkonis, P. A. (1977). Shyness, public and private, and its relationship to other measures of social behavior. *Journal of Personality, 45,* 585–595.

Pryor, J. B., Gibbons, F. X., Wicklund, R. A., Fazio, R., & Hood, R. (1977). Self-focused attention and self-report validity. *Journal of Personality, 5,* 513–527.

Sarason, I. G. (1975). Anxiety and self-preoccupation. In I. G. Sarason & C. D. Spielberger (Eds.), *Stress and anxiety* (Vol. 2, pp. 27–44). New York: Wiley.

Sattler, J. A. (1965). A theoretical development and clinical investigation of embarrassment. *Genetic Psychology Monographs, 71,* 19–59.

Scheier, M. F. (1976). Self-awareness, self-consciousness, and angry aggression. *Journal of Personality, 44,* 627–644.

Scheier, M. F., Buss, A. H., & Buss, D. M. (1978). Self-consciousness, self-report of aggressiveness and aggression. *Journal of Research in Personality, 12,* 133–140.

Scheier, M. F., & Carver, C. S. (1977). Self-focused attention and the experience of emotion: Attraction, repulsion, elation, and depression. *Journal of Personality and Social Psychology, 35,* 625–636.

Scheier, M. F., & Carver, C. S. (1980). Private and public self-attention, resistance to change, and dissonance reduction. *Journal of Personality and Social Psychology, 39,* 390–405.

Scheier, M. F., Carver, C. S., & Gibbons, F. X. (1979). Self-directed attention, awareness of bodily states, and suggestibility. *Journal of Personality and Social Psychology, 37,* 1576–1588.

Scheier, M. F., Carver, C. S., & Gibbons, F. X. (1981). Self-focused attention and reactions to fear. *Journal of Research in Personality, 15,* 1–15.

Schlenker, B. R. (1980). *Impression management: The self-concept, social identity, and interpersonal relations.* Monterey, CA: Brooks/Cole.

Schlenker, B. R., & Leary, M. R. (1982). Social anxiety and self-presentation: A conceptualization and model. *Psychological Bulletin, 92,* 641–669.

Snyder, M. (1974). Self-monitoring and expressive behavior. *Journal of Personality and Social Psychology, 30,* 526–537.

Spence, K. W. (1956). *Behavior theory and conditioning.* New Haven, CT: Yale University Press.

Tetlock, P. E., & Manstead, A. S. R. (1985). Impression management vs. intrapsychic explanations in social psychology: A useful dichotomy? *Psychological Review, 92,* 59–77.

Turner, R. G., Gilliland, L., & Klein, H. M. (1981). Self-consciousness, evaluation of physical characteristics, and physical attractiveness. *Journal of Research in Personality, 15,* 182–190.

Vallacher, R. R., & Solodky, M. (1979). Objective self-awareness, standards of evaluation, and moral behavior. *Journal of Experimental Social Psychology, 15,* 254–262.

Wegner, D. M., & Giuliano, T. (1982). The forms of social awareness. In W. J. Ickes & E. S. Knowles (Eds.), *Personality, roles, and social behavior* (pp. 129–157). New York: Springer-Verlag.

Wicklund, R. A. (1975). Objective self-awareness. In L. Berkowitz (Ed.), *Advances in experimental social psychology* (Vol. 8, pp. 233–275). New York: Academic Press.

Wicklund, R. A. (1978). Three years later. In L. Berkowitz (Ed.). *Cognitive theories in social psychology* (pp. 509–521). New York: Academic Press.

Wicklund, R. A. (1979). The influence of self-awareness on human behavior. *American Scientist, 67,* 187–193.

Wicklund, R. A. (1980). Group contact and self-focused attention. In P. B.

Paulus (Ed.), *Psychology of group influence* (pp. 189–208). Hillsdale, NJ: Lawrence Erlbaum.

Wicklund, R. A., & Gollwitzer, P. M. (1987). The fallacy of the private–public self-focus distinction. *Journal of Personality, 55*, 491–522.

Wine, J. D. (1971). Test anxiety and direction of attention. *Psychological Bulletin, 76*, 92–104.

Wojciszke, B. (1987). Ideal-self, self-focus, and value-behaviour consistency. *European Journal of Social Psychology, 17*, 187–198.

5

The evolution and manifestation of social anxiety

PAUL GILBERT and PETER TROWER

Fear is a vital evolutionary legacy that leads an organism
to avoid threat, and has obvious survival value
– Marks (1987, p. 3)

Threats to an animal come from different sources: from natural situations (e.g., heights and fire), from predation, and from members of the
same species (conspecifics) that are in competition for resources. Social
(or conspecific) anxiety may be viewed as one aspect of a defensive
response system that evolved to deal with threat (Marks, 1987). Although anxiety conditions can be classified in various ways, in this chapter our emphasis highlights the differences between social anxiety and
other forms of anxiety/fear.

First, consider the appraisal of threat. Non-social threat is conveyed
largely through sensory information from sources such as smells, sudden
sounds, or movements, and there may be little in the way of detailed
cognitive processing. That is, there is a largely automatic component to
these kinds of fear responses. Generally, however, social threats are not
conveyed by sensory information, although scent marking of territory
may be an exception to this rule, in that some animals show anxiety on
entering another animal's territory (Marks, 1987). Social anxiety, on the
other hand, at least in the higher mammals, depends on decoding
complex social signals that require more detailed, less automatic, cognitive processing (Leventhal & Scherer, 1987; Ohman, 1986).

Second, the potential responses to social threats (e.g., shyness, embarrassment, shame) appear to be more complex and have under-
gone fundamental adaptations with the evolution of the reflective self-
awareness that is allowed by consciousness. These adaptations are not
mirrored in the responses to non-social threats (i.e., self-presentation is
not related to either evaluation or response in dealing with physical
danger). Indeed, self-awareness may have evolved from social living
(Crook, 1980).

In this chapter we focus on social anxiety as an evolved capacity for

144

coping with social threat. We hypothesise that the situations and roles that elicit social anxiety are those that have, or would have had, special meaning for survival and satisfactory adaptation; in other words, social anxiety falls in the area of a prepared phobia (Seligman, 1971).

Evolutionary processes and social anxiety

This section focuses on the evolutionary processes that may have given rise to social anxiety. We shall review the role of sexual selection on breeding patterns and how these in turn have exerted important effects on the way animals live within proximity to each other. Sexual selection has given rise to two forms of breeding organisation: territorial living and group living. Group-living breeding organisations can in turn be differentiated into agonic (threat-based) and hedonic (co-operation/affiliation-based) modes. We shall argue that the ability to be able to decode and to respond to the different types of social signals that are characteristic of the agonic and hedonic modes requires the existence of innate competencies (appraisal-response systems). When an animal evaluates and responds to a threat, this is facilitated by the operation of the defence system (Gilbert, 1989; Marks, 1987). When an animal evaluates social signals as non-threatening or conferring reassurance, pro-social behaviour (e.g., co-operation, sharing) is facilitated by the safety system (Gilbert, 1989). We shall suggest that the previously mentioned factors are important for an understanding of the nature and meaning of social anxiety.

Sexual selection and breeding structures

Darwin (1871) proposed that species change their forms over time (evolve) by processes of selection. There are two salient processes involved: natural selection and sexual selection. Natural selection involves the inheritance of characteristics that give survival advantage over the non-social or natural domain (e.g., ability to avoid predation, ability to cope with climatic factors). Sexual selection has two components. The first is called intrasexual selection. This involves the inheritance of characteristics that convey advantage in the competition with members of the same sex for breeding resources (e.g., physical strength, size). The second is called intersexual selection. This involves the inheritance of characteristics that confer advantage in making one sex attractive to the other (e.g., plumage). The rules for mate attractiveness among humans appear to follow those predicted by evolutionary theory (Buss, 1987, 1988).

Sexual selection can be hypothesised to have played a major role in the evolution of social anxieties and other psychopathologies (Gardner, 1988; Gilbert, 1989; Price, 1988; Trower & Gilbert, 1989). This is partly because both intersexual and intrasexual selections operate on the display behaviour of the animal. It is via successful display behaviour that conspecifics are able to exert control over breeding resources and opportunities. Indeed, it is probable that it is intrasexual selection that has given rise to those motives that often are referred to as power motives (McClelland, 1985). We shall hypothesise that it is the evaluation of our own display behaviour and the expected social responses to it that are at the heart of social anxiety (Schlenker & Leary, 1982).

Territorial breeding structures. Sexual selection strategies, which are expressed in patterns of breeding behaviour, have given rise to two fundamentally different forms of social organisation: territorial living and group living (Chance, 1984). The most primitive is territorial. In this situation, conspecifics compete for the ownership of a territory, home base, or nest site. The most successful contestants have the better territories and are better placed to attract mates. Mates (usually females) are attracted by both the mating (courting) display and the territory occupied (Hinde, 1982). In other words, mates are attracted into the territory and towards each other. Courtship rituals appear necessary to keep the sexes from attacking each other as if they were competitors, but even these courtship displays can be dangerous, and fighting can break out (Hinde, 1982).

Contesting a territory between conspecifics of the same sex, however, involves displays to keep others out. To achieve this, conspecifics display to each other their strengths and abilities to gain or hold a territory (i.e., to win any ensuing contest). These behaviours have been called "resource-holding potential" (RHP) signals (Parker, 1974; Price, 1988; Price & Sloman, 1987) and are expressed in various postural behaviours: upright postures, head bobbing, gaze fixation, strutting, ground stamping, and so on (Harper, 1985; MacLean, 1985). These displays are enacted in what has been called ritualistic agonistic behaviour (Price & Sloman, 1987). Social signals or displays that are designed to reduce the RHP of a contestant have been called catathetic signals (Price, 1988). In general, then, as Gardner (1988) points out, social communication can serve the purpose of either linking (attracting to) or spacing.

Of special importance is the fact that conspecifics have to be able to evaluate the strength and nature of the RHP or catathetic signals being emitted by others. Without this, every conflict or competition would be resolved only by actual fighting. Furthermore, animals must also be able to generate estimates of their own relative or comparative RHPs. Those that estimate that they have higher (or favourable) RHPs relative to

opponents are freed to engage in aggressive or agonistic challenge behaviour toward the opponents (i.e., they are likely to emit catathetic
signals toward the opponents). Those that evaluate their opponents to be
superior (i.e., they estimate that they themselves have unfavourable
relative RHPs) must either yield to the superior opponents or flee the
territory. In other words, an unfavourable estimate of relative RHP
activates escape/flight action tendencies. This results in dispersion of
conspecifics. Importantly, then, it is not necessary that every dominance
encounter be settled with actual fighting. Rather, fighting can be ritual-
ised, enabling contestants (e.g., via strutting and posturing) to "weigh
each other up". Indeed, serious fighting may break out only when both
contestants evaluate that they are relatively equal.

The competency to evaluate one's own relative strength (RHP) and
ability to cope with the challenge of a contestant seems to be the root of
much intrasexual behaviour. It is perhaps the most primitive form of
social comparison. The ability of animals to be able to make this kind
of comparison has clear advantages; for example, it avoids pointless
fighting and risk of injury. But there are other implications to the
evolution of this ability or competency. Most important is the fact that
an unfavourable evaluation or social comparison of RHP activates various defensive repertoires, such as yielding and flight.

We should emphasise that this evaluation is something that goes on
inside an individual and therefore needs to be understood as a psychological process. In species whose common form of breeding is territorial,
those that estimate that they have low RHP have only two innate
response options; they may resort to flight, or, if that is not possible
because of limited territory or other factors, they may exhibit a major
change of state called yielding (Price & Sloman, 1987).

Group breeding structures: The agonic mode. The other form of breeding
organisation involves the evolution of group-living social structures (i.e.,
there is no contest for individual territories). This marks a dramatic shift
to social living. There appear to be two fundamentally different ways in
which the infrastructures of group-living animals are organised. These
have been called the agonic mode and the hedonic mode (Chance, 1984,
1988).

In the agonic mode, social groups are organised around a dominance
hierarchy of power and threat (with the most powerful reaching the
higher ranks). The agonic mode represents the situation where the
predominant way in which individuals relate to each other is *mutual
defensiveness and threat*. In this mode the structure of social attention is
co-ordinated around those who have the higher RHP.

The term *mode* refers to the structure and organisation of conspecifics;

that is, it refers to a description of social behaviour at the group level. In the agonic mode, dominance hierarchies are organised in a way different from that of the territorial species (e.g., they are not organised into individually owned territories). Group living is made possible by the evolution of two important adaptations to the escape/flight and yielding options consequent to an evaluation of unfavourable RHP. These are submission and reverted escape.

In submission, the animal that believes that it has a lower RHP relative to a contestant can signal its recognition of that fact by acting submissively. For rats, this involves flipping onto its back when the animal believes that it has lost a dominance encounter; that is, the animal stays put, but displays its recognition of having lost by displaying a submissive posture. Primates display their evaluated inferior status in various ways, such as gaze avoidance, crouching, presenting, showing the fear grin denoting appeasement, withdrawing (or shying away), refraining from initiation, and so forth (Harper, 1985). These kinds of action tendencies, postures, and display behaviours can also be noted in the repertoires of shy, embarrassed, and socially anxious humans (Ohman, 1986) and those experiencing shame (Lewis, 1986). Indeed, we can recognise that individuals are undergoing these aversive social experiences by observing their non-verbal behaviours (e.g., gaze avoidance, lowering the chin, and turning away).

The second adaptation to the flight option is called reverted escape (Chance, 1988). In this situation, a subordinate may have been threatened by a dominant and may have withdrawn for a while, but is motivated to return to the source of the threat (the dominant), enacting various appeasement and submissive behaviours (e.g., presenting). This acts to reduce the fight tendencies of the dominant and the flight tendencies of the subordinate – tendencies that if acted on in these species would result in dispersion and collapse of the social structure and a regression to territorial breeding patterns.

Subordinate animals show patterns of physiological activity different from those of dominants. They have high circulating concentrations of cortisol, for example (Gilbert, 1989; Henry & Stephens, 1977). This may be related to their need to be vigilant to the possibility of conspecific threat from the more dominant. The state of being vigilant to such threat has been called "braced readiness", in that the subordinate must remain ready to take defensive action in case its behaviour provokes hostility from the more dominant (Chance, 1980, 1984); see Trower, Gilbert, and Sherling (in press) for a further discussion of the relation between braced readiness and social anxiety. Although we use the terms *dominant* and *subordinate* in a general sense, the reader should note that these concepts are not as straightforward as they appear, especially in primates (e.g., de Waal, 1988; Dunbar, 1988).

Group breeding structures: The hedonic mode. Not all group structures are organised around the most powerful; for some primates, dominance hierarchies may be very loosely defined. Furthermore, the social organisations of certain species (especially chimpanzees) are marked by high levels of mutual, positively reinforcing behaviours, where the more dominant send reassurance signals to the more subordinate. Relationships are marked by a good deal of hedonic (fun-loving) joint explorative and foraging behaviours and a relative absence of the aggressiveness noted in agonic groups. Furthermore, de Waal (1988) points out that aggressive encounters can be followed by a good deal of mutual reassurance (e.g., grooming, kissing), which increases affiliative behaviour between previous adversaries.

The hedonic mode represents those social structures in which the previously described social behaviours and interchanges predominate (Chance, 1980, 1988). In the social displays of these groups, it is often the dominants that are responsible for sending reassurance signals to the more fearful. This has important effects, because it acts to decrease the subordinates' natural defensiveness, braced readiness, and threat monitoring. In the presence of reassurance signals the subordinates are able to relax and direct their attention to exploration and mutually beneficial activity. This is especially apparent in the foraging primates and hunter-gatherer groups (Power, 1988). Hence, whereas in the agonic mode conspecifics relate to each other with a good deal of defensiveness, in the hedonic mode the style is one of *mutual dependence.* Indeed, co-operative behaviour, at which humans excel, depends on reassurance if the society is not to regress to power and compliance relations.

Two other aspects of the hedonic mode should be noted. The first is that in response to some external threat, such as a predator, hedonic chimpanzees come together, cuddling and holding each other in order to gain confidence to harass the predator. In other words, the response to such threats is a group response rather than an individual response (Chance, 1980). Interestingly, a recent television documentary has suggested that one of the attractions of horror films is that they are usually watched in groups, and it is the nature of this group (reassurance) experience of the "horror" that is reinforcing.

The second adaptation centres on the immense importance of reconciliation. Reconciliation has a number of aspects. First, it tends to follow an agonistic encounter, with one member acknowledging subordinate status to the other. Second, it increases close-proximity behaviour, which has clear affiliative components, such as grooming and holding (de Waal, 1988). Indeed, young chimpanzees that have been threatened or attacked by a more dominant may subsequently pester the dominant for stroking and reassurance and may throw tantrums if such reassurance is not given (Goodall, 1975). Such reassurance, one may presume, operates through the reward system, because the effect is to calm and reassure and to allow return to exploration and non-aggressive relations. In other words, one needs to consider the sequence of behaviours that precede and follow aggressive interactions to understand the full meaning of submission in group-living animals (de Waal, 1988).

The defence and safety systems

The defence system

So far, we have discussed the major forms of social behaviours that have emerged as a result of evolution. We have highlighted two distinct social modes: the agonic and the hedonic. In this section we discuss the innate competencies that exist within individuals – competencies from which these behaviors (threatening, submitting, reassurance) are generated. In other words, the social behaviour patterns that exemplify the two modes arise out of innate appraisal and response competencies.

At the simplest level these competencies are concerned with whether stimuli are potentially punishing or positively reinforcing and with the selection of appropriate responses. As a general rule, the individual possesses classes of appraisal and response options that are oriented to defence and safety. That is, an individual is innately equipped to be able to discern what is threatening to it (e.g., from an innate capacity to recognise the meaning of facial and postural displays) and is able to select the appropriate defensive action (e.g., fight/flight, freeze/faint, camouflage, submission, reverted escape) and to determine which stimuli are positively reinforcing and safety-conferring (Gilbert, 1989).

In brief, then, we can argue that the organisation of social behaviour arose from the evolution of important evaluative competencies (Gilbert, 1989) and complex options for response. The uniquely social nature of these competencies becomes clear when it is recognised that submission and reverted escape are not options for coping with predator threats or heights. Nor are submissive behaviours displayed before feared animals of a different species (e.g., chimpanzees do not show submissive behaviour to baboons, even though they may fear baboons) (de Waal, 1988). Nor are submissive or reconciliatory behaviours possible in, say, reptiles, because they simply have not evolved this option within their brains. Therefore, submissive behaviour is a special-purpose behaviour that depends on a specific kind of evaluation – conspecific threat – and also on a species having submission (or signalling awareness of threat and lower rank) as a potential option of defence.

Central to our analysis is the social-comparative, social-evaluative nature (matching an evaluation of one's own RHP/fighting ability with that of a contestant) of the intrasexual and competitive strategies. It is this evaluation that gives rise to the appraisal of threat and to the kinds of social signals and behaviours emitted. To put this another way, it is the competency for behaving towards others as a member of a ranked social structure and hence for organising behaviour in line with what the animal determines its rank to be.

There is now increasing evidence that much of what we regard as psychopathology arises from the (often inappropriate) activation of innately available appraisal-response systems (Bailey, 1987; Beck, Emery, & Greenberg, 1985; Chance, 1980, 1984, 1988; Crook, 1980; Gardner, 1982, 1988; Gilbert, 1984, 1988, 1989; MacLean, 1985; Marks, 1987; Ohman, 1986; Price, 1988). Gilbert (1989) has proposed that many of the attentional, appraisal, and response options that are involved with threat are part of, or a mentality of, a defence system that operates through the punishment and behavioural inhibition (the septohippocampal stop system, Gray, 1971, 1985) areas of the brain. A similar view was put forward by Marks (1987).

The reasoning for this point of view cannot be outlined here, although it should be noted that successful escape, in so far as it brings relief, may operate via the reward areas (Gray, 1971). Suffice it to say that threat arousal involves various patterns of psychobiological changes that are shared across various situations (e.g., cardiac changes). Hence, the response options of submissiveness and reverted escape are part of the defensive system. Because they are part of a system, they may be coupled with other response and defensive options, such as freeze or faint (Beck et al., 1985; Marks, 1987).

What evidence is there that the socially anxious do recruit the evaluative and response potentials that are coded in the defence system? There is growing evidence that the socially anxious are prone to recruit the submissive options in various social encounters they evaluate as threatening (Alden & Cappe, 1981; Alden & Safran, 1978; Glasgow & Arkowitz, 1975; Sutton-Simon & Goldfried, 1979). Depressed individuals appear to do likewise (Forrest & Hokanson, 1975). Vitkus and Horowitz (1987) utilised Leary's notion (1957) that interpersonal behaviour results from the interaction of two independent dimensions (dominance–submission and love–hate) to explore the idea that lonely people tend to enact a role of submissive behaviour. They reviewed the evidence that this role is chosen even though a person may know how to act assertively. In their view, the choice of this role is related to a poor self-image. Such a view is in accord with the ideas expressed here – that the choice of expressed behaviour is linked with social-comparative self-estimates (e.g., relative RHP).

It would also seem the case that low-assertive people are inordinately concerned with the effects of any assertive behaviour they may express. They are preoccupied with how others see them and appear to be especially concerned with the fear that assertive behaviour might result in an escalation of conflict (Schwartz & Gottman, 1976). However, the submissive behaviour that may result from this fear can be self-defeating in the long run (Forrest & Hokanson, 1975; Gilbert, 1984; Vitkus & Horowitz, 1987), in that it may result in other people behaving more dominantly towards them or finding them "unattractive".

It is important to note, however, that it is not only self-evaluation that is important, or the image one thinks one is creating in another (Trower et al., in press), but also the evaluation of the situation that recruits the defence system. This, in turn, depends on how a sequence of expressed social behaviours is role-constructed (Ingraham & Wright, 1987). For example, one may feel relaxed or excited when talking about one's ideas to a group of friends, but feel quite anxious when one is asked to give the same talk to a group of unfamiliars at a conference. In the latter case, one may see the conference as clearly relating to ranking, because in this context status may be evaluated as being very much on the line. One might fear that there would be others who would know more and who might use that knowledge to disrupt or undermine or belittle one's display – an outcome not expected from one's friends. With one's friends, one may construct the role as that of sharing knowledge rather than competing, whereas at a conference one may construct the same behaviour as engaging in a more competitive bid for attention. Furthermore, with one's friends, one may have well-developed affiliative tendencies that are not present at a conference. These may act to give reassurance that would not be present at a formal conference.

In general, then, we can suggest that in contexts that are evaluated as potentially competitive (i.e., have ranking implications), and where the structure of the group or some part of it is believed to function in an agonic way, the defence options are primed. Anxiety regarding those that are seen to have more favourable RHPs (i.e., seen as superior in some way) is an essential capacity if animals are to live in groups. Hence, social anxiety is far from abnormal in those species whose dominance hierarchies are organised around power and threat.

The safety system

The safety system functions through the positive reinforcement system. In social situations where the safety system is activated, individuals are attracted to each other, find proximity rewarding, and are generally supportive. Primates also are able to form alliances with other members of the group, and these alliances are at the heart of friendship (Crook, 1980; Gilbert, 1989). Feeling safe with others and having a basically social disposition seem to be related to our sense of happiness and well-being (Argyle, 1987). Hence, though it is true that conspecifics can be sources of threat and challenge, it is also the case that other humans can reduce our arousal by sending reassurance signals and messages of support, and they can be sources of attachments and friendships.

Gilbert (1989) has suggested that there are two components to the social safety system. The first relates to attachment behaviour and the way in which related individuals can seek support from and remain in close proximity to each other. The attachment system may in fact be an important component of subsequent peer group forms of friendship (Heard & Lake, 1986). Certainly, the experience of positive attachments in early life appears to facilitate positive peer behaviours (Rohner, 1986). The second component may relate to co-operative behaviour. People can form positive relationships on the basis of their ability to send supportive and valuing signals to each other. Furthermore, humans have the ability to respect each other (e.g., respecting each other's rights when standing in queue) and to refrain from attacking each other even though they may not have any form of attachment with each other. In other words, although attachment and friendship facilitate positive social relations, they are not necessary in order to feel safe in the presence of others.

It would, of course, be incorrect to suggest that ranking does not occur in the hedonic mode. However, its nature and structure are quite different from those in the agonic mode. Hedonic ranking is based on recognising and valuing the positive attributes of others, not on threat possibilities. In the hedonic mode, rank arises out of respect, rather than fear, though some individuals appear to confuse these two forms of ranking, as in the case of individuals who believe that they will be respected only if they demonstrate some form of strength and threat potential.

Hedonic styles of relating would not be possible were it not for the fact that we have evolved appraisal–response systems that make these positive forms of conspecific relating possible. Unless we are innately prepared to be able to engage others in essentially positive ways, the hedonic mode cannot exist. Obviously, reptiles do not make supportive friends, because they are not biologically equipped to do so. Hence, it is because we can experience others as essentially supporting that humans are able to feel relatively safe in most contexts with their fellows. However, this safety clearly is not felt in situations of social anxiety. Whereas it is comparatively easy to understand social anxiety as related to activation of the defence system, we might also consider the result of failure of an individual to be able to recruit the safety system in social encounters. In other words, social anxiety can represent an increase in threat evaluation and/or a failure to feel safe in the presence of others. This failure to feel safe may exist even in the absence of threatening cues from others.

Social anxiety may be increased in contexts that represent a loss of the ability to evaluate others as supportive or reassuring. In other words, social anxiety may represent a failure in the recruitment of our safety competencies (Trower & Gilbert, 1989). There are at least four ways in which this can occur.

The first may arise when an individual is not able to acknowledge the superiority of a conspecific without also evaluating this negatively as a sign of personal inferiority and self-dislike (e.g., "I must succeed or be seen as a 'wimp'"), or when reassurance seeking is socially constructed within the culture as a sign of weakness ("strong people never give in or seek reassurance"). Furthermore, even though some autocrats in human society seem to desire that others behave submissively towards them, they may also punish efforts at reassurance. This can be quite common in families in which there is a poverty of affective sharing (Rohner, 1986).

The second context may arise when there appears little opportunity for seeking reassurance in subsequent encounters. Human culture is such that the kinds of continual social interactions (especially the frequent reunions following foraging) noted in primates and hunter-gatherers (Power, 1988) often are broken and discontinuous. We can avoid each other for long periods of time. For example, if I give a poor presentation during a talk at a conference, I may not be close enough to others to be reassured by them or to have subsequent opportunities to show that actually I am not so daft as my 20-min presentation may have suggested. Also, a poor performance may suggest that one is not fit for a particular job upon which others may depend – a concern hardly at issue in chimpanzees.

Third, the kinds of dominant–submissive interactions considered by ethologists usually have focused on dyadic encounters. However, humans often function in dyads that are enacted within a larger social group. For example, consider the kind of experiment in which an individual knows that he or she is being observed in a social dyadic encounter. A subject may be willing to express subordinate behaviour in an unobserved situation, but may be concerned about how that will be perceived by observer(s) of the interaction. In other words, human social behaviour is not only targeted to specific individuals but also oriented towards attempting to create certain impressions in an audience who may be watching the interaction (Baumeister, 1982).

Finally, individuals may come to various social encounters with poorly developed safety competencies, perhaps as a result of a history of aggressive or neglectful social experiences or because of unrealistic ideas about what is necessary to display in order to avoid conflict, rejection, or hostility. Individuals may be unable to decode potentially supportive or pleasurable contexts and may approach most social encounters with highly amplified desires to impress others (Trower & Gilbert, 1989).

To return to our overview of the evolutionary perspective, we can suggest that the higher primates have innate abilities to send, evaluate, and be calmed by reassurance signals and to find co-operative/friendly behaviour positively reinforcing. These capacities, along with those of attachment, can be regarded as parts of a (social) safety system (Gilbert, 1989). Indeed, the more that individuals who co-operate with each other come to like each other, the more they may behave with attachment-like behaviour (Heard & Lake, 1986). The safety system works primarily through the positive reward areas, making attachments and friendships essentially pleasurable and positively motivating. Under threat, escape behaviour is likely to be exhibited towards those that are seen as supportive or from whom reassurance is sought, rather than producing dispersion.

If it is true that the defence and safety systems are utilising different brain structures, as seems likely, then conflict between approach and avoidance motives can be aroused. In our view, social anxiety arises in situations in which it is believed that one's self-presentation may be subject to attack or humiliation. In these circumstances, the individual may respond with either aggression or submissiveness. An understanding of this requires consideration of why the socially anxious find social situations threatening and, having done so, why they act submissively or withdraw. This exploration is the concern of the rest of this chapter.

The importance of display

Concerns about self-presentation or "display" form a crucial component of social anxiety (Schlenker & Leary, 1982). Furthermore, this self-presentation is focused on the image created in the eye of the observer (Trower et al., in press). We have stressed the point that the sexual selection strategies operate through display behaviour. It is our display behaviour that is paramount in social anxiety, in that the anxious person is concerned with what "the other" can see and how the other evaluates and will respond to what is seen. In human group contexts (e.g., the academic conference), dominance and competitive behaviour are not usually conducted with physical threats. Rather, the interest is to "spoil the display" of the other to make him or her appear stupid, silly, or incompetent. Any "attack" is therefore aimed at undermining confidence and reducing the attention that others may pay to an individual, in other words, to reduce the person's attractiveness to others as a social actor in that particular arena.

It is not surprising, therefore, that among the most stressful social events are those in which there could be or has been a "spoilt display". This has been studied by social psychologists (Goffman, 1963) and in the extreme constitutes the condition of stigma. In display behaviour, either intrasexual or intersexual strategic behaviour can be operative. To put this another way, we may become anxious because we feel unable to defend our status, related to intrasexual and dominance activity, or we may become anxious when we attempt to appear "attractive" to others, especially members of the opposite sex, and elicit positive (approach) behaviour from them (related to intersexual activity).

A positive (attractive or attracting) display, rather than threat, is the major strategy of intersexual behaviour, because, as we argued earlier, these displays are designed to attract mates towards the displayer. In humans, however, positive displays have other advantages. One advantage of a positive display is that it is able to direct positive attention to the self, called "positive attention-holding potential" (Gilbert, 1989). The self is seen as valued and desired. In these situations, one is able to attract potential mates, allies, and friends (or hold those one has), is allowed access to resources (e.g., successful students get to pursue advanced study), and gains prestige (Hill, 1984). That is, one gains access to resources both personal and material by being held "in high regard". Even in chimpanzees, high regard, in so far as this facilitates access to resources, is not dependent solely on aggressive potential (de Waal, 1988). Hence, when individuals are engaged with others in an essentially safety-conferring manner, they do not attempt to gain dominance by threat display, but rather by displaying that which has social attention-holding potential. They attempt (amongst other things) to display competency or attributes that others will find attractive. In this sense they gain status rather than dominance (Harper, 1985).

It is important that an individual engaging in positive display does not expect to be punished for such display, but to be reinforced by the target audience. The desired effect is acceptance, admiration, appreciation, or some positive recognition. It is, in this sense, a form of positive bestowing of value via the positive responses of the other. If this display provokes envy or is seen as a threat by the more dominant members, as may happen in those with type A personality (Price, 1982) or when young members of a profession are attempting to push for a paradigm shift, then hostility of some form may break out. At the very least, the dominant will begrudge the success of the younger and may try to spoil the younger's display and thereby undermine his or her self-presentation and hence attractiveness to others. This may be achieved with sarcasm or belittling comments, made either directly or behind his or her back, or by refusal to offer assistance. This situation is not difficult to detect, because the more dominant often forego rational debate and engage more in open hostility. In fact, self-handicapping, submissive gestures, and perhaps "false modesty" may be deliberate tactics to inhibit envious attacks. This may be especially so if one doubts one's ability to cope with such attacks.

The desire to be valued by one's colleagues introduces a complication, for now it may be that social anxiety can be induced in any situation that may invoke a negative reaction from another and hence potentially reduce a person's sense of attractiveness. Indeed, the feared response from the other need not be hostility as such. In fact, in our experience, patients are just as anxious about inducing disgust or contempt in others as they are about provoking aggression or envious attacks. That is, they may fear being devalued or being seen as unattractive, in some way, by others.

An example of this was provided by a socially anxious patient of ours who feared breaking out in heavy perspiration in company, such as in restaurants or trains. During therapy, he revealed that he thought other people would see him as different and possibly as having something contagious. He elaborated this by saying that he thought other people would be repelled by him. During therapy, it turned out that he had some minor deformities that he believed made him abnormal, and if these were revealed and seen by others, he would induce disgust and rejection responses from others. This anxiety was heightened in potentially sexual encounters.

We believe that the nature of the feared response from the other needs to studied in more detail. For example, it may be that the experience of feeling worthless relates to being seen as having very low rank. This appears to be associated with a lack of potency or power or positive attributes. In this situation the person may simply fear being ignored or regarded as a "nothing" or nonentity. This would go with loss of control over valued incentives. However, the construction of "badness" carries an idea of negative potency. If I am worthless, I am not worth bothering with, but if I am bad, then I may be subject to attack and being made an out-group member. Hence, we might be able to contrast those conditions in which a person evaluates a lack of potency or positive attributes with those conditions in which a person is seen as being someone to be positively rejected.

Evolution and mental mechanisms

So far, we have argued that by considering how conspecifics relate to each other, we can discern certain consistent properties of group structures and that these depend on underlying appraisal–response competencies. First, we looked at how the territorial species tend to exist in home-based territories that they must protect and defend. Second, are the agonic groups, which depend on individuals working out their relative rankings and co-ordinating their social behaviour accordingly. In these social structures, social anxiety is necessary to enable subordinates to express submissive behaviours to the more dominant. Third, we noted the evolution of hedonic groups. In these groups, individuals must be able to evaluate and form co-operative relations and bring agonistic encounters to a satisfactory resolution by reconciliation.

Is it necessary to understand these forms of breeding structures in phylogenetically ancient species and the appraisal-response systems that allow for their existence in order to understand social anxiety? We believe so, for a number of reasons. First, it has been the pressure of breeding that has led to the evolution of group-living social structures within which social behaviour has become so important. Indeed, it has been these breeding structures that have facilitated social behaviour and "society" as we understand it today. Second, much of human display behaviour has clear antecedents in other animals (Morris, 1977) – even the threat postural displays of the reptile have suggestive similarities to the human military goose step (MacLean, 1985). Third, evolution rarely throws anything away; rather, old ways are adapted to new ways and are not deleted. Nowhere does this seem more true than in the structures of the brain. Bailey puts it this way:

... we must acknowledge that our species possesses the neural hardware and many of the motivational-emotional "proclivities" ... of our reptilian ancestors, and, thus our drives, inner subjective feelings, fantasies, and thoughts are thoroughly conditioned by the emanations from the R-complex [the reptilian hindbrain of humans]. The reptilian carry-overs provide the automatic, compulsive urgency to much of human behavior, where free will steps aside and persons act as they have to act, often despising themselves in the process for their hatreds, prejudicies, compulsions, conformity, deceptiveness and guile. (Bailey, 1987, p. 63)

In other words, conscious intent may play but a small role in the way we act, especially in the face of perceived threat. Rather, in socially threatening situations we have innate tendencies to act, as did our animal ancestors, with mixtures of aggression, anxiety, submission, flight/ withdrawal, and so on. Another important aspect of the evolutionary perspective is that there is increasing evidence that the capacity to display and recognise emotions is innate. The most important source of this information is the face (Izard, 1977; Tomkins, 1981). The face is the most easily seen area for emotional display (Ohman, 1986), and facial expressions carry important meanings in various encounters. It seems reasonable to suggest that the emotions are so wired into facial motor systems because of the enormous importance of conspecific signalling in social behaviour (Gardner, 1988; see Castelfranchi & Poggi, this volume, for the signals that may be conveyed by blushing).

Finally, we should note that there is one further complication that we should introduce into our analysis. This concerns the fact that humans are able to perform in various contexts and to enact diverse roles (Gardner, 1988). We are able to elicit help/care from others, and we are able to offer care/help to others. We can develop co-operative relations with others and act in an essentially moral way by respecting others and their rights. It is unlikely that all these different ways of responding to the varied social contexts we inhabit can be understood as the products of a learning history that does not have some prepared basis to it. Furthermore, studies of brain-damaged people suggest that the competencies to understand and enact these roles are represented in different brain structures.

In fact, there has been growing recognition that the brain is a mixed modular system; that is, it appears to be organised in terms of a specialisation of appraisal–response competencies. Different brain areas do different jobs and are concerned with different motivational concerns. Ornstein (1986) has aptly referred to this as "multimind". Gilbert (1989) has pointed out that this aspect of brain organisation may be considered in terms of varied mentalities. For example, we have mentalities for evaluating friendship signals, for eliciting care, and for competitive signals. These mentalities are necessary to enact the varied social roles that are part of the human potential, such as helping others, co-operating with others, attracting potential partners, and so forth. Even though an individual may consciously desire to receive or send friendship signals (i.e., to act in a friendly role with conspecifics) and may "know" that a certain situation is not a competitive (agonistically derived ranking) situation, the particular mentality that is involved in evaluating ranking, and co-ordinating defensive responses (e.g., submission, blushing) may override these conscious desires.

This may be because the competitive-ranking mentality, which we have argued is one of the most primitive mentalities, is highly sensitised to responding to certain contexts as representing potential threats to the self. In this situation the output/behavioural options for dealing with conspecific threat (e.g., fight/flight, submission) are recruited into the person's expressive display. Efforts to keep action tendencies, such as blushing, hand tremors, sweating, and so forth, from being noticed may be the source of further threat evaluation. In other words, individuals monitor the types and degrees of threats arising in the social domain with the use of special-purpose mentalities. A more detailed consideration of this aspect and how different forms of evaluation relate to stimulus and outcome expectancies is available (Trower & Gilbert, 1989).

The self, the other, and context

In the first part of this chapter we have suggested that social anxiety is part of an evolved competency for recognising and coping with social threat and conflict. In humans, the source of this threat may relate to hostility, but probably more often to loss of value, positive attention holding, or attractiveness. We have shown how evolutionary processes have shaped the social organisations of groups and the display behaviours of individual members of those groups. This evolutionary approach, if substantiated by further research, may require a reappraisal of the social sciences, especially in regard to "the self", "the other", and the "social context". In the following sections we outline some principles in a first attempt at such a re-apprasial of these areas.

The self

We now wish to explore notions of self-knowledge. This is because most research into social anxiety has been concerned with self-presentation and self-image, these being essentially internal constructive processes. However, we would emphasise that the concept of self-processes does not liberate humans from their phylogenetic past. Rather, we suggest that the evolved phylogenetic structures that are present in the brain define the boundaries and typical forms for the construction of self-knowledge and self-expression. Our intent so far has been to highlight the evolution and preponderance of agonic (ways of evaluating ranking) styles of social relationships in many non-human animals, but also to highlight how in humans the capacity to make social arenas safe by the exchange of safety and reassurance signals is of paramount importance. Further, we wish to put the view that, for various reasons, social anxiety represents a loss of safety and an evaluation of loss of positive attention holding or attractiveness. This invokes the recruitment of a more primitive competitive mentality (power ranking) – a mentality that constructs the social arena in which the person is acting as one of potential threat to self-presentation and from which reassurance is not possible.

We have emphasised that humans are concerned not only to avoid provoking aggression with which they could not deal but also to avoid having their display behaviours destroyed by invoking disgust or contempt in others. Individuals may be fearful that if a display is scrutinised too closely, they might reveal undesired (or unattractive) aspects of themselves, leading others to experience disgust or contempt towards them. In this case, individuals perceive that they would lose friends or the opportunity to form attachments, because disgust is experienced as an emotion that is essentially distancing and involves "getting rid of".

We have argued that attention, appraisal, and response in the socially anxious are controlled by the defence system. Under normal circumstances, however, it is the positive reward and safety system that exerts primary control over social behaviour; for example, we are relatively optimistic about the effects of our display behaviours on others, and even if we do not do so well, we are able to elicit reassurance. However, the defence and safety systems may both be activated, as perhaps in public speaking, where we are both hopeful of making a good impression and fearful of not; hence, we are excited and have "butterflies".

Social anxiety, then, is significantly controlled by the defence system. This system evolved specifically to facilitate the recognition of threat and to coordinate defensive action. However, as we have argued, to activate the defence system within a social context, the individual has first to make some kind of comparative evaluation of self and other(s). Furthermore, one must determine that the other is (potentially) capable of inflicting some kind of damage on one's display behaviour. In other words, to suffer social anxiety one must evaluate the context of the social arena as one of potential conflict; that is, one's display behaviour is subject to negative evaluation, and hence social anxiety is sometimes called evaluation anxiety (Beck et al., 1985). This leads us to consider three main areas: the construction of the self, the construction of the other, and the evaluation of context.

Aspects of the self. The self is a hypothetical construct that, as Neisser (1988) points out, is multifaceted and full of apparent contradictions. It refers to different processes of knowledge organisation and different goals and motivations. It has been suggested elsewhere (Gilbert, 1989) that whereas all aspects of self-appraisal are essentially actively constructed, our ways of understanding and knowing ourselves are derived from knowledge stored in the various innate mentalities of human nature that have been developed and articulated by experience. For example, if during my early family life I have experienced relations as essentially competitive, hostile, or shaming, then into my construction of self comes knowledge of how I succeeded or coped with these relations. I am biologically predisposed to fight, submit, or withdraw when faced with a threat. Further, I may tend to construct interpersonal relations and construct my self-identity with the mentality that is most familiar to me. In other words, I may doubt my ability to direct positive attention to myself or believe that I can do so only with outstanding performances or displays.

We suggest that at least three forms of self-referent schemata are important in understanding social anxiety. The first relates to the private self that draws on internal sources of information about aspects, attributes, competencies, and qualities that are owned or believed to be part of the individual. These are essentially coded as "I am" beliefs, which may be positive ("I am intelligent, attractive, caring, etc.") or negative ("I am stupid, ugly, uncaring, etc."). The private self also has access to autobiographical information, that is, memories of good or traumatic events that occurred to the individual over the life cycle.

Schemata in the second set relate to the ideal self. This reflects the attributes or qualities the self would like to have or be able to display. These are coded as "I would like to be" ("I would like to be intelligent, attractive, caring, powerful, dominant, etc."). The ideal self is oriented to the future. Attributes for an ideal self may arise from social comparisons (Swallow & Kuiper, 1988). They reflect elements of modelling on valued others. They may also reflect a distance from how one would not like to be, or, as Ogilvie (1987) has termed it, the undesired self (weak, uncaring, ignorant, etc.).

Third, there are the schemata of the public or interpersonal self. Neisser (1988, p. 41) defines the interpersonal self as "the self as engaged in immediate unreflective social interaction with another person". The interpersonal self also reflects knowledge of the kinds of display behaviours that the person habitually adopts in interpersonal contexts. These, in turn, reflect beliefs about how one evaluates the social domain one inhabits, for example, expectations of how others will react to certain types of display behaviours. In a sense, the public/interpersonal self reflects those selections of attributes or possibilities encoded in the private self but displayed with the hope of positive social reinforcement. The interpersonal/public self is the domain of self-presentation.

In social anxiety, it is the self-presentation that is the focus of concern. Self-presentation is essentially related to display behaviour and an attempt at the projection of a valued identity. Baumeister (1982) has suggested that there are two main motives in self-presentation behaviour; the first relates to desires to please the target audience, and the second is to construct a public image as close to that of the ideal self as possible. These two goals may be in conflict, as in the person who wishes to regard himself or herself as assertive (ideal self) but fears that to act assertively would produce some kind of negative reaction in the target audience. Hence, as Baumeister put it,

another irony in the relationship between publicity and conformity is that although people apparently conform and yield to influence because of concern with the opinions of others, it is undesirable to be recognised by others as being conforming and yielding. (1982, p. 8)

Hence, though it may be the case that most people are motivated to conform to general social rules and social expectations because it is undesirable to gain the reputation of behaving inappropriately, "it is also undesirable, however, to build the reputation of yielding to changing, contradictory and arbitrary influences; such a reputation portrays one as weak, gullible, and unreliable" (Baumeister, 1982, p. 8).

Such considerations suggest that self-presentation involves a complex balancing act between the three sources of self-knowledge. Evidence to be discussed later suggests that socially anxious individuals are especially prone to suffer from heightened conflict between these sources of self-knowledge because they have high, excessively idealised self-standards and are, at the same time, inordinately sensitive to their social audiences.

Schlenker and Leary (1982, 1985), for example, are among a number of authors who have found that socially anxious individuals have unrealistically high self-standards. The socially anxious individual would seem to have a heightened desire to impress others as one of the domains of the ideal self. This may link with psychoanalytic concepts of narcissistic difficulties. These individuals are believed to have somewhat grandiose aspirations as part of their ideal self-presentations; yet they also suffer from a deep sense of inferiority and shame when these behaviours are carried out incompetently or when there is some form of censure or lack of admiration from their social audiences (Adler, 1986; Gilbert, 1989).

Evidence also suggests that the socially anxious are inordinately sensitive to the reactions of their social audiences. They are particularly attentive to the emotional displays of their audiences and are engaged in a constant search for social information, such as certain facial expressions (Ohman & Dimberg, 1984), that may indicate acceptance or censure of their display behaviours. Basically the socially anxious are more fearful of social evaluation (Trower & Gilbert, 1989) and, furthermore, are more likely to predict and recall negative appraisals from others, as compared with those who are not socially anxious (e.g., Carver & Scheier, 1981; Halford & Foddy, 1982; Lucock & Salkovskis, 1988; Mathews & Macleod, 1987).

The foregoing considerations suggest that there are difficulties in the construction of an ideal self, as well as the interpersonal/public self. But again, this is only part of the story, for the socially anxious are also concerned with concealment of those characteristics that would bring scorn or censure (i.e., that would make them appear unattractive to others). Hence, the socially anxious not only are concerned with projecting a highly idealised positive image but also fear revealing negative aspects of the private self. This brings us to the role of shame in social anxiety.

The role of shame. Shame has been the neglected area in the study of social anxiety, although Beck et al. (1985) regard shame as an important aspect of social anxiety. They also make the important point that anxiety is heightened before and during an encounter, whereas shame is heightened during and after an encounter. The experience of shame can produce significant rumination on a "spoilt identity" following the termination of social relations.

Shame is concerned with concealment of characteristics of the private self from public observation; it relates above all else to fear of exposure. Recently, increasing attention has been given to the phenomenology and experiences of shame (Lewis, 1987; Nathanson, 1987). Shame has often been compared with the experience of guilt. Although these emotions often go together and become fused, there are also differences that help to highlight the nature of shame.

Wicker, Payne, and Morgan (1983) asked 152 students to recall personal experiences of shame and guilt and rate them according to various characteristics. Overall, the differences between them were small, especially on aspects such as pain, tension, and arousal. Nevertheless, some interesting differences were found. Shame was related to feelings of inferiority and was regarded as the more overpowering and incapacitating emotion. Shame was associated with a sense of weakness and of being "smaller", with desires to hide and conceal the self. Shame was associated with confusion over how to act appropriately, a greater sense of being "under scrutiny", and greater self-focused attention (especially of physical sensations like blushing) and self-consciousness. Shame also tended to increase the desire to punish the other and seek revenge. In contrast, guilt motivates efforts at reparation. In shame, the other is seen as more powerful and as the cause of injury, whereas in guilt it is the self that has caused hurt.

The experience of shame, perhaps more than any other, captures the feeling and evaluation that others perceive the self as an object of disgust or contempt. Indeed, in those cases where shame is prominent, the person often will discuss the characteristics of the private self in terms of disgust. This is particularly true when the shame relates to some physical aspect. For example, victims of sexual abuse often make the evaluation that they have been "spoiled" and feel an inner sense of disgust with this spoiled identity. They also believe that if these facts became known about them, others would feel disgusted and view them as contemptible. Abuse is one of the most traumatic events one can experience, and individuals often try to conceal it (Jacobson & Richardson, 1987); yet such concealment can be the source of increased distress and pathological sequelae (Pennebaker & Beall, 1986).

Shame in relation to body shape, such as the feelings of being fat that are prominent among those with eating disorders (Silberstein, Striegel-Moore, & Rodin, 1987), and shame deriving from experiences of the private self also reflect the experience of disgust. A prominent concern here is how an individual attributes blame for traumatic events or aversive private experiences. Characterological self-blame, as opposed to behavioural self-blame, is more associated with shame (Hoblitzelle, 1987) and depression (Brewin, 1988). As yet we do not know if shame relates to fears of being made an outcast, but attributions that others will not share one's experiences and will behave with scorn if one reveals them do seem to provide one reason why depressed individuals do not risk gaining what could be consensus validation for their experiences. Moreover, they may experience themselves as being different from others (Brewin & Furnham, 1986). Also it may be that consensus validation bears some relationship to reassurance. The experience of revealing some aspect of the self and finding acceptance may act in a similar way as reassurance, in that it reduces arousal and facilitates more positive exploration following agonistic encounters. However, more research is needed on this general approach to psychopathology.

Lewis (1986) suggests that shame is related to a complex of affect-cognitive states that include embarrassment, humiliation, mortification, chagrin, disgrace, and shyness, where shyness is associated with the notion of "shying away" and avoidance. More research is needed on the relationships among these different experiences, but evidence does suggest that shame is indeed highly correlated with the affects suggested by Lewis (Hoblitzelle, 1987; Crozier, this volume).

In summary, we can say that the socially anxious person has an inordinate concern with pursuing an idealised self and fears social disapproval when this ideal is not attained, but is also concerned with the possibility of exposures that would provoke shame and the experience of a "spoilt identity" (Goffman, 1963).

It is therefore not surprising that the socially anxious closely monitor their own display behaviours and are especially sensitive to their own overt behaviours that might provoke any evaluation of weakness, inferiority, or disgust. As discussed elsewhere (Beck et al., 1985; Trower & Gilbert, 1989), this self-monitoring leads to a defensive "fear of fear" cycle. In other words, the individual fears the intrusion of unwanted overt behaviours into his or her display and self-presentation. These intrusions, which may arise from memories and knowledge stored in the private self that the person would rather keep private, can include hand tremors, loss of voice control, having the mind "go blank", sweating, needing to defecate or urinate, vomiting, and so forth. In essence, they are all symptoms of anxiety that relate to loss of bodily control. These intrusions into self-presentation become the focus of evaluation and self-monitoring because they are perceived to cause catastrophic loss of the pursued ideal self and to represent a spoiled identity.

It is as yet unknown how far these experiences relate to latent schemata of the private self-evaluation system. However, there is anecdotal evidence that would support such a proposition. Consider this extract from a therapy session:

> My therapist was asking me to describe an incident from the past week, when I had felt extremely uncomfortable at a social gathering. Rather than just asking me to describe it, as he normally did, however, he asked me to close my eyes and to attempt to imagine the situation as clearly and as vividly as possible. As I described the incident, he probed for images and feelings and helped me to relive the experience. The palms of my hands became sweaty, and I became aware of a choking sensation in my throat. I experienced that all-too-familiar feeling of panic and desperation that so often used to leave me feeling paralysed. *I had this image of myself as this pathetic little creature, worthy only of contempt.* As my therapist continued to probe, I was able to verbalise some painfully self critical thoughts. (Greenberg & Safran, 1987, pp. 5–6, italics added)

The other

It is common in clinical psychology and psychiatry to pursue investigations of "the individual with the symptoms", as if the source of a disorder lies totally within. However, as we have emphasised, humans have innate propensities to relate to others and to establish certain *kinds* of relationships, and social anxiety plays an important role in some of these kinds of relationships. It is therefore of some importance that the roles played by "the other" be considered when undertaking any analysis of social anxiety (for a different approach to the same issue, see Ingraham & Wright, 1987).

There are at least three ways in which the other can create or influence the circumstances in which social anxiety may be triggered. The first is through developmental processes by which individuals learn which aspects of their display behaviours are approved of or elicit punishment. Second, there are cultural attitudes and rules about social behaviour and display that represent the agonic style of social organisation; we refer to this as the "culture of command". Third, there are cultural and group aspects by which the group agrees to regard some actions or experiences of others as evidence of inferiority or as shameful. In other words, shame can be used purposefully and deliberately as a means of social control. We refer to this aspect as the manipulation of values.

Developmental issues. The first form of influence concerns "the other" in the role of parent or developmentally significant other. This influence is transmitted through the development of a child's self-esteem and general attitudes and expectations about life (Rohner, 1986). There are various ways in which experiences of early childhood can facilitate healthy self-esteem. Early research suggested that one aspect of self-esteem in children is self-liking. There is no doubt that the experience of being parented is crucial (Rohner, 1986). Children with high self-esteem have parents who are authoritative (in contrast to authoritarian) and are able to facilitate self-reliance, and yet set realistic limits and show warmth. Children with low self-esteem tend to have authoritarian parents who are poor or inconsistent at setting limits, are controlling, expect submissive behaviour from their children, and are less warm or empathic to their children (see Bee, 1985, for a review).

In fact, research has suggested that poor parental control and lack of warmth often are part of the history of many who suffer from various psychological difficulties, including social anxiety (Rohner, 1986; Bowlby, 1988). Of special interest is the capacity to provide reassurance, with physical comfort, following any agonistic encounter. Failure to do so, as is likely in the case of parents who are low in regard to warmth, may leave the child in a permanent state of fearful arousal, as appears to happen in chimpanzees (Goodall, 1975). We suggest that these early experiences lead to various negative evaluations in the private self. The private self operates primarily in an agonic and defensive way, with uncertainty of self-presentation and fears of being revealed as weak, inadequate, contemptible, or bad.

Kohut (1977) has pointed to an important developmental stage that he calls the exhibitionist stage. At this time, children are eager to display to significant others. For example, young children enjoy directing parental attention to their ability to perform somersaults or to newly acquired skills (e.g., "Look at me mummy, watch me do this"). The parent, by

positive mirroring and pride in the child (positive reinforcement), enables the child to internalise a positive sense of self in that the child is
optimistic about the positive reinforcement contingent on display behaviour. This means that many of the private self-constructs develop in
the safety system. Failures of display (e.g., mistakes and errors) are
handled compassionately and with reasssurance. This leads to the development of healthy and realistic self-esteem (see Kahn, 1985, for a
clear account of this process) and a generally positive internal private
self. It should also be considered that in so far as social anxiety can
relate to a fear of being perceived as unattractive, parenting may serve
the very important role of helping the child develop positive schemata of
the self. Indeed, in personality disorder, one of the commonest forms of
difficulty is that the person has very poorly formed positive schemata of
the self, and such patients often show a history of parental neglect
(Rohner, 1986).

   In the absence of positive mirroring and in presence of extensive
parental control, often maintained through threats and punishment, the
child learns that various aspects of his or her displays may provoke
punishment. Furthermore, negative labelling ("You are a stupid child")
leads to negative schemata being laid down as part of a private self that
is encoded in the defence system. Hence, the motivation to exhibit
self-competencies and be admired is heavily tainted with the fear of
being punished. Punishment may be avoided only if the performance is
perfect or of a very high standard. One's private self is therefore concerned with deciding which parts of the (private) self can be revealed,
which competencies or autobiographical details can be enacted or revealed, and which are to be hidden from view. Such an approach gives
some suggestions as to why the socially anxious set such high standards
and are inordinately concerned with the responses of others, as discussed
earlier.

   It is not possible here to review the work on developmental processes
as they pertain to social anxiety, and in any case research in this specific
area has been scant. Nevertheless, enough has been said to offer the
following hypotheses. As children mature, they learn the meaning (the
reward/safety or punishment/defensiveness valence) of their social behaviours. Those who grow in emotionally distant and controlling environments tend to develop self-constructs that recruit the competitive
schemata of the agonic mode. Hence, they are prone to judge the world
as populated with inferiors and superiors, and those who have power can
inflict injury on those who do not. They must either compete with others
or be ready to submit and withdraw. In some personality disorders,
these options – dominant-grandiosity or rage and shame-submission –
can oscillate with great intensity (Adler, 1986).

In other words, they come to see the world as essentially a competitive arena in which others can add to or subtract from their self-presentation. Their desire in display remains somewhat grandiose, as in the child's exhibitionist stage, because of unrealistic self-esteem (Kahn, 1985), and they often confuse admiration with love. Basically, then, as pointed out elsewhere (Gilbert, 1989; Trower & Gilbert, 1989), there is a failure regarding the maturity and development of the safety system. Much of the private self is deemed unsafe and should remain hidden. The results of this are that trust is difficult, and many pro-social contexts (e.g., going to a party) are seen as potential areas for humiliation from failed or incompetent displays, rather than as positively reinforcing opportunities.

In brief, then, the other, in the form of parents and other significant figures, must take some responsibility for how individuals come to use and develop their innate social competencies (e.g., competitive, co-operative, affectionate).

The culture of command. The second way in which the other can influence the circumstances that elicit social anxiety is via culture, by manipulation of the fact that people do have a desire to conform and please their social audiences (Baumeister, 1982) and to be compliant in certain social contexts. Many human and non-human social structures are organised around issues of power. Individuals often try to behave in such a way as to avoid attacks or rebukes from those seen as more powerful, by submitting and complying. Nowhere was this more forcefully demonstrated than in Milgram's experiments (1974) on obedience. When confronted with the choice of obeying or disobeying an experimenter, who could ask a confederate to deliver apparently painful or potentially lethal electric shocks, most subjects obeyed the request. This was in spite of personal distress, in some subjects, in carrying out the actions requested. Should we regard this compliance as a form of submissive social anxiety? We think so.

It would seem that the culture of command, with power invested in authority figures, remains a salient social organising process: Humans, like most animals, are fearful of disobeying those seen to be more powerful. Here lies one of the most problematic aspects of human behaviour; it facilitates destructive behaviour and inhibits moral behaviour (Hampden-Turner, 1970; Sabini & Silver, 1982).

The manipulation of values. The third way in which the other can influence the recruitment of social anxiety is by deliberately setting up a system of rules governing the expression of behaviour and ensuring, by the use of censure and scorn, that certain behaviours will not be displayed. The best examples of this are those social systems that implicitly or explicitly let it be known that personal distress itself is shameful. For example, in the helping professions, individuals who express personal distress in the form of anxiety or depression are prone to censure, sometimes to such an extent that an extra source of distress may arise from efforts to keep these personal experiences secret (Rippere & Williams, 1985).

This reveals the subtle, but often denied, tendency for those with psychological difficulties to be regarded as inferior or at least as unworthy of being vested with authority. As a result, some individuals struggle on for years, fearful that they may be discovered as incompetent, weak, or "of inferior quality". It is, however, important to note that although all cultures have various systems of rules, different cultures are, to some degree, free to choose their precise values. For example, in analogy with the preceding example, it should be recognised that in other cultures the experience of the personal suffering of the healer or shaman is taken as evidence of an ability to heal. Indeed, a struggle to overcome personal suffering may be expected of those who set themselves up as healers and is certainly not a mark of inferiority (Ellenberger, 1970).

Context

Having discussed the self, the other, and the roles and forms of interactions that can be played between them, we now turn attention to the evaluation of context. It is obvious that individuals vary in regard to the contexts that will provoke anxiety in them (Beck et al., 1985). Some feel confident at parties, provided that they do not have to eat in public. Others feel confident provided that they have ready access to a lavatory. Others feel confident if escape routes are open, but not if they are enclosed or trapped. Others are fearful of their display behaviour in general in any new context, and some become fearful only if called on to be the centre of attention, as in public speaking. Yet others are happy with members of the same gender, but are prone to shyness, embarrassment, or fear with members of the opposite sex. Hence, social anxiety must be understood in terms of its context and meaning.

One way of determining context is with the distinctions of intimate, personal, social, and public zones suggested by Hall (1979). Some individuals are confident in intimate one-to-one encounters and "deep" relationships, but become anxious in a larger, more public arena (Bryant & Trower, 1974). At the other end, some individuals are very confident when acting publicly, controlling others, and engaging in multiple superficial relations, often closely role- or work-prescribed; however, they may become particularly anxious when they are engaged in intimate relationships that may involve disclosure of fears, anxieties, and aspects of themselves that they would rather keep private. This appears a particular problem for type A men, who tend to use work as a way to avoid intimacy and the sharing of feelings (Price, 1982). There may, in fact, be a deep experience of shame involved in the recognition of intimate needs, and these may never be acknowledged. A patient or the patient's spouse may complain of an inability to show feelings. Compassion, love, and vulnerable desire may be viewed as anti-masculine or "wimpish".

Can these aspects be regarded as forms of social anxiety? We believe that they can. Somehow, however, our culture does not seem to regard such difficulties as worthy of scorn. Indeed, in spite of the very serious impoverishment of emotional life that type A behaviour can involve, the tendency for type A men to see others, especially their wives, as subordinates (Price, 1982), and the clear links between type A and narcissistic personality disorder (Gilbert, 1989), some men seem only too willing to admit to it. To call oneself type A seems almost an act of bravado by one who perceives the neglect of the emotional life that it involves as a positive trait. Here may be a mirror to our society and evidence that pathology is in the eye of the beholder – that cultural values are important determinants of what is regarded as pathological. Even a serious difficulty can be paraded as evidence of a positive self in a culture that is competitive and encourages its members to think in terms of winners and losers. The effects, both short-term and long-term, that these individuals may have on their intimates – their spouses and children – by their emotional unavailability may go relatively unnoticed.

It is also the case that the complexities of the social life that we now enjoy, as a result of technology and cultural change, represent major changes from those of hunter-gatherer societies from which we sprang. It was perhaps those early societies that best fitted our nature. Today, however, humans are called on to play numerous roles, to present themselves as competent in ever-changing arenas, where they may feel anything but competent. Furthermore, perhaps in response to this pressure and/or as a result of evolution, humans tend to find it easy to form out-groups and in-groups; in lay terms, we are "cliquey". In primitive societies it was usual for individuals to grow in relatively small bands, and transitions from one group to another usually were infrequent or were clearly prescribed (e.g., initiation rituals into adulthood). Growing up was not a problem of continually meeting large numbers of individuals and impressing them (often in terms defined differently with each new group), but of finding ways to live harmoniously with a small number of familiars. It is not surprising that social anxiety is a condition of our age.

Hence, when it comes to considering context from an evolutionary point of view, it is important to consider how entry into the technological age has greatly changed the contexts of social life. It may be that the hedonic, co-operative life style flourishes only under certain ecological conditions, and when those change, as they have in recent times, the evolved propensities for hedonic life are significantly compromised.

Conclusion

In this chapter we have cast a wide net, at times speculatively. We have suggested that humans are animals whose social behaviours have evolved out of adaptations to breeding structures. Successful breeding requires two skills: the ability to gain and hold resources in competition with others and the ability to present oneself as attractive to potential mates and, in certain species, allies and friends. We have outlined two basic forms of social organisation in group-living animals: a hierarchical and ranked system, called the agonic mode, and a system derived from mutual dependence and reassurance, called the hedonic mode. Although this runs the risk of being a gross oversimplification, nevertheless it provides at least a beginning towards exploration into the evolutionary mechanisms of social anxiety. We have also suggested that our abilities to be able to anticipate and evaluate social signals and organise our social behaviours are results of innate competencies for appraisal and response.

Based on these distinctions, we have attempted to outline how social anxiety may represent a failure of reassurance: The person operates (at least in some contexts) with a predominantly competitive but defensive mentality. We have explored some possible reasons why some individuals may fail to feel safe with others (e.g., developmental factors, the context). Furthermore, some individuals may become anxious only if they believe that relationships are likely to switch to a more agonic form. In these individuals, there may be excessive effort to keep relations friendly in order to maintain the hedonic mode. Unfortunately, in doing so they may run the risk of behaving submissively. The degree to which the socially anxious confuse friendly with submissive responses requires further research. We have also suggested that in the hedonic mode, anxiety may arise from fear of being seen as not having value or positive attributes, which makes one unattractive to others; whereas in the agonic mode, the fear may be of invoking aversive (e.g., conflicts that one may lose) reactions from others.

We have argued that social anxiety can take many forms and cannot be understood as something that is only a characteristic or "disorder" of the individual in isolation from social interaction and the social context. An individual comes to any situation with a history that has been shaped by the actions of others. Furthermore, individuals find themselves embedded in a culture that positively affirms some experiences and behaviours and scorns others. Social anxiety may be one factor in our predisposition to act cruelly to our fellow human beings in part because of our fear of authority and need for approval. These approving and value-bestowing audiences are themselves not socially decontextualised beings, but are the conveyors of the values of the culture they inhabit (Sampson, 1988).

Social anxiety may show itself in many areas of life, ranging from the fear of expressing our individuality and making bids for resources and the attention of others with whom we may be in competition, to the way we try to present ourselves as attractive to others. But the study of social anxiety provides more than an important insight into personal suffering. Social anxiety may also be apparent in the fear of acting morally, the fear of disobeying, shown in part in the preparedness to harm others, the fear of being shamed, and the avoidance of the truly social and compassionate life that is capable of seeking, finding, and giving reassurance.

REFERENCES

Adler, G. (1986). Psychotherapy of the narcissistic personality disorder patient: Two contrasting approaches. *American Journal of Psychiatry, 143*, 430–436.

Alden, L., & Cappe, R. (1981). Nonassertiveness: Skill deficit or selective self-evaluation? *Behavior Therapy, 12*, 107–114.

Alden, L., & Safran, J. (1978). Irrational beliefs and nonassertive behavior. *Cognitive Therapy and Research, 2*, 357–364.

Argyle, M. (1987). *The psychology of happiness.* London: Methuen.

Bailey, K. (1987). *Human paleopsychology: Applications to aggression and pathological processes.* Hillsdale, NJ: Lawrence Erlbaum.

Baumeister, R. F. (1982). A self-presentational view of social phenomena. *Psychological Bulletin, 91*, 3–26.

Beck, A. T., Emery, G., & Greenberg, R. (1985). *Anxiety disorders and phobias: A cognitive perspective.* New York: Basic Books.

Bee, H. (1985). *The developing child* (4th ed.). New York: Harper & Row.

Bowlby, J. (1988). Developmental psychiatry comes of age. *American Journal of Psychiatry, 145*, 1–10.

Brewin, C. R. (1988). *Cognitive foundations of clinical psychology.* Hove, Sussex: Lawrence Erlbaum.

Brewin, C. R., & Furnham, A. (1986). Attributional versus preattributional variables in self-esteem and depression. *Journal of Personality and Social Psychology, 50*, 1013–1020.

Bryant, B. M., & Trower, P. (1974). Social difficulty in a student sample. *British Journal of Educational Psychology, 44*, 13–21.

Buss, D. M. (1987). Sex differences in human mate selection criteria: An evolutionary approach. In C. Crawford, M. Smith, & D. Kerbs (Eds.), *Sociobiol-*

ogy and psychology: Ideas, issues, and applications (pp. 335–351). Hillsdale, NJ: Lawrence Erlbaum.

Buss, D. M. (1988). The evolution of human intrasexual competition: Tactics of mate attraction. *Journal of Personality and Social Psychology, 54*, 616–628.

Carver, C. S., & Scheier, M. F. (1981). Self-consciousness and reactance. *Journal of Research in Personality, 15*, 16–29.

Chance, M. R. A. (1980). An ethological assessment of emotion. In R. Plutchik & H. Kellerman (Eds.), *Emotion: Theory, research and experience* (Vol. 1, pp. 81–111). New York: Academic Press.

Chance, M. R. A. (1984). Biological systems synthesis of mentality and the nature of the two modes of mental operation: Hedonic and agonic. *Man–Environment Systems, 14*, 143–157.

Chance, M. R. A. (1988). Introduction. In M. R. A. Chance (Ed.), *Social fabrics of the mind* (pp. 1–35). Hove, Sussex: Lawrence Erlbaum.

Crook, J. H. (1980). *The evolution of human consciousness.* Oxford: Clarendon Press.

Darwin, C. (1871). *The descent of man and selection in relation to sex.* London: Murray.

de Waal, F. (1988). The reconciled hierarchy. In M. R. A. Chance (Ed.), *Social fabrics of the mind* (pp. 105–136). Hove, Sussex: Lawrence Erlbaum.

Dunbar, R. I. M. (1988). *Primate social systems.* London: Croom Helm.

Ellenberger, H. F. (1970). *The discovery of the unconscious: The history of and evolution of dynamic psychiatry.* New York: Basic Books.

Forrest, M. S., & Hokanson, J. E. (1975). Depression and autonomic arousal reduction accompanying self-punitive behavior. *Journal of Abnormal Psychology, 84*, 346–357.

Gardner, R. (1982). Mechanisms in manic-depressive disorder: An evolutionary approach. *Archives of General Psychiatry, 39*, 1436–1441.

Gardner, R. (1988). Psychiatric syndromes as infrastructure for intra-specific communication. In M. R. A. Chance (Ed.), *Social fabrics of the mind* (pp. 197–225). Hove, Sussex: Lawrence Erlbaum.

Gilbert, P. (1984). *Depression: From psychology to brain state.* Hillsdale, NJ: Lawrence Erlbaum.

Gilbert, P. (1988). Psychobiological interaction in depression. In S. Fisher & J. Reason (Eds.), *Handbook of life stress, cognition and health* (pp. 559–579). Chichester, Sussex: Wiley.

Gilbert, P. (1989). *Human nature and suffering.* Hove, Sussex: Lawrence Erlbaum.

Glasgow, R., & Arkowitz, H. (1975). The behavioral assessment of male and female social competence in dyadic heterosexual interactions. *Behavior Therapy, 6*, 488–498.

Goffman, E. (1963). *Stigma: Notes on the management of spoiled identity.* Englewood Cliffs, NJ: Prentice-Hall.

Goodall, J. V. (1975). The chimpanzee, In J. V. Goodall (Ed.), *The quest for man* (pp. 131–170). London: Phaidon Press.

Gray, J. A. (1971). *The psychology of fear and stress.* New York: McGraw-Hill.

Gray, J. A. (1985). Issues in the neuropsychology of anxiety. In A. H. Tuma & J. D. Maser (Eds.), *Anxiety and anxiety disorders* (pp. 5–25). Hillsdale, NJ: Lawrence Erlbaum.

Greenberg, L. S., & Safran, J. D. (1987). *Emotion and psychotherapy*. New York: Guilford Press.

Halford, K., & Foddy, M. (1982). Cognitive and social skills correlates of social anxiety. *British Journal of Clinical Psychology, 21*, 17–28.

Hall, E. T. (1979). Proxemics. In S. Weitz (Ed.), *Nonverbal communication* (2nd ed., pp. 293–312). Oxford University Press.

Hampden-Turner, C. (1970). *Radical man*. London: Duckworth.

Harper, R. C. (1985). Power, dominance and nonverbal communication. In S. C. Ellyson & J. F. Dovidio (Eds.), *Power, dominance and nonverbal behavior* (pp. 29–48). New York: Springer-Verlag.

Heard, D. H., & Lake, B. (1986). The attachment dynamic in adult life. *British Journal of Psychiatry, 149*, 430–438.

Henry, J. P., & Stephens, P. M. (1977). *Stress, health and the social environment*. New York: Springer-Verlag.

Hill, J. (1984). Human altruism and sociocultural fitness. *Journal of Social and Biological Structures, 7*, 17–35.

Hinde, R. A. (1982). *Ethology*. London: Fontana.

Hoblitzelle, W. (1987). Differentiating and measuring shame and guilt: The relation between shame and depression. In H. B. Lewis (Ed.), *The role of shame in symptom formation* (pp. 207–235). Hillsdale, NJ: Lawrence Erlbaum.

Ingraham, L. J., & Wright, T. L. (1987). A social relations model test of Sullivan's anxiety hypothesis. *Journal of Personality and Social Psychology, 52*, 1212–1218.

Izard, C. E. (1977). *Human emotions*. New York: Plenum Press.

Jacobson, A., & Richardson, B. (1987). Assault experiences of 100 psychiatric inpatients: Evidence of the need for routine inquiry. *American Journal of Psychiatry, 144*, 908–913.

Kahn, E. (1985). Heinz Kohut and Carl Rogers: A timely comparison. *American Psychologist, 40*, 363–381.

Kohut, H. (1977). *The restoration of the self*. New York: Karger.

Leary, T. (1957). *Interpersonal diagnosis of personality*. New York: Ronald Press.

Leventhal, H., & Scherer, K. (1987). The relationship of emotion to cognition: A functional approach to a semantic controversy. *Cognition and Emotion, 1*, 3–28.

Lewis, H. B. (1986). The role of shame in depression. In M. Rutter, C. E. Izard, & P. B. Read (Eds.), *Depression in young people* (pp. 325–339). New York: Guilford Press.

Lewis, H. B. (Ed.). (1987). *The role of shame in symptom formation*. Hillsdale, NJ: Lawrence Erlbaum.

Lucock, M. P., & Salkovskis, P. M. (1988). Cognitive factors in social anxiety and its treatment. *Behaviour Research and Therapy, 26*, 297–302.

McClelland, D. C. (1985). *Human motivation*. Dallas: Scott, Foresman.

MacLean, P. (1985). Brain evolution relating to family, play and the separation call. *Archives of General Psychiatry, 42*, 405–417.

Marks, I. M. (1987). *Fears, phobias and rituals: Panic, anxiety and their disorders*. Oxford University Press.

Mathews, A., & Macleod, C. (1987). An information-processing approach to anxiety. *Journal of Cognitive Psychotherapy, 1,* 105–115.

Milgram, S. (1974). *Obedience to authority.* New York: Harper & Row.

Morris, D. (1977). *Manwatching: A field guide to human behaviour.* London: Triad Granada.

Nathanson, D. L. (Ed.). (1987). *The many faces of shame.* New York: Guilford Press.

Neisser, U. (1988). Five kinds of self-knowledge. *Philosophical Psychology, 1,* 35–59.

Ogilvie, D. M. (1987). The undesired self: A neglected variable in personality research. *Journal of Personality and Social Psychology, 52,* 379–385.

Ohman, A. (1986). Face the beast and fear the face: Animal and social fears as prototypes for evolutionary analysis of emotion. *Psychophysiology, 23,* 123–145.

Ohman, A., & Dimberg, U. (1984). An evolutionary perspective on social behavior. In W. M. Waid (Ed.), *Sociophysiology* (pp. 47–86). New York: Springer-Verlag.

Ornstein, R. (1986). *Multimind: A new way of looking at human behavior.* London: Macmillan.

Parker, G. A. (1974). Assessment strategy and the evolution of fighting behaviour. *Journal of Theoretical Biology, 47,* 223–243.

Pennebaker, J. W., & Becall, S. K. (1986). Confronting a traumatic event: Toward an understanding of inhibition and disease. *Journal of Abnormal Psychology, 95,* 274–287.

Power, M. (1988). The cohesive foragers. In M. R. A. Chance (Ed.), *Social fabrics of the mind* (pp. 75–103). Hove, Sussex: Lawrence Erlbaum.

Price, J. S. (1988). Alternative channels for negotiating asymmetry in social relationships. In M. R. A. Chance (Ed.), *Social fabrics of the mind* (pp. 157–195). Hove, Sussex: Lawrence Erlbaum.

Price, J. S., & Sloman, L. (1987). Depression as yielding behavior: An animal model based on Schjelderup-Ebb's pecking order. *Ethology and Sociobiology, 8,* 85–98.

Price, V. A. (1982). *Type A behavior pattern: A model for research and practice.* New York: Academic Press.

Rippere, V., & Williams, R. (1985). *Wounded healers: Mental health workers' experiences of depression.* Chichester, Sussex: Wiley.

Rohner, R. P. (1986). *The warmth dimension: Foundations of parental acceptance-rejection theory.* Beverly Hills, CA: Sage.

Sabini, J., & Silver, M. (1982). *The moralities of everyday life.* Oxford University Press.

Sampson, E. E. (1988). The debate in individualism: Indigenous psychologies of the individual and their role in personal and societal functioning. *American Psychologist, 43,* 15–22.

Schlenker, B. R., & Leary, M. R. (1982). Social anxiety and self-presentation: A conceptual model. *Psychological Bulletin, 92,* 641–669.

Schlenker, B. R., & Leary, M. R. (1985). Social anxiety and communication about the self. *Journal of Language and Social Psychology, 4,* 171–192.

Schwartz, R. M. & Gottman, J. M. (1976). Toward a task analysis of assertive behavior. *Journal of Consulting and Clinical Psychology, 44,* 910–920.

Seligman, M. P. E. (1971). Phobias and preparedness. *Behavior Therapy, 2,* 307–320.

Silberstein, L. R., Striegel-Moore, R. H., & Rodin, J. (1987). Feeling fat: A woman's shame. In H. B. Lewis (Ed.), *The role of shame in symptom formation* (pp. 89–108). Hillsdale, NJ: Lawrence Erlbaum.

Sutton-Simon, K., & Goldfried, M. R. (1979). Faulty thinking patterns in two types of anxiety. *Cognitive Theory and Research, 3,* 193–203.

Swallow, S. R., & Kuiper, N. A. (1988). Social comparison and negative self-evaluation: An application to depression. *Clinical Psychology Review, 8,* 55–76.

Tomkins, S. S. (1981). The quest for primary motives. *Journal of Personality and Social Psychology, 41,* 306–329.

Trower, P., & Gilbert, P. (1989). New theoretical conceptions of social phobia. *Clinical Psychology Reviews, 9,* 19–35.

Trower, P. Gilbert, P., & Sherling, G. (in press). Social anxiety, evolution and self-presentation: An interdisciplinary approach. In H. Leitenberg (Ed.), *Handbook of social anxiety.* New York: Plenum Press.

Vitkus, J., & Horowitz, L. M. (1987). Poor social performance of lonely people: Lacking a skill or adopting a role? *Journal of Personality and Social Psychology, 57,* 1266–1273.

Wicker, F. W., Payne, G. C., & Morgan, R. D. (1983). Participant descriptions of guilt and shame. *Motivation and Emotion, 7,* 25–39.

PART II

An emphasis upon embarrassment

6

Embarrassment:
A conceptual analysis

ROM HARRÉ

Introduction

The study of embarrassment may seem a small and insignificant enterprise, and yet it raises some important psychological, moral, and philosophical issues. It turns, in part, on the nature of the human self and its relation to the fact of embodiment. Embarrassment often is a very bodily emotion. This is not only through the emphasis on the body's presence on occasions of embarrassment but also through the way that my personal presence is mediated to others by my visible, audible, tangible, tastable, and smellable body. In our culture, smell and taste are not usually signs of the tangible presence of bodies. For us, it is the fact that I can be looked at, that the lumpish presence of my body can never be denied when I am in company, that means that I can hardly achieve presence without vulnerability. Hence the importance of masks, burkhas, cloaks, and so on in the achievement of presence without the chance of embarrassment. Where would a Mozart opera be without them?

But embarrassment is also an emotion characteristic of situations in which personal conduct becomes an object of a public consideration and judgement of which the actor is either aware or believes himself or herself to be aware. I hope to be able to show through the study of embarrassment how conduct and personal appearance are linked through the grounding of rules and conventions of propriety in conceptions of personal honour. This should provide a general account of the emotions of self-attention that will transcend the enormous variety of kinds of conducts and bodily exposures that are locally taken to be discrediting.

However, I want to go further, to suggest that in the study of this apparently minor emotion we can find indications of profound and widespread changes in the basis of social order. It is commonplace to say that shame is a form of social control. But I believe that shame is everywhere giving place to embarrassment as the major affective instrument of conformity. In the shift from shame to embarrassment we see a sign of the widespread recognition of the conventionality (and hence relativity) of morality and of the triviality of breaches. At the same time, embarrassment is shifting in focus from bodily disclosures to conduct, and this, I hope to show, is indicative of changing social attitudes towards women and the social location of women.

To get clear about the concept of embarrassment will call for a quite modest application of the techniques of philosophical analysis. Apart from the grand themes I have touched on, such studies have a more practical value. Embarrassment can trouble people; indeed, it can become destructive and even pathological. Clarity in concepts may have a role to play in the ordinary decent business of improving the quality of human life. There are complexities in the "logic" of the concept, complexities that illustrate a general point about the nature of emotions, a point of some importance in the practical applications of an analysis such as I propose. Emotions are not just bodily perturbations. Embarrassment is not just blushing and squirming. It is a particular case of the interplay among social conventions, moral judgements, and bodily reactions. The analysis will enable us to juxtapose conventions governing bodily exposure and those concerning character manifestations within the same conceptual framework and to see how they are sometimes psychologically equivalent. The distribution of credit, however, follows crooked paths. We are embarrassed by public attention to those matters that are creditable to us as well as those that are discreditable. It has often been remarked that a display of embarrassment, and of its more potent kin, shame, may itself be creditable and even be prescribed. It may be necessary to remind someone that one need not always blush for one's blushes.

I want to argue that there has been a shift away from and then back towards a Victorian relation between displays of bodily parts and attributes and embarrassment. The characterological importance of concealment of the sexual parts has declined remarkably (more particularly in Europe than in the United States), while the significance of the signs of careful bodily cultivation for character attributions has been enormously amplified. In these Jane Fonda days an excessively flabby and ill-kept body is an object of embarrassment (and perhaps shame), both to its possessor and to those who might be unfortunate enough to catch a glimpse of it. Jane and her like have taught us to tie body and character together in an almost Victorian way. Though the content is vastly different, the underlying structure is similar to the self-attentive bodily emotions of the Victorians. Something bodily serves as a public index of character.

Some classical accounts of the emotions of discredit

Shame has attracted much more attention from philosophers and psychologists than has embarrassment. Both are occasioned by painful public attention to something about ourselves and are manifested in similar displays. A brief look at some of the treatments of shame will help to clarify the grammar of embarrassment while leaving open the question how they are to be differentiated.

In the *Nicomachean Ethics* (1128b) Aristotle defines "shame" as a kind of "fear of disrepute [which] produces an effect similar to that produced by fear of danger; for people who feel disgraced [that is, think themselves disgraced] blush, and those who fear death turn pale". It is "in a sense a bodily condition" and so a passion.

Aristotle remarks on the "double ought" involved, in that we "praise young people who are prone to that passion". His more detailed treatment in the *Rhetoric* (Bk II, 1383b–1385a) lists many bad actions that can be sources of shame, but does not mention immodest appearance. In the *Rhetoric* there are three nice additions to be *Nicomachean* definition. Aristotle observes that it is the disgrace, not the consequences of the disgrace, from which we shrink, that the others whose opinions of our actions are germane to our feelings are those whose opinions we respect, and that when we are ashamed for others, they are people socially linked to us in some way.

Aristotle mentions two kinds of infractions: serious transgressions, such as fleeing from the battlefield, about which one would be rather more than embarrassed, and the merely socially tiresome, such as boastfulness.

One is tempted to think of shame at one pole of a continuum, with embarrassment at the other. That would imply that embarrassment is just a species of shame, the shame we feel when we notice that some relatively trivial transgression is publicly noticed. Though this feature does serve to mark one dimension of difference between them, two other important differences will emerge. Parenthetically, it is worth reminding ourselves that in ancient Greek there was no word for our most common sense of embarrassment, namely, that which the dictionary calls "constrained feeling or manner arising from bashfulness or timidity". The ancient Greek *aporein* picks up only that sense of embarrassment that the *Oxford English Dictionary* defines as "perplexity or hesitation". It is as if the gap between morality and nature, which we fill with convention, did not exist for the Greeks.

For the most recent important discussion of shame, I turn to Sartre's writings. So far as I know, Sartre nowhere discusses embarrassment (the French *rougissement*). The French language, like Spanish, does not mark a distinction between blushing and embarrassment. Embarrassment as a public display of confusion is a different concept. Ricks (1974) suggests, on the basis of literary evidence, that the concept of embarrassment as such has no application to French life. Be that as it may, Sartre's interest is in shame, particularly in the structure of the interpersonal relations within which shame occurs. He pays no attention to the modes by which shame is displayed. There are two structural conditions for shame:

1. "... shame is shame of oneself *before the other*. These structures are inseparable" (Sartre, 1943/1956, p. 303). The inseparable structures are the reflexive and the interpersonal.
2. The former is modelled on the sufferer's beliefs about the latter. "The experience of my gesture as vulgar is to borrow the other's judgement of it" (Sartre, 1943/1956, p. 303).

Sartre is unclear about shame itself. Is the experience referred to in the second condition the expression of shame? Or is the experience made possible by the satisfaction of conditions 1 and 2 the occasion for another experience, the experience of shame? I think it must be the latter.

The ubiquity of "the Look", actual or potential, in which I see "the Other" seeing me as a person, necessitated by its engagement in every relationship in which I take myself to be in human company, would seem to entail that every encounter is potentially an occasion for shame. Not so – Sartre is at pains to implicate the same sociopsychological *structure* in the genesis of a great many other emotions. The structure *seems* to present me with an opportunity for an intimacy with another, by way of grasping the world, including myself, as part of it, from another point of view. But the bulk of Sartre's famous text is devoted to showing that all attempts to realise the common structure in this way are doomed to failure. "I am guilty first when beneath the Other's look I experience my alienation and nakedness". In a very long subsequent passage, this tantalising combination of the apparent opportunity offered by the realisation of the existence of the basic structure and my inevitable failure to make use of it in the way I and everyone else wants is argued to be the source of hate.

Sartre's analysis supports a point I was at pains to develop in *Personal being* (Harré, 1983): that the reflexivity upon which the entire range of self-regarding emotions depends is not an external relation between two ontologically distinct beings, say "I" and "me", but rather a bringing together of two points of view, mine and my conception of the points of view of other people. Or, to put the matter in Wittgenstein's way, the duality is grammatical, not ontological.

Embarrassment proper

Starting from the blush as an expression common to this cluster of emotions, Darwin seems to be concerned more with embarrassment than with shame. In contrast to Aristotle's emphasis on conduct, it is bodily presence and physical appearance that Darwin mostly finds salient in the occasions for blushing. In *The Expression of the Emotions in Man and Animals* (Darwin, 1872/1955, p. 325) Darwin remarks that "it is not the simple act of reflecting on our own appearance, but the thinking of what others think of us, which excites the blush" (the Sartrean point). Whereas Aristotle focuses on demeaning actions as sources of shame, Darwin is mostly concerned with demeaning appearances as sources of embarrassment, though he sometimes speaks of "appearances and conduct" in the same breath. The apparent relative salience of bodily presence and appearance to embarrassment rather than conduct might be thought to give us a second dimension for distinguishing embarrassment from shame. But this observation draws attention to one of the analytical problems in understanding embarrassment. One can see how honour is tied up with the conduct, but how is the *value* of the self tied up with appearance? Darwin does not touch on this question at all. It will become clear only when we see embarrassment in the context of virtue. However, it is not, in Darwin's account, an actual unfavourable assessment of our appearance or conduct that is at the root of embarrassment, but the dread of the possibility of it. An adolescent does not blush because anyone has explicitly remarked on his or her bodily presence, only at the thought that that presence might be unfavourably received.

These considerations suggest that embarrassment and shame are not neatly distinguishable by reference to discreditable bodily appearances, on the one hand, and disgraceful actions, on the other. Bodily shame, on this view, will occur when a wrong appearance in the eyes of others is so tied to personal moral standing that it casts doubt on the virtues of the person involved; that is, the others take exposure to be a sign of defective moral character. So if I become aware of (or merely believe in) their taking up such an attitude towards my delict, shame must follow, if I am of good character. Of course, if I am a "brazen hussy" or an "arrogant son of a bitch", it will not. So my lack of shame is a second dereliction.

The tie between appearance and self has to do with intentions and the attribution of fault. Making a distinction between embarrassment and shame in this way needs rather careful statement. In many cases of inadvertent breach, neither the action nor the breaching of the convention is intended. Sometimes we intend an action but do not realise that it is in breach of a convention. But in cases where the action or disclosure is shameful, the action is deliberate and the breach not accidental. (There are hard cases where the fault is grave, but the breach unintended.) But we can reasonably be expected to realise in the moment of fleeing from the battlefield that our flight is disgraceful.

Errol Bedford (1956–7) has a nice, sharp example: "Davies was said to be 'to his mild embarrassment' the original of Peter Pan". He could hardly be said to have been ashamed of this role, whatever his feelings and overt behaviour. The concept of "shame" includes fault, and it was not his fault that Barrie picked him as a model. And we have also noticed that not to display shame at a fault is also a fault, just as not to be embarrassed at an infraction of conventions is also an infraction of conventions.

But there are contexts in with the shame or embarrassment one feels is tied in with the delicts of others. Armon-Jones (1986) makes the point that whereas she would feel ashamed if she saw a manifest Englishman dead drunk in the streets of Paris, she would only be embarrassed by the similar condition of a Frenchman. One might add that in Peking, both delicts would be occasions for shame, because the relevant moral community would no doubt be European. The shame arises through the manifest fact that Ms. Armon-Jones and the drunk belong to some relevant common category. It is as a member of that category that she is shamed, whatever the relevant category might be. Again, Aristotle clearly anticipated this refinement in his remarks on vicarious shame.

There are some reflective emotions in other cultures that are startlingly general. Spaniards place great emphasis on *vergüenza ajena*, an intense "shame/embarrassment" brought on by the foolish or self-demeaning behaviour of a stranger. It is the common membership of the human race that creates the moral community. Translating "embarrassed" into Spanish is not easy. *Embarazada* means "pregnant", and the Spanish language tends to favour the flustered behaviour of the embarrassed rather than their blushes as the core semantic concept. For instance, the semantic range covers *desconcertar* (to be disconcerted), *aturrullar* (to be bewildered), *avergonzar* (to be shamed), and *estorbar* (annoying). In Spain, one might guess, embarrassment is not a separate category from shame, because, through *dignidad*, character is always "on the line".

We are now in a position to make a tentative distinction between shame and embarrassment. Two axes of difference will be needed, and each represents a continuum of distinction. The "space" of shame/embarrassment might look as in Figure 6.1. There are many more locations in the space than those I have singled out, and for which we have no specific descriptive terms. Nevertheless, I am fairly confident that they represent psychologically real emotional phenomena. We can relate what is proper more tightly to circumstances by turning to the

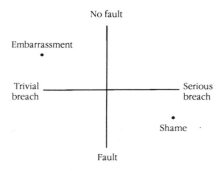

Figure 6.1. The "space" of shame/embarrassment.

ever-popular dramaturgical model, the analogy of life to the stage. This opens up the idea of seeing a strip of life as a *performance* put on before others. And we can perform well or ill, regardless of what it is we are actually doing. Drawing on Goffman's famous essay on face work (1967), Silver, Sabini, and Parrott (1987, p. 58) propose the following definition: "Embarrassment is the flustering caused by the perception that a flubbed [botched, fumbled] performance, a working consensus of identities, cannot, or in any event will not, be repaired in time".

Two additions to the Aristotle–Darwin treatment, summarised in the two-dimensional space in Figure 6.1, are implied. Infractions of social conventions cannot, in general, be ignored. They must be remedied. Goffman suggests that remedies are needed to dispel the threat of an inference to the conclusion that the participants (and sometimes even the onlookers) are not committed to the local conventions, either though vice or ignorance. One shows that one is the right sort of person, the kind of person with whom others might wish to consort, by putting right one's own infractions and tactfully assisting others to do the same with theirs. Silver et al. (1987) suggest that while the mutual work of face-saving proceeds smoothly, embarrassment does not occur. So it is not the mere fact of failing to maintain the conventions that occasions embarrassment.

Time is required to get remedial work under way. An infraction may be forced into public notice just because there has not been time to do the remedial work, be it verbal or practical. The 'working consensus' of the foregoing definition must be about the virtues, qualities, and characters of the persons involved. Thus, what is at issue because it is at risk is an unfavourable assessment of character. Unless the skirt is pulled down in time, or the self-deprecatory remark is dropped in fairly soon after the public congratulation, one runs the risk of being taken to be a "shameless floozy", a "brash oaf", and so on, contrary to the working consensus as to the kind of persons we are and consort with. So, in the end, embarrassment has little to do with what has been done or not done, in itself, but with how what is done or not done about what has been done provides evidence for assessments of character.

This point is well taken, but Silver and associates overlook the "double ought" that governs displays of embarrassment. The display may, *in itself*, be sufficient remedy for the infraction, supplying evidence in default of explicit face work to support an attribution of good character and virtue. One is not embarrassed because the remedy cannot be carried out in time; being embarrassed *is* the remedy. However, incompetence (the demeaning attribution occasioned by a botched performance) is an example of the kind of milder dereliction that we have been looking for to open up a gap between embarrassment and shame on the dimension of seriousness. One is more than merely embarrassed when caught out in a deliberately intended and morally debased action. Yet one is less than ashamed when one arrives at a formal dinner in tee shirt and jeans.

But the restriction of occasions of embarrassment to the public display of incompetence in a noticeably botched performance without public remedy is both too narrow and too vague. Wrong appearances are just as embarrassing as wrong actions and just as much in need of remedy. The embarrassment occasioned by a violation of a local modesty convention is oddly drawn under the concept of a botched performance. Keeping one's clothing in order is taken for granted, and unintended background to action, hardly a sustained performance. But nevertheless one's honour can be at stake if clothing is ill-adjusted.

Furthermore, Silver and associates invoke only one aspect of the embarrassment display: fluster (Darwin's "confusion of thought"). They have nothing to say about blushing. Experience suggests that these modes of display are semantically equivalent, in that either will do as a manifestation of embarrassment. They often occur together, and Darwin gives a physiological account of why that might be, but there are many occasions when disorderly gestures and muddled speech are not accompanied by blushing. And there are other occasions when a blush is all there is to show that someone is embarrassed.

The dramaturgical analysis does bring out the important principle behind the fact that a display of embarrassment is a last-ditch remedy for a breach of convention. It is better to lose one's reputation for poise than one's character as a modest sort of person.

A still sharper distinction between embarrassment and shame emerges from the apparent anomaly that one can be embarrassed as much by public attention attracted to one's successes as to one's delicts. I think the concepts do not admit of one being said to be ashamed at public attention to one's success, unless it has been achieved by discreditable or dishonourable means. Then it is the means, not the success, that occasions the shame.

The explanation of anomalous embarrassment involves the virtue of modesty. A display of self-satisfaction in success would breach the modesty conventions. Public attention to oneself in the moment of success opens up the possibility that one's natural pleasure in one's achievement may appear to others as immodest self-satisfaction. Hence, one's successes are occasions of threat to one's character as a proper modest person. There are cultures in which it would be considered improper not to boast about an achievement or triumph over a defeated rival.

This accounts for the mapping of embarrassment onto the more trivial breaches of the code, while shame is mapped onto the more serious. Modesty is a less "serious" virtue for us nowadays than, say, honesty or integrity. However, this is a recent change in the hierarchy of virtues, and later I shall come back to reflect more deeply on the nature of bodily modesty.

Occasions, conditions, and resolutions of embarrassment

A catalogue of some of the conditions under which it seems proper to say that someone has been embarrassed can be distilled from these accounts:

1. One has become the focus of (apparently excessive) attention from others whose opinions one values with respect to what one has said or done or how one appears.
2. One has become aware that others have taken the sayings, doings, or appearances in question to be abnormal.
3. The attention of others has been attracted by the deviance of one's actions or appearance, but it is not that the way one looks or speaks or acts is unusual – one sees the others as seeing what one has done, and so forth, as an infraction of a rule or convention adherence to which is a mark of good character and moral virtue.

The question whether or not the sufferer's beliefs conforming to these three conditions are true has only a marginal role to play in our understanding of the significance of embarrassment. So three parallel conditions of merely thinking that the preceding three objective conditions are verified are also enough for a blush.

4. One can be just as embarrassed when one is loudly congratulated as when one is quietly advised to "zip up". There is no paradox in this case, because too ready a display of self-satisfaction in one's achievements is in itself a mark of bad character, and public

attention of that sort provides room for it. A display of embarrassment immediately cancels that possibility.

There are three socially normative systems of conventions involved.
There is the system of conventions concerning appearance and conduct
whose violation will draw the attention of onlookers. To the sufferer, that
degree of attention is itself a violation of the rules of address and so, even
in the absence of any first-order infraction, can become embarrassing.
Then there is the normative principle that good character is demonstrated in a display of embarrassment. This, in turn, is relative to either or
both of the other two norms, because excessive complacency, when the
cynosure of all eyes, is a display of an unacceptable degree of self-
confidence.

People and cultures differ in degrees of embarrassability. In cultures
with high embarrassability, self-confidence, that quality of character
that protects against too readily succumbing to embarrassment, is
an equivocal virtue. Whereas self-confidence is a quality to be generally
admired, it must be displayed with caution, because it is perilously close
to some generally depreciated attributes such as "not giving a damn",
callousness, arrogance, indifference, contempt, and so on. Nevertheless,
the possibility of a life free from embarrassment particularly attracts the
easily embarrassed. Ricks (1974, p. 48) notices in the unembarrassed
display "a self-possession for which the ordinarily embarrassed are
grateful to the unembarrassable".

Surprise

Edelmann and Hampson (1979) placed great weight on the element of
surprise in the genesis of embarrassment. It is the sudden exposure that
embarrasses. To whom, though, is the surprise germane – the person
embarrassed, or the others, whose regard and attention, actual or potential, are the bothersome things? One way to tackle this is to consider
surprise as relative to the degree of expectation of an event. It is the
unexpected, rather than the merely sudden, that occasions surprise.
Indeed, something that creeps on the audience quite slowly may be quite
surprising. But not all surprises are embarrassing, as has been pointed
out in criticism of Edelman and Hampson. If the others are surprised by
what one does or exposes, it is surely because they do not expect it. But
what are they not likely to expect? Surely whatever violates the conventions appropriate to that kind of situation. It is not surprising to see
someone take off his trousers in the changing room of a gym, so it is not
an occasion for the kind of astonished regard that breeds embarrassment

either in actor or audience. A certain famous philosopher was forced to take off his trousers on the shoulder of a large and busy motorway because the pet gerbil he was transporting for one of his children had run up one leg. He reported this event as highly embarrassing. Surprise, then, is relevant only as a reflection that violations of current conventions on which both embarrassment and shame depend are unexpected.

Resolution and escape from embarrassment

I am indebted again to Ricks for opening up this issue with a brief remark on the complementary role that indignation can play to embarrassment. The idea seems to be roughly this: A display of embarrassment is, so to say, a mark to be entered in the public record, part of what Goffman called "character". It is ambiguous, in that although it serves to display sensitivity, it also contradicts such desirable impressions as that one is cool, sophisticated, and experienced. Not only is embarrassment a sign that one has realised that one has given an impression that is not up to some standard or other, but the embarrassment can itself be discrediting. Second-order discredit can be cancelled by cancelling the entry into the public record that one lacks savoir faire. One way of doing that is to display indignation, either on one's own behalf or on someone else's behalf.

Nevertheless, as Aristotle noticed, a display of embarrassment may incur second-order credit, because it shows our awareness of what is proper, if that awareness is a mark of a creditable stage on the way to maturity. As Goffman (1967, p. 108) puts it, "when an individual, receiving a compliment, blushes from modesty, he may lose his reputation for poise but confirm a more important one, that of being modest". Hence, as Aristotle observes, the young are to be praised for blushing, though a similar blush would be discreditable among the mature. Is this because the blush shows that I know what I should have done or how I should have appeared, but that I failed to follow the rules and I know it? Or does the blushing of the older person manifest a childish degree of insecurity of social place or a lack of the nonchalance one would expect from a socially experienced person?

There are two face-saving routes out of embarrassment. In one, creditable embarrassment is its own resolution. In the other, discreditable embarrassment is displaced by an attack on the Sartrean Other, whose self-appropriation of the right to judge led to the blush in the first place – "How dare you presume to judge me!" "Take that superior smile off your face!" Most of us just slink away.

Empathy and sympathy

There are marked differences in the degrees to which the peoples of different cultures are embarrassable. We have also noticed the moral ambiguity of immunity to embarrassment. Coolness and ignorance can look much the same, but Ricks has argued that there are differences in the degrees to which cultures admit embarrassment among the stock human reactions. He has suggested that embarrassability is high among the English and low among the French, building his case by reference to the moral preoccupations of novelists and poets. I cannot take the intercultural question any further here.

Can personal differences in embarrassability be related to any other psychological traits? Sartre emphasises that "assuming the point of view of the other" is an essential condition for the possibility of experiencing a reflexive emotion. But what is the source of my beliefs as to how I look to them – beliefs which against the background of norms of appearance and conduct, lead on to embarrassment? Modigliani (1968) explored the idea that capacity for empathy may be the psychological condition for high degrees of embarrassability. Though his research was methodologically rather slap-dash, it did seem to show that the degree of empathic sensitivity was not correlated with the degree of embarrassability. Modigliani's result is hardly surprising if we reflect on what seems quite obvious: that our beliefs about the opinions of others need not be true to be effective in the genesis of embarrassment.

However, a capacity for sympathy may be behind the degree of embarrassability that some people suffer with respect to the evident embarrassment of others. Burgess (1839, cited in Darwin, 1872/1955, p. 332) remarks how "when we see the cheek of an individual suffused with a blush in society, immediately our sympathy is excited towards him; we feel as if we were ourselves concerned, and yet we know not why". But there are cases in which the embarrassment occasioned by the embarrassment of another is not to be explained by reference to fellow feeling. Most embarrassment displays are embarrassing because of the threat they pose to yet other people's readings of our characters, as associates of the one whose blushes or flustered behaviour and speech are generally indicative of a lack of maturity and social skill.

Displaying embarrassment: The blush

This fascinating response has not drawn much attention from psychologists in recent years; yet blushing is the usual sign of embarrassment. It is one of the most striking phenomena of adolescence. It is unknown in infancy. Babies' reactions to being the focus of attention do not include blushing. Infants are also in complete command of the fixed, unwinking stare. Burgess (1839, cited in Darwin, 1872/1955) was the first to emphasise that blushing is a physiological response found in all humans, even those with dark skin, in whom the blush may be invisible.

Darwin remarks that one cannot control blushing. As he says, "blushing is not only involuntary; but the wish to restrain it, by leading to self-attention, actually increases the tendency" (1872/1955, pp. 310–11). The corollary, that blushing cannot be brought on deliberately, means that embarrassment cannot be feigned. This fact has long been known to actors and actresses, and it has been suggested as the origin of the use of rouge. (The French verb *rougeir* means both to blush and to apply a cosmetic blush.)

Another curiosity is that blushing is confined to the face and those parts of the upper body that are normally exposed to view without embarrassment. But the hands have never been observed to blush. When suffering from acute embarrassment, some people report tingling and suffusion of warmth over the whole body, but this is not accompanied by any visible blush. Though all people blush, whether their skin be dark or light, it is not known, even to this day, if in those climes where people go nearly naked blushing is still confined to those body areas characteristic of the European blush.

Suggestions as to the evolutionary origins of the phenomenon, if it is indeed biological and not a learned response, have come to grief on the fact that because of its invisibility on the dark skins of the majority of people it could not be an ethologically accountable signal of submission, say (Castelfranchi & Poggi, this volume). Nor, for the same reason, could it have been sexually selected, though Darwin reported that those Circassian women who blushed the most vividly fetched a higher price in the slave markets of Turkey. Darwin was impressed by the evidence that thinking attentively about some part of the body often led to a dilation of the capillaries in that region. The face, he conjectured, was the usual target of the assessing and critical look, and so blushing could be explained as a biologically accidental consequence of the social phenomenon of critical self-attention triggered by the looking of others.

Darwin added a similar explanation for the confusion of thought and muddle that seems to accompany embarrassment: The blush arises because of a diversion of the blood supply to the face, and a fortiori away from the brain, leading to depressed neural functioning. The social basis of the emotion of embarrassment, which is an integral part of this explanation, he supports by citing the fact that people rarely blush when alone, when they are sleeping or dreaming, or even when they are reading about something embarrassing. Without the look from the Sartrean Other, no blush will mantle the damask cheek.

Though Darwin (1872/1955, p. 325) seems to have posed the pure biologist's question ("how it has arisen that the consciousness that others are attending to our personal appearance should have led to the capillaries, especially those of the face, instantly becoming filled with blood?"), his answer is essentially a social answer.

Displaying embarrassment: Fluster

Disorder in speech and gesture is as much a display of embarrassment as is the blush. The behavioural aspects of displays of shame and embarrassment include squirming, rubbing one foot over the other, casting down the eyes, and so on. Bodily awkwardness is both an occasion for and a manifestation of embarrassment, feeding on itself. Goffman, following Lord Chesterfield, argues that squirming and casting down of the gaze are best seen as part of the repertoire for concealing emotion, hiding the blush. According to Goffman, "the fixed smile, the nervous hollow laugh, the busy hands, the downward glance that conceals the expression of the eyes, have become famous as signs of the attempt to conceal embarrassment". In some cultures the whole face may be covered by the hands. And so these acts become as clear a part of the display of embarrassment as the blush itself. Goffman (1967, p. 102) quotes Lord Chesterfield, who, icily contemptuous of the middle classes, to whom embarrassment is endemic, as it is to adolescence, speaks of these actions as "tricks to keep in countenance" and notices that "every awkward, ill-bred body" has them.[1]

I owe to S. B. Thomas (personal communication) the idea that the same terminus would be reached from a directly functional analysis of embarrassment displays. In displaying confusion of mind, they make manifest an exculpable lack of poise; in the blush they manifest a recognition of the modesty rules. Content and arousal are "internally" connected in a Wittgensteinian way.

Dismembering the cluster of related concepts

We rarely find an important concept existing in isolation from others with which it forms a system of terms ordered by similarities and differences. Darwin, for example, ties blushing, and so embarrassment, to modesty, shyness, and shame. Chagrin, too, must be added to this cluster. People who are shy, modest, or chagrined tend to be embarrassed when subject to public gaze. Those who are coy may appear embarrassed, but can feign only the superficial squirmings of the embarrassed and lack the telltale blush. Whereas the former are creditable emotions and attributes of character, coyness is discreditable. But shame (a creditable emotion for discreditable acts) and embarrassment are linked, as I have brought out already, whereas modesty is a virtue implicated with both. Those who are pert, proud, bold, brassy, shameless, and brash earn our disapprobation at least as much for their unrepentant attitude as for that which they are unperturbed at displaying.

Embarrassment and its contraries are concepts that necessarily involve an element of display. Their logical grammar excludes their use for hidden feelings and emotions. To be embarrassed is both to blush and to be discombobulated, whereas to be bold as brass is both to exaggerate one's décolletage and to seem not to give a damn about anyone taking a longish look. I think the element of display is crucial, because the importance of these styles of behaviour in social life lies not so much in the feelings they betray as in the characters they disclose. Because embarrassment is not a subjective matter, its display is not a sign or even an expression of an inner state, the "real embarrassment". The concept does not admit of concealed or suppressed embarrassment on the model of concealed or suppressed anger. And this fits with Darwin's important observation that the manifestation of embarrassment – the blush – can be neither inhibited nor feigned.

Modesty and shyness are the character attributes with which embarrassment is typically associated. Shame and chagrin are two emotions whose similarities to and differences from embarrassment were mentioned earlier. Both shame and embarrassment can occur in cases where my blush is occasioned not by my realisation that you are attending to my public gaucherie, immodesty, or incompetence but by my attention to yours. However, I can hardly feel chagrin for your failures, unless we are very closely linked socially.

We tend to associate displays of embarrassment with the virtue of modesty. Many of the expressions from the cluster have two characteristic contexts of use, illustrating the systematic ambiguity of the concept of "modesty". There is the context set by the sense of unwelcome attention being paid by others to some infraction of the local rules of bodily presence and display. But there may also be attention to our reactions to the attention of others to our first-order infractions. We assign the virtue of modesty as follows: A modest young lady would normally pull down her skirt *and* be embarrassed by it riding up, whereas a shameless hussy would let us see her knickers and not give a damn. The same duality of context occurs in more abstract matters. A truly modest colleague would keep quiet about his receipt of an honorary degree, and he would display some measure of embarrassment when others brought it up. An arrogant son of a bitch would both publicly broadcast the news and show nothing but self-satisfaction at the perhaps reluctant congratulations of his peers. However, academic honours are not exactly like underwear. A modest pride is acceptable, but it is a tricky note to strike.

Whereas the study of modesty helps to bring out the "double ought" in embarrassment, the phenomenon of bodily modesty has further features that are of interest in their own right, being relevant to the larger question whether the emotions are "natural" or "cultural".

The *Oxford English Dictionary* has amongst the glosses on "modesty" the following: "Womanly propriety of behaviour; scrupulous chastity of thought, speech, and conduct (in men or women); reserve or sense of shame proceeding from instinctive aversion to impure or coarse suggestions". I shall return to the issue raised by the use of "shame" rather than "embarrassment" in this definition and the framing of modesty within the womanly. It is notable that the author of the gloss takes it for granted that modesty arises out of an instinctive aversion, by which I take it he or she means something natural. There are two aspects to this: first, that a person is naturally put out when others notice something that ought not to be seen; second, that there is a common catalogue of bits and pieces of the body that would, if accidentally displayed, lead to embarrassment or perhaps shame.

Many commentators have suggested that modesty is an effect of custom, not its cause. Westermark (1901), for instance, says that "the feeling of shame, far from being the cause of man's covering his body is, on the contrary, a result of this custom". Helvetius went so far as to suggest that "modesty is only the invention of a refined voluptuousness", that is, that the body is covered to draw attention to it. Mantegazza remarks that "covering body parts is an (unconscious) way of emphasising or drawing attention to them". But though that may be true, it is far from explaining why shame and embarrassment attend accidental display. However, these suggestions, if sound, do put paid to the idea that body shame or embarrassment is natural.

It is also worth reminding ourselves of the enormous diversity of parts of the body whose display would be thought to be shameful or immodest. Here is a short list: For Islamic women it is the face and elbow, not the breasts; for traditional Chinese it is the bare feet. For traditional Tahiti, clothing is irrelevant – only an untattooed body is immodest. In traditional Alaska (indoors, of course) only lip plugs are essential for modesty. In Melanesia, clothing is indecent, whereas in Bali, for women to cover the bosom is coquettish at best and a mark of prostitution at worst. Turkish women were once required *by law* to cover the back of the hand, though the palm could be displayed without shame or embarrassment.

Historically, our own culture has also shown great diversity. Just one simple contemporary example: Many women wear nothing "on top" when swimming in the United Kingdom or continental Europe, whether in municipal baths or at the beach. This change has occurred only in the last 15 years. The female bosom is now no cause for embarrassment. But not to wear a white bow tie at an Oxford degree giving would be cause for the most acute embarrassment.

The realisation that the occasions for display of the virtues of modesty are culturally specific and historically variable has been very recent. Readers may enjoy the opinion of Judge Phillips in the case of the United States versus Harman (45 Fed. Rep. 423, 1891), which runs as follows:

There is in the popular conception and heart such a thing as modesty. It was born in the Garden of Eden. After Adam and Eve ate from the fruit of the Tree of Knowledge they passed from that condition of perfectibility which some people nowadays aspire to, and, their eyes being opened, they discerned that there was both good and evil "and they knew that they were naked, and they sewed fig-leaves together, and made themselves aprons". From that day to this, civilized man has carried with him a sense of shame – the feeling that there were some things which the eye – the mind – should not look, and where men and women become so depraved by the use, or so insensate from perverted education, that they will not veil their eyes, nor hold their tongues, the government should perform the office for them in protection of the social compact and the body politic.

As recently as 1935, the following event was reported in Associated News despatches of 16 and 17 June of that year:

SHOCKED YONKERS[2] STARTS ROUNDUP OF GIRLS IN SHORTS

Five young women, handed summonses today for appearing on the streets of Yonkers in shorts, will be treated to the sight of themselves as others see them – and in the movies at that.

The women were ordered into court tomorrow on the complaint of Alderman William Slater who said he had been besieged by the objections of citizens at having their Sunday afternoon veranda-gazing monopolized by young women in bare legs sauntering about the streets.

I have several times remarked on the fact that many of the authors I have cited have taken shame rather than embarrassment as the exemplary reflexive emotion. Earlier, in my general treatment, I suggested that shame is appropriate in cases of serious derelictions that would, if publicly noticed, lead to assessments of character so unfavourable as to permanently depreciate one's honour. Embarrassment is the emotion proper to the violation of mere convention, a code of manners. It would be absurd to say that one who failed to wear a white bow tie at an Oxford degree giving was dishonoured by that dereliction. Reputation for savoir faire would be lost, but hardly moral character.

Reminding ourselves of this distinction can help to explain why earlier writers tended to discuss bodily exposure and the consequent disturbances in terms of shame rather than embarrassment. Particularly when women's honour was at stake, modesty was linked to chastity in a tightly knit conceptual cluster. Exposure of the female body was treated as dishonourably provocative, and so one was careful to avoid even accidental exposure of some forbidden part of herself for fear of being mistaken for the kind of slut who deliberately does so. Once the connection between bodily exposure and womanly honour dissolves (or where in many non-Western societies it has never existed) and the conventionality regarding which bits to cover up is recognised society-wide, then only embarrassment can ensue from violation of some sumptuary rule. I remind the reader that in Bali it is immodest for a woman to cover the upper part of her body; that device is a trick of "street girls" to entice clients.

Shyness

So far, we have seen the grammar of the word "embarrassment" to be controlled by the principle that it should be used for disturbances that occur on occasions of sudden and excessive public attention to something personal that society decrees should be kept hidden, or least unattended and unemphasised, attention to which threatens the self via the possibility that the attention is critical and the regard, in itself, denigratory. We tend to call people "shy" when they display some kind of disturbance (something like the marks of embarrassment) on *any* occasion of public attention, and with respect to *any* or *all* personal attributes. Mere bodily presence in the public domain, if noticed, say by address, is enough.

For instance, someone might refuse to appear in the presence of others at all, with the claim that "I'm shy!" Or such a refusal might be accounted for by someone else with "He's shy!" Like any alibi talk, this sort of remark can be studied against the distinction between excuses and justifications. An excuse serves to admit a fault and to give a reason why it was committed, whereas a justification is a claim that the action was not a fault at all. To shrink from the public gaze is, I think, to be accounted a fault. One has a duty to some measure of sociality. So "I'm shy" or vicariously "He's shy" is an excuse, not a justification. It belongs with "I was too scared", not with something like "Don't be so picky; punctuality is neurotic" or "Come on, everyone tries to beat the customs!"

It seems to follow that whereas "embarrassment" is a proper emotion and indeed a mark of certain virtue, shyness is verging on the pathological. Thus, with respect to the "double ought" principle, whereas embarrassment is a feeling one ought to have, shyness is not.

In the case of shyness, it is the normality of what is exposed to view (and the whole person is a special case of that normality) that lies at the root of the social disapproval and the mildly pathological rating of shyness. Is there anyone who ought to be shy?

I think not, though its polar opposite, "showing off", is also to be deprecated. It goes something like this: Although shyness is something one ought not to feel and even less display, still it is something that children are expected to exhibit at some passing stage of life. Thus, as in many cases in the moral order, normality and propriety are not in one-to-one correspondence. Notice, too, that shyness is generally preferred to showing off, in that shyness is excessive modesty, whereas showing off is tied in with unacceptable character traits like boasting, arrogance, and the like. But there are cultures where boasting is proper, even virtuous. Showing off can reasonably be deprecated in the young, and their shyness is endured with some sympathy. In a way, shyness could be thought of as a kind of apprenticeship to proper modesty.

Chagrin is associated with and typical of the realisation that one has failed in the context of an expectation of success. The worst case occurs when the expectation of success has been publicly declared, and note that that declaration can be retrospectively redefined as boasting if one fails. So failure is deadly for two reasons: first, the loss of esteem, honour, and so forth, consequent on the failure itself; second, the loss of one's reputation as a modest person, which, as the dictionary says, denotes "a reserve springing from an unexaggerated estimate of one's qualities". Failure encourages a retrospective redefinition of one's public and optimistic estimate of success as mere boasting. If one brings off a declared project, one cannot be said to have boasted.

In summary, the structure of the conceptual system underlying embarrassment seems to be the following: The virtue involved is modesty, which, having both a characterological sense and a behavioural sense, is bimodal. The emotions involved are the following:

1. Shame – occasioned by the realisation that others have become aware that what one has been doing has been a moral infraction, a judgement with which I, as actor, concur.
2. Embarrassment – occasioned by the realisation that others have become aware that what one has been doing (in a qualified sense) has been a breach of convention and the code of manners, a judgement with which I, as actor, concur.

We can make sense of this complexity with the thesis that in our culture improper body displays are taken as prima facie evidence of attributions of bad character.

There is a link between character modesty and body modesty that explains why we have two kinds of modesty; it is the concept of honour, which is tied in with one's reputation in the judgement of others. Violations of the modesty code, the general form of which are failures to adhere to the rule of non-self-emphasis, in either mode, threaten a loss of honour. This explains the Balinese anomaly – why covering the bosom is immodest; a good woman with her bosom covered would be mistaken for a tart.

It also explains why body modesty has been a more restrictive code for women than for men, in our culture, because, notoriously, there are more "good-time girls" than gigolos. But more important, the old double-standard morality amplified the need to disambiguate accidental disclosures that would have been deliberately provocative if they had been made by a woman of dubious reputation. Accidental disclosure of normally hidden body aspects can be mistaken for deliberate disclosure, with a consequent risk of misattribution of character and the Sartrean realisation that has occurred.

Complexities of embarrassment

Iterated emotions

Students of embarrassment, such as Darwin and Goffman, have re-marked on how embarrassing it is to be embarrassed or to watch the embarrassment of others. It seems to me, however, that one cannot be ashamed of one's own shame, though I am not so sure about the shame of another. So far as I know, no work has been done on the general question of iterated emotions, in particular the question of why some emotions can be iterated (one can be angry at being angry) and some cannot. One can hardly be sad at being sad. There are also nested emotions, such as being ashamed of being angry, embarrassed at being envious, proud of being sympathetic, and so on.

What is the principle behind these cases? The first point to notice is that the embedded emotion is always one in the conditions for which the double-ought principle applies. Being embarrassed at being embarrassed is fairly easily accounted for via the principle that in many cases the infraction that one is embarrassed about is one that someone with more savior faire, more worldly experience, and so on, would not find embar-rassing. A well-brought-up American lady might feel iterative embarrass-ment when dressed for the beach European style. In the double-ought cases, the second ought can be prescriptive or proscriptive; so the embedding emotion can be a show of consonance of character with the original act (proud of being compassionate) or of dissonance of character with the original act (ashamed of being shy). Once again, the issue at issue is the conventional assignments of character and virtue at risk in the event. Thus, the embedding emotion may be itself a contribution to face work, a remedy, or, in the case of the prescribed embedded emotion, a confirmation.

Paradoxes and inversions of embarrassment

Embodiment opens up the possibility of being looked at, in person, so to say. The fact that our appearance and our honour are tied up with one another has been treated thus far as a source of threat. But every shrinking violet also needs to be noticed, to have his or her existence confirmed. Embarrassment is the adolescent emotion par excellence. The predicament of adolescence is precisely the ambiguity of visibility. The enlarged and clumsy body seems only too visible, and hence the blush; yet identity as a publicly noticeable being is confirmed only by being seen to have been seen (and, in lesser ways, heard to have been heard). Is it too indelicate of me to draw the reader's attention to the way that the smell of children changes from babyhood to infancy, from childhood to adolescence? No, because smell, too, is an occasion for embarrassment. To capture this dark moment of adolescence, I borrow a phrase from Ricks (1974, p. 27) concerning the "ereutophobe who yet longs to be stared at, and who plays with fire, her [his] cheeks on fire".

So far, I have drawn attention only to the way that our and others' embarrassment can be itself a source of embarrassment. But the embarrassment of others can also be fun. Perhaps this can throw light on the curious practice of teasing, where the embarrassable and the shy are much at risk, like the fiery and the feeble. "Teasing is testing", as someone once remarked. It probes for certain socially undesirable vulnerabilities, such as tendencies to anger and embarrassment, and mercilessly punishes them. Real (and imaginary) shortcomings become the focus of attention of all the world, for that is what the tease is. In teasing, I suggest, we have a coarse-grained model of the general structure of embarrassment. The teaser forces the victim to attend to the demeaning nature of the defect, not just the defect itself, by forcing attention to the mocking attention that the teaser is giving to it. For adolescents, the defect can be mere bodily presence. (O! that this too too solid flesh would melt, might quote the embarrassed one in an agony of self-awareness.)

Ricks, again so sure and sharp in his observations (1974, p. 42), remarks that "an intense self-awareness is both bred from and breeds embarrassment". And here again is the paradox of adolescence – a proper self-awareness is a prerequisite for the kind of control Goffman called "impression management". And the acquisition of it opens up the possibility of a sensitivity to the regard of others that can only too readily invoke the "critical stare". I think it is a mistake on the part of some authors to concentrate on the sexuality of adolescence as the focus of self-awareness. The range of that which can be embarrassing is wide, from the new voice in boys to the mere bulky presence of either sex in the physical world.

Vicarious emotions

An important distinction among emotions is whether or not it makes sense to imagine them as experienced vicariously. Some, such as an anger, are readily seen to be possible vicariously; I might well be angry on your behalf, as I sense a transgression against you. But I am quite unable to conceive of vicarious jealousy. The source of this intuition must lie somewhere in the grammar of the concepts. Some light can be thrown on this by noticing that vicarious embarrassment and perhaps shame are routine, though strongly culturally variable in intensity. However, vicarious shyness is, so far as I know, never reported nor felt. Why?

Malicious pleasure in your discomfiture is not an unknown emotion. Under what conditions am I likely to experience it? It seems to me that there must already exist some other hostile relationship between us. But if there is no such relationship, then fellow feeling is, in the absence of any reason to the contrary, taken for granted in our moral system. Our normative expectations assume that within certain bounds, my good is your good, and particularly my moral standing is tied in with yours. We have looked at this already in relation to the conditions for face work and for the fellowship condition on feeling embarrassed by the behaviour of someone to whom we can be seen to have some social tie. In the case of vicarious embarrassment, it is not that I am embarrassed by your behaviour but that your behaviour might as well have been mine as an occasion for embarrassment.

But we have already seen that shyness is not a proper emotion prescribed for occasions on which I am acutely aware of real or imagined attention being paid to me. Indeed, that emotion is generally proscribed and tolerable only as a stage through which we pass to a proper modesty. It is only as seen as on the way to that state that it is tolerable at all. Shyness, then, cannot be associated with a common set of normative expectations that have been violated accidentally in your case, and so, through fellow feeling, can be felt as if the violation were relative to me.

Now to take this thought back to the intuition that distinguished anger and jealousy. Anger may, in certain circumstances, be a pre-scribed emotion. It reflects the sense of proper outrage at an improper infraction of my honour, body space, rights, and so forth. Jealousy, at least for us, is a proscribed emotion, and so far as my intuition goes, this admits of no exceptions. It would be too much to say that shyness is proscribed; it is not important enough for that, but it is a mode of display that one generally deprecates while one understands it.

I have already suggested that the fact that embarrassment has appeared only recently as a topic for serious study may have its roots in quite profound social changes of which this may be an indicator. We may be witnessing a collapse of the distinction between manners and morality. Relativism in matters of ethics would be expressed as conventionalism, which is as much as to say that a morality is just the manners and customs of this or that tribe. Bodily modesty, then, becomes a locally variant set of conventions, not a virtue deeply embedded in the very quality of womanhood. The collapse of the distinction between manners and morality would explain the recency of an interest in embarrassment and a decline of attention to shame.

There are cultures that do not make the distinction. Catherine Lutz (1986) tells us that the Ifaluk do not distinguish manners from morality, and that is reflected in their indigenous emotion clusters. Shame does not exist as a distinctive emotion, and whatever we comprehend under the concept is parcelled out into an anger cluster *song* and a fear cluster *metagu*. Jude Dougherty (personal communication) reminded me that classical China was a civilisation in which manners rather than morality regulated interpersonal relations under Confucian influence. A study of the self-reflexive emotions of social delict in that culture would be worth making.

By way of final summary, I return to Sartre's way of defining all emotion occasions as deprivations of "freedom". The freedom to formulate judgements ad libitum gives Sartre a ground for distinguishing shame from hate. In shame, I accept the presence of the Other and the restrictions that are imposed, through "the Look", on my range of reflexive judgements. In the case of hate, I do not accept the restrictions and long for the destruction of the Other to restore my freedom. It is worth noticing that this is a formal distinction only. No content is involved. But for embarrassment to emerge as a separate emotion, there must be a working distinction, so I argue, between manners and morality. It is infractions of the conventions of the former that engender it. Sartre quite fails to pick up the virtue involved. I suggested that in the closed society of French intellectuals, the manners–morality distinction is not drawn, and that character in the old-fashioned sense is in jeopardy, even from the unintentional vulgarity of a gesture, to take Sartre's own and telling example. Unlike women whose lives have shifted from the moment-by-moment regulation of a morality to the gentler and culturally malleable influence of a code of manners, the Sartre circle treated manners as a morality. In this respect they regressed, and I suppose regressed gladly, to the moral condition of the women of the Victorian era, where virtue was held to be at stake in the lightest deed. Stephen J. Ross (personal communication) has asked why there are no strategies for converting issues of morality into issues of manners. The answer brings out a paradox. While morality rules character, no such strategies will be wanted, because they would themselves be signs of a loose character.

Once morality has ceased to rule, such strategies will be otiose. What powers the transition from the one state of order to the other I leave to historical sociology to discover.

ACKNOWLEDGEMENT

I am grateful to "Mike" Dillon for his generous help in understanding Sartre's theory of emotions.

NOTES

1. It is well to bear in mind that modesty conventions have always been class-related (Grant Webster, personal communication). Embarrassment is stronger among the middle classes, because in terms of character they have more at hazard.
2. The city of Yonkers is immediately north of New York City.

REFERENCES

Aristotle (1953). *Nicomachean ethics* (trans. J. A. K. Thomson). Harmondsworth, Middlesex: Penguin.

Aristotle (1941). *Rhetoric, the basic works of Aristotle* (ed. R. McKean). New York: Random House.

Armon-Jones, C. (1986). The thesis of constructionism. In R. Harré (Ed.), *The social construction of emotions* (pp. 32–56). Oxford: Blackwell.

Bedford, E. (1956–7). Emotions and statements about them. *Proceedings of the Aristotelian Society, 57,* 281–304.

Darwin, C. (1955). *The expression of the emotions in man and animals.* New York: Philosophical Library. (Original work published 1872)

Edelmann, R. J., & Hampson, S. E. (1979). Changes in non-verbal behaviour during embarrassment. *British Journal of Social and Clinical Psychology, 18,* 385–390.

Goffman, E. (1967) *Interaction ritual.* Harmondsworth, Middlesex: Penguin.

Harré, R. (1983). *Personal being.* Oxford: Blackwell.

Lutz, C. (1986). The domain of emotion words on Ifaluk. In R. Harré (Ed.), *The social construction of emotions* (pp. 267–288). Oxford: Blackwell.

Modigliani, A. (1968). Embarrassment and embarrassability. *Sociometry, 31,* 313–326.

Ricks, C. (1974). *Keats and embarrassment.* Oxford: Clarendon Press.

Sartre, J.-P. (1956). *Being and nothingness* (trans. H. E. Barnes). New York: Pocket Books. (Original work published 1943)

Silver, M., Sabini, J., & Parrott, W. G. (1987). A dramaturgic theory of embarrassment. *Journal for the Theory of Social Behaviour, 17,* 47–61.

Westermark, E. (1901). *The history of human marriage.* London: Longmans.

7

Embarrassment and blushing: A component-process model, some initial descriptive and cross-cultural data

ROBERT J. EDELMANN

Embarrassment is generally regarded as a form of social anxiety closely related to shyness, audience anxiety, and shame. These variants of social anxiety have many overlapping features, including the involvement of self-presentational concerns (Leary & Schlenker, 1981; Schlenker & Leary, 1982), although there have been many attempts in the literature to highlight crucial differences. Thus, the links between audience anxiety and shyness, on the one hand, and embarrassment and shame, on the other, have been noted by a number of authors (Buss, 1980; Edelmann, 1987a; Schlenker & Leary, 1982).

It has been argued that those who *anticipate* a discrepancy between their perceived self-presentation and their desired self-presentation are likely to experience shyness or audience anxiety (Asendorpf, 1984, also this volume; Schlenker & Leary, 1982), depending upon the nature of the encounter. Shyness may occur in those situations in which our behaviours are *contingent* upon the responses of others, whereas audience anxiety is restricted to *non-contingent* encounters (i.e., encounters that are primarily guided by internal plans, such as when delivering a prepared speech).

Cutting across the shyness and audience anxiety dimensions are social emotions that result from unintentional and undesired predicaments or transgressions (Schlenker & Leary, 1982; Semin & Manstead, 1981, 1982). The social anxiety that results from such predicaments has been termed embarrassment or shame, depending upon the nature of the event. "Shame" usually refers to a private feeling, whereas "embarrassment" involves interpersonal exposure (Goffman, 1956; Modigliani, 1966; Vallelonga, 1976). Thus, Modigliani (1966) comments that "one is primarily ashamed of oneself, while one is primarily embarrassed about one's presented self" (p. 10). This suggestion of overlapping but different concepts is also raised by Vallelonga (1976). He suggests that although both shame and embarrassment entail a discrepancy "between who one is and who, according to one's lived self-projects one 'must' be" (p. 57), embarrassment additionally involves interpersonal exposure, "loss of face", and a desire to escape, hide, or disappear. For Goffman, too, it is the public presentation of a discrepant self-image that gives rise to embarrassment.

Embarrassment is thus likely to occur in some kind of real or imagined social interaction when there is an anticipated or perceived discrepancy between one's current self-presentation and one's standard for self-presentation as a result of an undesired and unintentional social accident or predicament that has occurred or that the person fears may occur (Edelmann, 1987a).

Given these many facets to the experience of embarrassment, it is clear that the process involved is likely to be a complex phenomenon, the key components of which need to be carefully unpacked before a clear understanding can be achieved. This chapter thus analyses the process or chain of events that constitute the experience of embarrassment. Preliminary descriptive data for a group particularly vulnerable to embarrassment are presented, in addition to cross-cultural data; both these data sets evaluate specific aspects of the model. As a starting point, however, it is necessary to consider the chain of events associated with the experience of embarrassment.

Embarrassment as a process

There have been numerous attempts to conceptualise the process underlying embarrassment (e.g., Goffman, 1955, 1956; Edelmann, 1985, 1987a; Modigliani, 1968, 1971; Semin & Manstead, 1981, 1982), the majority of which have tended to emphasise the occurrence of a social act defined as being potentially embarrassing to the actor. Thus, the starting point for Modigliani's model is an assumption that an incident has occurred that is the immediate cause of embarrassment, whereas for Semin and Manstead the starting point is the occurrence of a public violation of a taken-for-granted social rule that is part of the actor's repertoire. It is undoubtedly the case that embarrassment is frequently evoked by a clearly defined faux pas, impropriety, accident, or transgression that results in the actor's projected image creating an undesired impression. As noted elsewhere, however (Edelmann, 1987a), it is also clear that some actors experience embarrassment even in the absence of a clearly defined antecedent event. Thus, it is possible to induce embarrassment (or at least to elicit the behavioural display of embarrassment) by informing the interactant that he or she looks embarrassed, even if the situation itself is not defined as embarrassing.

The "look" of embarrassment, which has frequently been noted in the literature, is characterised by a well-defined behavioural display. Eye contact is reduced, body movements and speech disturbances are increased (Edelmann & Hampson, 1979, 1981), and facial flushing occurs; in fact, blushing has been described as the hallmark of embarrassment (Buss, 1980). It does appear, however, that it is possible to experience embarrassment without blushing and to blush without being embarrassed. However, in certain instances blushing seems to precede the experience of embarrassment – the latter emotion is then experienced in the absence of any clearly defined external antecedent event. It seems, therefore, that stimuli that can evoke feelings of embarrassment can be either external (a faux pas, impropriety, social transgression, etc.) or internal (bodily and facial cues).

A further component of embarrassment that is noted in the literature is the use of impression management strategies, which can be invoked by the actor to deal with his or her predicament. Goffman (1955) has referred to this as "face work". In general, this consists of attempts to correct, minimise, explain away, or excuse the behaviour (either externally or internally elicited) that has given rise to embarrassment. Though such remedial tactics frequently involve verbal comments, several authors have discussed the way in which smiling or laughter may be used as a response or alternative to embarrassment within an interaction (e.g., Emerson, 1970). The interactions among these coping attempts, the initial non-verbal display, and evoking stimuli clearly need to be taken into account in any comprehensive model of embarrassment.

The experience of embarrassment thus necessitates that the actor make appraisals of the social event (i.e., the social setting, expected behaviours, expectations of others, the rules of conduct), the behavioural and physiological consequences of that event (i.e., the behaviours associated with the negative consequences of failure to follow the rules of conduct), and the behaviours associated with subsequent attempts to rectify the situation once a negative event has occurred. The label "embarrassment" can be assigned as a result of the subjective experience of the actor, as well as on the basis of an evaluation of the event that precipitated the experience and/or an evaluation of the behavioural display that resulted from the event. Components of the non-verbal and physiological reaction may thus play a central part in defining the nature of embarrassment.

Non-verbal behaviour and embarrassment

It is widely acknowledged that embarrassment is characterised by a well-defined behavioural display. These behaviours may well serve func-

tions similar to the functions of those occurring in association with social anxiety in general (Leary, 1982, 1983; Schlenker & Leary, 1982).
Schlenker and Leary have grouped the behaviours into three functional
classes: nervous responses, disaffiliative behaviours, and image protection. In the case of embarrassment, fidgeting and stammering could be
regarded as nervous responses; avoiding eye contact or covering one's
face could be viewed as behaviours that decrease social contact with
others and hence are disaffiliative; smiling may in some cases be an
attempt to protect one's image following a disruption of social routine.
In the case of embarrassment, however, there are added complexities
that require explanation. Firstly, as mentioned, it is possible to elicit
embarrassment by informing the actor that he or she looks embarrassed,
even if that is not the case and/or the situation itself is not defined as
embarrassing. Secondly, the experience of embarrassment can be heightened by making the actor aware that he or she is embarrassed. Thirdly,
it is possible to become embarrassed as a result of blushing, even in a
situation that is not deemed by others who are present or by the actor to
be intrinsically embarrassing.

In order to account for these issues, Edelmann (1985, 1987a) has
suggested that one's overt embarrassment can be perceived and labelled
as such by using information from one's facial expression and other
expressive behaviours (body motion, smiling, speech patterns), as well as
visceral cues (alerting to environmental events) and memory from past
experience (knowledge of social rules and others' reactions to rule-
breaking episodes). The suggestion is that embarrassment can be elicited
by the situation and/or the display, with the display intensifying the
experience of embarrassment (i.e., via facial feedback).

The notion that feedback from one's facial expressive behaviours gives
rise to the experience of the emotion has had a long and checkered
history, with a wealth of contradictory evidence produced. The issues
have been reviewed and commented upon elsewhere (Buck, 1980; Edelmann, 1987a; Laird, 1984), and it is beyond the scope of this chapter to
repeat them here. Inevitably, in light of the controversial nature of the
topic, there are those who support (or who claim that the evidence
supports) some version of the facial feedback hypothesis and those who
are less convinced by the available evidence. Although it may be difficult
to assert that facial expression *is* the emotion, it seems clear that expressive behaviour can add to or accentuate emotional experience. As Leventhal (1979, 1980) points out, some form of expressive-motor mechanism
is likely to be central to the generation of affect, even if this takes the
form of intensifying or sustaining emotional experience rather than caus-
ing it.

The notion that feedback from facial and bodily signs of emotions plays a central part in the experience of embarrassment has received some support from two lines of evidence. First, the limited clinical literature on chronic blushing suggests that for certain individuals, blushing can give rise to embarrassment. Thus, Timms (1980) refers to a client who comments as follows: "I come on all red ... as red as that pencil ... people associate redness with embarrassment, and when I'm red I think people think I must be embarrassed and then I do get embarrassed, but I'm not embarrassed to start with" (p. 59). The sequence of events clearly involves blushing, followed by the client's own evaluation of that blushing, which is labelled as embarrassment even in the absence of an intrinsically embarrassing situation. Obviously, the part played by the client's cognitive appraisal of the behaviour is central, a point that will be discussed later.

The second line of reasoning is drawn from Tomkins's updated theory of affect. As he points out, "I have come to regard the skin in general and the skin of the face in particular as of the greatest importance in producing the feeling of affect" (Tomkins, 1981, p. 386). He further adds that "changes in hotness, coldness, and warmth would undoubtedly be involved but there may well be other, as yet unknown, specific receptors, which yield varieties of experience peculiar to the affect mechanism" (p. 389). It is thus possible that skin temperature changes associated with blushing play a part in influencing the intensity of reported embarrassment. It is, of course, a further inferential leap to assume that the facial flush leads directly to the experience of embarrassment. Whether or not other aspects of facial expression and body movement serve a similar function is a matter of speculation. Of central importance is likely to be the part played by cognitive factors in evaluating the bodily and situational cues available, and perhaps creating embarrassment from these factors.

Cognitive appraisal and embarrassment

Theories emphasising the importance of cognitive or inferential decisions in building up emotional experience stress the importance of three central elements: the existence of some perceptible internal state that differs from one's base-line state, the focusing of sufficient attention on the internal state to result in awareness of its existence, and the use of some knowledge structure to interpret the state. In interpreting feelings of embarrassment, autonomic arousal and cognitive interpretation undoubtedly play an important part. Drawing on Bem's self-preception theory (1967, 1972), it is likely that we infer our current state from observing our actions and the circumstances in which we act. Not only are there likely to be individual differences in the salience of particular

cues used to identify one's emotional state, but also situational or personal cues may differ in their importance on separate occasions.

Individual difference factors associated with increased salience of
personal cues are likely to be those that reflect a concern with the way
we are evaluated by others: over-concern with one's public image, sensitivity to and over-awareness of the evaluations of others, and a tendency
to believe that others' evaluations of one's behaviour are likely to be
negative (Edelmann, 1987a). In the case of chronic blushers, the posses-
sion of such a set of characteristics may be associated with a predisposition to attend to bodily cues for information.

One assumption that is often noted in the literature is that we have a
relatively fixed amount of attention to allocate to our object of focus
(whether ourselves or the environment) (Duval & Wicklund, 1972;
Scheier, Carver, & Matthews, 1983; Gibbons, this volume). Assuming
that a person has only a limited amount of attention to allocate to a
particular stimulus, increasing the salience or input from one source of
information will of necessity decrease the salience or input from other
sources. Thus, as attention inward to the self increases, attention outward to others in the environment will decrease.

One possibility (Hull & Levy, 1979; Scheier et al., 1983) is that our
attention is shifting between ourselves and environmental cues on a
continual but non-random basis. Thus, if a social accident, transgression, or faux pas has occurred, attention may initially be directed towards
an appraisal of the event itself. This may be quickly followed by an
inward focus of attention directed specifically at those aspects of the
self that are presumed to be associated with embarrassment (blushing,
trembling, averted gaze, stammering). Subsequently, attention may
again be directed towards the environment, but on this occasion guided
by a search for the evaluation or reaction of others. Subjective appraisal
may partially alternate with environmental appraisal and partially occur
in parallel. The sequence of appraisals obviously may be initiated both
externally and internally, and the fact that the process can be repeated
may also serve to increase the subjective experience of embarrassment.

There is indeed evidence that attending to one's inner state can make
that experience more intense, whereas distraction can alleviate the feeling. This seems to be the case for both situationally induced self-focus
(e.g., Scheier, 1976, found that self-focus induced by experimental manipulation led to increased feelings of anger) and individual differences in
self-attention (e.g., Scheier & Carver, 1977, found that individuals with
a tendency to be self-attentive experienced greater repulsion when viewing emotive slides than did their low-self-attentive counterparts). In the
same way, chronic blushers may focus on internal cues to the exclusion
of other valid emotional determinants and hence overestimate the salience of their embarrassed feelings.

There is evidence that this occurs in the case of social anxiety. McEwan & Devins (1983) divided socially anxious subjects into two groups (high and low levels of concomitant somatic symptoms) on the basis of self-report measures of the intensities of seven somatic anxiety symptoms (palpitations, perspiration, difficulty breathing, trembling, nausea, urinary urgency, bowel sensations). It was found that socially anxious individuals with elevated somatic symptoms believed that they displayed greater numbers of visible signs of anxiety, as measured via a behavioural checklist, than were actually noticed by their peers.

In two further studies (Jerremalm, Jansson, & Ost, 1986; Ost, Jerremalm, & Johansson, 1981), socially phobic subjects were classified as "behavioural reactors", "physiological reactors", or "cognitive reactors" based on scores obtained from three sets of measures. The behavioural measures consisted of 17 items concerned with voice, posture, gesture, proximity, orientation, speaking, and turn-taking derived from videotape recordings of a brief interaction between the subject and one male and one female confederate. The physiological measure consisted of a continuous record of the patient's heart rate taken during the interactions with the confederates. The cognitive component was measured on a scale consisting of 10 negative and 10 positive examples of thoughts to be rated for frequency of occurrence during the test on a 0–4 scale.

In the first study (Ost et al., 1981), the "physiological reactors" were patients with high heart rate reactions but small overt behavioural reactions, whereas the "behavioural reactors" had large behavioural reactions but little or no heart rate reactions. In the second study (Jerremalm et al., 1986), the "cognitive reactors" were patients with a low heart rate but a negative thought pattern, and the "physiological reactors" had a high heart rate reaction but a positive pattern of thoughts. It does not seem unreasonable to assume that the three groups of subjects rely on different cues to indicate the salience of their anxiety.

In the case of embarrassment, the three systems of behaviours, cognitions, and arousal may also operate to some extent in parallel, with cue salience varying as a function of both situational and individual differences. A summary model has recently been suggested to account for these diverse dimensions of embarrassment (Edelmann, 1987a).

A component-process model of embarrassment

A detailed account of the derivation of the model is given elsewhere (Edelmann, 1987a), and only a brief résumé of the salient features of the model itself will be provided here.

In line with the preceding discussion, the initial stimulus giving rise to a subjective feeling of embarrassment can be either an external event, such as a social accident, trangression, or faux pas that is labelled as embarrassing by the actor and observer, or an internal event, such as a bodily reaction in the apparent absence of an external embarrassing event. During the appraisal process, the salience of particular cues will be influenced by a range of factors, including the individual's past learning history and personality and the intensity of the initial stimuli.

The comparative initial impact of external or internal cues will be largely influenced by factors affecting self-awareness. The salience of internal cues may be enhanced when a particular aspect of the environment prompts self-focus (e.g., the presence of a high-status, expert audience) or in the case of individual differences that predispose the actor to be self-attentive. External cues are clearly salient in the event of a social transgression, faux pas, or accident. The speed with which the actor subsequently switches attention to internal cues may similarly be influenced by factors affecting self-awareness. For some people ("chronic blushers") attending to internal cues may be sufficient to generate the subjective experience of embarrassment.

In line with both Leventhal's perceptual motor theory of emotion (Leventhal, 1979, 1980; Leventhal & Mosbach, 1983) and Carver and Scheier's control theory approach to behaviour (Carver & Scheier, 1981; Scheier & Carver, 1982; Scheier et al., 1983), attention will subsequently alternate between environmental and internal cues. This can lead to both reactions from the environment (i.e., the reactions of others) and feedback from one's own behaviour (i.e., facial expressions, blushing, body movements, etc.) modifying initial perceptions of the stimulus. If the initial evoking stimulus is internal (i.e., I am blushing), subsequent appraisal will involve both an evaluation of external reactions to this event (i.e., Have others noticed? How are they reacting?) and an appraisal of one's own subsequent reaction (visceral arousal, bodily reaction, etc.).

If the initial evoking stimulus is external (i.e., a social transgression), subsequent appraisal will involve both an evaluation of one's initial internal state and an ongoing evaluation of changes that might occur.

One aspect of importance within the model is the part played by distorted cognitions. When making an evaluation of a particular eliciting stimulus, there is a tendency for the actor to assume that cue salience will be similar for the actor and for an observer. Thus, a "chronic blusher" will assume that everyone is noticing and evaluating his or her blushing behaviour; an actor with a high personal standard for presentation whose current presentation is below that standard will assume that observers are evaluating his or her performance negatively and may experience embarrassment as a result. In both examples the cues may not be salient to the observers, and the cause of any resultant embarrassment may be evident only to the actors themselves.

A further factor of importance involves the use of strategies for coping with embarrassment that may well be invoked following a re-appraisal of the evoking stimuli and one's own reaction to these events. The use of particular strategies may well depend on both the nature of the initial eliciting stimulus and the initial reaction to this event. For example, coping with a discernible external eliciting stimulus may be easier than coping with an internal event. The tendency to over-concentrate on internal cues may be mediated by individual difference factors, which are rather more difficult to modify. Further, because of cognitive distortions, the actor may believe that the observer is noticing the extreme blushing and hence may attempt to hide or decrease it (which, given the alternating attentional focus referred to, may be difficult), whereas an external event (which is clearly noticed) can be coped with by verbal or non-verbal comment (e.g., laughter).

The salience of particular cues in the experience of embarrassment clearly requires examination, and a number of strategies could be adopted. Given the dearth of studies in this area, there is evidently a need for basic descriptive data as well as carefully conducted studies investigating the salience of physiological, non-verbal, and environmental cues in the experience of embarrassment and the ways in which these can be modified. The remainder of this chapter presents some initial descriptive data dealing with chronic blushing and self-reported physiological/non-verbal reactions and strategies for coping with embarrassment across cultures. Further laboratory studies evaluating cue salience are currently being conducted.

A description of chronic blushing

Background

As a preliminary investigation of the cognitive situational factors and consequent coping attempts associated with blushing, self-reports were generated from a sample of self-defined chronic blushers (Edelmann, 1987b). The initial sample pool consisted of 500 people who had written requesting a fact sheet entitled "Blushing, what it is and what to do about it", as advertised in an article published in a well-known women's magazine. Returned to each person with the fact sheet was a request for factual information concerning chronic blushing. Of the initial 500 subjects, 100 returned sufficiently detailed information to allow for data to be generated. Given both the method of recruiting subjects and the low response rate from the initial sample, it may well be the case that the final sample was not representative of either the general population or the population of chronic blushers. It could be argued with equal force

Table 7.1. *Age of respondent, age of onset of blushing as a problem, severity of problem, and time for blush to subside*

Variable	Mean	S.D.	Min.	Max.
Age	29.8	9.9	15	55
Age of onset	12.6	4.7	5	27
Severity	2.5	0.9	1	4
Time to subside	2.6	1.1	1	4

Note: Figures for age and age of onset are in years and months. Severity: 1 = not very; 4 = extreme. Time to subside: 1 = <1 min; 2 = 1–5 min; 3 = 5–60 min; 4 = >60 min.

that the sample was biased either towards less severe sufferers who did not mind revealing information about their blushing or more severe sufferers who perhaps felt that revealing information about themselves would generate further assistance for their problem. The sample was large enough, however, to provide some preliminary descriptive data.

Each subject was asked to provide information in the following 10 areas:

1. age
2. age of onset of blushing as a problem
3. gender
4. thoughts when blushing
5. situations in which blushing occurs
6. effects of blushing on everyday life
7. severity of blushing
8. time before a blush subsides
9. methods used for making a blush go away
10. methods for coping with the problems of blushing

Blushing: Cognitions and coping

The basic description of the sample concerning current age, age of onset, severity of blushing (rated 1 = not at all to 4 = extreme), and time for blushing to subside (1 = <1 min; 2 = 1–5 min; 3 = 5–60 min; 4 = 60 min) is presented in Table 7.1. (Given that the article that elicited the sample appeared in a women's magazine, it is perhaps not surprising that all but three of the respondents were female.) Severity ratings indicated moderate difficulties over the group, which suggested that the respondents might not in fact be biased in the ways referred to earlier.

The average age of recalled onset of blushing was during early adolescence. The increased occurrence of blushing during adolescence has been noted by a number of authors (e.g., de Beauvoir, 1957; Van den Berg, 1955); further, Horowitz (1962) found that the greatest numbers of embarrassing incidents remembered by high school and college students had occurred between the ages of 11 and 15 years. Whereas it is no doubt the case that retrospective reports may not produce reliable data, adolescence does seem to be a peak time for blushing/embarrassment difficulties. No longer being a child and not yet an adult, the adolescent has yet to develop a familiar repertoire of behaviours. Aware of his or her potential deficiencies, blushing at the slightest provocation, the adolescent may well be inclined to be over-attentive to his or her internal state and hence over-react to an initial mild response.

In order to gain a clearer impression of the thoughts associated with blushing, subjects' responses were coded into those that specifically mentioned concern about their own responses ("I'm going red", "I want to hide", etc.) and those that specifically mentioned fears about how others were evaluating them ("What must they think", "Everyone is looking", etc.); a third category consisted of those who mentioned both their own and others' responses. The numbers coded in each of the three main categories, with specific reactions mentioned, are shown in Table 7.2.

In order to examine the effect that blushing had on an individual's life, responses were coded into those that contained a cognitive (worry) component and those that contained a behavioural (avoidance) component; a third category consisted of those mentioned both worry and avoidance.

Situations that gave rise to blushing were coded according to whether respondents referred to people or to temperature changes. Many subjects specifically referred to the fact that there was no actual situation that elicited blushing, the crucial factor being any situation in which a potential observer was present.

Methods for coping with a current blush were coded according to whether respondents referred to behavioural avoidance, cognitive techniques, or physiological strategies (the majority, however, reported that they were unable to cope). General methods for dealing with blushing were also coded into the preceding categories, with additional categories referring to medical intervention, hypnosis, and the use of makeup.

Blushing: An evaluation

Respondents clearly had little difficulty eliciting cognitions associated with blushing, and specific comments tended to reinforce the notion that

Table 7.2. *Thoughts and situations associated with blushing, the effects of blushing, and coping with blushing*

(a) Thoughts associated with blushing		
About own reaction		37% of respondents
Specific reactions mentioned:		
Panic/"Oh no"	$(n = 3)$	
I'm going red	$(n = 21)$	
I want to run and hide	$(n = 7)$	
I feel annoyed	$(n = 6)$	
About others' reactions		46
Specific reactions mentioned:		
They think I'm an idiot	$(n = 6)$	
They think I'm pink	$(n = 10)$	
What must they think	$(n = 14)$	
Everyone is looking	$(n = 12)$	
Everyone is laughing at me	$(n = 4)$	
Both own and others' reactions		17
(b) Effects of blushing on life		
Constant worry		45
Specific worries mentioned:		
About meeting people	$(n = 5)$	
What others are thinking	$(n = 40)$	
Avoidance		30
Specific avoidance mentioned:		
Avoid visiting	$(n = 7)$	
No social life	$(n = 20)$	
Avoid shopping	$(n = 3)$	
Constant worry plus avoidance		25
Specific category mentioned:		
What others are thinking + lack of social life	$(n = 25)$	
(c) Situations causing blushing		
Any situation involving people		84
Hot rooms		2
People + hot rooms		11
Rudeness		2
Unspecified		1
(d) Method for coping with current blush		
Unable to cope		62
Behavioural avoidance (leaving room)		17
Cognitive (distraction)		10
Physiological (relax, breathe slowly)		9
Combinations of above		2
(e) General methods for dealing with blushing[a]		
Totally unable to deal with blushing		22
Behavioural avoidance		3

Table 7.2. (*cont.*)

Cognitive (ignore and/or put up with it)	12
Hypnosis	11
Physiological (e.g., relaxation, yoga)	13
Mention of GP and/or tranquillisers	22
Wearing makeup	22

[a] Some subjects mentioned more than one strategy; the percentages thus are not cumulative.

relativity) of morality and of the triviality of breaches. At the same time, a central problem for these individuals was over-concentration on their own bodily reactions and/or over-concern with the reactions of others. For example:

When I blush I think that people think I'm an idiot, and I feel like one too, but I also think that people think I'm guilty of something too. (35-year-old woman)

When I blush I think of what the other people must be thinking. Things like – she has gone bright red or she is blushing or she must be really embarrassed or even why is she blushing? (30-year-old woman)

I'm going red! Why? I wish I could stop. I'm getting hot; come on don't be silly, I'm too old to blush. (26-year-old woman)

The fact that these cognitions generated further concern is evident in the worry/avoidance reaction associated with a fear that blushing might occur. This, again, was reinforced by specific comments:

The fear of blushing is awful. I hate going to places where I am likely to meet other people. I even worry about meeting friends or relations who I have not seen for a while. (30-year-old woman)

I can't seem to get through a day without blushing. I feel as though I don't want to talk to new friends, as I know I will blush. I can't even laugh at something without blushing. (16-year-old woman)

Blushing affects me very much, I can't do things that I would like to do. It hurts to see people having a good time and that I can't be part of it. I'm scared to talk to people 'cause I know I will blush. (22-year-old woman)

The absence of any clear external eliciting stimuli was also suggested by the responses. The only stimulus required was the presence of an observer, who was seen in an evaluative capacity; the subjective feeling of discomfort was generated by an overconcentration on and fear of one's own likely reaction. This is clearly illustrated in the following comments:

It occurs if I'm introduced to any new person or even buying something in a shop. Really any occasion where it is likely that people will notice/look at me. (19-year-old woman)

No particular situation really; I just seem to blush easily. I can be talking to friends and I think don't start going red and then I blush and wish the ground would open up and swallow me. (35-year-old woman)

The fact that many chronic blushers are unable to cope with their difficulty is no doubt partly due to a lack of knowledge about how to cope and the use of inappropriate strategies. It is also likely that coping is made more difficult by a predisposition to blush and cognitive distortions concerning the likely cue salience of blushing. Difficulty in coping may explain why many referred to specific physical remedies:

The only thing I've done about my problem is go to my GP. He prescribed tranquillisers which seem to stop my blush from being so deep or from lasting as long. (27-year-old woman)

I've found a product which helps me cover up my blushes – it's a colour corrective moisturiser which you wear under your normal makeup and it tones your blushes. (22-year-old woman)

A few people mentioned trying hypnosis or attempting to relax, but other psychologically related strategies were rarely citied. Given the important cognitive component involved in the unpleasant nature of chronic blushing, the importance of cognitive techniques in reducing self-attention is likely to be an important factor. Clearly, this is an intervention issue that requires careful scrutiny.

Given the importance of cognitive factors in apparently creating an unpleasant subjective state from the visible display of blushing, a central question that needs to be answered is whether or not there is something fundamentally different between blushing as exhibited by chronic blushers and blushing as exhibited following a social accident, transgression, or faux pas by those who are not chronic blushers. Whether or not one can differentiate between the two groups in skin temperature changes or other signs of bodily arousal clearly warrants careful examination. In relation to the model outlined previously, however, the current descriptive evidence seems to support the notion that for some individuals embarrassment can be experienced in the absence of a clearly defined external stimulus, with cognitive appraisal of internal events creating the subjective state of embarrassment. If bodily cues are indeed of such importance, the question arises whether or not these are culture-specific; perhaps alternative cues are associated with embarrassment in different cultures, cues that operate in a similar way to blushing within the United Kingdom.

Cross-cultural aspects of embarrassment

Background

One of the major controversies that have dominated the history of emotion research is the debate over universality versus cultural determinism. The belief that emotions are expressed in the same forms in different cultures and that emotional expressions are innate can be traced to the work of Darwin (1872). More recently, Ekman (1972, 1973) has presented evidence to support Darwin's claim. Others, however (e.g., Birdwhistell, 1971), have rejected the innateness notion, pointing to the fact that both the incidences and meanings of expressions vary between different social groups.

In an attempt to reconcile possible innate and learned aspects of emotional expression, Ekman (1972, 1977) has put forward what he calls a neuro-cultural model of emotional expression. Although the antecedent events may differ across cultures, he assumes the existence of at least six fundamental emotions with innate expressions. He also argues that it is possible to modify these innate expressions by the learning of "display rules".

With regard to cultural differences in the reported physiological symptoms and behaviours associated with embarrassment, previous suggestions are also contradictory. Eibl-Eibesfeldt (1972) points to similarities in the expression of embarrassment across cultures:

Another complex of behaviour patterns which is similar in a diversity of cultures is that of coyness, embarrassment and flirting. One pattern of embarrassment is the hiding of the face or just the mouth behind one hand. I have filmed this in Europeans as well as in Samoans, Balinese, Africans, Papuans and Waika Indians. (p. 302)

The fact that there may also be cultural differences in expressions of embarrassment was pointed out by La Barre: "Modern Chinese, in South China at least, protrude the tongue for a moment and then retract it, to express embarrassment at a *faux pas*" (1947, p. 59). If bodily cues are important in determining the subjective state of embarrassment, then one would expect close similarities in expressions across cultures. Attempts at controlling or regulating embarrassment obviously will depend upon the individual's perception of the expressive behaviour that is to be controlled or regulated and on the basis of rules of performance that are determined by cultural norms. In line with Ekman's suggestion, the expression might be constant across cultures, whilst attempts at control might vary. Our recent studies have addressed this possibility; full details of those studies have been presented elsewhere (Edelmann

Table 7.3. *Sample sizes and sample characteristics across cultures*

Variable	Greece	Italy	Japan	Spain	United Kingdom	West Germany
Number of subjects	96	108	200	196	100	200
Male subjects (%)	33	42	46.5	47	34	50
Female subjects (%)	67	58	53.5	53	66	50
Mean age in years	19.6	21.5	19.3	26	22.3	22.9
S.D. in years	2.2	3.2	2.6	8.4	3.8	3.2

et al., 1987, 1989; Edelmann & Iwawaki, 1987), and only a summary of relevant details will be presented here.

The questionnaire and subjects

Data concerning cross-cultural aspects of embarrassment were collected by questionnaire from 900 subjects in six countries. All subjects had lived since childhood in the countries concerned (Greece, Italy, Japan, Spain, United Kingdom, and West Germany), and they were native speakers of the languages in question. Details of the samples are given in Table 7.3.

The questionnaire was an adapted and extended version of a questionnaire used in a study of the antecedents and components of emotion (joy, anger, fear, sadness) by Scherer, Summerfield, and Wallbott, (1983). Equivalent forms of the questionnaire were developed in Greek, Italian, Japanese, Spanish, English, and German. The questionnaire itself was divided into sections dealing with the circumstances surrounding the event, the reaction associated with embarrassment, and coping attempts. Specific aspects of the reaction and coping attempts will be discussed here.

Questions of relevance to the current discussion asked for descriptions of (1) physiological and non-verbal reactions, the amount of verbalisation, the intensity and duration of the emotion, the amount of control attempted, and the success of these attempts at control and (2) non-verbal coping strategies.

Because most of the questionnaire consisted of free response items, it was necessary to develop coding schemes for a systematic analysis of responses. An adapted and extended version of a coding scheme used by Scherer et al. (1983) was developed, and the coding was performed in each location by the co-investigators. It should be kept in mind that the results are based upon self-reports rather than observed behaviour. As

Table 7.4. *Differences in reaction categories between nations*

Symptom group	Greece	Italy	Japan	Spain	United Kingdom	West Germany
Temperature	54	49	60	60	79	58
Mouth	3	2	1	2	1	3
Chest	65	43	35	43	46	42
Stomach	9	4	1	2	1	5
Muscles	36	30	21	33	28	31
Voice	43	45	46	49	53	38
Face	43	42	49	37	38	33
Eyes	29	12	13	30	49	31
Body	11	16	3	13	18	9
Motor behaviour	9	6	12	10	6	6
Posture	12	9	19	17	18	7

Note: Figures represent percentages coded in the respective categories for each nation.

such, they may represent socially normative behaviours, actual behaviours, or a combination of both. If the reports represent normative behaviours, they may represent the "best possible option" in a given culture; actual behaviours may, on occasion, be discrepant from the desired option. It seems fair to assume, however, that reports will represent a combination of both actual behaviours and normative behaviours and as such will give a fair indication of the behaviour that might be anticipated in a given culture.

Cross-cultural comparisons

Physiological symptoms and non-verbal behaviour. Because the symptom and expression codes were elaborate, with many possible alternative symptoms and reactions, the frequencies with which many categories were reported were quite small across countries. These categories were thus combined according to the body part mentioned: voice, face, eyes, body (gestures, movement), motor behaviour (orientation), posture, and physiological symptoms (temperature, chest, stomach, and muscles). These categories are broadly comparable to those used by Scherer et al. (1983). Table 7.4 shows the frequencies of these reaction groups for each culture.

Reactions rarely mentioned by any sample included "mouth symptoms" (e.g., lump in throat, swallowing), "stomach symptoms" (churning stomach, butterflies, etc.), specific body movements, motor behaviour, and posture. The small numbers in these categories meant that statistical analysis would not be very meaningful.

Table 7.5. *Most important physiological symptoms and non-verbal behaviours across samples (mentioned by at least 15% of the sample in one location)*

Symptom type	Greece	Italy	Japan	Spain	United Kingdom	West Germany
Temperature:						
Rise in temperature	13	4	13	25	15	11
Blushing	25	29	30	21	55	34
Chest:						
Heart beats faster	50	39	32	33	38	40
Muscles:						
Tension of muscles	22	25	18	23	25	24
Face:						
Laugh	4	4	15	4	19	10
Smile/grin	33	33	25	35	37	20
Eyes:						
Averted gaze	12	8	11	11	41	22
Body:						
Face touching	2	8	2	2	16	4

Note: Figures represent percentages coded in the respective categories for each nation.

Chi-square tests were performed on the six remaining reaction groups, comparing observed percentages across nations with expected frequencies under the assumption of equal distributions, compared with theoretical χ^2 values with five degrees of freedom. Although there were some variations between the reaction groups across the six samples, the only difference that reached significance was for eye reactions ($\chi^2 = 34.2$, $p < .01$), reflected by the lower frequency reported by the Italian and Japanese samples and the higher frequency reported by the U.K. sample.

The most frequently mentioned changes in all samples involved "temperature" symptoms (particularly a rising body temperature and blushing), "chest" symptoms (particularly heart beating faster), "muscle" symptoms (particularly muscle tension), "voice" symptoms, for which no particular category predominated, and "facial" symptoms (particularly smiling and grinning). The most frequently reported sub-categories are shown in Table 7.5. Although there were overall similarities in the specific reactions reported, blushing, averted gaze, and face touching predominated in the U.K. sample, whereas a faster heart rate predominated in the Greek sample. Laughter as an embarrassed response was reported to be unlikely to occur in Greece, Italy, or Spain. Although differences existed in self-reported reactions across cultures, these were quite small and mirrored

Table 7.6. *Comparisons of amount of verbalisation, intensity, duration, control, and success of control for embarrassment across cultures* ·

	Greece	Italy	Japan	Spain	United Kingdom	West Germany	F	P
Amount of verbalisation[a]	4.0	3.5	3.0	3.2	3.0	3.4	7.5	0.001
Intensity[b]	3.9	3.3	3.4	3.2	3.0	3.6	9.5	0.001
Duration[c]	1.9	1.7	2.0	1.7	1.3	1.5	6.2	0.001
Control[b]	3.4	2.9	2.8	2.9	3.0	3.3	7.0	0.001
Success of control[b]	3.0	2.5	2.3	2.9	2.3	2.8	8.4	0.001

[a] Amount of verbalisation: 1, saying nothing; 2, verbalisation (word/part word); 3, exclamation (swearing, "Oops", etc.); 4, utterance/part sentence; 5, discussion/conversation.
[b] Intensity, control, and success of control: scale from 1 (not at all) to 5 (extremely).
[c] Duration: 1, 5 min or less; 2, 5 min to 1 hr; 3, 1 hr to 1 day; 4, several days or longer.

similarities of self-reported symptoms associated with other emotions across cultures (Scherer, Wallbott, & Summerfield, 1986).

Amount of vocalisation, intensity and duration of the emotion, amount of control, and success of control. In the questionnaire, these data were obtained either by rating scales directly (for intensity, amount of control, and success of control, 1 = not at all, and 5 = extremely) or by coding of open-ended answers that could all be translated into a semi-interval scale (for verbalisation, 1 = saying nothing, and 5 = discussion/conversation; for duration, 1 = under 5 min, and 4 = several days or longer).

Each variable was analysed by a two-way ANOVA; the between-subject variables were gender and country (Greece, Italy, Japan, Spain, United Kingdom, and West Germany). There were no significant main effects of gender, nor were any of the interactions significant. The mean scores for variables for each country, together with significance levels, are presented in Table 7.6.

The amounts of verbalisation showed interesting cultural differences. Post hoc comparison of means using a Newman–Keuls test showed that the Greek, Italian, and West German subjects reported saying significantly more than did the U.K. sample, with the Greek sample saying significantly more than any of the remaining five samples.

The intensity of embarrassment reported by the U.K. sample was significantly less than that reported by any of the other five samples. The Spanish sample reported experiencing significantly less intense embarrassment than did the Greek or West German sample, the latter of which also reported experiencing less intensity of embarrassment than did the Greek sample.

For duration of embarrassment, the U.K. sample reported that their embarrassment lasted for significantly less time than did that among the Greek, Italian, Japanese, or Spanish sample. The Greek and Japanese samples also reported embarrassment of significantly longer duration than did the West German sample.

The amount of control attempted was significantly less for the Italian, Japanese, Spanish, and U.K. samples than for the Greek or West German sample. The Japanese and U.K. samples felt that they were significantly less successful than the Greek, Spanish, and West German samples at controlling their embarrassment, and the Italian sample felt that they were significantly less successful than the Greek and West German sample.

It seems, then, that there are greater variations between nations in variables associated with the experience of embarrassment (intensity, duration, verbalisation, control, and success of control) than in the reported display of embarrassment itself. This may well be a reflection of Ekman's display rules (1972), that is, the conventions, norms, and habits that develop regarding the management of emotional responses. Thus, the lack of verbal response and the less intense embarrassment of shorter duration reported by the U.K. sample may illustrate the playing down of emotions stereotypically noted in the United Kingdom (i.e., the notion of the "stiff upper lip"). As Harper, Wiens, and Matorazzo (1978) point out, the British are noted for their "understatement" of emotion; one might similarly suggest that the Greek sample showed evidence of "over-statement". The underlying physiological/non-verbal reaction of embarrassment did, however, show a great deal of overlap across nations.

Non-verbal coping strategies. As with the non-verbal reaction, categories were combined according to body part mentioned: face, eyes, body (gesture, movement), motor behaviour (orientation, locomotion), and posture. Table 7.7 gives the frequencies across the six samples, in addition to the most frequently cited "symptoms" within each category. Involvements of body movement, motor behaviour, and postural re-actions in coping attempts were not reported with any frequency in any of the six samples, and the small numbers in each category meant that statistical comparisons would not be very meaningful.

Chi-square tests were performed on the remaining reaction groups, comparing observed percentages across nations with expected frequen-cies under the assumption of equal distributions, compared with theo-retical χ^2 values with five degrees of freedom.

There were significant variations in the use of facial displays to cover

Table 7.7. *Non-verbal reactions as attempts to cover or hide embarrassment across samples, with most frequently cited specific reactions within each group*

	Greece	Italy	Japan	Spain	United Kingdom	West Germany
Face:	54	13	34	40	43	38
Smile/grin	44	11	17	33	23	29
Eyes:	26	36	9	23	40	31
Seek eye contact	16	12	1	8	6	9
Avoid eye contact	9	18	8	14	34	22
Body	9	5	3	11	6	5
Motor behaviour	7	6	7	17	12	8
Posture	12	6	9	10	9	8

Note: Figures represent percentages coded in each category for each nation.

embarrassment ($\chi^2 = 24.8$, $p < .01$), reflected by less smiling/grinning in the Italian and Japanese samples and more smiling/grinning in the Greek sample, in comparison with the Spanish, U.K., and West German samples ($\chi^2 = 26.5$, $p < .01$).

There were also significant variations in the use of eye gaze to cover embarrassment ($\chi^2 = 21.4$, $p < .01$), reflected by the frequent reporting of averted gaze by the U.K. sample and the infrequent mention of eye gaze variations by the Japanese sample in relation to the other five samples.

Non-verbal coping attempts for each nation involved a combination of smiling, grinning, or laughing and avoiding eye contact, although with some marked variations. Smiling/grinning were reported infrequently by the Italian and Japanese samples, and eye gaze variations were rarely reported by the Japanese sample. Seeking eye contact was as likely as avoiding eye contact in Greece and Italy, but avoiding eye contact predominated in the United Kingdom and West Germany.

Overall, these results could be interpreted as suggesting a degree of similarity across cultures in the self-reported reactions of embarrassment, but with wider cultural variations in both the associated variables and control attempts. These findings fit with Ekman's notion (1972, 1977) of an innate expression modified by "display rules", although further research in a wider range of cultures, relying upon data other than those derived from self-reports, is clearly still required. Initial data, however, further highlight the possibility that behaviours associated with embarrassment play an important part in the experience of the emotion. Carefully controlled laboratory studies are needed to further evaluate this suggestion.

Concluding comments

The aim of this chapter has been to present a model that views embarrassment as a complex interaction of events and appraisals of those events. The importance of internal as well as external cues in generating the experience of embarrassment has been emphasised. Given the possibility that in certain cases attending to internal cues may be sufficient to generate the experience of embarrassment, two lines of preliminary research were described. The first examined self-reports derived from self-defined chronic blushers in order to clearly describe the thoughts and actions associated with this response. The second examined self-reports concerning the response and coping attempts associated with embarrassment across cultures. The similarity in responses across nations and the meaning attributed to facial reddening by chronic blushers could be interpreted as indicating that blushing and possibly other behavioural manifestations of embarrassment play some central part in the generation of embarrassment. Clearly, this suggestion requires further, more systematic research. Whether the self-reported nature of blushing and the reaction of embarrassment across cultures correspond to naturally occurring or laboratory-induced blushing and embarrassment remains to be seen. Certainly, within the United Kingdom, grinning, smiling, or laughing and avoidance of eye contact were associated with embarrassment in laboratory studies (Edelmann & Hampson, 1979, 1981). Further, carefully controlled studies will be required to evaluate the responses associated with embarrassment across cultures, as well as to (1) evaluate the precise physiological responses associated with embarrassment, (2) describe the relationship between facial skin temperature changes and subjectively reported embarrassment, and (3) compare the physiological responses experienced by "chronic blushers" and the responses associated with "normal" embarrassment produced by a faux pas, social accident, or transgression. If, as Tomkins (1981) suggests, the skin of the face is particularly important in producing feelings of affect, then blushing and embarrassment may provide a good empirical test for the facial feedback hypothesis.

REFERENCES

Asendorpf, J. (1984). Shyness, embarrassment, and self-presentation: A control theory approach. In R. Schwarzer (Ed.), *The Self in anxiety, stress, and depression* (pp. 109–114). Amsterdam: North Holland.

Bem, D. J. (1967). Self-perception: An alternative interpretation of cognitive dissonance phenomena. *Psychological Review, 74,* 183–200.

Bem, D. J. (1972). Self-perception theory. In L. Berkowitz (Ed.), *Advances in experimental social psychology* (Vol. 6, pp. 1–63). New York: Academic Press.

Birdwhistell, R. L. (1971). *Kinesics and context.* London: Allen Lane, Penguin Press.

Buck, R. W. (1980). Nonverbal behavior and the theory of emotion: The facial feedback hypothesis. *Journal of Personality and Social Psychology, 44,* 13–21.

Buss, A. H. (1980). *Self-consciousness and social anxiety.* San Francisco: Freeman.

Carver, C. S., & Scheier, M. F. (1981). *Attention and self-regulation: A control theory approach to human behavior.* New York: Springer-Verlag.

Darwin, C. (1872). *The expression of the emotions in man and animals:* London: Murray.

de Beauvoir, S. (1957). *The second sex.* New York: Knopf.

Duval, S., & Wicklund, R. A. (1972). *A theory of objective self-awareness.* New York: Academic Press.

Edelmann, R. J. (1985). Social embarrassment: An analysis of the process. *Journal of Social and Personal Relationships, 2,* 195–213.

Edelmann, R. J. (1987a). *The psychology of embarrassment.* Chichester, Sussex: Wiley.

Edelmann, R. J. (1987b). *Chronic blushing: A model and some preliminary descriptive data.* Paper presented at the British Psychological Society London conference.

Edelmann, R. J., Asendorpf, J., Contarello, A., Georgas, J., Villanueva, C., & Zammuner, V. (1987). Self-reported verbal and non-verbal strategies for coping with embarrassment in five European cultures. *Social Science Information, 26,* 869–883.

Edelmann, R. J., Asendorpf, J., Contarello, A., Zammuner, V., Georgas, J., & Villanueva, C. (1989). Self-reported expression of embarrassment in five European cultures. *Journal of Cross Cultural Psychology, 20,* 357–371.

Edelmann, R. J., & Hampson, S. E. (1979). Changes in non-verbal behaviour during embarrassment. *British Journal of Social and Clinical Psychology, 18,* 385–390.

Edelmann, R. J., & Hampson, S. E. (1981). Embarrassment in dyadic interaction. *Social Behavior and Personality, 9,* 171–177.

Edelmann, R. J., & Iwawaki, S. (1987). Self-reported expression and consequences of embarrassment in the U.K. and Japan. *Psychologia, 30,* 205–216.

Eibl-Eibesfeldt, I. (1972). Similarities and differences between cultures in expressive movements. In R. A. Hinde (Ed.), *Nonverbal communication* (pp. 297–315). Cambridge University Press.

Ekman, P. (1972). Universal and cultural differences in facial expression of emotion. In J. R. Cole (Ed.), *Nebraska Symposium on Motivation* (pp. 207–283). Lincoln: University of Nebraska Press.

Ekman, P. (1973). Cross-cultural studies of facial expression. In P. Ekman (Ed.), *Darwin and facial expression* (pp. 169–222). New York: Academic Press.

Ekman, P. (1977). Biological and cultural contributions to body and facial movement. In J. Blacking (Ed.), *The anthropology of the body* (pp. 39–84). London: Academic Press.

Emerson, J. P. (1970). Behavior in private places: Sustaining definitions of reality in gynecological examinations. In H. P. Dreitzel (Ed.), *Recent sociology. No. 2: Patterns of communication behavior* (pp. 74–97). New York: Macmillan.

Goffman, E. (1955). On face-work. *Psychiatry, 18*, 213–231.

Goffman, E. (1956). Embarrassment and social organisation. *American Journal of Sociology, 62*, 264–271.

Harper, R. G., Wiens, A. N., & Matorazzo, J. D. (1978). *Nonverbal communication: The state of the art.* New York: Wiley.

Horowitz, E. (1962). Reported embarrassment memories of elementary school, high school, and college students. *Journal of Social Psychology, 56*, 317–325.

Hull, J. G., & Levy, A. S. (1979). The organization functions of the self: An alternative to Duval and Wicklund's model of self-awareness. *Journal of Personality and Social Psychology, 37*, 756–768.

Jerremalm, A., Jansson, L., & Ost, L.-G. (1986). Cognitive and physiological reactivity and the effects of different behavioural methods in the treatment of social phobia. *Behaviour Research and Therapy, 24*, 171–180.

La Barre, W. (1947). The cultural basis of emotions and gestures. *Journal of Personality, 16*, 49–69.

Laird, J. D. (1984). The role of facial response in the experience of emotion: A reply to Tourangeau and Ellsworth, and others. *Journal of Personality and Social Psychology, 47*, 909–917.

Leary, M. R. (1982). Social anxiety. In L. Wheeler (Ed.), *Review of personality and social psychology* (Vol. 3, pp. 97–120). Beverly Hills, CA: Sage.

Leary, M. R. (1983). *Understanding social anxiety.* Beverly Hills, CA: Sage.

Leary, M. R., & Schlenker, B. R. (1981). The social psychology of shyness: A self-presentation model. In J. T. Tedeschi (Ed.), *Impression management theory and social psychological research* (pp. 335–358). New York: Academic Press.

Leventhal, H. (1979). A perceptual-motor processing model of emotion. In P. Pliner, K. R. Blankstein, & I. M. Spigel (Eds.), *Advances in the study of communication and affect. Vol. 5: Perception and emotion in self and others* (pp. 1–46). New York: Plenum Press.

Leventhal, H. (1980). Toward a comprehensive theory of emotion. In L. Berkowitz (Ed.), *Advances in experimental social psychology* (Vol. 13, pp. 139–207). New York: Academic Press.

Leventhal, H., & Mosbach, P. A. (1983). The perceptual-motor theory of emotion. In J. T. Cacioppo & R. E. Petty (Eds.), *Social psychophysiology: A sourcebook* (pp. 353–387). New York: Guilford Press.

McEwan, K. L., & Devins, G. M. (1983). Is increased arousal in social anxiety noticed by others? *Journal of Abnormal Psychology, 92*, 417–421.

Modigliani, A. (1966). *Embarrassment and social influence.* Unpublished doctoral dissertation, University of Michigan, Ann Arbor.

Modigliani, A. (1968). Embarrassment and embarrassibility. *Sociometry, 31*, 313–326.

Modigliani, A. (1971). Embarrassment, facework, and eye contact: Testing a theory of embarrassment. *Journal of Personality and Social Psychology, 17*, 15–24.

Ost, L.-G., Jerremalm, A., & Johansson, J. (1981). Individual response patterns and the effects of different behavioural methods in the treatment of social phobia. *Behaviour Research and Therapy, 19,* 1–16.

Scheier, M. F. (1976). Self-awareness, self-consciousness, and angry aggression. *Journal of Personality, 44,* 627–644.

Scheier, M. F., & Carver, C. S. (1977). Self-focused attention and the experience of emotion: Attention, repulsion, elation and depression. *Journal of Personality and Social Psychology, 35,* 625–636.

Scheier, M. F., & Carver, C. S. (1982). Cognition, affect and self-regulation. In M. S. Clark & S. T. Fiske (Eds.), *Affect and cognition* (pp. 157–183). Hillsdale, NJ: Lawrence Erlbaum.

Scheier, M. F., Carver, C. S., & Matthews, K. A. (1983). Attentional focus in the perception of bodily states. In J. Cacioppo & R. E. Petty (Eds.), *Social psychophysiology: A sourcebook* (pp. 510–542). New York: Guilford Press.

Scherer, K. R., Summerfield, A. B., & Wallbott, H. G. (1983). Cross-national research on antecedents and components of emotion: A progress report. *Social Science Information, 21,* 355–385.

Scherer, K. R., Wallbott, H. G., & Summerfield, A. B. (Eds.). (1986). *Experiencing emotion. A cross-cultural study.* Cambridge University Press.

Schlenker, B. R., & Leary, M. R. (1982). Social anxiety and self-presentation: A conceptualisation and model. *Psychological Bulletin, 92,* 641–669.

Semin, G. R., & Manstead, A. S. R. (1981). The beholder beheld: A study of social emotionality. *European Journal of Social Psychology, 11,* 253–265.

Semin, G. R., & Manstead, A. S. R. (1982). The social implications of embarrassment displays and restitution behaviour. *European Journal of Social Psychology, 12,* 367–377.

Timms, M. W. H. (1980). Treatment of chronic blushing by paradoxical intention. *Behavioral Psychotherapy, 8,* 59–61.

Tomkins, S. S. (1981). Affect theory. In P. Ekman (Ed.), *Emotion in the human face* (2nd ed., pp. 353–395). Cambridge University Press.

Vallelonga, D. (1976). Straus on shame. *Journal of Phenomenological Psychology, 7,* 55–69.

Van den Berg, J. H. (1955). *Phenomenological approach to psychiatry.* Springfield, IL: Thomas.

8

Blushing as a discourse: Was Darwin wrong?

CRISTIANO CASTELFRANCHI and
ISABELLA POGGI

The aim of this chapter is to consider the social and biological functions of shame and the communicative value of its most typical expression, blushing, while arguing against Darwin's theory of blushing, which would deny it any specific function.

Embarrassment, shame, and guilt

Before elaborating on our topic we wish to define our sense of the word "shame" as opposed to "embarrassment". A common element in shame and embarrassment is that they are unpleasant social emotions. They may be called social in that they have the function of cognitive mediators of the individual's social behaviour (Castelfranchi, Conte, Miceli, & Poggi, 1989): Through the unpleasant feelings they inflict they lead one to avoid or remediate possible misfunctioning in one's relationships with other people.

Apart from this common element and the fact that they may occur at the same time in many situations, one may view shame and embarrassment as largely distinct emotions as to their antecedents, feelings, somatic expressions, and social and biological functions. Yet, as several chapters in this volume have indicated, there is no consensus in the literature that they are different. Some authors (e.g., Goffman, 1967; Zimbardo, 1977) group them in a single category; others distinguish them in terms of severity of inadequacies, with embarrassment experienced for minor flaws and shame for severe flaws (Buss, 1980; Harré, this volume); alternatively, embarrassment is linked to etiquette, and shame to moral worth (Schlenker & Leary, 1982).

In attempting to draw a clearer distinction between the two emotions we find it useful to start with linguistic issues. It is our impression that the semantic areas linked to the words for embarrassment and shame in English and Italian do not completely overlap (Figure 8.1).

The English word "embarrassment" seems to cover at least some part of the meaning that in Italian is borne by *vergogna*, the word for

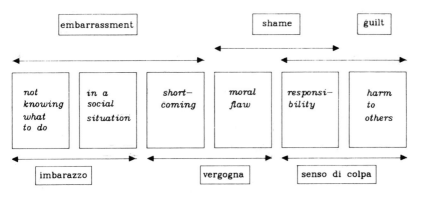

Figure 8.1. The semantic area of embarrassment, shame, and guilt, in English and Italian.

"shame". In particular, the English "embarrassment" seems to include the idea of some shortcoming of the individual, some inadequate feature or behaviour, that in Italian is implied by the word *vergogna*, but not necessarily by the word *imbarazzo*. The minimum necessary core of meaning of *imbarazzo* does not even refer to an emotion; it may simply mean a conflict among different choices: One does not know what to choose or what to do because all choices are equally good (or bad). This element of a decision conflict is still present in *imbarazzo* as an emotion (Zammuner & D'Urso, 1986): In a social situation one may experience some conflict among different goals, often among one's own goal and those of others. Suppose a very boring and dull scholar often intrudes in a conference with lengthy silly and irrelevant questions. This may cause people to be embarrassed (or at least *imbarazzati*), but not, we think, because they feel inadequate. They merely feel uncomfortable because they do not know what to do in such a situation: They are experiencing a conflict between the goal of telling the bore to shut up and the goal of being polite, of not offending the bore. This conflict between two goals, one Ego-oriented and the other Alter-oriented, is, in our view, the crucial semantic element of the Italian word *imbarazzo*. This word, then, covers a more restricted area than the English "embarrassment" because it does not necessarily imply any shortcoming on the part of the embarrassed person. That semantic area is covered, instead, by *vergogna*. Thus, in comparison, "embarrassment" seems to trespass on the area of *vergogna*.

On the other hand, and unlike "shame", *vergogna* may refer not only to moral flaws but also to simple clumsiness. In this, "shame", with its stress on moral matters, looks closer to "guilt", with which it seems to share a semantic element of responsibility (Silver, Sabini, & Parrott, 1987). This is one further divergence of "shame" from *vergogna*, which may refer to physical defects, or even to one's good luck, for which one is not responsible.

Finally, from a linguistic point of view, "guilt" and its Italian match *senso di colpa* seem to overlap much more than do the words for embarrassment and shame, the crucial element in both being responsibility for harm to others.

The mental state of shame

Darwin (1872/1965), consistent with his analysis of other expressions of emotions, proceeds from blushing (the expression) to shame (the emotion). We follow the opposite path of making predictions concerning the functional and phenomenological aspects of blushing on the basis of our theoretical analysis of shame (Castelfranchi, 1988). We start from a cognitive analysis of the mental state of shame, in terms of the goals and assumptions holding within the mind of the ashamed person,[1] from which we derive functional hypotheses about the mental state of shame and about its expression, the blush.

In our view, the most famous functional explanations, the evolutionary explanations provided by ethology and sociobiology, though important and stimulating, are somewhat misleading or weakened because they cut out the cognitive mediator of social and biological facts: the individual's mind. A functional hypothesis about some behaviour, emotion, or verbal or non-verbal communication can, instead, be enhanced and rendered more sophisticated if entities and processes of the mind are taken into account and the mind itself is seen as a mediator, at the level of the individual organism, of social and biological functions. Because goals are what determine external behaviour (Parisi & Castelfranchi, 1984), goals inside the mind may be seen as corresponding to goals outside the mind, therefore acting as their cognitive mediators and, functionally, as their sub-goals (Castelfranchi, 1981). That is why an important parallel can be drawn between, say, an analysis of the mind of the ashamed and blushing person, on the one side, and an analysis of the functions of shame and the blush, on the other side.

In sum, the analysis of the mind is essential, in our opinion, in order to gain a deeper understanding of behaviours and emotions and to reduce their endless variability for theoretical ends. People may be ashamed about an infinite number of things in the various cultures and situations, but the analysis of shame as a state of mind can be abstract and general.

The ashamed person's mind

According to our analysis (Castelfranchi, 1988), shame is an emotion implying regret or fear of being thwarted in one's goal of esteem and/or self-esteem.

As is well known (Izard, 1977; Plutchik, 1980; Scherer, 1983a,b; Scherer & Ekman, 1984), an emotional state includes several aspects: physiological arousal, leading to visceral and somatic responses, a state of physiological and motivational readiness, a subjective feeling, an expressive display of this internal state, and so on. All of these responses are plausibly triggered by a perception of one's state of mind, that is, of the set of one's goals and assumptions. Our analysis focuses on this aspect of the emotion.[2]

Specifically, shame may be a kind of regret – the emotion felt when the individual has been thwarted in one of his or her goals – or it may be a kind of fear – the emotion felt as one assumes that one is risking being thwarted in some goal, namely, the goal of esteem and/or the goal of self-esteem. In other words, we are ashamed when we regret or fear a loss of face before others or ourselves.[3] In this sense, shame is an alarm system for face-saving, and its function is to protect our goals of esteem and self-esteem, in that the pain it causes us informs us when we are thwarting those goals or are about to thwart them.

The goals of esteem and self-esteem are defined, respectively, as the goals of being evaluated positively by others and by ourselves with respect to our values (Castelfranchi, 1988); that is, the goals of showing others and ourselves that we are able to achieve some goals – some norms and expectations.

A goal approach provides us with a tool to simply and precisely define such notions as image, evaluation, value, esteem, and self-esteem. The definition of shame as an emotion aimed at protecting the goals of esteem and self-esteem may lead to predictions about

1. what one is ashamed of – we can be ashamed only about things that cause, or may cause, a negative evaluation of ourselves,
2. those who can feel shame and those who cannot – only people who have some goal of esteem and self-esteem (not infants, for example) can experience shame,
3. those before whom we are ashamed – we can be ashamed only before those whose esteem we seek (including ourselves).

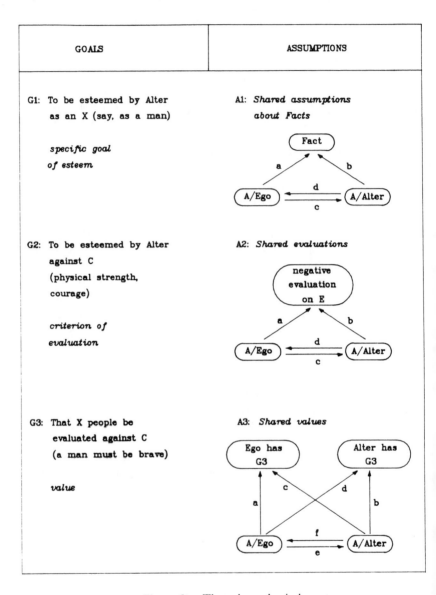

GOALS	ASSUMPTIONS
G1: To be esteemed by Alter as an X (say, as a man) *specific goal of esteem*	A1: *Shared assumptions about Facts*
G2: To be esteemed by Alter against C (physical strength, courage) *criterion of evaluation*	A2: *Shared evaluations*
G3: That X people be evaluated against C (a man must be brave) *value*	A3: *Shared values*

Figure 8.2. The ashamed mind.

The goals and assumptions of shame

As is shown in Figure 8.2, at least three goals and three assumptions must be represented in a person's mind for him or her to be ashamed. Both goals and assumptions generally involve three arguments: E (Ego), the ashamed person; A (Alter), the person before whom E is ashamed; and F (Fact), the fact about which E is ashamed. Here, then, are Ego's goals (as summarised in Figure 8.2, left):

G1: E has the goal of being esteemed by A as an X, that is, as a member of the class X.

He may, for example, want to be considered a *real man* by A. Being considered a worthy member of the class of men is the "specific goal of esteem" of E before A. Coupling that with all other specific goals of esteem of E before A yields a "general goal of esteem of E before A", the whole of positive evaluations E wants to elicit by A.

From goal G1 stems goal G2 – a sub-goal of G1 – in E's mind:

G2: E has the goal of being evaluated positively (esteemed) by A with respect to the criterion of evaluation C.

In our example, E may wish to be judged positively with respect to the criterion of physical strength and courage. A goal that one must be able to fulfill in order to belong to some class can be taken as a criterion of evaluation (Miceli & Castelfranchi, 1989). Being considered a man entails being strong and brave, and anyone unable to do so cannot be considered a real man. So, being evaluated positively against the criterion of courage (i.e., being evaluated as a brave person) is a sub-goal of being considered a man, and for E it also becomes a goal G2, in that it is a necessary means to attaining E's goal G1. This holds, however, only if E also has goal G3, that is, if the evaluation criterion C is also one of E's values:

G3: E has the goal that people who want to belong to the class X are evaluated against criterion C.

In E's view of what it takes to be a man, courage is a value (i.e., a criterion of evaluation that rightly and necessarily applies to being a man). A value is defined, in fact, as a criterion of evaluation against which one has the goal of evaluating, and of being evaluated by others and oneself (Miceli & Castelfranchi, 1989).

We now come to the assumptions of the ashamed Ego.[4]

A1: Assumptions about facts. Generally, if E is ashamed before A, E assumes that he and A share the same assumptions about facts. Suppose

E is a doctor and A is his patient, and A asks him about some new medicine; E is forced to admit that he does not know anything about it and feels ashamed. In this case, E assumes some fact F, that is, that he does not know the medicine (see arrow *a* in Figure 8.2, right, box A1). E assumes that A also assumes F (arrow *b*); but, also, E assumes that A assumes it (*c*), and assumes that A assumes that E assumes it (*d*).

As far as assumptions about facts are concerned (but, as we shall see later, values and assumptions about values are the most crucial ones), assumption *a* would be sufficient for E to be ashamed before himself only. If the doctor tries to bluff his way out of it, pretending he knows the new medicine, he may nonetheless be ashamed in his own eyes; self-shame may be felt even in the absence of assumptions *b*, *c*, and *d*. (On the contrary, as we shall see later, assumption *a* is not a necessary condition to experience shame before others.)

A2: Assumptions about evaluations. Other assumptions by E that are relevant to shame are evaluations – the evaluating assumptions deriving from facts. For E to be ashamed before A, E not only must assume the fact F but also must assume that such a fact naturally leads to a negative evaluation about criterion C. In our example, E not only assumes that he does not know the new medicine but also assumes that such a shortcoming is enough to warrant judging him to be incompetent as a doctor; he assumes that such a fact F can lead to a negative evaluation of himself (Figure 8.2, right, box A2, arrow *a*).

As was the case for assumptions about facts, shame of E before A also requires, first (arrows *b* and *c*), that E assumes that A shares E's negative evaluation resulting from the fact F and, second (arrow *d*), that E assumes that A assumes that he also assumes that evaluation.

A3: Assumptions about values. We now come to the third and, in our model, most crucial assumption related to shame: the assumption about values (Figure 8.2, right, box A3). E cannot be ashamed, before A or himself, if E has not accepted the criterion of evaluation C as one of E's values, as a goal against which E thinks people should be evaluated; and E cannot be ashamed before A if he does not share the criterion of evaluation that E assumes to be a value for A.

In our example, let us assume that E knows that patient A's criterion for evaluating the competence of a doctor is some status symbol, say a luxurious office or a big car. If E does not agree that this is a good criterion for his goal of esteem of being judged a good doctor, this will not be included among his own values, and he will not feel proper shame, either before himself or before A, when going to visit patients in a ramshackle car.

On the other hand, he may be ashamed only in his own eyes if he does not know about a new medicine – for him a relevant criterion – even if A does not use this as a criterion in forming A's opinion. Finally, he will be ashamed before both A and himself in the circumstances outlined in box A_3 – if values are shared. Here, both E and A assume (arrows a and b) that they have G_3 (i.e., the goal that every doctor be judged a good doctor according to the criterion C of medical competance). Furthermore, they each assume the other to have the goal G_3 (arrows c and d), and, finally, E assumes that A assumes E's sharing of value (arrow e) and assumes (arrow f) that A also assumes E's assumption e.

The conditions of shame

According to this analysis of the ashamed mind, three conditions are relevant to being ashamed before others:

1. when assumptions about facts are shared,
2. when paths from facts through evaluations are shared, and
3. when values are shared.

E is ashamed before A if he assumes that he and A share assumptions about some trait or behaviour of E and also assumptions about this fact leading to a negative evaluation against some shared value.

The crucial point we make in this analysis is that the sharing of values (condition 3) is a necessary condition of shame before others, whereas the sharing of assumptions about facts (condition 1) and the sharing of their evaluations (condition 2) are not. If doctor E is only being absent-minded at the moment, but actually does know the new medicine, he may not be ashamed about not answering A readily; likewise, he may not be ashamed if he believes that an overall opinion of medical incompetence should not be based on ignorance of a single new drug.

Moreover, shared assumptions about facts and evaluations are neither necessary nor sufficient conditions for shame to occur; one is not necessarily ashamed even if one has actually been evaluated negatively or criticised in fact. Doctor E may be perfectly aware of the negative evaluation attached to driving an old car. But because he does not agree that surface appearance is a good criterion for judging a doctor, he may not be ashamed of his car and may even drive about in it ostentatiously. In fact, because some criteria of evaluation are values to others, but not to oneself, one can show one's contempt for those criteria by nonchalantly and openly flouting them.

Blushing and the sharing of values

From our analysis of the goals and assumptions in the ashamed person's mind we can draw the following predictions regarding the feeling of shame before others and oneself, and hence the occurrence of blushing.

As values are shared, one may be ashamed before both others and oneself, or only before others. The latter case occurs when values are shared but assumptions about facts or evaluations are not. Suppose a man E saves a girl from drowning and gives her mouth-to-mouth respiration; passer-by A might think that E is taking advantage of the situation. If E has a clear conscience – he knows that is not the case – he does not share the assumption about the fact, and so he will not be ashamed before himself, but he might be before A.[5] Here, shame only before others is caused by failure to share assumptions about facts. The other case of shame only before others occurs when evaluations are not shared, as in the example of the absent-minded doctor, where a momentary lapse of memory does not mean, for him, a serious gap in his medical competence.

Our prediction is that blushing will occur any time shame before others is felt, whether or not one also feels shame before oneself. Instead, blushing will not occur when shame is felt only before oneself, which may happen in three cases:

1. E does not care about A's judgement (E has no goal of esteem before A),
2. A does not share E's value, or
3. A does not know the fact.

An example of the first case arises when a woman E takes an examination on topics she likes and wants to know well, but fails because her examiners are dishonest and make things difficult for her. She despises her examiners, does not have the goal of being esteemed by them at all, but has lost her challenge to herself; so she is ashamed before herself, but not before the examiners. Now suppose that E esteems her examiners, and in the course of the examination she discovers that she cannot remember a topic that is very important to her, but not to them. Again, she may be ashamed before herself, but not before them: The value is not shared. Finally, she may be ashamed before herself only, if she is aware of an important topic she cannot remember, whereas the examiners are not aware of this gap in her knowledge.

In sum, as the goal of esteem is lacking, or as assumptions about values or facts are not shared, shame may be felt only before oneself, and blushing is not likely to occur.

Darwin's view on blushing

Darwin (1872/1965) holds blushing to be "the most peculiar of all expressions" (p. 309), one that is different from others and cannot be elicited by any physical means, such as laughing caused by tickling, or frowning caused by receiving a blow:

It is the mind which must be affected. Blushing is not only involuntary; but the wish to restrain it, by leading to self-attention actually increases the tendency. (p. 310)

Darwin reviews the relative spreading of the blush through the body (on face, cheeks, neck, ears, rarely on the breast, and only in some cases on the abdomen) and across ages (the young blush more than the old), sexes (women do so more than men), mental capacities (infants and idiots usually do not blush), and races (people of all races do, even when blushing cannot easily be seen, as in blacks). He also takes into account the concomitants of blushing: the movements and gestures aimed at concealment (the turning away of eyes, face, and the whole body) and the mental experiences accompanying blushing (desire for concealment and confusion of mind) (pp. 310–325). He goes on: "Nature of the mental states which induce blushing: These consist of shyness, shame, and modesty; the essential element in all being self-attention". And self-attention, in turn, is caused by "the thinking what others think of us" (p. 325). His hypothesis about blushing is that

originally self-attention directed to personal appearance, in relation to the opinion of others, was the exciting cause; the same effect being subsequently produced, through the force of association, by self-attention in relation to moral conduct. (p. 325)

Darwin contrasts his own theory of blushing with that of Dr. Burgess:

that it was designed by the Creator in "order that the soul might have sovereign power of displaying in the cheeks the various internal emotions of the moral feeling"; so as to serve as a check on ourselves, and as a sign to others, that we were violating rules which ought to be held sacred. (cited by Darwin, p. 336)

In Darwin's view,

the belief that blushing was specially designed by the Creator is opposed to the general theory of evolution. . . . Those who believe in design, will find it difficult to account for shyness being the most frequent and efficient of all the causes of blushing, as it makes the blusher to suffer and the beholder uncomfortable, without being of the least service to either of them.' (Darwin, p. 336)

Darwin's hypothesis, instead, is that because

our self-attention is excited . . . by the opinion of others, . . . whenever we know, or suppose, that others are depreciating our personal appearance, our attention is strongly drawn toward ourselves, more specifically to our faces. The probable effect of this will be . . . to excite into activity that part of the sensorium which receives the sensory nerves of the face; and this will react through the vaso-motor system on the facial capillaries. . . . Through the force . . . of association and inheritance our capillaries are relaxed, whenever we know, or imagine, that any one is blaming, though in silence, our actions, thoughts, or character; and, again, when we are highly praised. (p. 344)

Blushing as a communicative signal

Apart from its Lamarckian nuances in attributing blushing to inheritance of learned association (on Darwin's Lamarckian slips, see Ekman, 1972), there is a major flaw in Darwin's theory of blushing: According to him, blushing has no function and no meaning; it is a mere non-functional effect, a mere physiological by-product of self-attention, caused by concern for other people's opinions.

In our view, instead, blushing has a specific meaning: It is a signal with a specific communicative function, even if it bears, of course, a non-intentional communication, even a counter-voluntary one (here we agree with Darwin).

In particular, blushing has the function of communicating some aspects of the mental state involved in shame, namely, the individual's sensitiveness to others' judgements and, at the same time, the individual's sharing of their values. Those who are blushing are somehow saying that they know, care about, and fear others' evaluations and that they share those values deeply; they also communicate their sorrow over any possible faults or inadequacies on their part, thus performing an acknowledgement, a confession, and an apology aimed at inhibiting others' aggression or avoiding social ostracism. Such a view of shame and blushing is supported, among other things, by the existence of a prescription to feel and to show shame as one violates some important value. Such a prescription is given outward expression by imperatives such as "Shame on you!" and "Be ashamed, at least!", or by negative epithets such as "shameless", "cheeky", and so on.

Another flaw in Darwin's theory is the stress laid on a somewhat "conformist" view of the cause of blushing. He often states that blushing is excited by "the thinking what others think of us", by "a sensitive regard for the opinion of others". This seems to us as arbitrary as the well-known misleading trend in anthropology of viewing guilt as the emotion sustaining morality, with shame instead sustaining mere formal outward conformity to others' opinions (Leighton & Kluckhohn, 1947; Mead, 1937); for a criticism of which, see Piers and Singer (1971).

One may find the same view expressed by different authors, for example, Buss (1980), with his claim that shame is linked to evaluation by others, or Goffman (1967), with his dramaturgical model that seems to underestimate the importance or even existence of self-image. In Goffman's view, people, much like puppets, are merely supposed to play roles, and it is only when this role-playing is in some way jeopardised, and when the projected social self is discredited, that shame or embarrassment is felt.

Actually, Darwin rightly sees, in our terms, that the assumptions about facts may not be shared in blushing: "It is not the sense of guilt, but the thought that others think or know us to be guilty which crimsons the face" (1872/1965, p. 332). As we maintained, too, one can be ashamed and blush for some fault others attribute to one, even while knowing that in fact one is blameless.

What Darwin does not see, instead, is that value sharing is a necessary condition for blushing. If a doctor thinks that a luxurious office is not the right criterion on which to be judged a good doctor – if this is not a value of his – he will not be ashamed or blush to receive his patients in a basement flat. Darwin's view thus leads to an interpretation of blushing as mere caring about the opinions of others, which could even be instrumental, opportunistic, and hypocritical.

In fact, other expressive signals of shame, such as averting one's eyes or lowering one's head, can be simulated; they can be performed even if one is not sincerely ashamed – even if one does not subscribe to the values by which one is being judged. A blush, instead, cannot be voluntarily produced, and hence simulated (precisely as noted by Darwin). Such a character of involuntariness must have a function, in our view: Blushing lets others know that some value against which we are, or are believed to be, inadequate is nonetheless a value to us, a value we sincerely share. Thereby they can distinguish us, sincere maintainers of the group's values, from other potentially dangerous individuals who only pretend to share such values, but in fact do not, and therefore do not have the right to belong the group.

Our view about a communicative function of blushing supports Izard's view of the functions of shame:

Shame sensitizes the individual to the opinions and feelings of others and thus acts as a force for social cohesion. It assures the group or society that the individual will be responsive to criticism. (1977, p. 400)

But shame can assure present and future responsiveness to criticism only if it assures the individual's lasting and sincere acceptance of some value, and the group can best be assured about that only by an expression of shame that is not under voluntary control: an expression that cannot be simulated.[6]

Darwin's possible objections, and our counter-objections

What might be Darwin's objections to our view of blushing as a communicative signal? First, he would object that the blush has no function at all: It is completely useless, or even dangerous, because it causes embarrassment to both the blusher and the beholder. And, one might add, it may well be dangerous also because the individual's inadequacies, even when passed unnoticed, may be unmasked by a blush. Furthermore, there exists a prescription, one that is partly contradictory to that of feeling and showing shame, not to be too sensitive to shame, and not to show one's shame even when it is felt. Not to do so becomes a value in its turn, and violating it becomes a source of shame accordingly: a "meta-shame" (i.e., shame of one's shame) (Castelfranchi, 1988). Very briefly, this meta-shame is caused (1) by the somewhat masochistic fact that shame unmasks one's faults and (2) by the fact that shame, as a type of fear, is partly seen as a childish emotion, one not worthy of an adult, and one pointing to an over-sensitivity to the opinions of others. An implicit consideration of this phenomenon may have led Darwin to his observation of the embarrassment caused by the blush in both blusher and bystanders and to his claim of its uselessness for both Ego and Alter.

Against that, we argue, in the first place, that the tendency or desire to conceal some emotion does not imply that feeling it, or even showing it, has no function at all. We usually do not like to show that we are afraid or scared, and we sometimes manage to conceal it; but that does not imply that feeling and sometimes displaying one's fear do not have a function! We therefore maintain, on the contrary, that blushing has a function for both Alter and Ego.

How is blushing of use to Alter? If we accept Izard's view that the group must be given assurance of the individual's responsiveness to criticism, it follows for Alter that it is necessary both to know that Ego is ashamed and to know that that shame (hence E's sharing of the supposed violated value) is sincere. Here lies the importance of blushing and of its involuntariness.

Let us see now why blushing is useful to Ego. As will be argued later, blushing, along with the other components of the expression of shame, such as lowering one's eyes and head, functions as a signal of appeasement. Appeased by a blush, which means an acknowledgement of a value and, possibly, an apology for its violation, the group is less likely to be aggressive towards or isolate the individual. So the blush is useful to the blusher because it protects the individual from the group's aggression or isolation.

One more possible objection by Darwin might be that blacks blush too, even if their blush is not easily visible. How could it have a communicative function?[7] Against that, one could argue, in the first place, that blushing may be still useful to the individual as a monitoring of one's behaviour and as a learning device. People sometimes feel that they are blushing even when a blush is not detectable by others, and this informs one that some value and some possibly negative evaluation of oneself is at issue. The goal of avoiding the unpleasant sensation of feeling oneself blushing, just like the goal of avoiding the unpleasant internal feeling of shame, may teach the blusher to avoid shameful behaviour in future.

Second, we put forward a hypothesis that it is up to biologists and anthropologists to verify: Could it not be the case that the expression of blushing came before race differentiation?

The expression of shame

Along with the blush, Darwin reviews the other components in the expression of shame, including the lowering of the face and averting of the eyes (Izard, 1977; Tomkins, 1962), and explains them in terms of concealment.

Such an interpretation is not completely plausible, in our opinion, for two reasons. First, we think that in principle it is important, in dealing with emotions, to distinguish the somatic response from the subjective experience (and the latter from the mental state): The "strong desire for concealment" does not necessarily imply that one actually performs acts of concealment. Second, it is just in the hypothesis of a concealing manoeuvre that blushing is not coherent with the averting and lowering of the eyes and head. As Tomkins (1962) points out, whereas the head-down, eyes-down posture inhibits facial communication and makes one look even smaller, the blush increases facial visibility. So the posture and the blush would appear to be logically and practically contradictory.

Yet, they can be interpreted coherently if they are viewed as a complex appeasement signal, in the sense of Eibl-Eibesfeldt (1970). Hanging one's head and shrinking are typical appeasement signals, and so is averting one's eyes: This means one gives up any claim of control over the other, and thus, again, one delivers oneself into the other's power. On the other hand, at least from an "etymological" point of view, we could perhaps see a meaning of powerlessness and defencelessness, hence inferiority, in it – again, a meaning of appeasement, a function of inhibiting the aggression of others.[8]

In this view, blushing and the posture of shame are coherent, and they co-operate in forming a complex non-verbal message that could be paraphrased in a discourse aimed at biological and social functions:

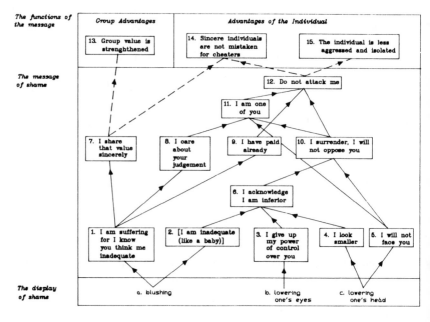

Figure 8.3. Blushing as a discourse.

avoiding aggression against and isolation of the individual, and avoiding the loss of one of the group's loyal members.

A non-verbal discourse

According to Parisi and Castelfranchi (1981), a discourse can be viewed as a hierarchy of goals. Every sentence is a speech act, a linguistic action, and as such it has a goal: to inform of something, to make some request, and so on. But beyond its literal goal (the one directly communicated by its surface meaning), every sentence may have one or more super-goals (superordinate goals of the literal goal) that may be inferred from the literal goal. So we can say that two or more sentences make a discourse when among their super-goals we can find at least one common goal. In such a case, those sentences form a linguistic plan, a hierarchy of goals in which the goals of all sentences directly or indirectly aim at the same final goal.

In this view, the different components in the expression of shame – blushing and the posture and movements of eyes and head – can be seen as forming a non-verbal discourse, in that their surface meanings (their literal goals), by communicating other meanings (their super-goals), all converge towards a unique, final super-goal: inhibiting possible group aggression over an alleged violation of some value. Moreover, such non-verbal discourse has a biological function and a social function in terms of individual and group advantages.

Let us see in detail what the goals and functions of the blush and the other expressions of shame are, as represented in Figure 8.3. In the first place, the component a of the shame expression, the blush, has goal 1: to communicate E's pain caused by E assuming that A thinks E to be inadequate when judged by a value that E shares (this captures the necessity of value sharing and non-necessity of shared assumptions about facts, which we have maintained as typical for blushing). At the same time, the "etymological" sense of the blush (I am like a baby) might possibly [hence the brackets] communicate goal 2: the acknowledgement of the alleged fault or inadequacy. Component b, the lowering of the eyes, communicates goal 3: the giving up of E's power over A (hence E's acceptance of inferiority). Component c, the head lowering, aims at goal 4 (looking smaller) and at goal 5 (giving up facing A).

Goals 2, 3, and 4 all converge towards super-goal 6, that is, acknowledging one's inferiority, which aims, in turn, at assuring super-goal 10: that the individual does not mean to oppose the group. At the same time, communication of goal 1 (i.e., pain for alleged violation) has three super-goals (7, 8, and 9): E is communicating to A that (7) E sincerely shares the value at issue, (8) E cares about A's judgement, and (9) E has already paid, through suffering, for the alleged fault. All three messsages argue for super-goal 11 (the individual maintains the right to continue to belong to the group), to which, in turn, also converges goal 10 (the giving up of the individual's opposition to the group).

Goals 9, 10, and 11 provide three important cores in the communication borne by the whole expression of shame. Individuals argue for their right to belong to the group (11) by informing that they do agree on one of its values, even if they happen to have fallen short of it (7 and 1); at the same time, they inform the group that they have been punished already by the pain of shame (9) and by surrender of any opposition (10). Through such goals, individuals aim at goal 12: requesting that they will not be attacked or ostracised by the group.

So the expression of shame may be viewed as the acknowledgement of a value and as a signal of appeasement, one comparable in its effects to apologies and justifications. And on the basis of this hypothesis, we may make the following empirical prediction: When a group assumes that one of its members has fallen short of some expectation or value, the aggressive reaction (anger and tendency to be aggressive towards or to isolate the member) will be weaker if the group also assumes that the member is ashamed of the violation; more specifically, anger is likely to be lessened by the assumption that the violator is ashamed, and possible aggression is likely to change in kind. In this, the effect of expressing shame should be similar to that of apologies and justifications, which function as inhibitors of aggression.

Of course, the communicative goals we listed probably are not intentional in the expression of shame, nor, perhaps, are they interpreted by a receiver on a completely conscious level; in fact, they might not be represented at all in E's and A's individual minds.[9] Yet they function as sub-goals to some social and biological functions, that is, to some advantages for the group and for the individual.

The individual's communication of having suffered pain for the (alleged) fault (1) and the communication of the sharing of the value (7) serve the external goal – the function – of strengthening the group's value (13). The request to refrain from attack (12) aims at the biological goal of the individual of not being subjected to aggression or being isolated (15), and at the same time, along with the guaranteed sincerity of the value sharing (7) provided by blushing, such a request avoids any aggression against the individual whose violation is due to an accident or mistake, not to contempt for the group's values in principle (14).

Conclusion

Starting from an analysis of the mental state underlying shame, in terms of the goals and assumptions in the ashamed person's mind, we put forward a hypothesis on blushing that differs from Darwin's theory of blushing.

According to our hypothesis, a blush is a communicative signal of shame, functioning as an appeasement signal, that is, one aiming at inhibiting aggression when the individual fears the group's blame for an actual or supposed fault with respect to some group value that the individual shares. So blushing is an act of submission, partly comparable to an apology; in addition, however, its involuntary nature bears witness to the individual's sincerity in showing regret for his or her fault. In this view, blushing, along with the whole posture of shame, the lowering of one's eyes and head, may be viewed as equivalent to a complex message bearing the meaning of a whole discourse, that is, of a coherent set of communicative acts, a message whose goals are ruled by social and biological goals impinging on the individual's mind.

Our hypothesis on blushing also has an important bearing on the theory of communication and action. Treating the blush as a communicative signal, and even one opposite to the individual's intentions, implies admitting that we can count not only behaviours ruled by internal voluntary, conscious goals of the individual – intentions – as communicative but also traits or behaviours that are ruled by some goal external to the individual's mind – some biological or social function (Castelfranchi, 1981; McFarland, 1983). At the same time, it is precisely the observation of such atypical signals as blushing that forces us to take into account such subtle but important distinctions as that between what is a communicative signal and what is not, and among communicative signals ruled by internal and external, intentional and non-intentional, conscious and unconscious goals (Castelfranchi & Poggi, 1987).

Coming back to the blush, it may be linked to other mental states besides shame proper: shyness and modesty. No mention has so far been made of such links (examined by Darwin at length) because we have treated the topic starting from the emotion and working towards its expression, not the other way round, as Darwin does. Yet, we believe that the core of our analysis may also help to explain how blushing is linked to shyness and modesty. As we shall see, in fact, fear of falling short of some value (and the consequent shame) is implicit in both cases.

Shyness may be considered the personality trait for which one tends to avoid exposure and interaction, particularly in order to avoid potential negative evaluation, hence potential shame (on shyness, see Zimbardo, 1977, and Crozier, 1982). Shy persons attach great importance to their goal of esteem, and that is why they fear negative evaluations more than do others. They are therefore persons particularly liable to shame, and particularly skilled in anticipating shame; this can explain the frequency of blushing in the shy.

A third elicitor of blushing is modesty (where Darwin distinguished two different senses). One is the "nineteenth-century modesty" that is given a specific term in many languages: *pudeur* in French, *pudore* in Italian, *Schamgefuhl* in German, *haidos* in Greek, and so on (Schneider, 1977). This is the goal of not showing one's private things, such as one's most intimate acts or parts of the body, or one's feelings, or one's qualities that may be subject to even positive evaluation. Depending on the extent to which this (innate?) goal is felt as a value, the idea of its violation itself may cause anticipation of shame, and therefore blushing.

The other sense of "modesty" is the goal of not showing off one's good qualities. This also appears as a value and a social command whose violation results in a special shame, most typically represented by the shame shown when being praised. Shame experienced because of praise might appear to be a counter-example to our hypothesis, because we said that shame always implies regret or fear of a *negative* evaluation. But we can, in fact, find something negative in praise. First, while being praised, one is in a situation where one is highly exposed to further evaluation, that is, a situation implying an increased risk of potentially negative evaluation, one caused not only by exposure per se but also by the increasing expectations induced in others. Second, one may know or fear that one does not deserve the praise, and that makes one ashamed of one's skill in deceiving people. Third, an actually paradoxical command seems to impinge on people: One must have the goal of being esteemed and of deserving praise, but not the goal of seeking praise, or at least one must not appear to be too glad when being praised. Some negative evaluation, hence potential shame, is thus also linked to this kind of blushing due to modesty.

In sum, even if this is an open issue, it seems to us that some kind of shame is present in all the blush-eliciting cases, in addition to shame proper.

Blushing due to shyness seems to indicate a high sensitiveness to others' opinions; it looks like begging indulgence and apologising in advance for breaches the shy are afraid of committing more often than others do. This is still blushing due to shame, albeit highly exaggerated and anticipated shame.

Blushing out of modesty (in both senses) also seems to be caused by a kind of shame; one form is caused by shame about being praised, the other by an anticipated shame about letting others into one's most private sphere: the sphere of one's self.[10]

Finally, while we spoke of blushing as the expression of shame, one could argue that the blush is also (or even only, see Buss, 1980) an expression of embarrassment. We do not share this view, but we could propose two reasons to account for such a divergence.

A first reason lies, in our opinion, in the linguistic differences, illustrated earlier, of the words for shame and embarrassment in English and other languages. If blushing is, as we maintain, an apology for some shortcoming, a blush has no reason to occur when a shortcoming is not at issue. In fact, no shortcomings of the individual are necessary in *imbarazzo*, but because the English "embarrassment" does seem to entail some shortcoming, it may well be linked with a blush.

The second reason might also explain why researchers often associate blushing with embarrassment: In empirical studies, blushing is often reported when speaking of embarrassment (Buss, 1980; Shields, Mallory, & Simon, 1989). This does not necessarily mean that blushing is triggered by embarrassment per se. It is well known that a blend of emotions is often experienced. Thus, one may be ashamed *and* embarrassed at the same time, or be embarrassed *because* of one's shame. The link between the two emotions is quite strong: Not knowing what to do because of embarrassment may subject one to negative evaluation and hence cause shame, and on the other hand, shame may prevent one from knowing what to do. In such situations it would not be easy for a subject to report whether blushing was caused by shame or embarrassment.

In conclusion, we regard shame and embarrassment as two distinct and somehow opposite emotions, in that the former aims to defend the individual's image, whereas the function of the latter is to avoid intrusion into the private sphere of others.

NOTES

1. By "cognitive aspects of the mind" we do not necessarily mean subjective or conscious aspects, and when we postulate goals or assumptions within the individual's mind, we do not imply that they are conscious.
2. It should be stressed that the aspect of the mental representations underlying emotions, and shame in particular, is usually overlooked: Many authors, among them Izard (1977), who paid particular attention to shame, tend to consider only the physiological, motivational, and subjective aspects.
3. We mean "before" not only in a physical sense; one may be ashamed "before" some person even when thinking ("What would he think of me if he knew x, y, and z?").
4. We borrow our formalism from Power (1984), in view of its clarity and schematicity, but with some modifications. As far as E's assumptions are concerned, we are representing only E's beliefs, not objective facts. We consider only the case in which E is ashamed before A, i.e., a case complicated by the problem that E represents to himself both his own assumptions and those that E assumes to be assumed by A. Of course, instead, the case for E ashamed only before himself is simpler, because no such split in assumptions is needed.
5. Strictly speaking, it is not necessary for E to assume the fact F, but it is necessary for E to assume that he gave A reason for assuming it. If E, on the other hand, besides knowing that the "fact" F is not true, also thinks that A has no reason to assume it, he may be angry, not ashamed, with regard to A.
6. Although we agree with Izard's view of shame as making the individual responsive to criticism, we are still suspicious of his words "opinions ... of others", which seem to push him too far towards an opportunistic view.
7. And yet the "watery eyes" often accompanying a blush, quoted by Darwin himself, provide a good cue for detecting shame in dark-skinned people.
8. Which is the origin of blushing? Could it originally have been a sexual and feminine signal, as MacCurdy (1930) hypothesises? Or can the reddening of the face be seen as a sign of babyishness? In that case, we could detect in it an "etymological" meaning of helplessness and inferiority.
9. Treating the expression of shame as a discourse means drawing a parallel between a structure of internal goals, a true plan of proper discourse, and a structure of external goals or functions; and such a link is metaphorical to some extent. We may distinguish two types of communication (Castelfranchi & Poggi, 1987): first, a non-cognitive communication, or communication "by signals", where the stimulus delivered by E has the goal of simply eliciting a reaction by A, without giving A any information about E's mind ("releasers" in animal behavior are good examples); second, a cognitive communication, or communication "by signs", where the stimulus delivered by E aims at

eliciting a reaction by A by providing A with some knowledge about E's mind, as is the case with human verbal communication. To which type of communication does the expression of shame belong? It might even be a simple releaser, with a very elementary cognitive mechanism, but as far as functional analysis is concerned, its structure may be analysed in all its complexity; in this it can be equated to a verbal message.

10. Although we think that the blushes in shame, shyness, and modesty are all one kind of blush, we think it is important to distinguish blushing from other reddening of the skin, differing in terms of location, eliciting circumstances, and mechanism. For instance, it should not be confused with flushing of the face or trunk due to physical causes or to anxiety.

REFERENCES

Buss, A. H. (1980). *Self-consciousness and social anxiety*. San Francisco: Freeman.

Castelfranchi, C. (1981). Scopi esterni. *Rassegna Italiana di Sociologia, 22*, 329–381.

Castelfranchi, C. (Ed.). (1988). *Che figura. Emozioni e immagine sociale*. Bologna: Il Mulino.

Castelfranchi, C., Conte, R., Miceli, M., & Poggi, I. (1989). *Emotions and goals*. Technical report, Istituto di Psicologia, CNR, Rome.

Castelfranchi, C., & Poggi, I. (1987). Communication. Beyond the cognitive approach and speech act theory. In J. Verschueren & M. Bertuccelli Papi (Eds.), *The pragmatic perspective* (pp. 239–254). Amsterdam: John Benjamins B.V.

Crozier, W. R. (1982). Explanations of social shyness. *Current Psychological Reviews, 2*, 47–60.

Darwin, C. (1965). *The expression of the emotions in man and animals*. University of Chicago Press. (Original work published 1872)

Eibl-Eibesfeldt, I. (1970). *Ethology: The biology of behavior*. New York: Holt, Rinehart & Winston.

Ekman, P. (Ed.). (1972). *Darwin and facial expression: A century of research in review*. New York: Academic Press.

Goffman, E. (1967). *Interaction ritual*. New York: Doubleday.

Izard, C. E. (1977). *Human emotions*. New York: Plenum Press.

Leighton, D., & Kluckhohn, C. (1947). *Children of the people: the Navaho individual and his development*. Cambridge, MA: Harvard University Press.

MacCurdy, J. T. (1930). The biological significance of blushing and shame. *British Journal of Psychology, 21*, 174–182.

McFarland, D. (1983). Intentions as goals. Open peer commentary to D. C. Dennett: Intentional systems in cognitive ethology: The Panglossian paradigm defended. *Behavioral and Brain Sciences, 6*, 369–370.

Mead, M. (1937). *Cooperation and competition among primitive peoples*. New York: McGraw-Hill.

Miceli, M., & Castelfranchi, C. (1989). Values: A cognitive approach. *Journal for the Theory of Social Behaviour, 19*, 169–193.

Parisi, D., & Castelfranchi, C. (1981). A goal analysis of some pragmatic aspects of language. In H. Parret, M. Sbisa' & J. Verschueren (Eds.), *Possibilities and Limitations of pragmatics* (pp. 551–567). Amsterdam: John Benjamins B. V.

Parisi, D., & Castelfranchi, C. (1984). Appunti di scopistica. In R. Conte & M. Miceli (Eds.), *Esplorare la vita quotidiana* (pp. 29–79). Roma: Il Pensiero Scientifico.

Piers, G., & Singer, M. (1971). *Shame and guilt*. New York: Norton.

Plutchik, R. (1980). *Emotion: A psychoevolutionary synthesis*. New York: Harper & Row.

Power, R. (1984). Mutual intention. *Journal for the Theory of Social Behaviour, 14*(1), 85–102.

Scherer, K. R. (1983a). Wider die Vernachlässigung der Emotion in der Psychologie. In W. Michelis (Ed.), *Bericht über den 32. Kongress der DGfP, Zurich, 1981*. Göttingen: Hogrefe.

Scherer, K. R. (1983b). La comunicazione non-verbale delle emozioni. In G. Attili & P. Ricci Bitti (Eds.), *Comunicare senza parole*. Roma: Bulzoni.

Scherer, K., & Ekman, P. (Eds.). (1984). *Approaches to emotion*. Hillsdale, NJ: Lawrence Erlbaum.

Schlenker, B. R., & Leary, M. R. (1982). Social anxiety and self-presentation: A conceptualisation and model. *Psychological Bulletin, 92*, 641–669.

Schneider, C. D. (1977). *Shame, exposure and privacy*. Boston: Beacon Press.

Shields, S. A., Mallory, M. E., & Simon, A. (1989). *The experience and symptoms of blushing in self-conscious emotions*. Unpublished manuscript.

Silver, M., Sabini, J., & Parrott, W. G. (1987). Embarrassment: A dramaturgic account. *Journal for the Theory of Social Behaviour, 17*, 47–61.

Tomkins, S. (1962). *Affect, imagery and consciousness*. New York: Springer.

Zammuner, V., & D'Urso, V. (1986). Imbarazzo. *Giornale Italiano di Psicologia, 13*, 351–382.

Zimbardo, P. G. (1977). *Shyness: What it is, what to do about it*. Reading, MA: Addison-Wesley.

PART III

An emphasis upon shyness

9

A definition of shyness and its implications for clinical practice

HENK T. VAN DER MOLEN

The evidence that the source of much, if not most,
emotional disturbances arises from the lack of good
human relationships is pervasive and generally acknowledged.
—Patterson (1980, p. 658)

Towards a definition of shyness

Introduction

"Shyness is a phenomenon so universally human that we can easily say:
someone who has never been shy or someone who, under certain circumstances, does not run the risk of becoming so is an abnormal person." That is the opening sentence in a book by Schouten (1935), one of
the first Dutch psychologists to take an interest in the specific problems
of shy people. He wrote that in his day, the 1930s, the problem was not
seriously discussed in the literature. Nowadays the situation is quite
different. We can find many publications under other, apparently more
impressive key words, such as "social anxiety" and "sub-assertiveness".

Yzermans (1982) has suggested that the increased interest in the
phenomenon of shyness can be explained by certain developments in
modern culture. These developments are supposed to have made Western people more demanding with respect to social contacts, with the
result that people more frequently come to the conclusion that social
skills are failing.

It is not possible to give a complete review of the literature. On
systematically searching the literature under the key words "timidity",
"social anxiety", and "(non)assertiveness", we found about 1,600 publications! Confronted with such an enormous number of publications, we
had to make a selection. In our study we have mainly used review
articles of the literature (e.g., Hersen, Eisler, & Miller, 1973; Rathus,
1975; Hersen & Bellack, 1976; Rich & Schroeder, 1976; Heimberg,
Montgomery, Madsen, & Heimberg, 1977; Crozier, 1979; Galassi &

Galassi, 1978; Brown & Brown, 1980) and a number of handbooks (e.g., Bellack & Hersen, 1979; Trower, Bryant, & Argyle, 1978).

After a thorough review of this literature, we found that shyness still needs elucidation: Clear definitions often are lacking, and there is no consensus among psychologists. So in this chapter our first goal is to find a clearer definition of the concept of shyness, and a second goal is to discuss the implications of this definition for clinical practice.

In the first section we give a global overview of the different theories about shyness. In the second section we present a basic definition. After that, we elaborate on the characteristic behaviours, thoughts, and feelings in the third section. In the fourth section, the question of the development and persistence of shyness is tackled. The fifth section deals with shyness-evoking situations. In the sixth section we mention several cultural factors; in doing so, we try to estimate the incidence of the phenomenon. Moreover, the question whether or not shyness should be regarded as a psychological problem is dealt with. In the seventh section we present a summarising working definition, which can be used as a basis for clinical practice and empirical research. Linking up with this definition of the problem, the second half of the chapter deals with training objectives and a training method that can be used in clinical practice. This training method has been applied in our "course for shy people" at the University of Groningen, The Netherlands. Finally, we briefly describe the results of our research into the effectiveness of this course.

Theories of shyness

As discussed in other chapters in this volume, there are several theories about the development of shyness (Zimbardo, 1977). The "nature – nurture" discussion seems to have raged in this domain as well. Most characterologists endorse the view that shyness is *congenital*. They believe that the shy type is born with an easily excitable and highly sensitive nervous system, which predisposes the shy individual to avoid conflicts and menacing situations. That theory, however, has received little empirical support. Zimbardo points out that nobody has ever demonstrated that individual differences in constitution between newborn children can predict which baby will develop into a "wallflower" and which into a "rose". In addition to the absence of empirical evidence, an even more questionable point is that this view has dissuaded many people from a systematic treatment of the complaint.

Behaviourists entertain the opposite view. They believe that shyness is not innate, but is *acquired*: Shy people have failed to acquire the social skills necessary for developing relations with others.

Additionally, there are sociologists who believe that shyness can best be seen as a matter of social programming: Social conditions cause a person to be shy. In this connection, it should be stressed that cultures differ strongly in their estimations of shyness. Whereas Western culture rewards assertive behaviour, certain Eastern cultures more appreciate modesty. Thus, Schouten (1935) discusses the Javanese as a people who regard shyness as a virtue. It will be evident that shy behaviour becomes a problem only when cultural norms and values mark such behaviour as less desirable.

Zimbardo defers judgement as to which theory he considers best, but he does think that each point of view can contribute to a better understanding of the phenomenon as a whole. For the rest, he proceeds pragmatically, in the sense that he picks from a theory only those elements that can be of use for framing programmes to contend with shyness.

A cognitive social learning concept of shyness. Zimbardo's pragmatism appeals to us. In our conception of shyness we leave room for different theoretical points of view. This conception links up with the general psychological insight that human behaviour is poly-determined. This also applies to shyness. Our view of the matter, however, has been coloured primarily by cognitive social learning theory in combination with social psychological views. An integrating element of cognitive social learning theory is the *interactionist* point of view: that behaviour is a function both of the individual and of the situation (Lewin, 1935; Mischel, 1968, 1973; Endler & Magnusson, 1976; Schlenker & Leary, 1982).

One reason for this choice pertains to the optimistic nature of learning theory, which assumes that shyness has been acquired and consequently can be conquered as well. In doing so, we do not adopt the jubilant tone detectable in so much of the literature about assertiveness training. Somewhat more modesty would have been appropriate. On the one hand, this somewhat conservative point of view has been inspired by the fact that evaluation research has not yet succeeded in proving beyond the shadow of a doubt that assertive trainers have reached the "promised land". On the other hand, this reservation may also have been induced by our own culture.

Our approach elaborates on recent developments in behavioural therapy that are described more thoroughly in a later section.

Summarising the literature, we can note that the social learning theoretical approach distinguishes three important aspects:

1. fear (phobic component, and attendant symptoms of physical tension),

2. social skills deficit (behavioural component), and
3. irrational thoughts (cognitive component).

Basic definition

The interactionist approach to the individual does not regard shyness as a stable character trait, in the sense of a feature firmly anchored in character, but rather as a possible way of handling interpersonal situations. The appearance of shyness depends not only on personal factors but also on situational factors. Pervin (1978) has expressed the interactionist view as follows:

> Whether a person exhibits a specific behaviour will depend on whether that behavior is a part of one's repertoire, if so, whether it is stable or varies according to the situation and, if variable, its relationship to the particular situation. (p. 471)

The theory of social learning starts from the principle that this "way of handling interpersonal situations" has been acquired.

Despite differences in theoretical perspectives, the literature appears to converge on four aspects: (1) a social aspect, (2) an emotional aspect, (3) an (inadequate) social behavioural aspect, and (4) a cognitive aspect.

We would like to suggest a basic definition that corresponds as much as possible with the lexical meaning and with a feature of current usage, namely, that shyness is primarily a question of personal experience, the individual's feelings and self-image. We believe that the individual is the most reliable expert on his or her own shyness; what others have to say about it is based on enquiries or (fallible) observations of behaviour.

As the concept to be defined, we choose the noun "shyness", not the phrase "shy behaviour", for "shyness" offers us the scope to regard the problem primarily as a concept of experience and only secondarily as a concept of behaviour. Even when a person's behaviour does not strike us as remarkable, he or she still can feel shy.

Individuals can safely be called shy if

1. they consider themselves (to a certain degree) shy, and
2. enquiry and/or observation of behaviour proves that in certain *kinds* of social situations they habitually have to contend with
   (a) feelings of tension, "diffidence", "feeling inhibited",
   (b) behavioural problems (not knowing how to behave in social situations or not daring to do what they really think they ought to do, particularly not daring to speak freely), and
   (c) negative thoughts about themselves.

Behaviours, thoughts, and feelings characteristic of shyness

In this section we consider more extensively the question of which behaviours, thoughts, and feelings accompany shyness as defined earlier.

Behaviour. The first area of consensus among psychologists pertains to the behavioural features described. Thus, shy persons seldom dare to strike up a conversation with a stranger. Whenever they do so, they often make a clumsy impression and hardly manage to conceal their embarrassment. Other noticeable features are avoidance of eye contact and a tendency to speak softly or inarticulately. Shy people often lack initiative; they prefer to wait until they are asked. Seldom making requests, refusing anything, criticising, expressing positive and negative feelings in general, or responding spontaneously, shy persons simply do not get around to such things. They lack the courage to do so. This illustrates the point that shyness can also find expression in exhibiting little or no characteristic behaviour. Thus, shy people evince little frankness. Social learning theory calls this lack of courage *avoidance behaviour*.

At the risk of labouring the obvious, we would like to emphasise that not all people who consider themselves shy exhibit all the sorts of behaviours we have mentioned. Likewise, we wish to underline that the degrees to which such behaviours occur can vary greatly among shy individuals.

Thoughts. Psychologists have also tended to emphasise the *thoughts* (cognitions) that shy persons entertain about themselves. Recent writings have used the phrases "irrational thought patterns" and "negative habits of thought". Whenever we review situations in which shyness manifests itself, we can make a primary distinction between the thoughts entertained before entering that social situation and the thoughts entertained after the situation has been entered. The former category includes the expectations that people hold about themselves and their functioning. The latter category can be characterised as afterthoughts or self-evaluations – self-evaluation in the sense that individuals somehow assess their behaviours in those situations. It is characteristic of shy persons that they often approach social situations with negative expectations. That in itself reduces the chances of engaging successfully. If successful behaviour consequently is not achieved, they judge their own behaviour adversely: "I have bungled it again". Such thoughts confirm or reinforce the poor opinions they have of themselves. Research shows that people are more kindly disposed towards themselves after positive experiences than after negative ones. They develop a more selective attention for positive information about themselves and thus gain greater self-satisfaction that can bear little relation to what has happened. After unsuccessful experiences, however, these people tend to display a more selective attention for negative information about themselves (Mischel, Coates, & Raskoff, 1968; Moore, Underwood, & Rosenhan, 1973). Being frequently exposed to negative experiences strengthens irrational thought patterns, such as "I shall never rise to the occasion" or "I shall always remain an uncommunicative person". Why are such thought patterns called irrational? Firstly, because thinking in terms of "never" and "always" is too absolute. Secondly – and this is even more important – because such thinking makes it even more difficult to achieve what is desirable.

Furthermore, we can distinguish between those irrational thought patterns that interfere with one's own functioning and those that interfere with what others think. The first category of thoughts proves to be amply present among shy people. It is characteristic of individuals' centrifugal thoughts that they constantly watch over their own functioning: "I probably *never* do it right". It is a question, then, of a high degree of "self-consciousness" of one's own presence, and also of the awareness that one cannot live up to one's (internalised) standards. This awareness restrains activity.

As far as the second type of irrational thought patterns is concerned, shy people often firmly believe that others judge them adversely. The very firmness of this conviction harbours an irrational element. After all, one cannot know for certain what others think unless one asks.

In conclusion, we can say that shy persons are alert both in relating their own behaviour to their own standards ("Do I act well in my own opinion?") and in relating their behaviour to the (supposed) standards of others ("Do I act well in the eyes of those who surround me?").

Feelings. The third point on which nearly all authors agree is that negative expectations about one's own behaviour, the "clumsy" realisation and the unfavourable evaluation of one's own behaviour, go hand in hand with negative feelings. These feelings manifest themselves physically through tension. The victim suffers from automatic muscle contractions that cause unpleasant sensations in the cardiac and gastric regions and may rigidify the facial expression, as well as obstruct speech. Shyness may even cause stammering. It may hamper a person's gait, induce trembling of the hands, and make other movements pass off less smoothly as well. Other symptoms are confusion of the senses, constriction or dilation of the blood vessels (blanching or blushing), and disorders of sweat and saliva secretion.

Whenever such symptoms occur, the individual in question is frequently the first to notice. He or she may also associate a particular emotional value with the physical condition perceived (Schachter & Singer, 1962): "How *tense* I am". "Oh, how *ashamed* I am". Taken by themselves, these thoughts are unfavourable again. The cognitivists (Ellis & Grieger, 1977; Mahoney, 1974; Meichenbaum, 1977) have pointed out that this thought is often followed by a second one: "How tense I am and what a nuisance to be so". "How ashamed I am; if only the others don't notice, for that would really be terrible". These two examples show that the first thought is evaluated with lightning speed, (i.e., is compared with a certain desirable standard). In these cases the standard is to feel no tension and not to be ashamed. The awareness of failing this standard often increases this tension and may even cause a sense of inferiority.

The development and persistence of shyness

In this section we deal with the question of which factors feature prominently in the development and persistence of shyness. It is difficult to answer this question because the development of shyness is a complex process that entails many factors. Human behaviour is poly-determined; this certainly applies to shyness. Our conception concerning the development of shyness links up with recent developments in learning theory and the behavioural therapy based on it. We have opted for a learning theoretical point of view because it offers several points of departure for *learning* how to remedy shyness.

Traditional learning theorists, such as Wolpe (1958) and Eysenck and Rachman (1965), account for shyness through a model in which two important learning processes play parts. First, a process of classic conditioning occurs, coupling a fear stimulus to one that was formerly neutral; this fear stimulus results in avoidance behaviour, which in its turn is reinforced through a process of operant conditioning on the basis of fear reduction. In this model, the essence of shyness resides in the conditioned fear stimulus.

More recently, authors have located the prime cause in a skill deficit in reacting to social situations. Curran (1979) speaks of a skill deficiency model in which people have not yet acquired the appropriate mental programmes to react to various situations. The concept of "mental programme" is interchangeable with "behavioural disposition" and "repertoire". We have derived these concepts from the terminology employed by the cognitivists, who regard humans as information processors. Such a repertoire, behavioural disposition, or mental process can be defined as a skill (stored in memory) to react appropriately to certain situations.

We can explain behavioural differences between people on the basis of the degrees to which they have acquired the disposition towards such behaviour. It seems rather odd to speak in this context of "skill" or to say that one has a "large repertoire of shy behaviours" at one's disposal. In our opinion, shyness can much better be seen as an *incapacity* to produce adequate social behaviour. The concept of "behavioural certainty" or "assertiveness" lends itself excellently to the purpose of conceptualising "the extension of repertoires". Those individuals who are considered "behaviourally certain" or "assertive" (that is, *not* shy) by their acquaintances evidently have a more extensive repertoire of social skills at their disposal than does someone who is regarded as "behaviourally uncertain" or "non-assertive" (shy), or they have *acquired fewer* socially *inadequate* behavioural patterns.

This model can be objected to because it does not explain why a person with an adeqate behavioural repertoire may fail to exhibit adequate behaviour. Another objection that can be levelled against both the classic conditioning model and the skill deficiency model is that they do not explain the "modelling effects" these people learn from observing other people's behaviours (Bandura, 1969). The cognitive social learning theoretical model takes these objections into consideration. On the basis of that conceptualisation we present our explanatory model of the development and persistence of sub-assertiveness (Figure 9.1).

In this model, two learning theoretical principles play important parts. The first is that people learn from the consequences of their deeds. This principle is of paramount importance for the self-image that the individual develops. People who perceive that their social behaviour is rewarded gain self-confidence, that is, a belief in the efficacy of their own behaviour. People who experience negative effects consequent to their deeds lose confidence and start to believe that their behaviour will again be ineffective in future.

The second learning theoretical principle is that people learn from examples (observational learning experiences). As far as shyness is concerned, some support can be found in the literature for the assumption that those who suffer from it often have been confronted with a shy behavioural model (Zimbardo, 1977).

Favourable and unfavourable expectations can both be related to specific situations, but may also have been generalised to various (similar) situations.

In the cognitive social learning theoretical model, the one-sided emphasis of the classic learning theory on (external) behaviour is compensated for, and room is made for "covert" processes (Ellis, 1973; Mischel, 1973). Moreover, it helps explain why people who have "mental programmes" or skills at their disposal occasionally *fail* to use these skills. Thoughts about possible adverse effects may restrain an individual

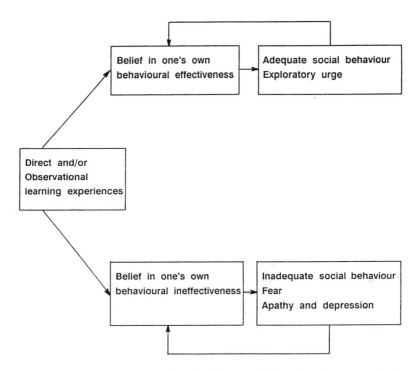

Figure 9.1. An explanatory model, based on social learning theory, concerning the development and persistence of sub-assertiveness.

from practising such behaviour. When the baleful effects have been properly assessed, the conduct chosen can be considered rational. The literature reports, however, that such adverse effects are frequently over-estimated; we are dealing, then, with irrational thoughts, which issue in a lack of courage (Ludwig & Lazarus, 1972).

Once shyness has developed, it becomes a vicious circle that is hard to break. All the aspects we distinguished in the preceding section contribute: clumsy behaviour in social situations gives rise to unfavourable thoughts about one's own functioning. These negative thoughts and self-evaluations go hand in hand with negative feelings, which physically manifest themselves in various kinds of tension. As a consequence, the individual anticipates such situations with tension; they are dreaded. This leads to avoiding those situations. The individual, consequently, does not practise his or her social repertoire in those situations, and that social repertoire is not rewarded. This, again, has as a consequence that the (anticipation) fear of such situations continues or even increases.

Moreover, the fear increases that others will judge adversely. It is precisely because of this decreasing openness and the limited number of contacts that one's thoughts of what others may think are no longer tested by reality.

Finally, we would like to discuss a social psychological process that plays an important role in the persistence of shyness: the so-called labelling process. People employ labels to categorise others. Their principal function is to reduce complex information. One kind of label is the social stereotype: "Some groups, including mental patients, the physically handicapped, and even the unattractive are stigmatized, through stereotyping" (Bellack & Hersen, 1979, p. 4). If people behave shyly, they will be considered shy by others and will even stigmatise themselves as such. This arouses certain expectations both in the stigmatised person and in others. Once shy people have permanently acquired the label, others come to see them as "dull": "How taciturn he is, what a dry stick!" Subsequently, the shy arrive at the same conclusion: "Nobody likes me; what a worthless person I am". That thought completes the circle, and so the process of stereotyping is difficult to reverse.

In what kinds of situations are people particularly liable to shyness?

Earlier we discussed the personal characteristics of shy people. Now we would like to pay attention to the question in which particular situations people are shy. It was Mischel (1968, 1973) who first pointed out that, to a large degree, differences in social situations create differences in social behaviours. "Character traits" like shyness prove to be particularly susceptible to situational influences. This situational specificity of human behaviour not only means that there are large differences between individuals with regard to the situations that cause shyness but also means that there are large variations within the individual in the way in which he or she responds to situations. According to this point of view, situations cannot simply be ranked according to the degree of shyness they cause. Acknowledging the importance of paying close attention to each person's idiosyncratic way of responding to situations, we can nevertheless ask the question whether or not shyness occurs more frequently in certain situations. To answer this question, we make use of some data gathered during our own research.

All trainees ($N = 87$) who participated in a training programme for shy people developed by our department were asked to write down what they considered the two most embarrassing situations they had experienced. We wanted to determine if their experiences of those situations had been altered by having attended the training programme. For classification of situations we used the following criteria:

Table 9.1. *Classification of embarrassing situations on four dimensions*

Dimension	Number of situations[a]	%
Size of the audience		
One person	52	30
Two to four persons	20	11
Five to 10 persons	64	37
More than 10 persons	34	20
Unscoreable	4	2
Degree of familiarity with the audience		
Very familiar	17	10
Vaguely familiar	101	58
Unfamiliar	44	25
Unscoreable	12	7
Response versus initiative		
Response	40	23
Initiative	104	60
Unscoreable	30	17
Formal versus informal		
Formal	35	20
Informal	123	71
Unscoreable	16	9

[a] $N = 174$ situations provided by 87 subjects.

1. the size of the audience,
2. the degree of familiarity with the audience,
3. formal versus informal situations,
4. initiative versus response (i.e., a situation in which one must take the initiative versus a situation in which one must respond to one or several people).

For analysis of the findings, listed in Table 9.1, we do not have available comparable material from people who are not shy. Consequently, we cannot say with absolute certainty to what extent the proportions found are characteristic of shyness. For that reason, the data can be used only for indicating some trends, although Zimbardo (1977) has presented evidence that shy and non-shy people agree in their rank-ordering of situations that are likely to elicit shyness. Table 9.1 shows that there is a wide variety of situations that can cause shyness. There is no clear order as far as the size of the audience is concerned. Examining the findings concerning the second dimension – degree of familiarity with the audience – we note that situations with vaguely familiar people were particularly considered embarrassing (58%). Psychologically, this can be easily explained. With casual acquaintances, people do not yet know exactly what can be expected, and they attach a certain importance to the impressions they will make. When the third dimension – response versus initiative – is analysed, it becomes evident that the trainees mentioned those situations in which they had to take the initiative.

What strikes us most about these data is that shyness particularly occurs in informal situations. Argyle, Furnham, and Graham (1981) suggest an explanation for this finding by pointing out that the more complex the situation, and the less familiar the individual is with the rules and rituals of the situation, the more difficult it becomes for the individual to select the appropriate behaviour and to behave freely. In such situations the individual cannot resort to a clear consensus regarding who should say or do what, whereas, in contrast, in a formal situation there would be clearer rules as to how to behave. Some of the informal situations mentioned were "new" situations, such as meeting strangers, a first training evening, and so forth. In a new situation, manners have yet to be defined by those present. People do not yet know where they are with each other.

It is clear that there is wide variety among the situations that can produce shyness. This can be explained because, strictly speaking, it is not the "objective" situation that elicits shyness, but rather the "psychological" situation (Lewin, 1935). This means that a person has to interpret a situation as menacing before experiencing shyness.

Is shyness a problem? Cultural factors

In the preceding sections we have spoken of adequate and inadeqaute social behaviours. In doing so, we left unresolved what exactly should be understood by these terms. In this section we endeavour to make clear that cultural factors are of the utmost importance for answering this question. Sociologists (e.g., Becker, 1963; Scheff, 1966) have pointed out that every culture or sub-culture has standards and values of its own and that individual behaviour is judged by the standards of that culture, both by the individuals themselves and by those around them. The individual's behaviour is considered adequate if it is consonant with those standards and values. This point of view implies that shy behaviour becomes problematic only if it is considered negatively deviant from those standards. To put it otherwise, appraisals of shyness can differ widely from culture to culture and from sub-culture to sub-culture. Thus, Schouten (1935) discusses the Javanese as a people who regard behaviour that we would consider shy as a virtue. This implies that in Javanese culture, shy behaviour is not considered problematical; on the contrary. In contemporary Western society, however, people seem to attach more and more importance to evincing assertive, extravert, and sociable behaviours. North American culture, in particular, seems to be dominated by this norm (Hall & Beil-Warner, 1978). In Western Europe, however, similar developments can be observed. One even speaks of the age of the "me" generation, with "assertive behaviour" as the latest standard for mental welfare. This may explain the enormous growth of interest in assertiveness training in the recent past (Heimberg et al., 1977).

When discussing the phenomenon of shyness in various cultures, we are faced with the question of whether or not we are dealing with a phenomenon that occurs all over the world. Although we are not acquainted with the details of all the countries and cultures in the world, research reported by Zimbardo (1977) seems to suggest that this question has to be answered in the affirmative. He administered the Stanford Shyness Survey in various countries (the United States, Japan, Germany, Israel, Taiwan, and Mexico) and in various sub-cultures (American students, Hawaiians, and American Jews). To the question whether or not the subjects considered themselves shy at the moment of investigation, none of the groups studied yielded less than 24% affirmative responses. Shyness proved to be most widespread in Japan, Taiwan, and Hawaii. The percentages of people from those regions who considered themselves shy at the moment of investigation were 60%, 55% and 60%, respectively. Shyness was most infrequent among Israelis (31%) and American Jews (24%). Zimbardo explains these remarkable differences as follows: In both the Japanese and Taiwanese cultures there is a strong competitive spirit; in addition, children are trained from a young age to keep their emotions under control, with obedience to rules and regulations being emphasised and restraint imposed on spontaneous activities. That gives rise to an exceptionally strong sense of duty, as well as fear of being judged adversely, especially when in the presence of authority figures. The percentages of shy subjects found among Israelis and American Jews contrasted dramatically with the percentages found among people from Eastern cultures. Zimbardo points out that these differences originate in the fact that among Jews, "chutzpah" and "spunk" (i.e., "guts") are cultivated, and people meet with approval if, without worrying about the possible thoughts of others, they express frankly and freely what they think themselves.

The preceding sections have made it clear that people can deal with shyness in various ways. Most people do not consider shyness a serious problem; for most people, the phenomenon may occur, but not habitually, and not in such a way that they are seriously troubled by it. For smaller numbers of people, however, shyness is very troublesome. These people are the main target group for the training method that is described in the second half of this chapter.

Summary and working definition

We now present a working definition, on the basis of the preceding sections; this working definition, which should be distinguished from the basic definition given earlier, is intended as a starting point for the training or therapy objectives and the evaluation problems closely interwoven with these objectives.

We say that someone suffers from shyness when it frequently is the case that he or she does not know how to cope with social situations. This "not knowing how to cope" may be caused by a deficit of (not having acquired or wrong use of) social skills, so that the individual does not *know* to act. This ignorance can also derive from inhibitions, from a lack of courage; the individual believes that he or she cannot cope with the situation, and the execution of the behaviours available from the repertoire is then, as it were, repressed. In both cases this "not knowing what to do" is attended by fear, negative thoughts (self-evaluations), and negative feelings that can be expressed physically in various ways: sweating, trembling, blushing, and so forth. As a consequence, the individual tries to avoid such social situations, or meets them with more (anticipatory) fear. A consequence of this evasive behaviour is that skills are not practised and subsequently not rewarded. A final consequence of meeting social situations with much (anticipatory) fear is that the chance of performing socially adequate behaviour is reduced.

The vicious circle thus described and its aspects that can be distinguished are shown in Figure 9.2 According to this model, we need to consider the following aspects of shyness (working definition):

1. *Experience*: fear, tension, lack of self-confidence
2. *Knowledge*: not knowing how to behave
3. *Skills*: not capable of executing the adequate behaviour
4. *Cognitions*: irrational thoughts before and during attendance at social situations; negative self-evaluations afterwards
5. *Physical aspects*: sweating, trembling, blushing, and so forth
6. *Avoidance behaviour*: not daring to execute (adequate) behaviour.

When formulating training or therapy objectives, we must consider all of these aspects.

A training programme for shy people

In this section we describe the objectives and the method of a training programme for shy people, developed at the Department of Personality

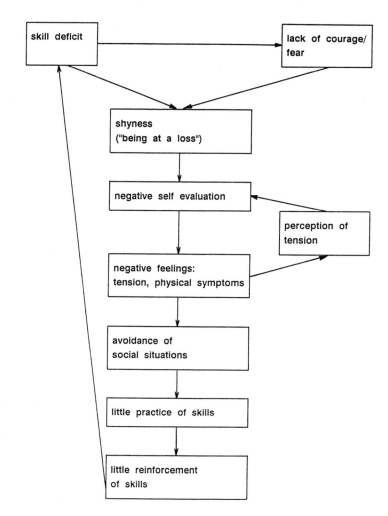

Figure 9.2. Processes within shyness: a vicious circle.

and Educational Psychology of the University of Groningen. This programme consists of 13 meetings, each lasting $2\frac{1}{2}$ hr.[1]

Objectives

The principal objective of the training programme is to reduce shyness. Linking up with the definition of shyness suggested earlier and the notion that what has not yet been learned can still be learned, and what has been wrongly acquired can still be corrected, we specify this objective by the following sub-objectives:

1. change of experience: a reduction of anxiety in social situations, an increase in self-confidence
2. increasing knowledge (concerning the phenomenon of shyness and communicative skills)
3. extension and greater sophistication of the repertoire of skills necessary for dealing with (difficult) social situations
4. reduction of irrational thoughts and negative self-evaluations
5. reduction of physical symptoms of tension
6. reduction of avoidance behaviour
7. insight into the situations that evoke shyness

Method

To realise these objectives, we have opted for a clear, structured approach that combines cognitive and behavioural working methods. We endeavour to break the vicious circle of shyness by breaking the various links in this circle (behaviour, thoughts, feelings of tension). We systematically elaborate the various elements of the method in the following sections.

Lucidity: Explanation of the theory, the objectives, and working method. Frank (1973) has pointed out that it is an important general characteristic of many forms of psychotherapy to work from a conceptual framework, a theoretical frame of reference and procedures associated with it. The efficacy of various forms of psychotherapy can then be understood as follows: Although the contents of the conceptual frameworks and procedures differ, they resemble each other in explaining the feelings and behaviours of the client, who in some way or other has nothing to hold on to, has lost control over his or her life. By being handed a structure, he or she regains this control.

In our method we have decided to introduce the trainees at the very beginning of the training to our conceptual framework and the working method deduced from it. This means that they are informed about the theory employed by the trainers, the training objectives, and the working methods used to realise those objectives. In this sense, the training can be called completely transparent.

The principal objective of this method is to inform the trainees what can be expected. We consider this important for three reasons. In the first place, clarity offers certitude. A person who knows what can be expected need not worry about what is going to happen. This is particularly important for shy people; we have already shown that these people often (needlessly) worry. In the second place, knowledge increases involvement, and that offers the trainers an opportunity to keep the trainees motivated and goal-oriented.

We also chose this working method for some ethical considerations. Firstly, we do not consider it desirable for trainers to pose as magicians with redemptive opinions. If trainers employ an implicit concept of human nature, the chance of indoctrination increases. Diekstra and Dassen (1976) have lucidly described how the images of human nature that lie at the heart of various forms of psychotherapy closely resemble religious dogmas. They maintain that psychotherapy in general is not much different from our "contemporary version of evangelisation".

Because we wish to indoctrinate as little as possible (it is virtually impossible to avoid it completely), we recommend explicating the theory from which we work. This contributes to the realisation of a second ethical principle closely related to the first: to regard our fellows as *responsible* human beings. Thus, they themselves must finally decide whether or not they wish to use what we offer them.

A structured programme. When we were framing this programme we opted for a high degree of structure. This structuring concerns both the division of time in the sessions and the method employed by the trainers. The structure is characterised by fixing a learning objective for each part of the programme. The trainees are continually informed about these objectives. The method we use can continually be divided into a number of stages, as described later. The reasons for this structured approach are the following:

In the first place, we consider a structured approach most efficient. We can make optimum use of the time available. Unstructured approaches often lead to wasted time.

In the second place, we have chosen a structured approach because we believe that it reduces anxiety. At the beginning of each meeting, the structure of the training programme is explained. Likewise, we make clear the principal aim of the meeting. We try to reduce as much as possible the trainees' uncertainty about what can be expected. This is considered vital in relation to the problem of shyness, which often makes the trainees very anxious.

In the third place, having a clear structure for the programme increases its *transferability*. Moreover, it enhances the possibilities for investigating the effects of the programme among various groups.

Combination of cognitive and behavioural approaches. In our training programme, cognitive and behavioural methods are combined. Throughout the training we try to relate the various aspects of shyness to each other on a cognitive level (particularly behaviour/skills, thoughts, and feelings). In addition, we explain during *lessons* the formation, content, and function of a repertoire of communicative skills. Finally, we hope to procure a deeper understanding of so-called irrational cognitions.

The behavioural aspect is highlighted during skills training. A "skill" (or conversational technique) ought to be regarded as a behavioural sequence that is partly of a cognitive (covert) nature and partly of an observable (overt) nature. Our approach employs Ivey's (1971) micro-teaching method (1971) and Goldstein's method (1973) of a "Structured Learning Therapy". The two methods show remarkable overlap and are characterised by the application of such learning theoretical principles as modelling and reinforcement. We have chosen this combination because these two methods are complementary. In contrast to Goldstein's method, the micro-training method makes use of audiovisual feedback; the Structured Learning Therapy uses so-called learning points. These are distinguishable "small steps" for the application of a skill. The presentation of learning points is lacking in the micro-training method. Before discussing our skills training method, which can be regarded as a synthesis of the two previously described methods, we first state which skills we have included in the training programme, and why.

Choice of skills. People who suffer from shyness experience difficulties in communicating. In a communicative process we can distinguish the "sender", the person who sends the message, and the "receiver", the person who receives the message, Schematically:

Analogously, we can distinguish between receiver skills (listening skills) and sender skills (conversational skills). The latter are also called assertive skills.

These assertive skills can be further differentiated into active skills, which help the individual in taking the initiative, and responsive skills, which help the individual to respond to others. An instance of the first type is to make a request; an example of the second type is to respond to criticism. One's progress in acquiring these skills can range from easy to difficult. Table 9.2 indicates which skills are involved.

We should add that the way in which the receiver responds can, in its turn, be understood as a message by the original sender. So the receiver turns into sender, and the sender into receiver. Whenever two interlocutors communicate, they interchange the roles of receiver and sender.

Both groups of skills have been included in the training course, for the following reasons:

RECEIVER SKILLS. It may seem somewhat paradoxical that we have included in a training course for shy people the skill of learning how to listen. After all, shy people are very quiet. In the first instance, that was also our trainees' response: "No, I have no difficulty listening". Never-

Table 9.2. *The repertoire of skills*

Receiver (listening) skills
  1. Listening: attentive behaviour, relaxed attitude, eye contact, follow verbally
  2. Minimal encouragements
  3. Asking questions
       Open
       Closed
  4. Paraphrasing the content
  5. Considering (reflecting on) feelings
  6. Integration of the listening skills

Sender (assertive) skills – initiative
  7. Telling something oneself
  8. Making requests
  9. Criticising: opinion, behaviour
  10. Expressing feelings
  11. Venting anger/annoyance
  12. Expressing affection

Sender (assertive) skills – responsive
  13. Refusing
  14. Responding to criticism
  15. Responding to anger
  16. Responding to affection

Specific skills
  17. Meta-communication: talking about the conversation

---

theless, we consider it important for this group of shy people to acquire insight into and proficiency at these skills so that they can get to grips with the conversational process. Listening "actively" does not mean that one remains silent, but that one responds appropriately to what somebody else says. In the second place, shy people, while listening to others, often are contemplating other questions: "What should I say now? How should I respond? What can I tell next?" Their preoccupation with such questions causes tension and prevents people from really listening to others. A more extensive repertoire of behavioural dispositions for listening well can counteract the development of such interfering thoughts. Knowing better how to respond can contribute to a feeling of self-confidence. Finally, it may be pointed out that practising listening skills contributes to the trainees' empathy, that is, their capacity to identify with others. This capacity should not be exclusively attributed to social workers and psychotherapists. Anyone who can listen well to others will have a better chance of receiving attention in return – "Do as you would be done by", as the proverb says. We are not quite alone in the choice of this group of skills. Both Lazarus (1971) and Jakubowski-Spector (1973) have emphasised the importance of emphathy.

SENDER SKILLS. In an earlier section we pointed out that shy people show little initiative. When in the company of others, they do not dare initiate stories of their own (Table 9.2, skill 7: telling something oneself); it will likewise cause shy people a great deal of trouble to make a request, as in borrowing something or agreeing to go out together (skill 8: to make a request). Criticising somebody's opinion or behaviour (skill 9) and expressing feelings in general (skill 10), and those of anger and affection in particular (skills 11 and 12), are all considered difficult.

The shy individual also has problems in reacting to delicate situations. He or she hardly dares to refuse a request (skill 13) and responds badly to criticism (skill 14), anger (skill 15), and affection (skill 16).

A final specific skill is meta-communication (Watzlawick, Beavin, & Jackson, 1970). This refers to the skill to see through and bring up for discussion what happens during the conversation. This is particularly necessary and useful when difficulties or obscurities occur, as when two people talk at cross purposes. We speak here of a "specific" skill because it is of a different order than the skills dealt with thus far, which take place on the first level, that is, direct communication between sender and receiver (speaker and listener). Schematically represented:

In meta-communication the conversation is put into some kind of perspective. Schematically:

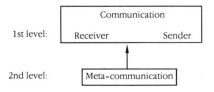

It is of importance for every skill distinguished to determine whether its non-utilisation is caused primarily by *ignorance* or by being *inhibited*.

We presume that some skills from the group of listening skills, such as eye contact, minimal encouragement, and the use of open and closed questions, may be stored in the shy individual's repertoire, though they may not be easy to handle on a conscious level. The shy person may have mastered a number of skills, but probably has never realised that what he or she has been doing can be called "a skill". So it seems, as far as these skills are concerned, that we are dealing primarily with a knowledge gap, particularly with a deficit in being able to choose consciously and at will from a variety of possible reactions. This certainly obtains for knowing the difference between open and closed questions, between paraphrasing the content and reflecting the feeling. However, application of these skills can also be inhibited by fear: A cognitive obstruction appears. This fear arises because one experiences the situation as menacing or because one is too preoccupied with oneself.

The assertive skills probably are more frequently hampered by cognitive obstructions than by a lack of knowledge. Taken individually, most people are capable of narrating, making a request, criticising, expressing feelings, refusing, and responding to criticism, anger, or affection. Frequently, however, it comes to nothing, because people do not dare to show these reactions. The contrast, however, cannot be conceived entirely in extremes, for in order to tell a story oneself, one must know how to do it. This also applies to criticising and reacting to criticism, expressing feelings and responding to those of others.

With respect to meta-communication, it should be observed that people often do not know what is meant by this. It also requires some insight into the processes of interaction between the interlocutors. Experience has taught us, however, that whenever one explains the concept simply and lucidly, it becomes quite clear even to people who have received only an elementary education.

In conclusion, we can say that in our opinion it is often a mixture of ignorance and inhibition that impairs the skills mentioned. It may be obvious that when people are ignorant, skills cannot be used, at least not consciously. If knowledge and skillfulness are present, they can still be repressed by fear. In both cases, *training* is useful – in the first case to make the behavioural mode available, in the second case to contend with fear.

Skills training: Combination of Ivey's micro-teaching method and Goldstein's Structured Learning Therapy. The micro-teaching method was developed in the United States by Ivey (1971). It is characteristic of Ivey that he studies certain professional types of conversation (particularly the interview and counselling interview) with respect to specific problems that people without any training in this type of conversation can experience. He subsequently translates these problems into skills, which have to be trained in order to better conduct the conversation. These skills are transferred to the trainees through a method of micro-teaching ("micro" because we are dealing with *sub-skills* that are essential for conducting a conversation). The micro-teaching is characterised by brief practise sessions of about 5 min in which one skill is central each time. Moreover, there is a clear system noticeable in the structure of these sessions. A final important characteristic of this method is the use of video equipment to illustrate specific comments.

In our course, the micro-teaching method is combined with Goldstein's Structured Learning Therapy. The most prominent addition to the latter method is that we have fixed a number of *learning points* for every skill. This combination of methods yields the following systematic structure:

1. Each lesson concentrates on a specific conversational skill and its function in the overall conversation. Written instructions are handed out.

2. The skill is *demonstrated* through examples on video (modelling). Two fragments are shown each time. The first, "wrong" example shows inadequate use of the skill. The second, "correct" example illustrates adequate use of the skill. By showing both examples, we aim at two learning effects. Firstly, we teach the trainees to distinguish between specific behavioural aspects as the relevant aspect is varied. Secondly, the correct example has a kind of model function with respect to the trainees' behaviour.

3. The *lesson* and *demonstration* are summarised in a number of *learning points*. The primary function of these points resides in the mediating part they play in the encoding and retention of the model behaviour and (covert) self-instruction (attention → encoding → retention → covert self-instruction → motor reproduction) (Bandura, 1977).

4. Subsequently the skill is practised in brief *role-plays* (of about 5 min) in which one primarily tries to practise the skill under discussion. Role-playing is chosen for this kind of work in order to sustain an informal atmosphere in which it will not seem so awful to make mistakes. People can learn how to experiment with their behaviour. These role-plays are recorded on video.

5. After having role-played, the trainee receives comments on his or her application of the skill from fellow trainees and from the trainer. In doing so, use is made of the video recording. During the evaluation, the good aspects of the trainee's behaviour are emphasised: correct use of the skill, improvements over preceding occasions. What did not go well is also discussed: Why did it not succeed? The principal purpose of this discussion is to find alternative ways of reacting. The trainer should take care that these alternatives are worded as concretely as possible.

6. At the end of each role-play, the trainer gives a summary in which the following questions are addressed:

(a) How has the skill been applied, considering its object?
(b) What (which behaviour) did the trainee practise correctly?
(c) What (which behaviour) can still be improved? At this point the
trainer offers instructions concerning points that need the trainee's
special attention during another exercise.

All in all, one can perceive in the foregoing a structured didactic approach. A large amount of empirical research (e.g., Ivey & Authier,
1978; Bandura, 1977) has shown that each element can enhance the
learning outcome. Also, we would like to draw the reader's attention to
the diversity of the method. It is plausible that this serves to keep the
trainees' attention concentrated.

To practise *listening skills*, we use a variation on this method that can
be termed "cumulative" micro-teaching. This method does not practise
one skill at a time (as Ivey suggested), but adds one skill to each
succeeding exercise in order to promote the integration and functional
use of skills.

In practising sender skills, we practise skills by themselves as much as
possible, although it is possible to integrate some skills (e.g., listening
and responding to criticism) even then. Two kinds of role-plays are
employed: the reconstructive and anticipatory. A reconstructive role-
play repeats a situation that has occurred. An anticipatory role-play
stages a situation that is expected to present itself in the near future.

Homework. In addition to training the various skills during the course,
extension of the behavioural repertoire is pursued by means of homework assignments. What primarily matters is the ability to make use of
what has been learned, that is, the transfer of training (Goldstein, 1973;
Bandura, 1977).

In the first part of the training course, people are told to study the
theory and to practise the skills presented. In the latter part of the
programme, the trainer gives homework assignments that are related to
a trainee's individual problems. The principal purpose of these assignments is to practise using the skills in situations that are difficult for the
individual and to discourage the avoidance of tense situations (objective
6). If all this sounds peremptory and schoolish, we would like to point
out that trainees are free to perform a given task or to refuse it. In doing
so, we aim as much as possible at a co-operative model in which the
trainer offers advice to the trainee on what is considered most desirable.
Occasionally that may put the trainer in an awkward position, for the
offer of consultation may be used by the trainees to "dodge it". We
cannot supply any laws of Medes and Persians, for we are convinced
that people profit more from the spur of necessity than from persisting

in their familiar, safe, but ultimately unsatisfactory, behaviours. It is, however, always the trainees who eventually must decide whether or not to carry out their assignments.

When discussing homework, every trainee gets the opportunity to report how he or she has performed the assignments, and those that have been successfully performed are reinforced by the trainer. This reinforcement should not be taken as "praising the good pupil", but should be related to the objectives pursued: "It's great that you succeeded in putting your plans into effect". Failures should not be highlighted. However, an attempt should be made to analyse the reasons why an assignment has failed. If the programme offers enough room, a reconstructive role-play can augment this analysis. Moreover, it should be pointed out that exhibiting the desired behaviour does not automatically lead to success. If the trainer asks good questions, the trainee need not give profusive answers; if one makes a request, that need not mean that one's request will be granted.

Lessons on irrational cognitions. In an earlier section we offered a cognitive social learning theoretical definition of shyness. A final cognitive point of view in the course methodology consists of lessons on irrational thoughts and anticipatory fear (objective 4). Shy people often excessively dread all kinds of situations. In thought, they already see themselves failing. Such thoughts often are based on previous experiences of failure. Although not quite inconceivable, these thoughts are irrational, because these people are assuming that they will *never* be able to do certain things, that they will *always* wear the label of "queer customer". Such premises consequently prevent shy people from taking steps; for example, they prefer staying at home rather than going to a party: "They won't like me anyway". This completes the circle. Shy individuals are also inclined to "think for others". Without testing the reality of their assertions, they start from the assumption that others entertain unfavourable thoughts about them. In the course of the training, we try to gain insight into this problem and effect a change in these negative thinking habits, among other things by employing the "Socratic dialogue", which provokes irrational thoughts: "Are you sure that you will *never* be able to do it?"

Relaxation training. With a view to reducing physical tension, relaxation is taught (objective 5) according to the "progressive relaxation method" (Jacobson, 1938). It is characteristic of this method to teach people how to relax by first tensing a group of muscles and then flexing them. The individual systematically works through the muscle bundles in arms, head, trunk, and legs. This exercise not only is carried out during the course sessions but also is performed during homework assignments, using a cassette on which the text of the exercise has been recorded.

Knowledge, attitude, and behaviour of the trainer. To a large extent, the execution of the method discussed in the preceding sections hinges on the trainer's expertise and dedication. In this sub-section we offer some observations on what is desirable in a trainer.

1. Trainers should have a thorough knowledge of the relevant personality theory that will shed light upon shyness, and of the methods that are based on cognitive social learning theory.
2. Rogers (1951) has advocated a basic attitude of accepting everybody's distinctive peculiarities. Genuineness, warmth, and empathy are here considered necessary but not sufficient – we also intervene more actively by imparting knowledge and practising skills. Nevertheless, the trainer should evince little dogmatism and certainly no attitude that would dictate unlearning shyness or standing up for oneself.
3. Clearly, trainers should be able to apply the skills they are teaching. This is important with respect to their modelling function. It should be added immediately, however, that we do not envisage a "whole" or "holy person" who is a model of assertiveness. Trainers who are somewhat shy themselves may be less authoritative but more acceptable to the trainees. Moreover, we are of the opinion that a course instructor can function more easily when the trainees regard him or her as an ordinary human being.
4. Trainers should also have a number of specific skills at their disposal: the ability to listen well, to explain lucidly, to impose structure, to concretise, to summarise, to lead a group discussion. We would add a last one: the ability to make a joke. Although it will depend on the trainer's individual style whether or not he or she is comfortable with such a manner, we would like to plead that trainers not shun such behaviour, for one of the functions of humour is to render sessions less charged with tension. Besides, it will be pleasant for shy people, who often contribute spasmodically during course sessions, to notice that some playfulness and lightness are possible. This does not mean, however, that the overall tone should not be serious. Those who want to change their shyness are fully entitled to do so.

Summary. Figure 9.3 charts the problem of shyness in connection with the approach employed in this course. It indicates that a reduction of negative affect is not the subject of special instruction. We expect that increases in knowledge, skills, adequate rational thoughts, and physical

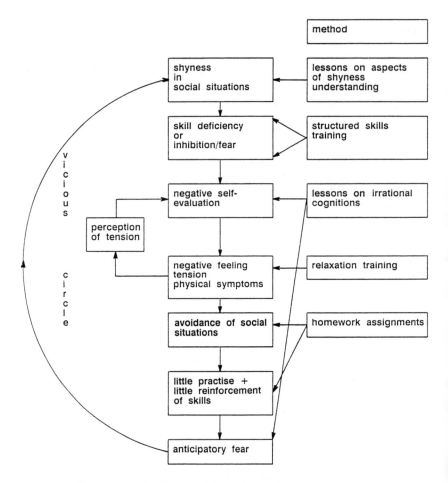

Figure 9.3. The theory of shyness and the course method.

relaxation will all contribute to reducing negative feelings. The method chosen links up with what James (1899/1962) wrote at the turn of the century:

Action seems to follow feeling, but really action and feeling go together; and by regulating the action, which is under the more direct control of the will, we can indirectly regulate the feeling, which is not. (p. 100)

Evaluation of the programme

The course described in the preceding sections has been evaluated thoroughly (van der Molen, 1985). However, we do not have space here to describe the complete research study. Therefore, we confine ourselves to a brief summary of the research findings.

In the evaluation research, the outcome for this programme (Course A) was compared with that for another programme (Course B) and with that for a waiting-list control group. Course B was based on humanistic and social psychological theories; the programme was less structured and followed the experience-divided thematic interaction approach developed by Cohn (1975). Both courses were directed at the same aims, as described in the preceding section. The main differences concerned the subject matters and coping strategies taught in the two courses.

Of central importance here was the kind of personality change considered to be necessary in both courses. Course A was based on the theory that enlargement of knowledge and of the repertoire of behavioural dispositions, combined with a decrease in irrational thought patterns (via lessons, social skills training, and rational emotive education), would lead to more positive experiences (less tension, more self-confidence). The theoretical position in Course B was that a deepening of general self-insight (via awareness exercises and Gestalt therapeutic techniques) would lead to release of blocked behaviour. Put in psychotherapeutic (instead of educational) terminology, Course A showed clear parallels with cognitive behaviour therapy, whereas Course B corresponded mainly with humanistic dynamic therapy.

In the evaluation research, we used a design involving pre-test, post-test, follow-up, and control-group elements. The subjects applied for the courses in response to advertisements in local newspapers. Half of the subjects participated in either Course A or Course B immediately after applying. The other half of the subjects were placed on a waiting list during that period. After the waiting period, the subjects in the second group were assigned to either Course A or Course B. A complete set of data was gathered for 87 subjects; 49 participated in Course A, 38 in Course B. The groups did not differ on background variables such as sex, age, educational level, and severity of problems. Contrary to what might be expected – subjects who *dare* to apply for a course are unlikely to be excessively shy – the severity of problems among the entire group was similar to the severity of problems among out-patients in psychiatric hospitals.

Seven instruments were used to evaluate the courses. Six of these yielded quantitative data (differences among pre-test, post-test, and follow-up scores). The seventh instrument yielded qualitative material: learning effects reported by the subjects themselves. Of the six instruments yielding quantitative data, three were intended to measure aspects of *experience*. The first explored experience of the two most shyness-provoking situations, the second explored general well-being, and the third explored feelings of tension in a comprehensive array of social situations. Two further instruments were used to measure *behavioural aspects*: avoidance behaviour and skill repertoire. The skill repertoire was measured by an objective behaviour test (a role-play with a "stooge"). The sixth quantitative instrument measured *knowledge*.

It was expected that Course A would be better able to achieve the pre-established course aims than would Course B. That hypothesis was based on two arguments. First, the content of Course A was considered to be clearer than that of Course B. Second, it was thought that the structured method of Course A would offer a better framework to shy people than would the less structured method in Course B, which made more use of spontaneous group processes.

The results show that both courses were effective and that the effects persisted over time. However, the effect of Course A proved to be stronger than that of Course B, and that was apparent immediately after the course was completed. Strong improvements were found for all the dependent variables: knowledge, experience of shyness-evoking situations, general well-being, feelings of tension, avoidance behaviour, and skill repertoire. When follow-up measurements were carried out, the difference in course effectiveness was even more pronounced. These results supported the hypothesis.

In order to obtain more insight into the relevance of the effects for practice, they were compared with effects reported in reviews of the literature (Shapiro & Shapiro, 1982; Miller & Berman, 1983). The effect of Course A proved to be stronger than the mean effect of psychotherapy and social skill training, as reported in those reviews. The effect of Course B corresponded with the reported mean effect.

The relevance of the effects for practice was also investigated in another way. A separate study was designed in order to assess which effects were expected by experts; the study was based on Hofstee's betting model (1980, 1984). Apart from experts who were already committed to the approach adopted in either Course A or Course B, three other groups were included in this study: social scientists who were sceptical about each of the approaches, journalists, and laypeople. Each group consisted of a number of individuals who were asked to predict the effects of each of the courses. A comparison was made between expected and observed effects. The most important result emerging from this investigation was the strong underestimation of the effects of Course A by most groups and the overestimation of the effects of Course B. Thus, the effects of Course A were stronger than were expected by all groups, including supporters of this course. Another point of interest was that most groups wrongly expected little difference between the effects of the two courses. The most accurate predictions were made by the group consisting of supporters of Course A. They received, in Hofstee's terms, the best group reputation. These results lead to the conclusion that the effect of Course A must be considered as very relevant for practice, whereas that of Course B must be judged as modest. Additionally, it was concluded that the results give more support to the theoretical position held in Course A than to that held in Course B.

NOTE

1. The complete training programme, with time schedules, lessons about skills, and homework assignments, will be described elsewhere (van der Molen & Trower, 1989).

REFERENCES

Argyle, M., Furnham, A., & Graham, J. A. (1981). *Social situations.* Cambridge University Press.
Bandura, A. (1969). *Principles of behavior modification.* New York: Holt, Rinehart & Winston.
Bandura, A. (1977). *Social learning theory.* Englewood Cliffs, NJ: Prentice-Hall.
Becker, H. S. (1963). *Outsiders: Studies in the sociology of deviance.* New York: Free Press.
Bellack, A. S., & Hersen, M. (Eds.). (1979). *Research and practice in social skills training.* New York: Plenum Press.
Brown, S. D., & Brown, L. W. (1980). Trends in assertion training research and practice: A content analysis of the published literature. *Journal of Clinical Psychology, 36,* 265–269.
Cohn, R. C. (1975). *Von der Psycho-analyse zur themenzentrierten Interaktion.* Stuttgart: Klett Verlag.
Crozier, W. R. (1979). Shyness as a dimension of personality. *British Journal of Social & Clinical Psychology, 18,* 121–128.
Curran, J. P. (1979). Social skills: Methodological issues and future directions. In A. S. Bellack & M. Hersen (Eds.), *Research and practice in social skills training* (pp. 319–354). New York: Plenum Press.
Diekstra, R. F. W., & Dassen, W. F. M. (1976). *Inleiding tot de rationele therapie.* Lisse: Swets en Zeitlinger.
Ellis, A. (1973). Emotional education at the Living School. In M. M. Ohlsen (Ed.), *Counseling children in groups* (pp. 79–93). New York: Holt, Rinehart & Winston.
Ellis, A., & Grieger, R. (1977). *Rational emotive therapy: Handbook of theory and practice.* New York: Springer.
Endler, N., & Magnusson, D. (1976). Toward an interactional psychology of personality. *Psychological Bulletin, 33,* 956–974.

Eysenck, H. J., & Rachman, S. (1965). *The causes and cures of neuroses.* San Diego: Knapp.

Frank, J. D. (1973). *Persuasion and healing: A comparative study of psychotherapy* (2nd ed.). Baltimore: Johns Hopkins University Press.

Galassi, M., & Galassi, J. (1978). Assertion: A critical review. *Psychotherapy: Theory, Research & Practice, 15,* 16–29.

Goldstein, A. P. (1973). *Structured learning therapy, toward a psychotherapy for the poor.* New York: Academic Press.

Hall, J., & Beil-Warner, D. (1978). Assertiveness of male Anglo- and Mexican-American college students. *Journal of Social Psychology, 105,* 175–178.

Heimberg, R. G., Montgomery, D., Madsen, C. H., Jr., & Heimberg, J. S. (1977). Assertive training: A review of the literature. *Behavior Therapy, 8,* 953–971.

Hersen, M., & Bellack, A. S. (1976). Social skills for chronic psychiatric patients: Rationale, research findings, and future directions. *Comprehensive Psychiatry, 17,* 559–580.

Hersen, M., Eisler, R. M., & Miller, P. M. (1973). Development of assertive responses: Clinical measurement and research considerations. *Behaviour Research & Therapy, 11,* 505–521.

Hofstee, W. K. B. (1980). *De empirische discussie. Theorie van het sociaalwetenschappelijk onderzoek.* Meppel: Boom.

Hofstee, W. K. B. (1984). A betting reconstruction of empirical research. *Acta Psychologica, 56,* 93–109.

Ivey, A. E. (1971) *Microcounseling. Innovations in interviewing training.* Springfield, IL: Charles C. Thomas.

Ivey, A. E., & Authier, J. (1978). *Microcounseling. Innovations in interviewing, counseling, psychotherapy and psychoeducation.* Springfield, IL: Charles C. Thomas.

Jacobson, E. (1938). *Progressive relaxation.* University of Chicago Press.

Jakubowski-Spector, P. (1973). Facilitating the growth of women through assertive training. *Counseling Psychologist, 4,* 75–86.

James, W. (1962). *Talks to teachers on psychology and to students on some of life's ideals.* New York: Dover. (Original work published 1899)

Lazarus, A. A. (1971). *Behavior therapy and beyond.* New York: McGraw-Hill.

Lewin, K. (1935). *A dynamic theory of personality.* New York: McGraw-Hill.

Ludwig, L. D., & Lazarus, A. A. (1972). A cognitive and behavioral approach to the treatment of social inhibition. *Psychotherapy: Theory, Research & Practice, 9,* 204–206.

Mahoney, M. J. (1974). *Cognition and behavior modification.* Cambridge: Ballinger.

Meichenbaum, P. (1977). *Cognitive-behavior modification: An integrative approach.* New York: Plenum Press.

Miller, R. C., & Berman, J. S. (1983). The efficacy of cognitive behavior therapies: A quantitative review of the research evidence. *Psychological Bulletin, 94,* 39–53.

Mischel, W. (1968). *Personality and assessment.* New York: Wiley.

Mischel, W. (1973). Toward a cognitive social learning reconceptualization of personality. *Psychological Review, 80,* 252–283.

Mischel, W., Coates, B., & Raskoff, A. (1968). Effects of success and failure on self-gratification. *Journal of Personality and Social Psychology, 10,* 381–390.

Moore, B. S., Underwood, B., & Rosenhan, B. L. (1973). Affect and altruism. *Developmental Psychology, 8,* 99–104.

Patterson, C. H. (1980). *Theories of counseling and psychotherapy.* New York: Harper & Row.

Pervin, L. A. (1978). *Current controversies and issues in personality.* New York: Wiley.

Rathus, S. (1975). Principles and practices of assertive training: An eclectic overview. *Counseling Psychologist, 5,* 9–20.

Rich, A. R., & Schroeder, H. E. (1976). Research issues in assertiveness training. *Psychological Bulletin, 83,* 1081–1096.

Rogers, C. R. (1951). *Client centered therapy.* London: Constable.

Schachter, S., & Singer, J. E. (1962). Cognitive, social and physiological determinants of emotional state. *Psychological Review, 69,* 379–399.

Scheff, T. J. (1966). *Being mentally ill.* Chicago: Aldine.

Schlenker, B. R., & Leary, M. (1982). Social anxiety and self presentation: A conceptualization and model. *Psychological Bulletin, 92,* 641–669.

Schouten, J. (1935). *De Verlegenheid.* Groningen: Wolters.

Shapiro, D. A., & Shapiro, D. (1982). Meta-analysis of comparative therapy outcome studies: A replication and refinement. *Psychological Bulletin, 92,* 581–604.

Trower, P., Bryant, B., & Argyle, M. (1978). *Social skills and mental health.* London: Methuen.

van der Molen, H. T. (1985). *Hulp als Onderwijs. Effecten van cursussen voor verlegen mensen.* Groningen: Wolters-Noordhoff.

van der Molen, H. T., & Trower, P. (1989). *How to deal with shyness.* Unpublished manuscript.

Watzlawick, P., Beavin, J. H., & Jackson, D. D. (1970). *De pragmatische aspecten van de menselijke communicatie.* Deventer: Van Loghum Slaterus.

Wolpe, J. (1958). *Psychotherapy by reciprocal inhibition.* Stanford, CA: Stanford University Press.

Yzermans, T. (1982). Sukkels van deze tijd. De last van de verlegenheid. *Intermediair,* pp. 1–3.

Zimbardo, P. (1977). *Shyness: What it is, what to do about it.* Reading, MA: Addison-Wesley.

10

Shyness and self-presentation

JAMES A. SHEPPERD and ROBERT M. ARKIN

There is growing recognition in all of psychology that cognitive processes play important roles in shaping the course and outcome of human behaviour. The ability to think about oneself, to fashion a coherent and pragmatic view of oneself, is the specific slice of this cognitive movement that serves as the impetus for a focus on the role of the self in social interaction. In short, one's human capacity to consider one's own identity, values, social image, personal worth, and the like, is a part of everyday life that influences the entire panorama of one's actions, often in subtle ways.

The purpose of this chapter is to address impression management (or self-presentation) processes and findings as they relate to social anxiety or shyness. This chapter is distinguished from many other approaches to social anxiety in that the locus of the motivational basis for behaviour is expressly social, or interpersonal; that is, the presentation of self in everyday life is one among numerous forms of social influence. This chapter begins with a brief review of the literature on social anxiety and self-presentation. This review is organised within a framework emphasising social anxiety as both an antecedent and consequence of self-presentation. Second, the attributional strategy of self-handicapping is discussed as an illustration of the relationship between the regulation of anxiety and the presentation of "the self" to others. The final section discusses social anxiety in two ways: as a reactive process in which the socially anxious individual responds to anxiety-producing circumstances in the environment, and as an active process in which the anxious individual actively engages in behaviours and seeks out circumstances that will serve to keep anxiety symptoms in check.

Social anxiety and self-presentation

The particular image an individual attempts to convey to others is determined by the specific interests or goals the presenter has in mind (Weary & Arkin, 1981). Moreover, the goals towards which self-presentation is directed are as diverse as they are numerous (Goffman,

1959, p. 3). The elicitation of specific audience reactions also seems to require presentations of the self tailored specially for the presentational goal (Jones & Pittman, 1982). Nevertheless, there is a common element underlying the numerous and diverse goals of self-presentation. A person will attempt to present the self in a socially desirable way. Specifically, people present themselves in a manner intended to elicit social approval, sustain the interaction, and maximise the likelihood that others will aid in the attainment of social and material needs.

However, recent theoretical and empirical work on the relationship between social anxiety, or shyness, and self-presentation suggests a second broad class of image maintenance strategies. Two approaches to linking self-presentation and social anxiety have been proposed. These approaches are complementary, in that one is focused on social anxiety as an antecedent of self-presentation (Arkin, 1981), and the other is concerned with self-presentation as an antecedent of social anxiety (Schlenker & Leary, 1982). Together, these two approaches imply that the behaviour of socially anxious individuals reflects an exception to the general rule suggested earlier.[1]

That is, the socially anxious individual's presentation of self is not characteristically directed towards eliciting social approval. Instead, the pre-eminent goal of the anxious individual ordinarily is to *avoid disapproval* rather than to *seek social approval*. We begin discussing the model by focusing on social anxiety as a precursor to stylistic differences in self-presentation. We focus next on evidence affirming these stylistic differences, and then examine the model concerned with self-presentation as an antecedent of social anxiety.

Social anxiety as an antecedent of self-presentation

There is some social risk inherent in all interpersonal relations. Failure, embarrassment, rejection, and losses in social status loom as potential outcomes of social relations. In most encounters, notably first encounters, the fear of loss competes for pre-eminence with the joys and pleasures of relating to others. The terms "acquisitive self-presentation" and "protective self-presentation" were coined (Arkin, 1981) to capture individual differences in reactions to this type of social risk. "Acquisitive self-presentation" refers to those instances in which an individual overcomes, or actually approaches and embraces, this risk, treating the presentation of self as a challenge. A person engaged in acquisitive self-presentation tries to present an image of the self that is the most favourable possible. In other instances, the social risk is minimal, and an individual may be blissfully un-self-conscious about his or her presentation of self. By contrast, the term "protective self-presentation" has been used to characterise social conservatism. An individual engaged in protective self-presentation attempts to create an impression that is merely "safe".

Whereas the traditional motive to achieve social approval was seen as underlying acquisitive self-presentation, the motive to avoid social disapproval was posed as the motivational basis for the protective self-presentational style. Specifically, it was proposed that all people from time to time (and some people chronically) would approach social situations intending merely to avoid social disapproval rather than to seek approval. Further, it was proposed that people would accomplish this pro-actively – by choosing, modifying, or creating social contexts such that social disapproval would be unlikely to occur.

The socially anxious individual has been posed as the prototypical sort of person inclined to adopt a conservative social orientation (Arkin, 1981). In proposing this link between social anxiety and disapproval concerns, self-doubts and shaky self-confidence were given prominent roles to play. Doubts about social competence are intimately linked with doubts about self-worth in general. Indeed, there are almost always inverse relationships between measures of shyness and measures of general self-esteem (e.g., Cheek & Buss, 1981; Zimbardo, 1977). Further, theory (e.g., Coopersmith, 1967) and research (e.g., Manis, 1955) have traditionally placed self-evaluation at the mercy of social evaluation (and thus social competence). Minimally, doubts about social competence should contribute to a subjective probability of engendering disapproval; this should at least raise doubts about general self-worth. Conversely, it seems axiomatic that low (or uncertain) self-esteem should raise doubts about social competence and thus produce concerns about engendering disapproval.

There is mounting evidence that socially anxious individuals tend to embrace a protective self-presentational style by avoiding or withdrawing from threatening social interactions. Specifically, a number of studies have demonstrated the tendency for socially anxious individuals to avoid social encounters or to leave such encounters quickly. For instance, students who score high on inventories of shyness and social anxiety date less frequently than do those who score lower (e.g., Curran, 1977). Similarly, socially anxious persons often express a preference to work alone rather than with others (e.g., McGovern, 1976).

In a similar vein, other studies have revealed that socially anxious individuals migrate to the fringes of social interaction, where they are better able to regulate its course and therefore its outcome. Dykman and Reis (1979) found that students scoring high in feelings of vulnerability and inadequacy tended to occupy seats near the rear and far sides of a college classroom. From such vantage points, anxious individuals can remain withdrawn and safe when uncertain, yet still be poised to enter the flow of classroom activity whenever it might turn to their advantage.

Once engaged in social interaction, socially anxious individuals appear unwilling to initiate and structure conversation. Several studies have shown that socially anxious people speak for a smaller percentage of time, take longer to respond to others' conversational sallies, contribute more to conversational dysfluencies (i.e., allow uncomfortable silences to continue unbroken), and tend not to interrupt, relative to their non-anxious counterparts (e.g., Natale, Entin, & Jaffee, 1979). Instead of speaking, they can be safe and avoid the social limelight by engaging in "back-channel responses", such as murmuring "uh-huh", smiling, nodding, or otherwise appearing attentive (Natale et al., 1979). It has been suggested that anxious persons tend to "bide their time" in this innocuous way and remain removed from the ebb and flow of social interaction. Only when they confront a safe conversational territory will they enter the interaction as a full, perhaps even dominant, participant (Efran & Korn, 1969).

One recent study directly implicated fear of disapproval in social avoidance and withdrawal, though it was not focused expressly on social anxiety (Bernstein, Stephenson, Snyder, & Wicklund, 1983). In that study, men were found to be far more willing to approach an attractive woman if their approach could occur under the guise of a motive other than a desire to be with the woman. Specifically, the men chose to watch the same movie as the attractive woman watched, and thus sit next to her, only when it appeared that they had joined her because they preferred the movie she had chosen over another film presented elsewhere. When the two movie options were the same, most of the men sat away from the attractive woman. Interestingly, a follow-up study implicated self-confidence as a determinant of these affiliation patterns. The only men willing to approach the woman in the same-movie condition, where no apparent cover for affiliating was available, were those rated by a group of independent raters as very high in physical attractiveness.

In addition to avoiding and withdrawing from social encounters, socially anxious individuals evidence a protective self-presentational style even where avoidance is not possible. For instance, by maintaining attitude neutrality, an individual can pro-actively engage in a protective manoeuvre. Ordinarily, people are perceived most favourably when they appear knowledgeable, authoritative, expert, and well informed. One way to accomplish this favourable presentation of the self is to have attitudes about things that are strong (though not dogmatic), that are well supported by facts, and that are at least somewhat different from the humdrum views of the majority or the average person (Jellison & Arkin, 1977; Myers, 1978). Yet socially anxious individuals do not appear to follow this strategy. Turner (1977) found that anxious individuals moderated their judgements (i.e., they endorsed neutral attitudinal positions) when they expected to be confronted by someone who supposedly held a strong opinion different from their own. By doing this, these individuals seized a part of the attitude scale that was safe: By appearing to have no attitude at all, one can avoid appearing to have the wrong attitude. A person who has no attitude can be persuaded, but cannot be attacked and embarrassed. By remaining neutral at the outset of a social encounter, socially anxious persons can avoid disapproval for the moment. Later it will be possible to adopt the position advocated by others and gain approval for being similar, or gain approval by allowing the others to enjoy the rewards of feeling persuasive (Cialdini & Mirels, 1976).

There also is evidence that individuals highly concerned about disapproval prefer conformity as an impression management strategy. As with attitude neutrality, conformity is a conservative strategy in that it minimises the risk of rejection associated with expressing divergent opinions or attitudes. By conforming, the individual adheres to a position that, because it is similar to that advocated by others, is likely to be safe. Santee and Maslach (1982) found that individuals scoring low on a measure of self-esteem or high on a measure of social anxiety conformed much more than did their counterparts. By contrast, their opposite numbers were much more likely to offer novel responses, reflecting a willingness to draw attention to themselves (and to acquisitively seek the approval of others).

In a related way, Arkin and Schumann (1983) found that socially anxious individuals wrote less in defence of a decision (relative to non-shy individuals) when the experimental situation was rigged so that they could only lose social approval they had gained earlier (i.e., their essays might produce disapproval). Interestingly, when subjects could gain social approval (i.e., their essays could only produce approval), socially anxious individuals wrote more than their non-anxious counterparts. On another measure, socially anxious persons took longer to get started writing a defence of a decision (i.e., were more cautious and hesitant) when they were facing the prospect of disapproval, but were even quicker getting started than their non-anxious counterparts when they could only gain approval.

Taken collectively, the studies described earlier provide intriguing support for the idea that socially anxious individuals chronically engage in behaviours typical of a protective rather than an acquisitive self-presentational style. By avoiding or withdrawing from social encounters, maintaining attitude neutrality, conforming, and so forth, socially anxious individuals virtually eliminate any chance of gaining social approval, but they are able to minimise the risk of social disapproval. Moreover, the findings of Arkin and Schumann (1983) suggest a link between fear of disapproval and protective self-presentation. When fear of disapproval was experimentally eliminated, socially anxious persons were even more acquisitive in their presentation of self than were their counterparts who were not socially anxious, a point that will be taken up again in a later section of this chapter.

Self-presentation as an antecedent of social anxiety

Schlenker and Leary (1982) propose that social anxiety is the product of a desire or motivation to impress others favourably, coupled with uncertainty regarding one's ability to achieve this goal. Specifically, a person should feel very insecure interpersonally (and therefore feel socially anxious) when that person (1) wishes to create some impression but is uncertain how to accomplish this goal, (2) believes he or she lacks the capacity to produce the desired impression, or (3) feels that some event will transpire to repudiate the intended presentation of self, thus producing embarrassment and a failed self-presentation. In short, the more that individuals subjectively feel that they will be unable to present themselves effectively, the greater the social anxiety that they will experience.

Naturally, an individual must assess the likelihood of achieving a preferred self-presentation, or else social anxiety should never occur. Schlenker and Leary (1982) therefore propose that an assessment process is triggered whenever a self-presentational goal is important to the individual and when some signal indicates that the social performance under way may be undermined. If the assessment process indicates that the desired image will be achieved, then the initial presentation of self is resumed. However, if the assessment process indicates that the desired image is not likely to be achieved, then withdrawal from the social situation is likely. If the individual is unable to withdraw from the social situation, however, he or she must "make the best of a bad situation" (1982, p. 658). To cope with such a predicament, the individual will adopt a cautious, innocuous, or non-committal presentation of self (Schlenker & Leary, 1982).

In short, Schlenker and Leary (1982) proposed protective self-presentation as a way to avoid disapproval and to keep feelings of social anxiety in check. But they introduced the switch from acquisitive motives to protective motives later in the self-presentational sequence than did the model of protective self-presentation described earlier (Arkin, 1981). Further, they tended to focus on the average, non-anxious individual's decision to switch from an acquisitive pattern to a protective pattern. The approach via self-presentational styles emphasises that the anxious individual is chronically engaged in an assessment process and therefore opts for the protective style in interpersonal relations from the outset. The shy individual is dispositionally inclined to see disapproval as likely. Thus, keeping feelings of social anxiety in check is of paramount importance cross-situationally. Nevertheless, the two approaches are identical in asserting that protective self-presentation is designed to minimise feelings of social anxiety. For the anxious individual, there are numerous strategies available for regulating the experience of social anxiety. The following section provides an illustration of one such strategy: self-handicapping.

An illustration: The relationship between self-handicapping and social anxiety

One means by which individuals can influence others' impressions of them is by attempting to influence the attributions made for their performance outcomes (Heider, 1958). For example, if an individual can lead others to believe that a successful performance occurred under adverse circumstances, then he or she can capitalise on the augmentation principle (Kelley, 1971). The individual will be seen as all the more able because the success will appear to have occurred despite the presence of impediments to successful performance. Similarly, if a failure occurs in the presence of adverse performance conditions, then the discounting principle (Kelley, 1971) permits the individual to assert that the impediment, not lack of ability, was the cause of the failure.

The term "self-handicapping" refers to such a claim or creation of inhibitory factors that interfere with performance (Jones & Berglas, 1978). The self-handicapping individual seeks out or creates a handicap (an external inhibitory factor that interferes with performance) and thereby obscures the link between performance and evaluation (at least in the case of failure). In this section we present a detailed discussion of the relationship of social anxiety to attributional strategies such as self-handicapping. Much of the recent research on self-handicapping has focused on the self-presentational aspects and has provided useful illustrations of the protective and acquisitive self-presentational styles and the stylistic preferences of socially anxious individuals.

Self-handicapping: A brief overview

A persuasive handicap to successful performance reduces the likelihood of success, but is attractive because it permits the handicapper to attribute an anticipated failure to a source other than lack of competence. Through self-handicapping, individuals can exert control over the attributions made for performance outcomes. Specifically, by acquiring or claiming a handicap that blocks the expression of ability, an individual can decrease the chances that lack of ability will be seen as the most plausible cause of the failure. In attributional terminology, self-handicapping is a strategy designed to "discount" lack of ability as an explanation for poor performance (Kelley, 1971). Further, any success enjoyed in spite of the handicap, albeit unlikely after the handicap has been introduced, carries added benefit: An individual who succeeds in spite of disadvantages is seen as all the more able (Heider, 1958; Kelley, 1971).

Self-handicapping is distinct from other attributional strategies, such as the "self-serving bias in causal attribution" (Weary & Arkin, 1981) and excuse making (Snyder, Higgins, & Stucky, 1983). Those strategies are undertaken with the goal of minimising the extent to which a failure can be attributed dispositionally to the actor/performer. In self-handicapping, an impediment to performance is displayed, and the audience is expected to infer that some non-ability factor is the cause of an anticipated failure, should it occur. It cases of self-serving bias and excuse making, personal responsibility for an unsuccessful outcome is denied, and external, non-ability factors are cited as the causes of failures that have already occurred. Both the self-serving-bias and excuse-making strategies are engaged in subsequent to some ability-relevant performance; self-handicapping, in contrast, is a pre-emptive coping strategy used prior to the commencement of some ability-relevant task.

The initial investigation of self-handicapping was conducted by Berglas and Jones (1978). In that study, subjects were informed that they had performed very well on a pre-test that measured intellectual ability. For half of the subjects, the pre-test was composed predominantly of solvable analogies; for the remaining subjects, the pre-test was composed predominantly of unsolvable analogies. Prior to taking a follow-up test, subjects were given a choice among taking a drug that was described as likely to facilitate test performance (called "actavil"), a drug that allegedly could interfere with test performance (called "pandocrin"), and a "neutral" drug that was described as likely to have no effect on test performance. Ostensibly, subjects were given the choice because the researchers were interested in the precise influences of those drugs on intellectual functioning. In fact, the alleged drugs were all placebos. Subjects who had been told they had performed well on the pre-test composed of solvable analogies believed that they had a reasonable probability of reproducing their performance on a follow-up test. By contrast, subjects who had been told they had performed well on the pre-test composed predominantly of unsolvable analogies could not understand how they had performed so well on the pre-test, and consequently they were doubtful about their ability to reproduce their performance on a follow-up test.

Subjects who presumably had performed well on the unsolvable problems were more likely to handicap their performance (by ingesting the "debilitating" drug) than were subjects who had been given the solvable problems. Ingesting the drug introduced the drug itself as an explanation for any subsequent failure. This undermined lack of ability as the sole, or most plausible, explanation for a subsequent poor performance.

Since the initial investigation by Berglas and Jones (1978), other researchers have demonstrated that individuals will handicap an upcoming performance by ingesting performance-debilitating drugs (Kolditz & Arkin, 1982), drinking alcohol (Tucker, Vulchinich, & Sobell, 1981), withholding effort (Frankel & Snyder, 1978; Harris & Snyder, 1986; Pyszczynski & Greenberg, 1983; Rhodewalt, Saltzman, & Wittmer, 1984; Snyder, Smoller, Strenta, & Frankel, 1981; Weary & Williams, in press), and choosing to listen to performance-debilitating music (Arkin & Shepperd, 1988; Shepperd & Arkin, 1989a,b).

One replicated finding within the self-handicapping literature is that self-handicapping appears to be motivated, at least in part, by self-presentational concerns (Arkin & Shepperd, 1988; Baumgardner, Lake, & Arkin, 1985; Kolditz & Arkin, 1982; Shepperd & Arkin, 1989b; Tice & Baumeister, 1984). For example, Kolditz & Arkin (1982) found that subjects who made their drug choices in total privacy, a context in which the choice of a performance-inhibiting drug could not serve as a self-presentational strategy, opted not to handicap. By contrast, a comparison group of subjects who made their drug choices in the presence of an audience (a standard, public setting) did handicap their performances. In short, self-handicapping appears to be a strategy designed, at least in part, to preserve a favourable public identity or public persona; in that study, it occurred only when the ploy could serve self-presentational ends.

The self-presentational component to self-handicapping has been illustrated in still another way: In an experiment conducted by Baumgardner et al. (1985), some subjects experienced an initial failure that was public. The public failure ensured a "spoiled public identity" and created conditions in which the utility of self-handicapping for preserving one's public identity on a subsequent re-test would be undermined. For other subjects, their initial failure was known only to the subjects themselves. Consistent with a self-presentational interpretation of self-handicapping, subjects whose initial failures were kept confidential handicapped themselves, protecting their public identities on the subsequent test, whereas subjects whose public identities were already spoiled did not.

Most recently, Shepperd and Arkin (1989b) used an individual difference approach to investigate the self-presentational component of self-handicapping. Specifically, subjects rated high and low in Public Self-consciousness, as measured by the Self-consciousness Scale (Fenigstein, Scheier, & Buss, 1975), were presented with an opportunity to handicap an upcoming performance described as either a valid or invalid measure of academic ability. Individuals high in Public Self-consciousness typically are concerned with the public images they portray to others, and they characteristically attend to those aspects of themselves that are open to the inspection and scrutiny of others. It was reasoned that if self-handicapping is motivated by self-presentational concerns, then individuals who are particularly sensitive to and concerned with their public images (i.e., high in Public Self-consciousness) would be prime candidates for self-handicapping.

The results confirmed that prediction. When the task at hand was described as valid, and consequently as potentially self-defining in the eyes of those observing the performance, subjects high in Public Self-consciousness self-handicapped, whereas subjects low in Public Self-consciousness did not. When the task was described as of unknown validity, and consequently as irrelevant to one's public image, neither group of subjects showed any tendency to manage their images by handicapping.

Theoretical approaches

Two conflicting predictions emerge when the literatures concerning social anxiety and self-handicapping are considered together. A case can be made for predicting that socially anxious individuals will be either more inclined or less inclined to handicap an upcoming performance. First, it could be argued that socially anxious individuals should be prime candidates for self-handicapping (Arkin, Lake, & Baumgardner, 1986). Through self-handicapping, one can protect one's self-image by shifting the responsibility for a poor performance from lack of ability to a non-ability cause – the handicap. Socially anxious individuals are uncertain about their capacity to succeed in social situations (Leary, 1983a). Further, socially anxious individuals place a premium on avoiding disapproval (Arkin, 1981). Through self-handicapping, the socially anxious individual can avoid the implications and repercussions of a poor performance.

From another perspective, however, it seems equally likely that social anxiety would tend to suppress the tendency to self-handicap. For instance, it has already been found that socially anxious individuals report far more modest attributions (attributing greater causality to themselves for failure than for success), especially when they anticipate close scrutiny of their attributions and behaviours (Arkin, Appelman, & Burger, 1980). This finding suggests that socially anxious individuals are unwilling to violate the "norm of internality" (Jellison & Green, 1981) by denying personal responsibility for an unsuccessful outcome. The act of publicly distancing oneself from failure is a tricky tactic of self-presentation. It may require greater social skills, or a greater sense of self-confidence, than the socially anxious individual believes that he or she possesses. When a person attempts to foster attributions that are at variance with objective reality, there is a risk of embarrassment. The individual may be called on to justify the misrepresentation of his or her actions, and that will draw unwanted attention to the self. Therefore, the conservative social orientation of the socially anxious individual will tend to militate against adopting such a risk-oriented self-presentational strategy. Instead, their protective orientation supports attempts to create an impression that is merely safe, rather than promotive.

Finally, of course, it may be that social anxiety both promotes and suppresses self-handicapping, depending on the circumstances of the social situation, the performance dimension, and the features of the handicap itself. Before discussing the evidence bearing on the relationship between social anxiety and self-handicapping, it may be useful to organise the self-handicapping strategies in some way. The following organisational scheme should provide insight into the circumstances under which social anxiety can be expected either to promote or to suppress self-handicapping.

An organisational scheme

Self-handicapping can be viewed along several dimensions. First, all efforts to self-handicap are designed to obscure the precise cause of failure; however, handicaps may differ in terms of whether they introduce ability-irrelevant *internal* attributions or ability-irrelevant *external* attributions (Arkin & Baumgardner, 1985). Examples of self-handicaps that shift the blame for a potential failure to some internal, non-ability factor include the following: reducing or withholding effort (Harris & Snyder, 1986; Rhodewalt et al., 1984; Weary & Williams, in press), self-reports of a debilitating internal state such as depression (Baumgardner et al., 1985), test anxiety (Smith, Snyder, & Handelsman, 1982), and the lasting results of traumatic childhood events (Smith, Snyder, & Perkins, 1983). Examples of self-handicaps that shift the blame for a potential failure to an *external*, non-ability factor include the

Source of Handicap

	Preexisting	Created or Constructed
Internal	– Social anxiety – Test anxiety – Personal disabilities – Physical complaints	– Withholding effort – Handicapping lifestyle (i.e. the chronic alcoholic or drug user)
External	– Poor performance conditions – Insufficient time	– Difficult goal choice – Occasional substance abuse – Debilitating music

Locus of Perceived Responsibility

Figure 10.1. Classification of self-handicaps.

selection of difficult goals or standards (Greenberg, 1985; Hamilton, 1974) and the assertion of the difficulty of a task.

Second, self-handicaps differ with respect to whether they are "created" by an individual prior to some performance or seem to pre-exist in some form prior to performance (see Arkin & Baumgardner, 1985, and Leary & Shepperd, 1986, for a slightly different distinction). By "created" we mean to imply impediments that are set in place or *constructed* by the individual prior to a performance. Created or constructed handicaps can include ingesting alcohol or drugs, choosing inhibiting performance circumstances, and preparing for some performance inadequately, as well as others. In contrast to constructed handicaps, handicaps can be *pre-existing* either within the individual or in the environment.[2] This class includes personal disabilities, physical complaints, and personality constraints such as test anxiety and social anxiety, as well as environmental impediments such as loud noise, poor lighting, and so forth.

Considering these dimensions together, self-handicaps can be classified into one of four quadrants: *internal pre-existing, internal constructed, external pre-existing,* and *external constructed* (Figure 10.1). What follows is a brief discussion of each of the four quadrants as they pertain to social anxiety. This is followed by a more detailed discussion of the implications of the internal/external and pre-existing/constructed dimensions for predicting and understanding the behaviour of socially anxious individuals. Next, there is a discussion of self-handicapping as it is related to other attributional strategies. Finally, we discuss self-handicapping in terms of the insights it provides for understanding social anxiety as an antecedent and consequence of self-presentation.

Evidence on self-handicapping and social anxiety

Internal pre-existing handicaps. Socially anxious individuals have a ready-made internal pre-existing handicap at their disposal: their anxiety. The anxious individual can assert his or her anxiety as an explanation for failure on a forthcoming performance and, through this, can undermine the ability implications of a poor performance. There is evidence to suggest that socially anxious individuals will pre-emptively claim their anxiety symptoms as in internal pre-existing handicap.

In one study, undergraduates high and low in social anxiety were instructed that they were to take a test of social intelligence. Some of the subjects were led to believe that anxiety symptoms would have no effect on test performance, and others were told nothing about the relationship between anxiety symptoms and test performance. In an additional group, subjects high and low in social anxiety also were given no information regarding the relationship between social anxiety and test performance; instead, they were provided instructions that de-emphasised the evaluative nature of the test (Snyder, Smith, Augelli, & Ingram, 1985). Prior to taking the test, all subjects were provided an opportunity to report their current levels of anxiety.

The researchers found that subjects high in social anxiety reported experiencing heightened anxiety symptoms in a setting in which their anxiety could serve as an excuse for poor performance. In the setting in which social anxiety was described as having no effect on performance, and in the non-evaluative setting, socially anxious individuals did not report heightened anxiety. Individuals low in social anxiety did not demonstrate this self-protective strategy in any instance. Rather, they reported relatively few anxiety symptoms regardless of how the test setting was characterised. To summarise, the study by Snyder et al. (1985) suggests that individuals high in social anxiety are willing to use their anxiety symptoms strategically as a pre-emptive excuse for failure on an upcoming test.

External pre-existing handicaps. In cases involving internal pre-existing self-handicaps, the handicapper reports some personal problem or disability (i.e., social anxiety) that handicaps an upcoming performance. By contrast, in cases involving external pre-existing self-handicaps, the individual pre-emptively asserts that some external factor (i.e., some feature of the environment or the social context) is preventing an optimal performance. To date, there have been no studies investigating the extent to which socially anxious individuals pre-emptively report external handicaps as an excuse for failure. However, there is mounting evidence that the presence of an external pre-existing handicap actually facilitates the interactions of socially anxious participants, freeing them to adopt an acquisitive self-presentational style (Arkin & Baumgardner, 1988). At the same time, the presence of an external pre-existing handicap serves as an impediment to smooth, facile behaviour on the part of the individual who is not socially anxious. For example, in one experiment, strangers rated high and low in social anxiety were exposed either to noise characterised as interfering or to noise characterised as non-interfering, and they engaged in both a structured encounter and a brief unstructured encounter. They were asked to express their attitudes on a variety of issues and were videotaped as they participated in the unstructured conversation.

Subjects for whom the noise was characterised as interfering made more unusual statements and more self-relevant statements during the course of the social interaction than did subjects who believed the noise was non-interfering. Apparently, subjects in the interfering condition believed that the noise would provide a persuasive explanation for a poor presentation. That fact diminished the risk associated with attempting an acquisitive presentation of self.

Further evidence that socially anxious individuals abandon their conservative orientation in the presence of a handicap was found in measures of subjects' attitudes. As mentioned earlier, socially anxious individuals typically exhibit the defensive posture of maintaining attitude neutrality (Turner, 1977) and initiating less conversation (Natale et al., 1979) than do their counterparts who are not socially anxious. By not endorsing strong attitudes, socially anxious individuals eliminate the likelihood that they will be rejected by others for how they think. By contrast, socially anxious subjects confronted with the "interfering" noise expressed more extreme attitudes, took more turns speaking, held the floor longer, and asked more questions when there was a handicap present than when there was none (Arkin & Baumgardner, 1988). These findings suggest that socially anxious individuals will use external pre-existing handicaps to their advantage, even adopting an acquisitive self-presentational style, if they believe it is safe to do so.

Additional research has revealed that socially anxious individuals not only will depart from their ordinarily conservative and protective orientation in the presence of a pre-existing handicap but also may actually experience less anxiety in this setting. Leary (1986) found that socially anxious individuals exposed to distracting noise that purportedly would interfere with their ability to interact with others were less anxious during a social interaction than were their counterparts not exposed to the "handicap". This somewhat counter-intuitive finding is based on the notion that failure is particularly threatening when it is likely to be attributed by oneself and others to one's incompetence. The

presence of an external factor that interferes with interpersonal behaviour, a handicap, releases socially anxious individuals from the negative social implications of a mediocre or sub-standard performance.

Further, from the perspective of the misattribution phenomenon
(Ross, Rodin, & Zimbardo, 1969), external impediments to successful
performance appear to temper evaluation apprehension and, ironically,
actually boost performance (Storms & McCaul, 1976, Weiner & Sierad,
1975). When arousal due to one stimulus (e.g., anxiety due to perceived
threat) is misattributed to some other factor (e.g., the difficulty posed by
some external impediment), the arousal itself tends to dissipate. The
intriguing result can be an increase in performance.

In a related way, socially anxious individuals seem to accrue other
supplementary benefits from the presence of a handicap. Because they
are less aroused, socially anxious individuals have been found to behave
more adroitly, and less awkwardly, in the presence of a persuasive
handicap than when no handicap exists. Leary (1986) found that socially
anxious subjects rated themselves more positively (friendly, responsible,
informed, intelligent, interesting, sociable, open-minded) subsequent to
an interaction in the presence of a handicap than when they interacted
without it. Further, Brodt and Zimbardo (1981) and Arkin and Baumgardner (1988) found that socially anxious individuals were judged by
their interaction partners to be less anxious when they believed that
interfering noise was distracting their performances than when they
believed that interfering noise had no effect on performance.

External constructed handicaps. The third class of self-handicaps is composed
of external environmental impediments to performance that are created
or acquired by the individual. An example of an external constructed
handicap is the choice of a difficult goal. In one study, subjects were
given success feedback following work on solvable (contingent success)
or unsolvable (non-contingent success) problems and then were allowed
to select the difficulty level of a second task (Greenberg, 1985). Consistent with previous research (Berglas & Jones, 1978; Kolditz & Arkin,
1982; Tucker et al., 1981), subjects given contingent success feedback
did not self-handicap. By contrast, subjects given non-contingent success
feedback handicapped by choosing a task with an extremely difficult
goal, but only when the task was presented as important to the self-
image. When the task was presented as irrelevant to the self-image,
individuals given non-contingent success feedback chose to pursue a
relatively easy goal. Other examples of external constructed self-
handicaps include some forms of occasional alcohol or drug use (Berglas
& Jones, 1978; Kolditz & Arkin, 1982; Tucker et al., 1981) and the selection of problematic performance conditions other than task difficulty.

There is evidence to suggest that socially anxious individuals are unwilling to attempt to discount their personal responsibility for an unsuccessful act by constructing an external self-handicap. In two experiments, subjects rated high and low in social anxiety were given a choice between listening to performance-enhancing or performance-debilitating music while taking a test measuring intellectual ability (Arkin & Shepperd, 1988). Whereas subjects rated low in social anxiety chose to listen to performance-debilitating music while taking the test, those rated high in social anxiety did not.

Internal constructed handicaps. The fourth and final class of self-handicaps includes those that are constructed by the handicapper (and thus presumably under personal control), yet reside within the handicapper or are reflections of the handicapper's character. An example of an internal constructed self-handicap is the reduction or withholding of effort. One familiar example is the student who does not prepare adequately for an examination and consequently is unable to perform at his or her best. A second example is the individual who embraces a self-handicapping life-style, such as the life-style of the alcoholic or drug abuser. In this example, the individual uses a handicap with such frequency that his or her identity becomes entwined with and defined in terms of the handicap. Though the handicap itself may be external, the frequency of its use leads others to conclude that it represents a stable trait of the individual and consequently to label that individual accordingly. Some forms of alcholism (specifically cases where the alcohol is used chronically as a pre-emptive excuse for failure) can be interpreted as an internal constructed means of self-handicapping. Though the alcohol itself represents an external constructed self-handicap, its chronic use (and the subsequent label of "alcoholic") can be viewed as reflecting a disposition of the individual. Therefore, it is perceived as internally determined.

Initially it might seem that chronic use of alcohol or drugs as a self-handicapping strategy (the self-handicapping life-style), because of its accompanying dispositional label, is no different from the category of internal pre-existing self-handicaps. A claim of anxiety symptoms by socially anxious and test-anxious individuals seems similar to an alcoholic's plea that the disorder or disease can interfere with effective performance (Weary & Williams, in press). However, the self-handicapping life-style may be conceptually distinct in that it represents behaviour constructed by the individual for instrumental reasons, at least initially, to set the stage for self-handicapping. By contrast, individuals who are test-anxious or socially anxious do not make themselves anxious in order to have a persuasive excuse for failure. They merely assert their pre-existing conditions as an explanation for a poor performance. In the examples we are using here, the handicapping life-style of the alcoholic is characterised as an *active* coping response; social anxiety and test anxiety have a more *passive* quality in which the individual is merely subject to situational forces, rather than being instrumental in creating them. Consequently, we might anticipate that individuals who embrace a handicapping life-style, such as the alcoholic, perceive some degree of control (albeit perhaps illusory) over their "handicap" that "pre-existing" conditions would not foster. The *mañana* fantasy of the alcoholic (e.g., Jones & Berglas, 1978) would seem to exemplify the illusion of control, whereas the sense of resignation of the shy person would seem to capture the element of passivity (Zimbardo, 1977).

To date, no research has focused on the relationship between social anxiety and internal constructed self-handicapping. However, it might be speculated that some socially anxious individuals may pre-emptively present themselves as shy to others in order to provide an excuse for any awkwardness in subsequent encounters. Specifically, socially anxious individuals may act reticent or shy *even when they actually feel calm*. By so doing, they can convey an image of shyness and provide others with the explanation that a stilted, awkward social encounter is attributable to their social anxiety, not to any other shortcoming of their character.

Analysis and comparison of the four quadrants

The research described earlier raises an interesting question: Why are socially anxious individuals willing to report their anxiety as a handicap (a pre-existing self-handicap) but not willing to engage in the conceptually similar behaviour of acquiring an external impediment to performance (a constructed self-handicap)? Both pre-existing self-handicaps and constructed self-handicaps provide a pre-emptive excuse for failure – the handicap. Should an individual perform poorly in the presence of either a pre-existing or constructed handicap, he or she can assert the handicap as a plausible cause. Moreover, the two forms of self-handicapping share the added advantage of embellishing one's ability should one perform successfully in the presence of the handicap. After all, success achieved in spite of a handicap is seen as an admirable accomplishment. Nevertheless, there are several plausible explanations for the inconsistent findings among socially anxious individuals across the two classes of self-handicaps.

First, there may be different costs associated with the two forms of self-handicapping. Specifically, the anxious individual who reports debilitating anxiety suffers no increased risk of failure by making such a claim. For the anxious individual, the probability that failure will ensue as a result of crippling anxiety remains the same regardless of whether the knowledge of this handicap is made public or kept private. Thus, in terms of the impact it has on actual task performance, claiming a pre-existing handicap is a relatively safe venture. Conversely, constructed handicaps, by definition, diminish the probability that the handicapper will perform successfully. Indeed, the handicaps that are likely to be most persuasive are the ones that debilitate task performance the most. In short, individuals who construct handicaps not only (1) must admit to embracing an action that, if it is to be persuasive as a handicap, is likely to be negatively sanctioned but also (2) diminish the likelihood that a successful performance on the task will occur. In weighing the costs and benefits associated with constructed self-handicaps, it seems likely that socially anxious individuals perceive the increased risk of failure as too costly. Consequently, they resist using this attributional strategy.

A second explanation is also based on the equation describing the relative costs associated with internal pre-existing versus constructed forms of self-handicapping. Constructed handicaps subject the handicapper to the risk of being caught practising deception. One who constructs a handicap runs the risk that an observer will call one's bluff, forcing one to attempt the task again unencumbered by the handicap. With one's handicap removed, one's true ability (or lack thereof) is laid open to the scrutiny of others. Should one continue to fail in the absence of the handicap, one is left with the short-term cost of the handicap (e.g., being perceived as lazy, as a drug or alcohol user), yet denied the long-term benefit of a non-ability attribution made for failure. With internal pre-existing handicaps, the handicapper's bluff can never be called. Though an audience may come to doubt the authenticity of a self-handicap that is merely reported, they can never conclusively exclude it as the cause of a failure. Thus, there is less risk associated with an internal pre-existing self-handicap, in that only the handicapper can know the impact it truly has on performance.

The same argument can be used to explain why socially anxious individuals are unwilling to deny personal responsibility for an unsuccessful outcome after it occurs (i.e., make self-serving attributions) (Arkin et al., 1980). As with acquiring a self-handicap, citing a cause other than lack of ability as the source of failure raises the prospect of being challenged. Individuals who assert extenuating circumstances (e.g., "My poor performance was due to not having enough time to do my best") as excuses for failure may be requested to repeat the task with the extenuating circumstances removed. Likewise, they may be faced with the prospect of an excuse not being judged credible; usually, excuses are offered to an expert, someone more powerful and knowledgeable, who presumably has a better understanding of what is and is not a viable excuse for failure. It is the resulting embarrassment and the risk of being labelled as one who "shirks responsibility" that may dissuade socially anxious individuals from making self-serving attributions. That is, socially anxious individuals are reluctant to violate the "norm of internality" (Jellison & Green, 1981) in this blatant way.

A third explanation for the inconsistent findings would prescribe that the two forms of self-handicapping tap different levels of sophistication in knowledge of attributional inference processes. Socially anxious individuals are characterised by a focus away from the task and on avoiding disapproval (Baumeister & Steinhilber, 1984). In a sense, they are very much like test-anxious individuals (Mandler & Watson, 1966; Wine, 1971). In a test situation, test-anxious individuals tend not to think about the test; rather, they focus on interfering thoughts such as how poorly they are doing on the test, the time constraints, the difficulty of the problems, how others have done on the test, and their level of ability (Sarason & Stoop, 1978). These interfering thoughts keep test-anxious individuals from concentrating on the test problems and consequently impede performance.

In a similar manner, the inordinate focus of socially anxious individuals on social disapproval may interfere with the tendency to make attributional links between behaviours and outcomes. The report of a pre-existing self-handicap (e.g., reporting anxiety symptoms as an impediment to performance, as in the Snyder et al., 1985, study) is a relatively simple means by which the socially anxious individual can influence the attributions made for a performance. It merely requires that the audience infer the appropriate attribution from the handicapper's verbal report of personal circumstances that debilitate performance. By contrast, constructing a self-handicap (e.g., taking a test while listening to distracting music, as done in the Arkin and Shepperd studies) is a more complex strategy, demanding that the handicapper engage in a more sophisticated attributional inference process. It requires that the handicapper not only be cognizant of the fact that a constructed handicap can serve as a persuasive excuse for a potential failure but also realise that observers of the handicap can be drawn into making non-ability attributions should failure occur. In sum, socially anxious individuals may fail to draw the conclusion that a constructed self-handicap can provide an excuse for failure on an upcoming task. Specifically, their intense concern with evaluation may cloud their ability to make the inference that creating a handicap can result ultimately in others making non-ability attributions for failure.

A continuum of self-presentational strategies

In the preceding section, an organisational framework was offered in which different forms of self-handicapping can be conceptualised systematically. In addition, the literature linking social anxiety and self-handicapping was discussed, and an attempt was made to resolve apparent contradictions in the literature. One explanation proposed for resolving the inconsistent findings asserts that the various forms of self-handicapping differ with respect to the costs or risks they present to the individual. It was suggested that some forms of self-handicapping (external constructed self-handicaps) may seem too risky, dissuading the socially anxious individual from undertaking the strategy.

At this point it seems possible to conceptualise the various strategies for controlling attributions (e.g., reporting a pre-existing self-handicap, constructing a self-handicap, making self-serving attributions) as falling on a continuum ranging from safe (there is little cost associated with employing the strategy) to risky (they expose the individual to undesirable consequences should this attempt at attributional control fail). Anchoring the safe end of the continuum are strategies such as pre-emptively claiming a handicap (e.g., social anxiety symptoms) to performance; anchoring the risky end of the continuum are the self-serving attributions for a previous performance (e.g., "I failed because I was unprepared"). Somewhere between these poles, perhaps more towards the risky end, are acquired, constructed forms of self-handicaps (e.g., ingesting a drug). When acquiring a self-handicap, individuals risk having their true ability exposed should they be called on to repeat the task with the handicap removed. When the risk of exposure is coupled with the negative attributions associated with acquiring a persuasive self-handicap, acquired self-handicapping becomes a risky venture – a risk that distances it from the safe end of the continuum. However, because acquired handicaps are constructed before the performance and thus do not appear to be mere excuses created expressly to shift responsibility subsequent to failure, they might be less likely to cause embarrassment should the individual be required to repeat the task with the handicap absent. Thus, acquired handicaps may be perceived as less risky than making self-serving attributions.

Social anxiety, self-handicapping, and the antecedent/consequence distinction

The purpose of this chapter is to cast social anxiety within a novel framework, one emphasising the interplay between social anxiety and self-presentation. In the first section, evidence was presented suggesting that social anxiety can be conceptualised both as an antecedent and as a consequence of self-presentation. In the second section, the attributional strategy of self-handicapping was introduced and discussed. The goal of that section was to illustrate the relationship between the regulation of one's anxiety and the presentation of the self to others through the use of a pre-emptive attributional strategy. We now return briefly to the antecedent/consequence distinction discussed in the first section of this chapter, drawing on the evidence from the self-handicapping literature to further explicate the two approaches to social anxiety.

Social anxiety as an antecedent to self-handicapping. The research on social anxiety and self-handicapping provides further evidence for the protective self-presentational style of socially anxious individuals. Prior to undertaking a task, socially anxious individuals appear less willing than their counterparts who are not socially anxious to risk engaging in the pre-emptive attributional strategy of constructing a handicap to performance (Arkin & Shepperd, 1988). The research by Arkin and Shepperd (1988) suggests that the increased risk of failure that accompanies constructed self-handicaps deters socially anxious individuals from undertaking this attributional strategy. Socially anxious individuals prefer to opt for the safer strategy of doing nothing to interfere with an upcoming performance. Indeed, Arkin and Shepperd (1988) found that socially anxious individuals chose to facilitate rather than interfere with their performances.

Social anxiety as a consequence of self-handicapping. Socially anxious individuals appear unwilling to embrace a handicap prior to a performance; however, should they be forced to perform in the presence of a handicap, they appear to derive supplemental benefits. Specifically, as noted earlier, Arkin and Baumgardner (1988) demonstrated that anxious individuals required to interact in the presence of an external pre-existing handicap were more comfortable and less shy in their interactions than were individuals who were not socially anxious. These anxious individuals appeared to exhibit behaviour more in line with an acquisitive self-presentational style. More importantly, the presence of the handicap appears to reduce the degree to which anxious individuals experience anxiety in social settings. In short, the consequences of performing in the presence of a handicap are a reduction in the anxiety symptoms characteristically associated with social interaction and the emergence of behaviours consistent with an acquisitive self-presentational style among socially anxious individuals.

Social anxiety: An active or reactive process?

Given that social anxiety can influence and be influenced by self-presentation, a question arises whether this process of mutual influence reflects a reactive process or can be conceptualised as an active process (e.g., Bandura, 1977). Specifically, it is conceivable that socially anxious individuals do not always respond passively to the social setting, but may pro-actively act upon the social setting in order to modify or regulate their anxiety symptoms.

Social anxiety as a reactive process

Traditionally, social anxiety has been portrayed as a reactive process – as a response by the individual to circumstances in his or her social environment. There are at least four distinct theoretical perspectives that define social anxiety as a reactive process (Leary, 1983a). One approach contends that social anxiety is a conditioned emotional response to a stimulus or class of stimuli (Zimbardo, 1977). According to this approach, the shyness and social apprehension an individual experiences in a particular situation can be traced to a specific aversive experience. For example, one can imagine a woman normally poised and confident who flubs badly when speaking in front of an audience for the first time. Consequently, she subsequently approaches another audience with increased apprehension and anxiety. In line with the classical conditioning approach, the real or anticipated presence of an audience comes to be associated with the embarrassment and anxiety experienced during the first speaking engagement.

A second approach, also characterising social anxiety as a reactive process, suggests that social anxiety results from a deficit in social skills (Arkowitz, Hinton, Perl, & Himadi, 1978). Leary (1983a) has noted three ways in which a social skills deficit can lead to social anxiety. First, individuals who are less adept in their social interactions are more prone to elicit negative responses from other participants in an interaction. These negative reactions are likely to produce social anxiety over future social interactions. Second, the social interactions of individuals who are unskilled in their interactions are likely to be more awkward, not only for them, but for all participants concerned. Frequent experiences of awkward, uncomfortable encounters are likely to elicit increased feelings of anxiety over future interactions. Third, the perception or awareness that one has difficulty interacting or is unable to interact smoothly in social relations is likely to produce social anxiety as one anticipates a social encounter. Regardless of the avenue by which a deficit in social skills leads to social anxiety, social anxiety is treated as a consequence rather than an antecedent of self-presentation.

The third approach represents a collection of hypotheses that are more cognitive in nature. The theme underlying each of these hypotheses is that the way individuals view themselves and the social world can elicit social anxiety. Leary (1983a) has classified the various cognitive approaches into three groups. For those in the first of these groups, it is proposed that social anxiety is a consequence of a negative self-evaluation. Specifically, when people perceive themselves negatively or believe that they are incapable of dealing with the demands of a particular social situation, they experience social anxiety (Clark & Arkowitz, 1975; Meichenbaum, Gilmore, & Fedoravicius, 1971; Rehm & Marston, 1968; Leary, 1983a). The second cognitive approach proposes that social anxiety is grounded in the irrational beliefs stemming from being excessively concerned with being liked by others (Ellis, 1962). Some people feel that it is important to be liked and approved of by virtually everyone. The inability to achieve full acceptance by everyone results in feelings of failure and unworthiness. Ellis argues that people who place an inordinate emphasis on achieving complete acceptance are likely to experience social anxiety in their social encounters, as they are never able to achieve acceptance by all. The third cognitive approach suggests that social anxiety is a consequence of holding unrealistically high standards (Bandura, 1969). According to this approach, anxiety results when individuals hold themselves to a high standard of self-evaluation or chronically compare themselves to others who are characterised by high levels of achievement. Consistent with each of the cognitive approaches to social anxiety is the assumption that social anxiety is a response arising from the way in which individuals view themselves or the social world.

The fourth approach characterising social anxiety as a reactive process was mentioned in an earlier section of this chapter. It proposes that social anxiety is a product of the desire to present a certain image of oneself and uncertainty that one can achieve the desired image (Schlenker & Leary, 1982). As the desire to create a certain image of oneself increases, and the certainty that one can succeed in doing so decreases, social anxiety results.

Social anxiety as an active process

The four approaches described thus far suggest that social anxiety is a reactive process representing a response by the individual to some aspect or feature of the social situation. However, rather than viewing socially anxious individuals as passive responders to their social environment, it is perhaps more appropriate to conceptualise chronically anxious individuals as taking an active role in constructing their social world. Specifically, in some circumstances socially anxious individuals may pro-actively act upon their social setting in order to regulate their anxiety feelings. Indeed, one can conceive of the protective self-presentational style of socially anxious individuals as a means of keeping anxiety symptoms in check. The conservative behaviours of socially anxious individuals perhaps represent a systematic attempt at self-regulation through which anxious individuals attempt to reduce their anxious feelings and to regulate their affective state.

The self-regulation of anxious feelings is distinct from the selective reporting of anxiety or shyness for strategic purposes, as discussed earlier. In the latter case, anxiety is pre-emptively claimed as an impediment to an upcoming social performance and thereby can mitigate the negative impact of any failure. From the self-regulation perspective, the anxious individual seeks out performance settings that are safe or engages in socially conservative behaviours in order to avoid or minimise anxious feelings.

The research by Arkin and Baumgardner (1988) provides some evidence for conceptualising social anxiety as an active process. Those researchers demonstrated that socially anxious individuals benefit from performing in environments characterised by pre-existing self-handicaps. The pre-existing handicaps provide an alternative, non-ability explanation for a poor self-presentation and consequently provide socially anxious individuals a safe environment in which to attempt an acquisitive self-presentational style. Their research suggests that if one is socially anxious, one can actively regulate one's affect by exerting control over features of the social environment.

On the basis of research by Arkin and Baumgardner (1988) it can be speculated that socially anxious individuals may go so far as to manage their anxiety symptoms by choosing performance circumstances in which handicaps already exist. By so doing, socially anxious individuals can provide themselves with an environment in which it is safe to abandon their conservative interaction style in favor of a more acquisitive style. In an environment characterised by pre-existing handicaps, any social discomfort or awkwardness in behaviour can be attributed to the handicaps present, rather than to personal inabilities or social inadequacies.

Summary and conclusion

The goal of this chapter has been to review the literature on social anxiety and self-presentation and to organise the literature within a framework conceptualising social anxiety as both an antecedent and consequence of self-presentation. In addition, we have attempted to portray social anxiety as more than a reactive process whereby the individual responds to anxiety-producing circumstances in the environment. It is also an active process in which the socially anxious individual actively manages circumstances that serve to keep anxiety symptoms in check.

Much of the research investigating self-presentation and social anxiety has been conducted only in the last decade. Numerous questions regarding social anxiety and various strategies and tactics for presenting the self remain unanswered. In this chapter we have attempted to provide a framework for viewing the bidirectional influences of the two processes. However, until more data are collected, the framework we have suggested for viewing self-presentation and social anxiety remains tentative. Obviously, more research is needed before a clearer picture of the relationship between social anxiety and self-presentation can be achieved.

NOTES

1. There is a third approach from which to view social anxiety and self-presentation. Specifically, social anxiety and self-presentation can be thought of as co-effects of a third process (such as the motive to be evaluated positively or to maintain self-esteem or social esteem). However, because of space limitations, this third model will not be discussed.
2. It is possible that a handicap that sounds as though it is pre-existing may in fact not exist. Rather, it merely may be claimed by the individual in order to provide a pre-emptive excuse for a potential failure. For example, in a test situation, individuals who are *not* chronically test-anxious may nevertheless claim to be. By so doing, they can redirect any negative attributions resulting from failure away from "lack of ability" and toward the fictitious handicap (being test-anxious).

REFERENCES

Arkin, R. M. (1981). Self-presentational styles. In J. T. Tedeschi (Ed.), *Impression management theory and social psychological research* (pp. 311–333). New York: Academic Press.

Arkin, R. M., Appelman, A. J., & Burger, J. M. (1980). Social anxiety, self-presentation, and the self-serving bias in causal attribution. *Journal of Personality and Social Psychology, 38*, 23–35.

Arkin, R. M., & Baumgardner, A. H. (1985). Self-handicapping. In J. H. Harvey & G. Weary (Eds.), *Basic issues in attribution theory and research* (pp. 169–202). New York: Academic Press.

Arkin, R. M., & Baumgardner, A. H. (1988). *Social anxiety and self-presentation: Protective and acquisitive tendencies in safe versus threatening encounters.* Unpublished manuscript, University of Missouri, Columbia.

Arkin, R. M., Lake, E. A., & Baumgardner, A. H. (1986). Shyness and self-presentation. In W. H. Jones, J. M. Cheek, & S. R. Briggs (Eds.), *Shyness* (pp. 189–203). New York: Plenum Press.

Arkin, R. M., & Schumann, D. (1983). *Self-presentational styles: The roles of cost orientation and shyness.* Paper presented to the American Psychological Association, Anaheim, CA.

Arkin, R. M., & Shepperd, J. A. (1988). *The role of social anxiety in self-presentational self-handicapping.* Unpublished manuscript, University of Missouri, Columbia.

Arkowitz, H., Hinton, R., Perl, J., & Himadi, W. (1978). Treatment strategies for dating anxiety in college men based on real-life practice. *Counseling Psychologist, 7,* 41–46.

Bandura, A. (1969). *Principles of behavior modification.* New York: Holt, Rinehart & Winston.

Bandura, A. (1977). *Social learning theory.* Englewood Cliffs, NJ: Prentice-Hall.

Baumeister, R. F., & Steinhilber, A. (1984). Paradoxical effects of supportive audiences on performance under pressure: The home field disadvantage in sports championships. *Journal of Personality and Social Psychology, 47,* 85–93.

Baumgardner, A. H., Lake, E. A., & Arkin, R. M. (1985). Claiming mood as a self-handicap: The influence of spoiled and unspoiled public identities. *Personality and Social Psychology Bulletin, 11,* 349–347.

Berglas, S., & Jones, E. E. (1978). Drug choice as a self-handicapping strategy in response to noncontingent success. *Journal of Personality and Social Psychology, 36,* 405–417.

Bernstein, W. M., Stephenson, B. O., Snyder, M. L., & Wicklund, R. A. (1983). Causal ambiguity and heterosexual affiliation. *Journal of Experimental Social Psychology, 19,* 78–92.

Brodt, S. E., & Zimbardo, P. G. (1981). Modifying shyness-related social behavior through symptom misattribution. *Journal of Personality and Social Psychology, 41,* 437–449.

Cheek, J. M., & Buss, A. H. (1981). Shyness and sociability, *Journal of Personality and Social Psychology, 41,* 330–339.

Cialdini, R. B., & Mirels, H. L. (1976). Sense of personal control and attributions about yielding and resisting persuasion targets. *Journal of Personality and Social Psychology, 33,* 395–402.

Clark, J. V., & Arkowitz, H. (1975). Social anxiety and self-evaluation of interpersonal performance. *Psychological Reports, 36,* 211–221.

Coopersmith, S. (1967). *The antecedents of self-esteem.* San Francisco: Freeman.

Curran, J. (1977). Skills training as an approach to the treatment of heterosexual-social anxiety: A review. *Psychological Bulletin, 84,* 140–157.

Dykman, B., & Reis, H. T. (1979). Personality correlates of classroom seating position. *Journal of Educational Psychology, 71,* 346–354.

Efran, J. S., & Korn, P. R. (1969). Measurement of social caution: Self-appraisal, role playing, and discussion behavior. *Journal of Consulting and Clinical Psychology, 33,* 78–83.

Ellis, A. (1962). *Reason and emotion in psychotherapy.* New York: Stuart.

Fenigstein, A., Scheier, M. F., & Buss, A. H. (1975). Public and private self-consciousness: Assessment and theory. *Journal of Consulting and Clinical Psychology, 43,* 522–527.

Frankel, A., & Snyder, M. L. (1978). Poor performance following unsolvable problems: Learned helplessness or egotism? *Journal of Personality and Social Psychology, 36,* 1415–1423.

Goffman, E. (1959). *The presentation of self in everyday life.* Garden City, NY: Doubleday.

Greenberg, J. (1985). Unattainable goal choice as a self-handicapping strategy. *Journal of Applied Social Psychology, 15,* 140–152.

312   JAMES A. SHEPPERD AND ROBERT M. ARKIN

amilton, J. O. (1974). Motivation and risk taking behavior: A test of Atkinson's theory. *Journal of Personality and Social Psychology, 29*, 856–864.

arris, R. N., & Snyder, C. R. (1986). The role of uncertain self-esteem in self-handicapping. *Journal of Personality and Social Psychology, 51*, 451–458.

eider, F. (1958). *The psychology of interpersonal relations.* New York: Wiley.

ellison, J. M., & Arkin, R. M. (1977). Social comparison of abilities: A self-presentation approach to decision making in groups. In J. M. Suls & R. L. Miller (Eds.), *Social comparison processes: Theoretical and empiricial perspectives* (pp. 235–257). Washington, DC: Hemisphere.

ellison, J. M., & Green, J. (1981). A self-presentation approach to the fundamental attribution error. *Journal of Personality and Social Psychology, 40*, 643–649.

ones, E. E., & Berglas, S. (1978). Control of attributions about the self through self-handicapping strategies: The appeal of alcohol and the role of underachievement. *Personality and Social Psychology Bulletin, 4*, 200–206.

ones, E. E., & Pittman, T. S. (1982). Toward a general theory of strategic self-presentation. In J. Suls (Ed.), *Psychological perspectives on the self* (pp. 231–262). Hillsdale, NJ: Lawrence Erlbaum.

elley, H. H. (1971). Attribution in social interaction. In E. E. Jones, D. E. Kanouse, H. H. Kelley, R. E. Nisbett, S. Valins, & B. Weiner (Eds.), *Attribution: Perceiving the causes of behavior* (pp. 1–26). New York: General Learning Press.

olditz, T. A., & Arkin, R. M. (1982). An impression management interpretation of the self-handicapping strategy. *Journal of Personality and Social Psychology, 43*, 492–502.

eary, M. R. (1983a). *Understanding social anxiety: Social, personality, and clinical perspectives.* Beverly Hills, CA: Sage.

eary, M. R. (1983b). Social anxiousness: The construct and its measurement. *Journal of Personality Assessment, 47*, 66–75.

eary, M. R. (1986). The impact of interactional impediments on social anxiety and self-presentation. *Journal of Experimental Social Psychology, 22*, 122–135.

eary, M. R., & Shepperd, J. A. (1986). Behavioral self-handicapping versus self-reported self-handicapping: A conceptual note. *Journal of Personality and Social Psychology, 51*, 1265–1268.

cGovern, L. P. (1976). Dispositional social anxiety and helping behavior under three conditions of threat. *Journal of Personality, 44*, 84–97.

andler, G., & Watson, D. (1966). Anxiety and the interruption of behavior. In C. D. Spielberger (Ed.), *The Self in Social Psychology* (pp. 263–288). New York: Academic Press.

anis, M. (1955). Social interaction and the self-concept. *Journal of Abnormal and Social Psychology, 51*, 362–370.

eichenbaum, D. H., Gilmore, J. B., & Fedoravicius, A. (1971). Group insight versus group desensitization in treating speech anxiety. *Journal of Consulting and Counseling Psychology, 36*, 410–421.

yers, D. G. (1978). Polarizing effects of social comparison. *Journal of Experimental Social Psychology, 14*, 554–563.

Natale, M., Entin, E., & Jaffee, J. (1979). Vocal interruptions in dyadic communications as a function of speech and social anxiety. *Journal of Personality and Social Psychology, 37,* 865–878.

Pyszczynski, T., & Greenberg, J. (1983). Determinants of reduction in intended effort as a strategy for coping with anticipated failure. *Journal of Research in Personality, 17,* 412–422.

Rehm, L. P., & Marston, A. R. (1968). Reduction of social anxiety through modification of self-reinforcement. *Journal of Consulting and Clinical Psychology, 32,* 565–574.

Rhodewalt, F., Saltzman, A. T., & Wittmer, J. (1984). Self-handicapping among competitive athletes: The role of practice in self-esteem protection. *Basic and Applied Social Psychology, 5,* 197–210.

Ross, L., Rodin, J., & Zimbardo, P. G. (1969). Toward an attribution therapy: The reduction of fear through induced cognitive-emotional misattribution. *Journal of Personality and Social Psychology, 12,* 279–288.

Santee, R. T., & Maslach, C. (1982). To agree or not to agree: Personal dissent amid social pressure to conform. *Journal of Personality and Social Psychology, 42,* 690–700.

Sarason, I. G., & Stoop, R. (1978). Test anxiety and the passage of time. *Journal of Consulting and Clinical Psychology, 46,* 102–109.

Schlenker, B. R., & Leary, M. R. (1982). Social anxiety and self-presentation: A conceptualization and model. *Psychological Bulletin, 92,* 641–669.

Shepperd, J. A., & Arkin, R. M. (1989a). Determinants of self-handicapping: Task importance and the effects of preexisting handicaps on self-generated handicaps. *Personality and Social Psychology Bulletin, 15,* 101–112.

Shepperd, J. A., & Arkin, R. M. (1989b). Self-handicapping: The moderating roles of public self-consciousness and task importance. *Personality and Social Psychology Bulletin, 15,* 252–265.

Smith, T. W., Snyder, C. R., & Handelsman, M. M. (1982). On the self-serving function of an academic wooden leg: Test anxiety as a self-handicapping strategy. *Journal of Personality and Social Psychology, 42,* 314–321.

Smith, T. W., Snyder, C. R., & Perkins, S. C. (1983). The self-serving function of hypochondriacal complaints: Physical symptoms as self-handicapping strategies. *Journal of Personality and Social Psychology, 44,* 787–797.

Snyder, C. R., Higgins, R. L., & Stucky, R. J. (1983). *Excuses: Masquerades in search of grace.* New York: Wiley.

Snyder, C. R., Smith, T. W., Augelli, R. W., & Ingram, R. E. (1985). On the self-serving function of social anxiety: Shyness as a self-handicapping strategy. *Journal of Personality and Social Psychology, 48,* 970–980.

Snyder, M. L., Smoller, B., Strenta, A., & Frankel, A. (1981). A comparison of egotism, negativity, and learned helplessness as explanations for poor performance after unsolvable problems. *Journal of Personality and Social Psychology, 40,* 24–30.

Storms, M. D., & McCaul, K. D. (1976). Attribution processes and the emotional exacerbation of dysfunctional behavior. In J. H. Harvey, W. J. Ickes, & R. F. Kidd (Eds.), *New directions in attribution research* (Vol. 1, pp. 143–164). Hillsdale, NJ: Lawrence Erlbaum.

314   JAMES A. SHEPPERD AND ROBERT M. ARKIN

Tice, D. M., & Baumeister, R. F. (1984). *Self-handicapping, self-esteem and self-presentation.* Paper presented to the Midwestern Psychological Association, Chicago.

Tucker, J. A., Vulchinich, R. D., & Sobell, M. B. (1981). Alcohol consumption as a self-handicapping strategy. *Journal of Abnormal Psychology, 90,* 220–230.

Turner, R. G. (1977). Self-consciousness and anticipatory belief change. *Personality and Social Psychology Bulletin, 3,* 438–441.

Weary, G., & Arkin, R. M. (1981). Attributional self-presentation. In J. H. Harvey, W. Ickes, & R. F. Kidd (Eds.), *New directions in attribution research* (Vol. 2, pp. 223–246). Hillsdale, NJ: Lawrence Erlbaum.

Weary, G., & Williams, J. P. (in press). Depressive self-presentation: Beyond self-handicapping. *Journal of Personality and Social Psychology.*

Weiner, B., & Sierad, J. (1975). Misattribution of failure and enhancement of achievement strivings. *Journal of Consulting and Clinical Psychology, 31,* 415–421.

Wine, J. D. (1971). Test anxiety and direction of attention. *Psychological Bulletin, 75,* 92–104.

Zimbardo, P. G. (1977). *Shyness: What it is, what to do about it.* Menlo Park, CA: Addison-Wesley.

11

Shyness as a personality trait

JONATHAN M. CHEEK and STEPHEN R. BRIGGS

In 1908, William McDougall published the first edition of *An Introduction to Social Psychology*. Paradoxically, the book presented his theory of personality. In the Preface to the 14th edition, McDougall defended his choice of that title by arguing that one cannot understand social psychology without first accounting for "the innate tendencies of human nature and their organization under the touch of individual experience to form the characters of individual men" (1919/1963, p. xvii). He continued throughout his career to maintain that dispositional tendencies must be considered as fundamental and indispensable postulates for all psychology (McDougall, 1938).

We agree with McDougall that understanding personality structure, development, and dynamics is prerequisite to explaining adult social behaviour. Many behaviourists, sociologists, and social psychologists, however, vehemently disagree with this core assumption of personality psychology and argue instead that behaviour is a function of the situation in which it occurs. As a result, the literature contains recurring cycles of debate about the existence and importance of personality traits (Allport, 1937, ch. 11; Magnusson & Endler, 1977; Mischel, 1968; Murphy, 1947, ch. 38; Sanford, 1956; Watson & McDougall, 1929). At present, the idea that internal dispositions have an important influence on behaviour appears to be enjoying increased acceptance (Kenrick & Funder, 1988; Rowe, 1987). Whether or not the status and popularity of personality psychology will continue to be cyclical, we believe that McDougall's conceptualisation must be taken seriously for the simple reason that it is essentially correct.

In this chapter we take the position that a trait approach is the indispensable foundation for a complete psychological understanding of shyness. We begin by considering the state–trait distinction and the definition of shyness as a personality trait. Next, we review research on the origins and development of shyness. Then we discuss the correlates and consequences of dispositional shyness. Finally, we describe the implications of the trait approach for treatment and future research.

316 JONATHAN M. CHEEK AND STEPHEN R. BRIGGS

States, traits, and situations

"Shyness" is the ordinary language term most often used to label the emotional state of feeling anxious and inhibited in social situations. As would be expected from a social psychological perspective, situations differ in their power to elicit reactions of social anxiety. Ratings of shyness-eliciting events reveal that interactions with strangers (especially those of the opposite sex or those in positions of authority), encounters requiring assertive behaviour, and explicitly evaluative settings (such as job interviews) provoke the strongest feelings of social anxiety (Russell, Cutrona, & Jones, 1986).

Viewed as an emotional state, shyness is an almost universal experience, with less than 10% of respondents to a cross-cultural survey reporting that they had never felt shy (Zimbardo, 1977). The ubiquity of shyness raises the question of its possible adaptive value. After quoting Darwin's account of shyness, William James concluded that "whether these impulses could ever have been useful, and selected for usefulness, is a question which, it would seem, can only be answered in the negative ... apparently they are pure hindrances ... they are *incidental* emotions, in spite of which we get along" (1890, p. 432).

Contemporary psychologists who take an evolutionary perspective on emotional development disagree with James. According to Izard and Hyson (1986), a moderate amount of wariness regarding strangers and unfamiliar or unpredictable situations has considerable adaptive value. As a *social* emotion, shyness helps to facilitate co-operative group living by inhibiting individual behaviour that is socially unacceptable (Ford, 1987). Moreover, the complete absence of susceptibility to feeling shy has been recognised as an antisocial characteristic since at least the time of the ancient Greeks (Plutarch, 1906). Situational shyness as a transitory emotional state thus appears to be a normal and functional aspect of human development and everyday adult life.

James's exclusively negative interpretation of shyness appears to apply better to the trait than to the state. Of the 30% to 40% of Americans who label themselves as dispositionally shy persons, three-quarters do not like being so shy, and two-thirds consider their shyness to be a personal problem (Lazarus, 1982; Pilkonis, Heape, & Klein, 1980; Zimbardo, Pilkonis, & Norwood, 1975). Indeed, shyness is generally rated as an undesirable personality trait, especially for men (Bem, 1981; Gough & Thorne, 1986; Hampson, Goldberg, & John, 1987). Recent research has supported this negative image of the trait by documenting how shyness can be a barrier to personal well-being, social adjustment, and occupational fulfillment (e.g., Jones, Cheek, & Briggs, 1986).

One way to approach the distinction between shy people and those who are not shy is simply quantitative: Dispositionally shy people experience physical tension, worry, and behavioural inhibition more frequently, more intensely, and in a wider range of situations than do people who do not label themselves as being shy (Cheek, Melchior, & Carpentieri, 1986b). This is a *descriptive* summary of the meaning of the trait, but we are more interested in shyness as an *explanatory construct* (Briggs, 1985). From this perspective, traits are not just labels for observed patterns of regularity in behaviour. They are "hypothetical constructs" or "latent variables" that contribute to the dynamic organisation of personality, which is defined as a motivational system that influences the individual's transactions with her or his environment (Allport, 1937, 1960; McDougall, 1938; Murphy, 1947). As Rowe (1987) put it, "like Rutherford's atoms, which could be detected by the scatter of atomic particles through a gold sheet, traits are inferred from their organizing effects on behaviour" (p. 219).

Crozier (1982) has pointed out that a successful explanation of dispositional shyness must account for two findings that have been common in the shyness literature: (1) Shy and non-shy people agree on the rank ordering of shyness-eliciting situations. (2) Almost all people who do not consider themselves shy still report experiencing some shyness symptoms in those situations. Concerning the first finding, the similarity of rank orderings does not necessarily mean that shy and non-shy people perceive each situation in exactly the same way. It would be a blow to the trait approach if they did, because the idea that personality dispositions profoundly influence the way different individuals perceive the same "objective" social situation is a fundamental assumption of many personality theorists (e.g., Hogan, 1976; Jung, 1933).

There is, however, ample evidence that this assumption is true for the personality trait shyness. For example, shy people perceive various situations as being inherently less intimate and more evaluative and perceive the same interpersonal feedback as being more evaluatively negative than do those who are not shy (e.g., Goldfried, Padawar, & Robbins, 1984; Smith & Sarason, 1975). These results suggest an affirmative answer to the questions Murphy (1947) formulated in response to the "situationist" challenge to personality psychology: "Is not each situation, as a functionally real thing, determined in part by the individual who confronts it? ... Is not the present situation, then, a projection into the present of the structure of past situations; are not individual heredity and past experience relevant to the definition of today's situation?" (p. 881).

The second issue raised by Crozier (1982) concerns how to explain the findings that most people who do not label themselves as shy do, nevertheless, experience social anxiety in many shyness-eliciting situa-

tions. Zimbardo (1977) suggested that when they encounter social difficulties, "shy people blame themselves; the not-shy blame the situation"
(p. 54). Numerous studies have demonstrated the validity of Zimbardo's
observation (for a review, see Cheek et al., 1986b). Ishiyama (1984)
proposed a related distinction between two phases in the experience of
shyness: The primary phase is the normal social anxiety experienced by
most people in difficult interpersonal encounters; the secondary phase
involves the dysfunctional cognitive processing that occurs only among
shy people, such as the self-blaming dispositional attribution of causality
for social failures. Shy people differ from those who are not shy not only
quantitatively, in terms of the frequency and intensity of shyness symptoms, but also qualitatively, in terms of how those symptoms are interpreted (Cheek & Melchior, 1990).

Although cognitive processes compose only one component of a dispositional tendency (McDougall, 1919/1963), the perceptions, expectancies, and attributions of shy people provide a good example of how a
trait contributes to the dynamic organisation of an individual's personality system. A trait approach also implies that feelings and actions can be
predicted. Indeed, when exposed to the same social situation, such as
meeting a stranger, high scorers on trait measures of shyness do tend to
talk less and feel more tense and inhibited than do low scorers (Cheek &
Buss, 1981; Pilkonis, 1977). But this does not mean that the trait is
monolithic, immutable, or unresponsive to situational influences. As
Kenrick and Funder (1988) have pointed out, such an interpretation
would be only an unproductive repetition of the "straw man" typically
set up for attack by critics of personality psychology.

Personality psychologists recognise that the extent to which a trait
influences behaviour may vary depending on the circumstances. Traits
are predispositions to respond in particular ways, but Allport (1937)
clearly stated that "traits are often aroused in one type of situation and
not in another; not all stimuli are equivalent in effectiveness" (pp.
331–332). As an example of this principle, consider the study of shyness
and creativity conducted by Cheek and Stahl (1986): Before writing a
poem, half of the subjects were told that their work would be judged by a
committee of poets and that they would receive a copy of this evaluation,
whereas no mention of evaluation was made to the other subjects. In the
evaluation condition, the pre-test measure of shyness correlated $-.57$
with creativity ratings of the poems, but in the control condition the
correlation was only $-.13$.

Another example of Allport's formulation of traits involved the influence of shyness on loneliness in a new situation. Cheek and Busch
(1981) found that shy college students reported significantly more loneliness than did those who were not shy, both at the beginning of a new

semester and it its end. However, the shy students' levels of loneliness did decline significantly during the semester, presumably because of habituation to the initially novel circumstances. The passage of time, by itself, appeared to ameliorate, but not to eliminate, the loneliness of shy people. Obviously, both traits and situations are important in the psychology of loneliness. Our general point here is simply that the personality tradition represented by Allport, McDougall, and Murphy, among others, does not ignore situational factors, but specifically includes them in a sophisticated, transactional approach to social behaviour.

The definition of shyness

The word "shyness", like other trait names, is a socially devised symbol for describing and explaining a salient aspect of human experience (Briggs, 1985). Its origin in ordinary language has, however, created a debate about the precise definition of shyness as a personality trait (Cheek & Watson, 1989). Harris (1984) argued that "it is clearly nonsense for psychologists to borrow a term from the lay person and then construct a definition of that term which enables them to subsequently inform the lay person that he or she is using the term incorrectly" (p. 174). On the other hand, psychologists are free to create technical definitions for their own terms, such as *interaction anxiousness* (Leary, 1983), *communication apprehension* (McCroskey & Beatty, 1986), or *threctia* (Cattell, 1965), as they see fit.

Many psychologists have preferred to stick with the term *shyness*, even though Pilkonis and Zimbardo (1979) concluded after 5 years of work on the topic that "shyness still remains a fuzzy concept that defies simple definition" (p. 133). Psychodynamic hypotheses about unconscious repression of aggressive and sexual impulses, narcissistic disturbances, and the behaviour of obnoxious individuals who may be compensating for their shyness have been particularly controversial and are difficult to verify (Kaplan 1972; Lewinsky, 1941). Nevertheless, considerable agreement exists among clinical, psychometric, experimental, and observational studies concerning the typical reactions of shy people during social interactions: global feelings of tension, specific physiological symptoms, painful self-consciousness, worry about being evaluated negatively by others, awkwardness, inhibition, and reticence (Briggs, Cheek, & Jones, 1986).

Disagreements among definitions of shyness centre around deciding which of these typical reactions should be considered the core characteristics that identify a person as being shy. Leary (1986) located 14 different definitions that emphasise various subsets of shyness symptoms.

and he speculated that more could be found elsewhere in the published literature. As both he and Harris (1984) have pointed out, the failure of many writers to define shyness explicitly in any way at all adds even more confusion to the proliferation of often contradictory definitions.

Perhaps the narrowest recent definition of shyness is found in the McCroskey and Beatty (1986) conceptualisation of this trait as a strictly behavioural tendency that is essentially equivalent to a quietness-versus-talkativeness dimension. Broader conceptualisations view shyness as a psychological syndrome that includes both the subjective experience of anxiety in social situations and awkward or inhibited social behaviour (Cheek & Buss, 1981; Jones, Briggs, & Smith, 1986). The syndrome approach raises the question of whether or not the simultaneous occurrence of behavioural inhibition and anxiety is necessary to define shyness. Leary (1986) concluded that the answer was yes and offered a new definition: *"shyness* is an affective-behavioral syndrome characterized by social anxiety and interpersonal inhibition that results from the prospect or presence of interpersonal evaluation" (p. 30).

We believe that Leary's specification of shyness is neither inclusive nor flexible enough to meet Harris's criteria (1984) pertaining to the professional usage of terms borrowed from ordinary language, for two reasons: First, the affective or social anxiety part of Leary's syndrome definition encompasses under one heading both the physical distress of emotional arousal and the cognitive processes of painful self-consciousness, self-deprecation, and worries about being evaluated negatively. The argument for distinguishing between somatic and cognitive components of shyness is based on the general distinction between symptoms of somatic anxiety and psychic anxiety (Buss, 1962; Schalling, 1975). This distinction continues to receive empirical support in research on trait anxiety and test anxiety (Deffenbacher & Hazaleus, 1985; Fox & Houston, 1983).

Concerning shyness, several surveys have revealed that somatic anxiety symptoms such as upset stomach, pounding heart, sweating, and trembling are experienced by only 40% to 60% of shy people (for a review, see Cheek & Melchior, 1990). As would be expected from these results, researchers have found it relatively easy to identify a subtype of shy people who are troubled by cognitive symptoms but not by somatic arousal (McEwan & Devins, 1983; Turner & Beidel, 1985). Moreover, distinguishing somatic anxiety from advanced cognitions is essential for the comparative study of shyness in young children (Greenberg & Marvin, 1982; Izard & Hyson, 1986) and in social animals such as dogs (Royce, 1955) and non-human primates (Buss, 1988). Therefore, we think it is necessary to distinguish three components of the shyness syndrome: somatic anxiety, cognitive symptoms and awkward or inhibited social behaviour.

Our second reason for disagreeing with Leary's approach (1986) to the definition of shyness concerns his requirement of the simultaneous occurrence of anxiety and behavioural inhibition. About two-thirds of the shy respondents in various surveys reported behavioural symptoms of shyness (Cheek & Melchior, 1990). Similarly, the results of several laboratory experiments indicate that not all shy people show obvious behavioural deficits, although most do think that others perceive them to be lacking in social skills (e.g., Cheek & Buss, 1981; Curran, Wallander, & Fischetti, 1980; Halford & Foddy, 1982). According to Leary's definition (1986), if individuals do not manifest the behavioural component, "they would not be labeled 'shy'" (p. 33). Yet it is precisely such usage of a professional definition of shyness, informing a substantial group of people who label themselves as shy that they are not shy, that motivated Harris's warning (1984) on the dangers of "psychological imperialism".

It is true that when viewed as a homogeneous group, shy people do report more symptoms of all three components – somatic, cognitive, and behavioural – than do those who are not shy (Fatis, 1983). Recent research has revealed, however, that some shy respondents rarely or never experience problems with one or two of the components (Cheek & Melchior, 1985; Cheek & Watson, 1989), even though the three components do converge both empirically and conceptually in specifying a meaningful psychological syndrome (Cheek & Melchior, 1990). Current research validates Buss's theoretical argument (1984) that it is reasonable to infer shyness when symptoms of at least one of the three components are experienced as a problem in social situations, as well as his contention that "it makes little sense to suggest that any one of the components represents shyness to the exclusion of the other two" (p. 40).

The three components of this syndrome model are represented in the following definition of the personality trait of shyness: the tendency to feel tense, worried, or awkward during social interactions, especially with unfamiliar people (Cheek et al., 1986b). Although the focus of this definition is on reactions that occur during face-to-face encounters, it should be noted that feelings of shyness may be experienced when anticipating or imagining social interactions (Buss, 1980; Leary, 1986). It also should be clear that discomfort or inhibition of social behaviour because of fatigue, illness, moodiness, or unusual circumstances, such as the threat of physical harm, is excluded from the definition of shyness (Buss, 1980; Jones, Briggs, & Smith, 1986).

Operational definitions of shyness

One representative measure of the trait is the Shyness Scale developed by Cheek and Buss (1981). Although the three-component model of shyness had not been articulated fully at that time, their original set of

Table 11.1. *Items from the revised Cheek and Buss Shyness Scale*

---

1. I feel tense when I'm with people I don't know well.
2. I am socially somewhat awkward.
3. I do *not* find it difficult to ask other people for information.
4. I am often uncomfortable at parties and other social functions.
5. When in a group of people, I have trouble thinking of the right things to talk about.
6. It does *not* take me long to overcome my shyness in new situations.
7. It is hard for me to act natural when I am meeting new people.
8. I feel nervous when speaking to someone in authority.
9. I have *no* doubts about my social competence.
10. I have trouble looking someone right in the eye.
11. I feel inhibited in social situations.
12. I do *not* find it hard to talk to strangers.
13. I am more shy with members of the opposite sex.
14. During conversations with new acquaintances, I worry about saying something dumb.

Note: The response format ranges from 1 to 5: 1 = very uncharacteristic or untrue; 5 = very characteristic or true. Items 3, 6, 9, and 12 are reverse-scored. Item 14 is a revised wording of one of the original 9 items that was not included in the 13-item version. The average item mean is 2.55.

nine items contained at least one for each of the somatic anxiety, cognitive, and behavioural categories of symptoms. Subsequent developmental work to improve the scale's reliability, content validity, and item wording resulted in 11-item and 13-item versions (Cheek, 1982, 1983). All 14 items employed in the development and revision of the Shyness Scale are shown in Table 11.1. Inspection of the questionnaire items in Table 11.1. will enable the reader to understand the type of operational definition used to identify participants as being dispositionally "shy" or "socially anxious" in the research we are reviewing in this chapter. The 13-item version of the Shyness Scale has a mean of 33 (S.D. = 9.2), an average inter-item correlation of .39, an α coefficient of .90, and a 45-day retest reliability of .88 (Cheek, 1983; Phillips & Bruch, 1988). It correlates between .66 and .81 with labelling oneself as a shy person, and .68 with aggregated ratings of the subject's shyness made by three to six friends and family members (Cheek, 1983). The versions of the Shyness Scale also predict relevant criteria of tension, worry, and behavioural inhibition in laboratory experiments (Arnold & Cheek, 1986; Cheek & Buss, 1981; Cheek & Stahl, 1986; Melchior & Cheek, 1990).

Jones, Briggs, & Smith (1986) found that the Shyness Scale correlated between .75 and .87 with the other major scales commonly employed in this domain of research (see Crozier, 1986, for a historical review). The crucial point here is that in spite of continuing debates among the test constructors about potentially important conceptual distinctions, these measures generally intercorrelate to an extent that permits us to consider them in our literature review as alternative operational definitions of the same global psychological construct. Factor analyses of shyness items from personality inventories usually yield only one major factor (Cheek & Buss, 1981; Jones, Briggs, & Smith, 1986), although some interesting efforts to score sub-scales have been made (e.g., Leary, Atherton, Hill, & Hur, 1986). At present, it appears that the best approach to investigating components of the shyness syndrome is to use symptom checklists or paragraphs describing each of the three components (Briggs, 1984; Cheek & Melchior, 1985, 1990).

Shyness and other constructs

Shyness is related to, but not identical with, a number of variables that together form a higher-order construct of adjustment that Maslow (1942) called "psychological insecurity": low self-esteem, depression, loneliness, test anxiety, fearfulness, embarrassability, and audience anxiety (for a review, see Cheek & Melchoir, 1990). The distinctiveness of shyness as a psychological construct is that it pertains specifically to insecurities about social interactions. For example, Jones, Briggs, & Smith, (1986) reported that the Shyness Scale correlated .50 with a measure of social fears (e.g., meeting someone in authority, and blind dates), but only .12 with a measure of non-social fears (e.g., high places, sharp objects, and germs). Moreover, Teglasi and Hoffman (1982) found that shy people made self-defeating causal attributions for social outcomes but not for work-related outcomes (see also Crozier, 1981; Efran & Korn, 1969). Overall, shyness has acceptable degrees of both convergent validity and discriminant validity in relation to other aspects of adjustment. It also tends to correlate around .40 with the Eysenck global neuroticism dimension (Jones, Briggs, & Smith, 1986).

Shyness is not the same thing as introversion or low sociability, although the degree of relationship between these constructs will vary depending on how they are operationalised by researchers. Shyness scales typically correlate about −.40 with the Eysenck extraversion dimension (see Briggs, 1988, for an item analysis). Other research indicates that the average correlation between shyness and various measures of sociability and affiliation motivation is around −.30 (Cheek & Zonderman, 1983; Cutler & Cheek, 1986; Hill, 1987). Moreover, shyness is only weakly related to private self-consciousness, which is a measure of thinking introversion rather than social introversion (e.g., $r = .10$ for Cheek & Buss, 1981).

Lewinsky (1941) observed that shy people often experience an approach–avoidance conflict in social situations, and she argued that "this ambivalent attitude seems of great importance in the understanding of shyness" (p. 106). We agree with Lewinsky that shy people experience their own social inhibition not as a voluntary choice but as a barrier that prevents them from participating in social life when they want or need to (Cheek & Melchior, 1990). In support of such a conflict model, it has been found that people rated high in *both* shyness and sociability sometimes experience the greatest difficulties during social interactions and report the most severe adjustment problems (Briggs, 1988; Cheek & Buss, 1981; Cutler & Cheek, 1986).

It is also worth noting that the presence of an approach–avoidance conflict towards social contacts appears to be a useful criterion for distinguishing clinical social phobia from schizoid or avoidant personality disorders (Bruch, 1989; Liebowitz, Gorman, Fyer, & Klein, 1985). We hope that the revisions currently being developed for DSM-IV will clarify the relationship between shyness and the relevant clinical diagnostic categories. Within the normal range of individual differences it is clear that shyness should not be equated with introversion or lack of affiliation motivation. The opposite of shyness is social self-confidence, not extraversion.

The development of shyness

Contemporary research and theory suggest both important continuities and significant discontinuities in the development of shyness. Buss (1980, 1986) has proposed a distinction between early-developing, fearful shyness and later-developing, self-conscious shyness. The fearful type of shyness typically emerges during the first year of life and is influenced by temperamental qualities of wariness and emotionality that include a substantial genetic component (Buss & Plomin, 1975; Plomin & Rowe, 1979). Shy, inhibited children have higher and less variable heart rates than do uninhibited children in laboratory testing situations, which suggests the hypothesis that inhibited children have lower thresholds of excitability in limbic system structures (Kagan & Reznick, 1986).

Buss's self-conscious type of shyness first appears around age 5, when the cognitive self has already begun to develop, and it peaks between 14 and 17 years as adolescents cope with cognitive egocentrism (the "imaginary audience" phenomenon) and identity issues (Adams, Abraham, & Markstrom, 1987; Cheek, Carpentieri, Smith, Rierdan, & Koff, 1986a). In contrast to the fearfulness and somatic anxiety that characterize early-developing shyness, the later-developing type involves cognitive symptoms of psychic anxiety such as painful self-consciousness and anxious self-preoccupation (Buss, 1986).

Surveys employing retrospective reports of college students revealed four findings relevant to Buss's conceptualisation: (1) About 36% of currently shy respondents indicated that they had been shy since early childhood. (2) Early-developing shyness is more enduring, with about 75% of those who said they were shy in early childhood reporting still being shy currently, but only about 50% of those who were first shy during late childhood or early adolescence saying that they were currently shy. (3) The early-developing shy respondents also had developed cognitive symptoms of shyness upon entering adolescence, so that they differed from those with later-developing shyness by having more somatic anxiety symptoms, but did not have fewer cognitive symptoms. (4) Early-developing shyness appeared to be more of an adjustment problem, with males in that group reporting the most behavioral symptoms of shyness (Bruch, Giordano, & Pearl, 1986; Cheek et al., 1986a; Shedlack, 1987).

The early–late distinction implies that the ordering consistency assessed by the test–retest stability of shyness should be high from infancy to age 5, more variable for assessments during middle childhood, depending on the exact age of each measurement, and then increasingly stable once again within adolescence and adulthood. Although no one has yet analysed longitudinal data specifically to test Buss's theory, Cheek and Melchoir (1990) have interpreted several existing studies as generally supporting this expectation. Damon and Hart's comments (1982) about qualitative changes in the trait of self-esteem across three stages of cognitive maturation also may apply to the development of shyness. According to McDougall's theoretical perspective (1919/1963), we should expect that cognitive affective sentiments, especially the self-regarding sentiment, will replace biological propensities as the prime organisers of behaviour during development (see Murphy, 1947, on the transition from "organic" to "symbolic" traits, for a more fully explicated systems theory of personality development).

Two prospective studies that traced the consequences of shyness from middle or late childhood into adulthood (average age about 35) found meaningful continuities in the trait and a coherent influence on the shy person's style of life, but uncovered little psychopathology (Caspi, Elder, & Bem, 1988; Morris, Soroker, & Burruss, 1954). Gilmartin's retrospective study (1987) of extremely shy adult men, however, demonstrated that early-developing shyness sometimes can have devastating consequences. These maladjusted men reported that their childhood relationships with *both* their peers and their parents, especially their mothers, were simply terrible. In contrast, the typical pattern for shy children is poor relationships with peers, but positive interactions at home, particularly with their mothers (Stevenson-Hinde & Hinde, 1986).

Thus, the home environment appears to be a decisive factor for developmental outcomes of shyness (Cheek & Melchior, 1990). We regard attachment, parental support, and sibling relationships as promising targets for future research on the development of shyness, which needs to be both cross-cultural and longitudinal. Even though the roots of shyness go back to biologically based individual characteristics and childhood experiences (Plomin & Daniels, 1986), the behavioural consequences of shyness are maintained and mediated by maladaptive cognitive processes, which we consider in the closing sections of this chapter.

Cognitive tendencies of shy people

One important reason why social psychologists should be interested in shyness as a personality trait is the distinctive pattern of self-relevant social cognitions typical among dispositionally shy people. In contrast to the approach recommended by McDougall (1919/1863), contemporary social psychologists tend to emphasise general statements about the processes underlying social behaviour, while ignoring or minimising the impact of personality development and systematic individual differences (Cheek & Hogan, 1983). The relevant example here is Greenwald's widely cited formulation of a general social psychological law called "beneffectance", which is based on the assumption that "the pervasiveness of cognitive biases that build and maintain an inflated sense of self-worth was demonstrated in a review by Greenwald (1980)" (Greenwald, 1988, p. 38).

We have summarised the large body of research on the cognitive tendencies of shy people in Table 11.2 (from reviews by Cheek et al., 1986b, and Cheek & Melchior, 1990). As an overview, Table 11.2 makes it clear that shy people suffer from a pervasive lack of "beneffectance" in their processing of self-relevant information. Rather than experiencing an inflated sense of self-worth, shy individuals expect that their social behaviour will be inadequate and that they will be evaluated negatively by others (e.g., Cacioppo, Glass, & Merluzzi, 1979; Leary, Kowalski, & Campbell, 1988; Smith & Sarason, 1975).

Shy people also tend to judge themselves more negatively than others judge them (e.g., Clark & Arkowitz, 1975). Liebman and Cheek (1983) found that shy college women under-estimated their levels of physical attractiveness as compared with observer ratings, whereas those who were not shy tended to over-estimate their attractiveness. This negative bias extends to explanations for social outcomes. Shy people typically reverse the general social psychological process known as "the self-serving bias in causal attribution" by accepting more personal responsibility for social failure than for success (e.g., Arkin, Appelman, &

Table 11.2. *Summary of shy people's cognitive and meta-cognitive tendencies before, during, and after confronting shyness-eliciting situations*

Unlike those who are not shy, dispositionally shy people tend to:
1. perceive that a social interaction will be explicitly evaluative
2. expect that their behaviour will be inadequate and that they will be evaluated negatively
3. hold "irrational beliefs" about how good their social performance *should* be and how much approval they *should* get from others
4. think about "Who does this situation want me to be?" rather than "How can I be me in this situation?"
5. adopt a strategy of trying to get along rather than trying to get ahead
6. become anxiously self-preoccupied and not pay enough attention to others
7. judge themselves more negatively than others judge them
8. blame themselves for social failures and attribute successes to external factors
9. accept negative feedback and resist or reject positive feedback
10. remember negative self-relevant information and experiences

Source: Adapted from Cheek & Melchior (1990).

Burger, 1980; Teglasi & Hoffman, 1982). Moreover, shyness is related to remembering negative information about oneself (Breck & Smith, 1983; O'Banion & Arkowitz, 1977). We should point out that these cognitive tendencies appear to be somewhat stronger among shy women than among shy men (Cheek et al., 1986b), which is one of several parallels between research on shyness and depression (Anderson & Arnoult, 1985; Ingram, Cruet, Johnson, & Wisnicki, 1988).

Perhaps the most damaging findings for the "beneffectance" hypothesis concern reactions to social feedback. Given that shy people expect to be evaluated negatively, we might anticipate that they would welcome some positive feedback. However, unlike those who are not shy, shy individuals more readily accept negative feedback than positive feedback, and they tend to resist, and to doubt the accuracy of, positive evaluations (Alden, 1987; Asendorpf, 1987; Franzoi, 1983; Lake & Arkin, 1983; Wurf & Markus, 1983). This striking pattern of consistent results strongly supports Epstein's proposal (1980) that "experiences that the individual regards as consistent with his or her evaluation of self are readily assimilated, while those that are regarded as inconsistent produce anxiety and are usually rejected" (p. 92). Therefore, we conclude that "beneffectance" is better conceptualised as a dimension of individual differences in intrapsychic personality rather than as a general law of social behaviour.

Meta-cognition and self-presentation

Crozier (1979) has argued that the defining characteristic of shy people is their tendency to spend so much time monitoring their own feelings and behaviour and worrying about how they appear to others that they become anxiously self-preoccupied. Several experiments have provided empirical support for Crozier's position (Arnold & Cheek, 1986; Melchior & Cheek, in press; Smith, Ingram, & Brehm, 1983). Even though shy individuals sometimes differ in their specific symptomatology, they seem to have broad commonalities at the meta-cognitive level of psychological functioning (Table 11.2). Meta-cognition is defined as higher-order cognitive processing that involves awareness of one's current psychological state or overt behaviour (Flavell, 1979). The distinctive self-concept processes of shy people suggest that maladaptive meta-cognition is the unifying theme in the experience of shyness (Cheek & Melchior, 1990; Hartman, 1986).

Anxious self-preoccupation influences social behaviour. Shy people typically choose to adopt a cautiously conservative or "protective" style of self-presentation (Arkin, Lake, & Baumgardner, 1986; Briggs & Cheek, 1988). They tend to conform to majority opinion, to change their personal attitudes towards the position advocated by an authority figure, and to avoid disclosing much information about themselves (e.g., Santee & Maslach, 1982; Turner, 1977; for a review, see Schlenker & Leary, 1985). When faced with a situation in which others hold high expectations of them, shy individuals may even fail strategically as a means of creating lower and safer standards of evaluation (Baumgardner & Brownlee, 1987). In general, shy people pursue a social strategy of getting along rather than getting ahead.

The impact of dispositional shyness extends far beyond reactions to psychology experiments. Passivity and caution also characterise the vocational development of shy people. Not only are shy college students uncertain about their vocational choices, but also they do not engage in appropriate information-seeking activities to explore the careers they might decide to pursue (Bruch et al., 1986; Phillips & Bruch, 1988). Shy adults tend to be unambitious, under-employed, and relatively unsuccessful once they have made a choice from the restricted range of careers that they are willing to consider (Caspi et al., 1988; Gilmartin, 1987; Morris et al., 1954). Next to loneliness and other relationship difficulties (e.g., Jones & Carpenter, 1986), dysfunctional career development appears to be the most severe long-term consequence of chronic shyness. In fact, shyness and its limitation of social support both affect one's ability to cope with involuntary unemployment in later life and to adjust to retirement (Hansson, 1986). In contrast to what goes on during the drama of psychology experiments, the influence of a trait such as shyness on one's overall style of life is presumably more habitual, less situationally contingent, and at least partly unconscious (Cheek & Hogan, 1983).

Conclusion

Although we are pleased that interest in social cognition and socially strategic goals (e.g., Pervin, 1989) appears to be bringing social psychology closer towards McDougall's theoretical perspective (1919/1963), we hope that this interest in cognition and conation (i.e. striving) soon will expand to incorporate the evolutionary, developmental, and affective aspects of McDougall's theory (Cheek, 1985). For example, it seems important to us that the cognitive behavioural strategy of social constraint identified by Langston and Cantor (1989) as central to predicting the relatively short term social outcomes of shy college students also has a long developmental history extending back into childhood (Funder, Block, & Block, 1983; Ludwig & Lazarus, 1983; Richard & Dodge, 1982). We disagree with Langston and Cantor's argument that the cognitive behavioural strategy unit should be granted the central (causal) status in the analysis of personality functioning, because we agree with McDougall's position (1919/1963) that "we cannot understand the intellectual processes without some comprehension of the organisation and working of the affective processes whose servants they are" (p. 487).

Shyness is the personality trait with the strongest genetic component (Plomin & Daniels, 1986), and it is also a trait involving consequential disturbances in conscious self-concept processes (Table 11.2). Future research appears likely to validate Allport's conceptualisation (1937) of personality traits as "neuropsychic entities" (Briggs, 1985; Haier, Sokolski, Katz, & Buchsbaum, 1987). Nevertheless, we think Rowe (1987) put it too strongly when he concluded that "genotypes must be the organizing force behind behavioral development" (p. 224). In our view, innate tendencies are the fundamental postulates for understanding social behaviour, not because they can explain behaviour directly but because they enter into the complex transactional processes of personality development and current self-interpretation (Cheek & Hogan, 1983).

Personality traits exist at different levels of biological, emotional, cognitive, interpersonal, and cultural functioning (e.g., Barkow, 1980; Hyland, 1985). This perspective helps to explain why combinations of various treatment strategies for overcoming shyness often are more effective than any one approach that focuses only on a single level (e.g., Cappe & Alden, 1986). Similarly, no single-level approach to the psychology of shyness, whether based on genetics, physiology, learning, emotion, self-esteem, psychodynamics, self-attention, or self-presentation, will succeed by itself. Instead, we need to continue along the path identified by McDougall, Allport, and Murphy towards a biocultural systems theory of personality and social behaviour.

REFERENCES

Adams, G. R., Abraham, K. G., & Markstrom. C. A. (1987). The relations among identity development, self-consciousness, and self-focusing during middle and late adolescence. *Developmental Psychology, 23,* 292–297.

Alden, L. (1987). Attributional responses of anxious individuals to different patterns of social feedback: Nothing succeeds like improvement. *Journal of Personality and Social Psychology, 52,* 100–106.

Allport, G. W. (1937). *Personality: A psychological interpretation.* New York: Holt.

Allport, G. W. (1960). The open system in personality. *Journal of Abnormal and Social Psychology, 61,* 301–310.

Anderson, C. A., & Arnoult, L. H. (1985). Attributional styles and everyday problems in living: Depression, loneliness, and shyness. *Social Cognition, 3,* 16–35.

Arkin, R. M., Appelman, A. J., & Burger, J. M. (1980). Social anxiety, self-presentation, and the self-serving bias in causal attribution. *Journal of Personality and Social Psychology, 38,* 23–35.

Arkin, R. M., Lake, E. A., & Baumgardner, A. B. (1986). Shyness and self-presentation. In W. H. Jones, J. M. Cheek, & S. R. Briggs (Eds.), *Shyness: Perspectives on research and treatment* (pp. 189–203). New York: Plenum Press.

Arnold, A. P., & Cheek, J. M. (1986). Shyness, self-preoccupation, and the Stroop color and word test. *Personality and Individual Differences, 7,* 571–573.

Asendorpf, J. B. (1987). Videotape reconstruction of emotions and cognitions related to shyness. *Journal of Personality and Social Psychology, 53,* 542–549.

Barkow, J. H. (1980). Sociobiology: Is this the new theory of human nature? In A. Montagu (Ed.), *Sociobiology examined* (pp. 171–197). Oxford University Press.

Baumgardner, A. H., & Brownlee, E. A. (1987). Strategic failure in social interaction: Evidence for expectancy disconfirmation processes. *Journal of Personality and Social Psychology, 52,* 525–535.

Bem, S. L. (1981). *Bem sex-role inventory professional manual.* Palo Alto, CA: Consulting Psychologists Press.

Breck, B. E., & Smith, S. H. (1983). Selective recall of self-descriptive traits by socially anxious and nonanxious females. *Social Behavior and Personality, 11,* 71–76.

Briggs, S. R. (1984, August). Components of shyness. In J. M. Cheek (Chair), *Shyness: Personality development, social behavior, and treatment approaches.* Symposium conducted at a meeting of the American Psychological Association, Toronto.

Briggs, S. R. (1985). A trait account of social shyness. In P. Shaver (Ed.), *Review of personality and social psychology* (Vol. 6, pp. 35–64). Beverly Hills, CA: Sage.

Briggs, S. R. (1988). Shyness: Introversion or neuroticism? *Journal of Research in Personality, 22,* 290–307.

Briggs, S. R., & Cheek, J. M. (1988). On the nature of self-monitoring: Problems with assessment, problems with validity. *Journal of Personality and Social Psychology, 54,* 663–678.

Briggs, S. R., Cheek, J. M., & Jones, W. H. (1986). Introduction. In W. H. Jones, J. M. Cheek, & S. R. Briggs (Eds.), *Shyness: Perspectives on research and treatment* (pp. 1–14). New York: Plenum Press.

Bruch, M. A. (1989). Familial and developmental antecedents of social phobia: Issues and findings. *Clinical Psychology Review, 9,* 37–47.

Bruch, M. A., Giordano, S., & Pearl, L. (1986). Differences between fearful and self-conscious shy subtypes in background and adjustment. *Journal of Research in Personality, 20,* 172–186.

Buss, A. H. (1962). Two anxiety factors in psychiatric patients. *Journal of Abnormal and Social Psychology, 65,* 426–427.

Buss, A. H. (1980). *Self-consciousness and social anxiety.* San Francisco: Freeman.

Buss, A. H. (1984). A conception of shyness. In J. A. Daly & J. C. McCroskey (Eds.), *Avoiding communication* (pp. 39–49). Beverly Hills, CA: Sage.

Buss, A. H. (1986). A theory of shyness. In W. H. Jones, J. M. Cheek, & S. R. Briggs (Eds.), *Shyness: Perspectives on research and treatment* (pp. 39–46). New York: Plenum Press.

Buss, A. H. (1988). *Personality: Evolutionary heritage and human distinctiveness.* Hillsdale, NJ: Lawrence Erlbaum.

Buss, A. H., & Plomin, R. (1975). *A temperament theory of personality development.* New York: Wiley.

Cacioppo, J. T., Glass, C. R., & Merluzzi, T. V. (1979). Self-statements and self-evaluation: A cognitive response analysis of heterosocial anxiety. *Cognitive Therapy and Research, 3,* 249–262.

Cappe, R. F., & Alden, L. E. (1986). A comparison of treatment strategies for clients functionally impaired by extreme shyness and social avoidance. *Journal of Consulting and Clinical Psychology, 54,* 796–801.

Caspi, A., Elder, G. H., & Bem, D. J. (1988). Moving away from the world: Life-course patterns of shy children. *Developmental Psychology, 24,* 824–831.

Cattell, R. B. (1985). *The scientific analysis of personality.* Baltimore: Penguin.

Cheek, J. M. (1982, August). Shyness and self-esteem: A personological perspective. In M. R. Leary (Chair), *Recent research in social anxiety.* Symposium conducted at a meeting of the American Psychological Association, Washington.

Cheek, J. M. (1983). *The revised Cheek and Buss Shyness Scale.* Unpublished manuscript, Wellesley College.

Cheek, J. M. (1985). Toward a more inclusive integration of evolutionary biology and personality psychology [Comment]. *American Psychologist, 40,* 1269–1270.

Cheek, J. M., & Busch, C. M. (1981). The influence of shyness on loneliness in a new situation. *Personality and Social Psychology Bulletin, 7,* 572–577.

Cheek, J. M., & Buss, A. H. (1981). Shyness and sociability. *Journal of Personality and Social Psychology, 41,* 330–339.

332   JONATHAN M. CHEEK AND STEPHEN R. BRIGGS

Cheek, J. M., Carpentieri, A. M., Smith, T. G., Rierdan, J., & Koff, E. (1986a). Adolescent shyness. In W. H. Jones, J. M. Cheek, & S. R. Briggs (Eds.), *Shyness: Perspectives on research and treatment* (pp. 105–115). New York: Plenum Press.

Cheek, J. M., & Hogan, R. (1983). Self-concepts, self-presentations, and moral judgements. In J. Suls & A. G. Greenwald (Eds.), *Psychological perspectives on the self* (Vol. 2, pp. 249–273). Hillsdale, NJ: Lawrence Erlbaum.

Cheek, J. M., & Melchior, L. A. (1985, August). *Measuring the three components of shyness*. Paper presented at a meeting of the American Psychological Association, Los Angeles.

Cheek, J. M., & Melchior, L. A. (1990). Shyness, self-esteem, and self-consciousness. In H. Leitenberg (Ed.), *Handbook of social and evaluation anxiety*. New York: Plenum Press.

Cheek, J. M., Melchior, L. A., & Carpentieri, A. M. (1986b). Shyness and self-concept. In L. M. Hartman & K. R. Blankstein (Eds.), *Perception of self in emotional disorder and psychotherapy* (pp. 113–131). New York: Plenum Press.

Cheek, J. M., & Stahl, S. S. (1986). Shyness and verbal creativity. *Journal of Research in Personality, 20*, 51–61.

Cheek, J. M., & Watson, A. K. (1989). The definition of shyness: Psychological imperialism or construct validity? *Journal of Social Behavior and Personality, 4*, 85–95.

Cheek, J. M., & Zonderman, A. B. (1983, August). Shyness as a personality temperament. In J. M. Cheek (Chair), *Progress in research on shyness*. Symposium conducted at a meeting of the American Psychological Association, Anaheim.

Clark, J. V., & Arkowitz, H. (1975). Social anxiety and self-evaluation of interpersonal performance. *Psychological Reports, 36*, 211–221.

Crozier, W. R. (1979). Shyness as anxious self-preoccupation. *Psychological Reports, 44*, 959–962.

Crozier, W. R. (1981). Shyness and self-esteem. *British Journal of Social Psychology, 20*, 220–222.

Crozier, W. R. (1982). Explanations of social shyness. *Current Psychological Reviews, 2*, 47–60.

Crozier, W. R. (1986). Individual differences in shyness. In W. H. Jones, J. M. Cheek, & S. R. Briggs (Eds.), *Shyness: Perspectives on research and treatment* (pp. 133–145). New York: Plenum Press.

Curran, J. P., Wallander, J. L., & Fischetti, M. (1980). The importance of behavioral and cognitive factors in heterosexual-social anxiety. *Journal of Personality, 48*, 285–292.

Cutler, B. L., & Cheek, J. M. (1986, March). *The independence of shyness and need for affiliation*. Paper presented at a meeting of the Midwestern Psychological Association.

Damon, W., & Hart, D. (1982). The development of self-understanding from infancy through adolescence. *Child Development, 53*, 841–861.

Deffenbacher, J. L., & Hazaleus, S. L. (1985). Cognitive, emotional, and physiological components of test anxiety. *Cognitive Therapy and Research, 9*, 169–180.

Efran, J. S., & Korn, P. R. (1969). Measurement of social caution: Self-appraisal, role playing, and discussion behavior. *Journal of Consulting and Clinical Psychology, 33*, 78–83.

Epstein, S. (1980). The self-concept: A review and the proposal of an integrated theory of personality. In E. Staub (Ed.), *Personality: Basic issues and current research* (pp. 81–132). Englewood Cliffs, NJ: Prentice-Hall.

Fatis, M. (1983). Degree of shyness and self-reported physiological, behavioral, and cognitive reactions. *Psychological Reports, 52*, 351–354.

Flavell, J. H. (1979). Metacognition and cognitive monitoring: A new area of cognitive-developmental inquiry. *American Psychologist, 34*, 906–911.

Ford, D. H. (1987). *Humans as self-constructing living systems*. Hillsdale, NJ: Lawrence Erlbaum.

Fox, J. E., & Houston, B. K. (1983). Distinguishing between cognitive and somatic trait and state anxiety in children. *Journal of Personality and Social Psychology, 45*, 862–870.

Franzoi, S. L. (1983). Self-concept differences as a function of private self-consciousness and social anxiety. *Journal of Research in Personality, 17*, 275–287.

Funder, D. C., Block, J. H., & Block, J. (1983). Delay of gratification: Some longitudinal personality correlates. *Journal of Personality and Social Psychology, 44*, 1198–1213.

Gilmartin, B. G. (1987). *Shyness and love: Causes, consequences, and treatment.* Lanham, MD: University Press of America.

Goldfried, M. R., Padawar, W., & Robbins, C. (1984). Social anxiety and the semantic structure of heterosocial interactions. *Journal of Abnormal Psychology, 93*, 87–97.

Gough, H. G., & Thorne, A. (1986). Positive, negative, and balanced shyness: Self-definitions and the reactions of others. In W. H. Jones, J. M. Cheek, & S. R. Briggs (Eds.), *Shyness: Perspectives on research and treatment* (pp. 205–225). New York: Plenum Press.

Greenberg, M. T., & Marvin, R. S. (1982). Reactions of preschool children to an adult stranger: A behavioral systems approach. *Child Development, 53*, 481–490.

Greenwald, A. G. (1980). The totalitarian ego: Fabrication and revision of personal history. *American Psychologist, 35*, 603–618.

Greenwald, A. G. (1988). A social-cognitive account of the self's development. In D. K. Lapsley & F. C. Power (Eds.), *Self, ego, and identity* (pp. 30–42). New York: Springer-Verlag.

Haier, R. J., Sokolski, K., Katz, M., & Buchsbaum, M. S. (1987). The study of personality with positron emission tomography. In J. Strelau & H. J. Eysenck (Eds.), *Personality dimensions and arousal* (pp. 251–267). New York: Plenum Press.

Halford, K., & Foddy, M. (1982). Cognitive and social skills correlates of social anxiety. *British Journal of Clinical Psychology, 21*, 17–28.

Hampson, S. E., Goldberg, L. R., & John, O. P. (1987). Category-breadth and social-desirability values for 573 personality terms. *European Journal of Personality, 1*, 241–258.

Hansson, R. O. (1986). Shyness and the elderly. In W. H. Jones, J. M. Cheek, &

S. R. Briggs (Eds.), *Shyness: Perspectives on research and treatment* (pp. 117–129). New York: Plenum Press.

Harris, P. R. (1984). Shyness and psychological imperialism: On the dangers of ignoring the ordinary language roots of the terms we deal with. *European Journal of Social Psychology*, *14*, 169–181.

Hartman, L. M. (1986). Social anxiety, problem drinking, and self-awareness. In L. M. Hartman & K. R. Blankstein (Eds.), *Perception of self in emotional disorder and psychotherapy* (pp. 265–282). New York: Plenum Press.

Hill, C. A. (1987). Affiliation motivation: People who need people … but in different ways. *Journal of Personality and Social Psychology*, *52*, 1008–1018.

Hogan, R. (1976). *Personality theory: The personological tradition.* Englewood Cliffs, NJ: Prentice-Hall.

Hyland, M. E. (1985). Do person variables exist in different ways? *American Psychologist*, *40*, 1003–1010.

Ingram, R. E., Cruet, D., Johnson, B. R., & Wisnicki, K. S. (1988). Self-focused attention, gender, gender role, and vulnerability to negative affect. *Journal of Personality and Social Psychology*, *55*, 967–978.

Ishiyama, F. I. (1984). Shyness: Anxious social sensitivity and self-isolating tendency. *Adolescence*, *19*, 903–911.

Izard, C. E., & Hyson, M. C. (1986). Shyness as a discrete emotion. In W. H. Jones, J. M. Cheek, & S. R. Briggs (Eds.), *Shyness: Perspectives on research and treatment* (pp. 147–160). New York: Plenum Press.

James, W. (1890). *The principles of psychology* (Vol. 2). New York: Holt.

Jones, W. H., Briggs, S. R., & Smith, T. G. (1986). Shyness: Conceptualization and measurement. *Journal of Personality and Social Psychology*, *51*, 629–639.

Jones, W. H., & Carpenter, B. N. (1986). Shyness, social behavior, and relationships. In W. H. Jones, J. M. Cheek, & S. R. Briggs (Eds.), *Shyness: Perspectives on research and treatment* (pp. 227–238). New York: Plenum Press.

Jones, W. H., Cheek, J. M., & Briggs, S. R. (Eds.). (1986). *Shyness: Perspectives on research and treatment.* New York: Plenum Press.

Jung, C. G. (1933). *Modern man in search of a soul.* New York: Harcourt Brace.

Kagan, J., & Reznick, S. J. (1986). Shyness and temperament. In W. H. Jones, J. M. Cheek, & S. R. Briggs (Eds.), *Shyness: Perspectives on research and treatment* (pp. 81–90). New York: Plenum Press.

Kaplan, D. M. (1972). On shyness. *International Journal of Psychoanalysis*, *53*, 439–453.

Kenrick, D. T., & Funder, D. C. (1988). Profiting from controversy: Lessons from the person–situation debate. *American Psychologist*, *43*, 23–34.

Lake, E. A., & Arkin, R. M. (1983, August). *Social anxiety and reactions to interpersonal evaluative information.* Paper presented at a meeting of the American Psychological Association, Anaheim.

Langston, C. A., & Cantor, N. (1989). Social anxiety and social constraint: When making friends is hard. *Journal of Personality and Social Psychology*, *56*, 649–661.

Lazarus, P. J. (1982). Incidence of shyness in elementary-school-age children. *Psychological Reports*, *51*, 904–906.

Leary, M. R. (1983). Social anxiousness: The construct and its measurement. *Journal of Personality Assessment, 47,* 66–75.

Leary, M. R. (1986). Affective and behavioral components of shyness. In W. H. Jones, J. M. Cheek, & S. R. Briggs (Eds.), *Shyness: Perspectives on research and treatment* (pp. 27–38). New York: Plenum Press.

Leary, M. R., Atherton, S. C., Hill, S., & Hur, C. (1986). Attributional mediators of social inhibition and avoidance. *Journal of Personality, 54,* 704–716.

Leary, M. R., Kowalski, R. M., & Campbell, C. D. (1988). Self-presentational concerns and social anxiety: The role of generalized impression expectancies. *Journal of Research in Personality, 22,* 308–321.

Lewinsky, H. (1941). The nature of shyness. *British Journal of Psychology, 32,* 105–113.

Liebman, W. E., & Cheek, J. M. (1983, August). Shyness and body image. In J. M. Cheek (Chair), *Progress in research on shyness.* Symposium conducted at a meeting of the American Psychological Association, Anaheim.

Liebowitz, M. R., Gorman, J. M., Fyer, A. J., & Klein, D. F. (1985). Social phobia: Review of a neglected disorder. *Archives of General Psychiatry, 42,* 729–736.

Ludwig, R. P., & Lazarus, P. J. (1983). Relationship between shyness in children and constricted cognitive control as measured by the Stroop color-word test. *Journal of Consulting and Clinical Psychology, 51,* 386–389.

McCroskey, J. C., & Beatty, M. J. (1986). Oral communication apprehension. In W. H. Jones, J. M. Cheek, & S. R. Briggs (Eds.), *Shyness: Perspectives on research and treatment* (pp. 279–293). New York: Plenum Press.

McDougall, W. (1963). *An introduction to social psychology* (31st ed.). London: Methuen. (Original work published 1908; 14th ed. published 1919)

McDougall, W. (1938). Tendencies as indispensable postulates of all psychology. In *Proceedings of the XI International Congress on Psychology: 1937* (pp. 157–170). Paris: Alcan.

McEwan, K. L., & Devins, G. M. (1983). Is increased arousal in social anxiety noticed by others? *Journal of Abnormal Psychology, 92,* 417–421.

Magnusson, D., & Endler, N. S. (Eds.). (1977). *Personality at the crossroads: Current issues in interactional psychology.* Hillsdale, NJ: Lawrence Erlbaum.

Maslow, A. H. (1942). The dynamics of psychological security–insecurity. *Character and Personality, 10,* 331–344.

Melchior, L. A., & Cheek, J. M. (in press). Shyness and anxious self-preoccupation during a social interaction. *Journal of Social Behavior and Personality.*

Mischel, W. (1968). *Personality and assessment.* New York: Wiley.

Morris, D. P., Soroker, M. A., & Burruss, G. (1954). Follow-up studies of shy, withdrawn children. I. Evaluation of later adjustment. *American Journal of Orthopsychiatry, 24,* 743–754.

Murphy, G. (1947). *Personality: A biosocial approach to origins and structure.* New York: Harper.

O'Banion, K., & Arkowitz, H. (1977). Social anxiety and selective memory for affective information about the self. *Social Behavior and Personality, 5,* 321–328.

Pervin, L. A. (Ed.). (1989). *Goal concepts in personality and social psychology*. Hillsdale, NJ: Lawrence Erlbaum.

Phillips, S. D., & Bruch, M. A. (1988). Shyness and dysfunction in career development. *Journal of Counseling Psychology, 35*, 159–165.

Pilkonis, P. A. (1977). The behavioral consequences of shyness. *Journal of Personality, 45*, 596–611.

Pilkonis, P. A., Heape, C., & Klein, R. H. (1980). Treating shyness and other psychiatric difficulties in psychiatric outpatients. *Communication Education, 29*, 250–255.

Pilkonis, P. A., & Zimbardo, P. G. (1979). The personal and social dynamics of shyness. In C. E. Izard (Ed.), *Emotions in personality and psychopathology* (pp. 133–160). New York: Plenum Press.

Plomin, R., & Daniels, D. (1986). Genetics and shyness. In W. H. Jones, J. M. Cheek, & S. R. Briggs (Eds.), *Shyness: Perspectives on research and treatment* (pp. 63–80). New York: Plenum Press.

Plomin, R., & Rowe, D. C. (1979). Genetic and environmental etiology of social behavior in infancy. *Developmental Psychology, 15*, 62–72.

Plutarch (1906). Of bashfulness. In *Plutarch's essays and miscellanies*. Boston: Little, Brown.

Richard, B. A., & Dodge, K. A. (1982). Social maladjustment and problem-solving in school-aged children. *Journal of Consulting and Clinical Psychology, 50*, 226–233.

Rowe, D. C. (1987). Resolving the person–situation debate: Invitation to an interdisciplinary dialogue. *American Psychologist, 42*, 218–227.

Royce, J. R. (1955). A factorial study of emotionality in the dog. *Psychological Monographs: General and Applied, 69* (22, Whole No. 407), 1–27.

Russell, D., Cutrona, C., & Jones, W. H. (1986). A trait-situational analysis of shyness. In W. H. Jones, J. M. Cheek & S. R. Briggs (Eds.), *Shyness: Perspectives on research and treatment* (pp. 239–249). New York: Plenum Press.

Sanford, N. (1956). Surface and depth in the individual personality. *Psychological Review, 63*, 349–359.

Santee, R. T., & Maslach, C. (1982). To agree or not to agree: Personal dissent and social pressure to conform. *Journal of Personality and Social Psychology, 42*, 690–700.

Schalling, D. S. (1975). Types of anxiety and types of stressors as related to personality. In C. D. Spielberger & I. G. Sarason (Eds.), *Stress and anxiety* (Vol. 1, pp. 279–283). Washington, DC: Hemisphere.

Schlenker, B. R., & Leary, M. R. (1985). Social anxiety and communication about the self. *Journal of Language and Social Psychology, 4*, 171–192.

Shedlack, S. M. (1987). *The definition and development of shyness*. Unpublished B.A. honors thesis, Wellesley College.

Smith, R. E., & Sarason, I. G. (1975). Social anxiety and the evaluation of negative interpersonal feedback. *Journal of Consulting and Clinical Psychology, 43*, 429.

Smith, T. W., Ingram, R. E., & Brehm, S. S. (1983). Social anxiety, anxious self-preoccupation, and recall of self-relevant information. *Journal of Personality and Social Psychology, 44*, 1276–1283.

Stevenson-Hinde, J., & Hinde, R. A. (1986). Changes in associations between characteristics and interactions. In R. Plomin & J. Dunn (Eds.), *The study of temperament: Changes, continuities, and challenges.* Hillsdale, NJ: Lawrence Erlbaum.

Teglasi, H., & Hoffman, M. A. (1982). Causal attributions of shy subjects. *Journal of Research in Personality, 16,* 376–385.

Turner, R. G. (1977). Self-consciousness and anticipatory belief change. *Personality and Social Psychology Bulletin, 3,* 438–441.

Turner, S. M., & Beidel, D. C. (1985). Empirically derived subtypes of social anxiety. *Behavior Therapy, 16,* 384–392.

Watson, J. B., & McDougall, W. (1929). *The battle of behaviorism.* New York: Norton.

Wurf, E., & Markus, H. (1983, August). *Cognitive consequences of the negative self.* Paper presented at a meeting of a American Psychological Association, Anaheim.

Zimbardo, P. G. (1977). *Shyness.* Reading, MA: Addison-Wesley.

Zimbardo, P. G., Pilkonis, P., & Norwood, R. (1975). The social disease called shyness. *Psychology Today, 8,* 69–72.

12

Social anxiety, personality, and the self: Clinical research and practice

LORNE M. HARTMAN and PATRICIA A. CLELAND

Introduction

"My fear of people is worsening to the point of getting the shakes when I go shopping, to the gas station or library; not to mention meeting friends and family. Nervous blotches even appear during phone conversations". This self-description is a good portrayal of social anxiety, a problem frequently experienced by persons seeking psychological help (Hartman, 1983). Socially anxious people experience intense discomfort in situations that involve interacting with others. Casual conversations, parties, public speaking, and many other interpersonal occasions of all sorts can be experienced as threatening and stressful (Turner, Beidel, Dancu, & Keys, 1986). They feel highly anxious and tense; they may be awkward and clearly inadequate in their performances; they may panic and escape from the situation, setting up an avoidance pattern for the future.

People who suffer from social anxiety often will blush, perspire excessively, or tremble, the "blood, sweat, and tears" symptom complex, when they feel exposed to scrutiny by others. And socially anxious persons are especially vulnerable to feeling exposed. They may be fully dressed, but psychologically experience the situation as if naked. They dwell persistently on their own internal dialogue. Negative self-statements and self-preoccupation are rampant. Even the most confident, self-assured individual can be made to feel a little shaky by increasing his or her self-awareness, a focusing on the self in social situations. But when someone has no confidence, feels unworthy and unacceptable, then the effects of self-observation can be paralysing. Even when their attention is turned outward, they search for a clue or sign that others have noticed their discomfort or awkwardness; their panic is only further fuelled.

The adverse effects of social anxiety can have an impact upon all facets of a person's life. Vocational, social, and family functions are all subject to disruption by this inappropriate sensitivity to self-presentation.

Clinicians who work extensively with socially anxious patients have

338

frequently identified a pattern of personality traits or features that are characteristic of the individual's overall manner of functioning and psychological make-up. These dispositional trends are fundamental in the sense that they are a part of the person's way of approaching and making sense of the world. Personality sets the stage for development and for one's degree of success in mastering the psychological challenges to form relationships, to function effectively, and to develop one's potential. Accordingly, the clinical features of the disorder, the presentation of social anxiety, are much better understood when we attempt to make sense of the greater personality context of the individual and his or her manner of psychological coping.

Differences in life-long coping styles predispose certain personality types to exhibit one set of symptoms rather than another. Of course, the correspondence between personality type and specific symptom groups or disorders is far from overwhelming. Individual life experiences and genetically mediated predispositions also account for a good deal of the variance. These are very complex, multivariate questions that defy simple solutions. It is clear, however, that fundamental and enduring patterns of perceiving, understanding, and approaching life can be identified that are powerful mediators of the extent to which we cope and thrive or succumb and retreat. Let us now examine the distinctive patterns of perceiving, encoding, attributing, and representing that in-fluence psychological state, physiology, and behaviour in social anxiety.

Characteristics of the socially anxious client

The principal descriptive features of the *avoidant personality pattern*, as presented in the *Diagnostic and Statistical Manual of Mental Disorders*, third edition (DSM-III) (American Psychiatric Association, 1980), are "hypersensitivity to potential rejection, humiliation, or shame; an unwill-ingness to enter into relationships unless given unusually strong guaran-tees of uncritical acceptance; social withdrawal in spite of a desire for affection and acceptance; and low self-esteem" (p. 323). The experienced clinician will readily acknowledge the apt characterisation portrayed here of clients presenting with symptoms of social anxiety and withdraw-al from interpersonal relationships.

Analytically oriented theorists working within an object-relations framework have referred to syndromes possessing features that are clear-ly dominant in the DSM-III avoidant personality. Klein (1970), for example, describes "the shy, socially backward, inept, obedient person who is fearful and therefore isolated but appreciates sociability and would like to be a part of the crowd ... with an emotional state com-pounded of anticipatory anxiety and low self-esteem" (p. 189).

As described by Millon and Millon (1974), the clinical picture of the avoidant pattern includes many of the behavioural features of social anxiety. Avoidant personalities are shy and apprehensive. They not only are awkward and uncomfortable in social situations but also actively withdraw from the reciprocal give-and-take of interpersonal relations. Avoidant personalities tend to be excessively introspective and self-conscious, unsure of self-identity and self-worth. Like social phobics, avoidant personalities are characterised as hyperalert, constantly scanning those with whom they come into contact in order to detect the most subtle hint of critical appraisal, denigration, or rejection.

According to the current analysis, one result of such perceptual vigilance is that the individual becomes flooded with irrelevant details and is distracted from attending to many of the ordinary but relevant features of social transactions. Thought processes are complicated further by cognitive fixations with the self that are intrusive and preoccupying and serve to divert attention away from important external stimuli. The result is a diminished capacity to cope with many of the ordinary, fundamental tasks of life. This cognitive interference is especially pronounced in social settings, where perceptual vigilance, emotional turmoil, and performance impairments are most acute.

Clearly, there are significant clinical ramifications for those individuals with social phobia. The disorder is not as circumscribed as DSM-III indicates. According to DSM-III, the social phobic avoids specific situations (such as public speaking). Broader disturbances where personal relationships in general, rather than specific situations, are the focal concern might meet the criteria for avoidant personality disorder. Not surprisingly, then, the issue of differential diagnosis between social phobia and personality disorder can be problematic.

In clinical practice, however, differential diagnosis is based on whether or not there are significant impairments in social, psychological, or occupational functions that are primarily attributable to persistent and maladaptive personality patterns or variations. That is, when the individual's characterological make-up or enduring style of "perceiving, relating to, and thinking about the environment or oneself" (DSM-III, p. 305) is maladaptive, then personality disorder is the primary diagnosis.

Turner et al. (1986) reported an empirical study on the relationship between these two diagnostic groups. On a number of situational tasks, those individuals with a diagnosis of avoidant personality disorder were found to be more sensitive interpersonally and exhibited poorer social skills than did the social phobic subjects. In addition, and contrary to DSM-III, social phobia was found to affect a variety of life areas and to produce emotional distress.

*Rationale for a performance-based emphasis in fostering behavioural,
affective, and cognitive change*

Elsewhere (Hartman, 1983), I have described social anxiety in terms of too much self-centred "meta-cognition"; that is, thinking *about* thinking, feeling, and doing. A grossly simplified mental image may be useful to illustrate this concept of meta-cognition. Think of meta-cognition as a "director" residing in the back of one's mind, above all other mental activity, observing what is occurring with the self, with the other, and in the interaction. The meta-cognitive director employs its data to direct behaviour. This includes issuing orders for response strategies, either verbal or non-verbal, and considering alternatives for the next behaviour while the current one is being executed. The director or meta-cognitive process constantly evaluates the results of actual behaviour, so that the effectiveness of such intervention is considered before issuing new orders. This process involves constant feedback at a high level and is available to the person's awareness. The individual is able to think about his or her thinking.

The problem in social anxiety is that the person is stuck in a closed loop of self-centred meta-cognition. The normally automatic functions of social discourse are disrupted because of the individual's excessive attention to other themes: "What will I say next?" "Now she knows I'm inadequate". "I feel defenceless". When self-awareness or "editing" becomes recursive in a social context, the individual is removed from the interactive process, and the result is anxiety and impaired social performance.

In proposing yet another approach to the treatment of social anxiety, it is important to ask this question: "What has to happen in order for this person to change?" The answer, according to the analysis presented here, is that he or she must be helped to break out of the self-preoccupation that is the source of resistive paralysis. Thus, the therapeutic strategy attempts to work with the resistance through inversion. That is, clients are helped to break out of their obsessive self-awareness by attempting to operate in an exaggerated, volitional other-centred style (i.e., think, feel, and perform). By attending differently to the social world, clients are helped to surrender themselves to disequilibrium, so that reorganisation and accommodation can occur. The specific medium utilised to achieve this objective is social skills training, a performance-based approach to initiating change.

In a group therapy format, clients are encouraged, taught, and given opportunities to practise insistent, willed, and even exaggerated attention towards others so that a decreased need for the exercise of external awareness will eventually be possible. Once established, the vigilant exercise of other-centred awareness, also meta-cognitively mediated, is less important, and the individual is readily able to integrate attentional needs.

Two sets of skills are basic ingredients in decentring: responding skills and initiating skills. In the area of responsiveness, therapy focuses on developing empathy. In part, this effort serves to enhance interpersonal sensitivity. But the primary objective of this therapeutic task is to short-circuit the self-centred attentional style. The basic skill set that underlies empathy, of course, is listening effectively. Accordingly, early interventions here emphasise the learning and practice of good listening. Structured group activities are extremely useful in this regard. Initiative basically involves seeing a goal and going after it. Clients are strongly encouraged to approach social opportunities as a testing ground for practising newly acquired interpersonal skills. This includes attempts to marshal "group process" in order to bolster self-confidence. Here, we are referring to the unique features of group interaction that contribute to feelings of commonality, support, and desire to change. Positive attitudes, affective change, and behavioural progress are identified, highlighted, and reinforced.

Socially anxious clients are thus trained to attend differently to interpersonal transactions. The techniques employed are those of traditional social skills training. The objective, however, is to channel perceptions and cognitions externally and to focus on the other person. Through this mechanism, individuals develop the means for improved control of their affective experience in social discourse. They are helped to be more attentive, expressive, and observant of others and to practise emotional responding. The salubrious results of such training occur through the effective blocking of self-centred meta-cognitions in order to conduct oneself as an other-centred interactionist. This is a performance-based treatment method derived from a cognitive analysis of social anxiety.

Assessment

Several excellent reviews of current assessment procedures specifically addressing social anxiety have now been published, and these permit a potentially useful comparison to be drawn between criticisms of these procedures, on the one hand, and current thinking in the field of personality assessment, on the other. Whereas it is now generally accepted that traditional approaches to personality assessment have promulgated a narrow, overly simplistic view of psychological functioning that has long outlived its usefulness (Mischel, 1968), behavioural strategies also suffer from limitations. Unidimensional conceptualisations of behaviour, regardless of their particular bias, focus only on the measurement of a single set of variables, virtually ignoring the influence of additional factors of importance.

The measurement approach currently employed in our research emphasises multiple determinants. This approach assumes that behavioural problems like social anxiety are multidimensional in nature and, as a result, pose obvious problems regarding the choice of an appropriate measurement strategy. As Fiske (1971) has pointed out, it is unlikely that any broad personality construct can adequately be assessed by a single measurement technique. Rather, he suggests an approach that differentiates global, unitary personality constructs in terms of smaller, more conceptually homogeneous sub-constructs, each of which has its separate measurement instruments. The "conceptual operational" strategy proposed by Fiske (1971) provides a framework within which to conceptualise and operationalise the multivariate concepts underlying the meta-cognitive model of social anxiety.

Another relevant principle from personality theory that has been incorporated into recent assessment approaches in our laboratory advocates the use of multiple methods of measurement. Convergence of evidence from various methods (including self-report, observer rating, behavioural and physiological data) lends greater confidence to the validity of findings pertaining to the construct being assessed. The multitrait/multi-method approach (Campbell & Fiske, 1959) is readily implemented in clinical research settings because of the accessibility of a wide variety of measurement techniques. In addition, as we shall shortly point out, the implications for treatment planning and evaluation pose potentially fruitful opportunities, especially with respect to matching or individually tailoring interventions to identified needs and deficits (Hartman, Krywonis, & Morrison, 1988).

Self-report methods and measures

Self-report indices of social anxiety that we employ include measures designed to assess each component process operative in interpersonal dysfunction. The Social Avoidance and Distress (SAD) and Fear of Negative Evaluation (FNE) scales developed and standardised by Watson and Friend (1969) are used as subjective indices of general interpersonal discomfort (anxious arousal as well as avoidance) and cognitive evaluative impairment, respectively. A review of data bearing on the psychometric properties of these scales suggests that both the SAD and FNE have adequate reliability and discriminant validity to support their use as screening and outcome measures. Both questionnaires list statements to which subjects respond "True" or "False". The SAD questionnaire contains 28 items concerning feelings of anxiety in the presence of others; for example: "I find it easy to relax with other people". "I often find social occasions upsetting". The FNE contains 30 items relating to self-perception and the perceptions of others, such as these: "I rarely worry about seeming foolish to others". "I am afraid that others will not approve of me". "I brood about the opinions my friends have of me". The wording of positive and negative statements is balanced in order to limit the effects of response set.

A broad-range, situationally specific self-report measure of skill level or social confidence, derived from the 105-item Social Anxiety Inventory (Curran, Corriveau, Monti, & Hagerman, 1980; Richardson & Tasto, 1976), is also administered to each subject. Items consist of descriptions of specific social situations, and respondents are asked to rate each situation on a Likert scale with respect to the degree of skill competency they would display. That is, subjects are asked to rate how skilfully they would handle the situations described in the items. The property of situational specificity with respect to skill level is especially important, because evidence suggests that individuals may, for example, be skilful in an intimate one-to-one encounter but be incompetent in a large social gathering (Eisler, Hersen, Miller, & Blanchard, 1975). Furthermore, situationally specific self-report measures of social skill have been found to show better correspondence with behavioural measures (McFall, 1982).

Factor analyses of anxiety components in the Social Anxiety Inventory (Richardson & Tasto, 1976) produced seven scales: (1) disapproval or criticism of others (e.g., "Someone acts as if he or she dislikes you"); (2) social assertiveness and visibility (e.g., "being interviewed for a job"); (3) confrontation and anger expression (e.g., "declining an invitation for a date or to a party"); (4) heterosexual contact (e.g., "caressing a member of the opposite sex all over; you are both nude"); (5) intimacy and interpersonal warmth (e.g., "telling someone that you really like them a lot"); (6) conflict with or rejection by parents (e.g., "Your mother or father acts cold towards you"); (7) interpersonal loss (e.g., "A good friend does or says something that hurts your feelings"). The reader may note, parenthetically, the obvious correspondence between these empirically derived factors and the discussion earlier in this chapter of the characterological features frequently evidenced by individuals suffering from social anxiety.

With respect to skill level, four factors appear to account for most of the variance (Curran et al., 1980): (1) social assertiveness and visibility, (2) the heterosexual contact scale, and (3) the intimacy and interpersonal warmth scale. A fourth factor dealing with negative emotional states (criticism, anger, conflict, rejection, or loss) emerges as well, with items loading on this skill factor from scales one (disapproval or criticism of others), three (confrontation and anger expression), six (conflict with or rejection by parents) and seven (interpersonal loss). In our work we have collapsed these factors into a single scale, and the entire questionnaire, which we refer to as the Social Skill Inventory (SSI), has been shortened to a 40-item version.

The tendency to experience maladaptive self-awareness as a trait that is stable across situations is assessed in our research with a self-report measure developed by Christensen (1982): the Self-consciousness Scale (SCS). The reliability and validity of the scale have been reported. Persons rated high in maladaptive self-consciousness, as measured by the SCS, were rated by their peers as more socially inadequate. In a dyadic interaction, high SCS scorers exhibited more ineffective social behaviour, reduced sensitivity to partners, and heightened self-perception of inadequacy (Christensen, 1982). Subjects are asked to rate each of 25 items describing a wide range of social and public situations on a 5-point scale (1 = not at all self-conscious, and 5 = very self-conscious).

The final self-report measure that is employed in our assessment protocol is the State-Trait Anxiety Inventory (STAI), From X-2 (Spielberger, Gorsuch, & Lushene, 1970). This scale is administered in order to obtain a more general measure of trait anxiety, of which social anxiety is considered a subset.

Behavioural methods and measures

Simulation or role-play procedures, following Wilson, Abrams, and Lipscomb (1980), may be used to assess social interaction and its physiological correlates. In our laboratory, the subject is comfortably seated in an armchair. A heart-rate-recording optical sensor is attached to the middle finger of the non-dominant hand. A second chair for a confederate is positioned directly in front of the subject at a distance of 5 feet. Behind the chair, a closed-circuit television camera is visible. The subject is first asked to indicate current level of anxiety on a scale from 0 (no anxiety) to 4 (extremely anxious). This is taken as the interaction baseline anxiety rating (AR). Next, the subject is informed that the session is being videotaped. He or she is requested to relax and await further instructions. Once the subject has settled down, four 10-sec heart rate samples, taken every 30 sec, are recorded as the base-rate measure. Preliminary instructions then describe the experimental task, which is speaking to an opposite-sex assistant for a few minutes with a view to making as favourable an impression as possible. The subject is informed that the assistant is a confederate in that he or she has been instructed to listen attentively, but not to talk during the interaction. The subject is instructed to avoid talking about the recording of the conversation. Two minutes later, the subject is instructed that the assistant will now enter the room, that he or she is to remain seated, and that he or she is not to converse with the assistant until told to begin. One minute after the interaction ends, the confederate leaves the room. The subject then completes two post-interaction questionnaires to be described later.

Previous research has raised questions about the validity of role-play procedures (Bellack, Hersen, & Lamparski, 1979a; Bellack, Hersen, & Turner, 1979b). Consequently, several strategies have been incorporated into the social interaction procedure in order to increase the likelihood that responses will reflect in vivo social functioning: (1) The situation is carefully designed to be relevant to the subject's naturalistic setting (a quasi-lounge facility is employed). (2) The task is relatively unstructured and thus more closely resembles real-life interactions. (3) Before enacting the scenario, subjects are asked if they can imagine themselves in the situation. If not, slight modifications are made to make it more realistic. (4) The enactments are extended, if necessary, through confederate prompts in order to increase realism.

Behavioural ratings include scoring of the subject's verbalisations for the percentage of time of the session during which the subject is speaking. In addition, videotape recordings of subjects during the social interaction are rated by judges for anxiety and other interpersonal cues based on fairly global perceptions of verbal and non-verbal behaviour.

Immediately after the interaction with the confederate, the subject is requested to again indicate his or her current level of anxiety on a 5-point scale. The subject is then requested to complete the Social Anxiety Thoughts (SAT) questionnaire (Hartman, 1984) as a self-report measure of dysfunctional self-statements and irrational thinking associated with the anticipation or experience of a stressful social interaction.

Finally, subjects complete the Exner (1973) Self-Focus Sentence Completion Test (SFSC) as an index of self-centredness induced by participating in an anxiety-provoking social interaction. The SFSC is a 30-item sentence-completion blank in which most of the items contain a self-reference (I, my, me, and so forth). It has been found to provide a useful index of egocentricity as a response orientation or style. Scores of particular interest are the S/E ratio (responses judged to be self-focusing versus those that are clearly external-world-oriented) and Sn (a subset of S representing those self-focusing responses that are negative in content). Exner (1973) reported data on scoring reliabilities with different groups of judges (graduate students in psychology, undergraduate psychology majors, secretarial staff, and Ph.D. clinical psychologists) indicating that whereas some inter-scorer differences do exist, they are generally modest

Table 12.1. *Mean scores on the screening battery and intake measures*

Screening battery	SA group	NSA group	t
SAD	19.2	7.9	8.41***
FNE	23.6	12.5	6.60***
STAI			
Trait sub-scale	58.9	42.5	6.60***
State sub-scale	55.3	37.0	7.01***
Intake measures			
Average annual income (thousand Canadian			
dollars)	18.3	25.9	−2.08*
Alcohol dependence scale	24.3	16.5	2.76**

*$p < .05$; **$p < .01$; ***$p < .0001$.

and within acceptable limits. Validation data on the SFSC show that it can discriminate among a variety of groups, both psychiatric and non-psychiatric. The S/E and Sn scores have been shown to change significantly with successful treatment in three separate studies with a pre-intervention/post-intervention design. The SFSC has also been found to have predictive validity in follow-up studies of service performance among Peace Corps volunteers. Finally, a third group of studies has shown SFSC performance to have concurrent validity with specific observed behaviours in interview and mirror-viewing situations.

Testing a model of social anxiety with problem drinkers

Although it has long been recognised that physiological arousal, negative cognitions, and behavioural factors are important mediators of social anxiety, it is unclear what role each plays with respect to the development, maintenance, and cessation of problem drinking. The assessment approach outlined here attempts to simultaneously assess behavioural, cognitive, and physiological reactivitiy in a stressful social situation. In as much as these parameters do not necessarily covary (Lang, 1968), this type of simultaneous situational assessment can be compared with trait-like, self-descriptive data in order to arrive at a more complete understanding of social anxiety in problem drinking.

Subjects for this assessment research were male patients seeking treatment for alcohol-related problems in the Clinical Institute of the Addiction Research Foundation in Toronto. Seventeen subjects who scored above the established cut-off scores indicative of clinical levels of anxiety on each measure of the screening battery (Table 12.1) composed the socially anxious (SA) group. Similarly, 59 subjects who scored below the cut-off scores on this same battery made up the group who were not socially anxious (NSA). Mean scores on the screening battery are listed in Table 12.1. As indicated by these scores, the level of social anxiety reported by individuals in the SA group represented a clinically significant problem. The individuals ranged in age from 21 to 61 years, with a mean of 38.7 years. The groups were equivalent with regard to age, race, years of education, age at first use of alcohol, and alcohol consumption (e.g., number of days since last drink at time of assessment, or number of drinking days in 2 months prior to assessment). There was no difference between the SA and NSA groups with regard to WAIS Vocabulary and Digit Symbol sub-tests. The NSA group reported a higher average income, and SA subjects showed greater alcohol dependence and negative impact of drinking on work, family, and personal adjustment.

The screening battery was composed of three inventories: the SAD (Watson & Friend, 1969), the FNE (Watson & Friend, 1969), and the STAI (Spielberger et al., 1970). Mean scores on the test battery for each group are shown in Table 12.1.

Each subject participated in a situational assessment designed to measure various parameters of social anxiety before, during, and following an unstructured, interpersonal interaction with an opposite-sex confederate. During this procedure, the level of physiological arousal, type of cognitions, and behavioural manifestations of skill and anxiety were monitored.

The tendency to experience maladaptive self-awareness as a trait that is stable across social situations was assessed using a self-report measure developed by Christensen (1982), the SCS, which was administered prior to the role-play assessment.

A version of the Social Anxiety Inventory (SAI) was administered to each subject prior to the role-play task (Curran et al., 1980; Richardson & Tasto, 1976). Finally, the subjects rated their levels of state anxiety before and after completion of the role-play task using a 5-point "fear thermometer", with 1 indicating complete calm, and 5 indicating a feeling of extreme anxiety.

Physiological reactivity was monitored continuously throughout participation in the behavioural task. Heart rate (HR) was measured with a "clip" sensor attached to the index finger of the non-dominant hand and was quantified on the basis of the average digital output of a cardiotachometer (Autogenic Systems) for each 10-sec interval throughout the role-play assessment.

The subject's performance during the role-play task was videotaped and rated by independent judges blind to group assignment. The behaviours were rated on 10-point qualitative scales developed by Trower, Bryant, and Argyle (1978) and included intonation, speech loudness, gaze, and overall skill. The scales were anchored with a rating of 10 indicating extreme inadequacy or high observed anxiety on that particular variable, and 1 indicating a high level of ability or a feeling of complete calm. The scales employed in this study had been used extensively in previous assessments of social skill (Wilson et al., 1980). In the analysis reported here, a global score was computed from the ratings by averaging over the 10 scales for both observers with each subject.

Immediately after the interaction with the confederate, each subject completed the Social Anxiety Thoughts (SAT-21) questionnaire developed by Hartman (1984) as a self-report measure of dysfunctional self-statements and irrational thinking associated with the experience of a stressful social situation. Finally, the Exner (1973) SFSC was used as an index of self-centredness induced by participating in an anxiety-provoking social interaction.

Self-consciousness, as measured by the SCS, was considerably higher within the SA group. Those subjects also estimated their levels of skill to be significantly lower than did the NSA group with respect to situations requiring social assertiveness, intimacy, and expression of negative emotion. Heterosexual contact, by comparison, was not perceived to be anxiety-provoking by highly socially anxious males. There were differences in pre-task levels of anxiety reported by SA subjects by comparison with NSA subjects that were not evident following the completion of the role-play procedure.

Mean HR data for the two groups at three different times during the role-play are shown in Table 12.2. The base line represents the final 10-sec interval prior to the confederate's entrance. The peak stress interval represents the first 10-sec period of the simulated interaction, and post-stress represents the final 10-sec period of talking. Differences in physiological reactivity between the two groups at each measurement period were in the expected direction, but not significant.

Group differences were not noted for judges' ratings of overall skill and anxiety during the unstructured role-play. The SA group was not perceived to be less skilful during the interaction than the NSA group.

The SA group experienced significantly more negative thoughts during the opposite-sex interaction. Though they did not engage in more self-focusing versus other-focusing during the interaction, to the extent that they did focus on themselves they were more likely to do so negatively. In contrast, the NSA group was more likely to exhibit an external focus of awareness in the context of the role-play task.

It is evident from the foregoing analyses that male problem drinkers exhibiting social anxiety manifest differences in self-perceived levels of

Table 12.2. *Differences in self-report, physiological reactivity, behaviour, and cognition between the SA and NSA groups*

Variable	SA Group	NSA Group	t
Self-report			
SCS	65.1	50.2	3.70**
SAI			
Social assertiveness	32.7	26.5	4.62**
Heterosexual contact	18.4	18.3	n.s.
Intimacy	33.3	27.6	2.99**
Negative emotion	37.9	31.8	3.81**
State Anxiety			
Rating			
Pre-task	2.3	1.5	2.84*
Post-task	1.9	1.3	n.s.
Physiological reactivity			
Base line	83.0	77.9	n.s.
Peak stress	92.4	88.5	n.s.
Post-stress	88.7	83.7	n.s.
Behaviour			
Average performance rating	4.37	4.08	n.s.
Cognition			
SAT-21	65.4	51.8	3.90**
SFSC			
Self-focus	6.7	7.5	n.s.
Negative self-focus	9.3	6.9	2.72*
External focus	7.0	10.0	−2.69*

$*p < .05; **p < .001.$

social skill and overall self-consciousness. These individuals operate cognitively with a highly sensitive editing apparatus; they tune themselves in and the environment out. To the extent that attention to external stimuli (particularly the other person or persons in a social interaction) occurs, it is self-focused, that is, looking for subtle indicators of rejection, disapproval, or negative evaluation. Not surprisingly, SA subjects were more anxious prior to engaging in social discourse.

The fact that interaction in the role-play task did not elicit significant differences between the groups in physiological arousal or behavioural skill is therefore significant. Despite evidence of perceived inability to cope, negative self-esteem, and heightened dispositional self-awareness, all of which contribute to the distress experienced during social encounters, these individuals are still able to perform effectively and without excessive physiological arousal. These findings lend further support to the seemingly paramount nature of a certain class of cognitive events – negative self-awareness in higher-order mental processes – as critical mediators of social anxiety and interpersonal malaise. Conceptual models that highlight meta-cognitive self-awareness in social anxiety (Hartman, 1983, 1986) are consistent with these descriptive data.

In summary, the purpose of this investigation was to determine if the level of physiological arousal, the type of cognition, and behavioural performances in social situations differed in the SA and NSA groups of male problem drinkers. The results indicate that the socially anxious do report more negative evaluatory cognitions and experience considerably greater negative self-awareness during a role-play interaction with an opposite-sex confederate. They do not, however, demonstrate higher levels of physiological arousal, nor are they perceived to be less skilful by independent evaluators. Still, the socially anxious perceive themselves to be less skilful (a pejorative self-efficacy appraisal) and to develop heightened self-consciousness as a prevailing personality trait that comes to characterise their presentations across a range of interpersonal situations. Future studies will be required in order to evaluate the manner in which relationships between response systems interact with treatment outcome. Clinical research using measures sensitive to change across independent response systems should, over time, contribute to better matching of treatment strategies for mitigating social anxiety in different client groups.

Treatment

A brief description of other-centred therapy has already been presented. Decentring interventions are designed to promote thinking and perceptual operations that are predominantly externally focused. The objective is to alleviate arousal and impairment arising from maladaptive self-awareness in social situations.

Cognitive, behavioural, and physiological strategies

The assumption that social anxiety is due to an inadequate repertoire of interpersonal behaviours has led to response acquisition approaches to treatment. An impressive collection of empirical studies attests to the efficacy of social skills training with respect to improved social competence and reduced social anxiety.

Of course, relaxation training has featured prominently in the behavioural treatment of social anxiety. It is important to note that relaxation as an active coping technique may enhance the individual's perception of personal control, which in turn will mediate improved social performance. Thus, simply providing alternative coping responses for use in interpersonal stress situations involving diminished perceived control may be an effective treatment for social anxiety. Along these lines, Klajner, Hartman, and Sobell (1984) have discussed the relationship among anxiety, control, and relaxation in the treatment of substance abuse.

Finally, attempts to modify faulty thought patterns are based on the premise that maladaptive cognitions mediate social anxiety and stress. Teaching new and appropriate self-statements that emphasise coping and adaptation (Meichenbaum, 1977) may facilitate more rational thought patterns, which in turn will improve social functioning. Alternatively, cognitive restructuring methods in general, and self-instructional training in particular, will directly address the individual's perceptions of control in stressful social interactions. Thus, enhanced self-efficacy may be the crucial mechanism mediating clinical improvement.

There is now a large and still growing literature attesting to the appropriateness and effectiveness of these treatment procedures. Except for other-centred therapy as a remedial technique, we have offered little in the way of innovative strategies. In the remainder of this section, therefore, an attempt will be made to elaborate further on a "clinical" orientation to treatment in which social anxiety is viewed within the context of personality structure.

An integrated, social psychological approach

First, our approach to therapy with socially anxious clients emphasises the importance of establishing a therapeutic relationship based on genuine trust. A minimum of six individual sessions is necessary prior to starting group therapy. Therapists are encouraged not to push matters too hard or too fast, somewhat inconsistent with a behaviourally oriented approach. Gradually, attention is turned to the client's positive attributes, addressing these as a means of building confidence and feelings of self-worth. This is a slow and arduous process, one that clients frequently resist. Long-standing anxieties, resentments, and perceived inadequacies need to be reworked. Typically, cognitive restructuring methods are employed in order to counteract the attributional roots of impaired self-esteem and, in time, to enable the client to reappraise these feelings more objectively.

Clients are assisted in arranging for a rewarding environment and facilitating the discovery of opportunities to enhance self-worth. "Homework" assignments involving social exposure are gently and carefully prescribed in a supportive therapeutic approach. Here, too, methods of cognitive reorientation designed to alter erroneous self-attitudes and distorted social expectancies come into play.

Early parental sensitisation frequently emerges as an important ingredient in the socially anxious client's view of himself or herself as psychologically inadequate. Where appropriate, family techniques can be usefully employed to moderate destructive patterns of communication that contribute to or intensify clients' problems, especially adolescent and young adult clients. Individually, therapy attempts to foster awareness, understanding, and, eventually, acceptance of developmental experiences that set the stage for a fragile identity and feelings of unworthiness. Finally, group therapy is an excellent medium for learning new attitudes and skills in a more benign and accepting social setting than is normally encountered.

Discussion and conclusions

Any attempt to systematically map the diverse life experiences that may give rise to social anxiety would be not only futile but also misleading. It is not so much the concrete events themselves nor the timing, setting, or source of these events that give them meaning. Rather, it is the message these experiences convey to the individual that is crucial. Diverse though they may be, these experiences possess one crucial theme in common: They depreciate the individual's sense of self-esteem through either explicit or implicit rejection, humiliation, or denigration. Moreover, repeated exposure to such events not only fosters a deflated sense of self-worth but also tends, ultimately, to produce the affective dysphoria, cognitive impairment, behavioural inadequacy, and active interpersonal avoidance so characteristic of social anxiety.

A primary source of these derogating experiences is parental rejection and depreciation. As a consequence of being reared in a family setting in which they are belittled, abandoned, and censured, these children learn to devalue themselves, and hence they develop little or no sense of self-worth. Opportunities for enhancing competencies and for developing effective social skills may remain intact, however, unless they experience rejection, isolation, or the devastating ridicule that so often occurs when children first encounter the challenge of peer group activities. Feelings of loneliness and inadequacy are then compounded by severe self-judgements of personal inferiority and unattractiveness.

To make matters worse, the coping manoeuvres utilised by socially anxious individuals prove to be self-defeating. They are painfully alert to signs of deception, humiliation, and depreciation. This hypersensitivity functions well in the service of self-protection, but fosters a deepening of social impairment and avoidance. As a result of extensive scanning of the environment, socially anxious individuals actually increase the likelihood that they will encounter precisely those stimuli they wish most to avoid. Their defensive vigilance allows them to pick up, transform, and distort what most people would overlook, thus intensifying rather than diminishing their anxiety. As a result, they become preoccupied with meta-cognitive fixations. By upsetting the smooth and logical pattern of perceptual and thought processes, meta-cognitive self-awareness further impairs efficient and rational social performance. No longer can one attend to the most salient features of the environment, nor can one focus on thoughts or respond rationally. Moreover, one cannot learn new ways to handle and resolve interpersonal difficulties, because the meta-cognitive process results in cluttered and scattered cognitive, affective, and behavioural mediation. Social communication takes on a tangential and unrealistic quality, and the individual begins to behave in an erratic and halting manner. The painful result is tremendous inner turmoil, impaired performance, and distorted thoughts. Eventually, social situations are avoided.

In summary, this chapter has attempted to pursue an understanding of social anxiety based on intrapersonal as well as interpersonal factors. Assessment and treatment procedures suggested by such an approach have been outlined. Although the measurement and intervention strategies identified here are empirically based and behaviourally oriented, the thrust of the analysis has been to emphasise a psychological understanding of the person. Accordingly, it is proposed that though we all possess psychological dynamics, some choose not to acknowledge them. For the psychological therapist, however, failure to recognise the importance of intrapersonal factors in the mediation of behaviour constitutes a professional disserve.

REFERENCES

American Psychiatric Association. (1980). *Diagnostic and statistical manual of mental disorders* (3rd ed.). Washington, DC: APA.

Bellack, A. S., Hersen, M., & Lamparski, D. (1979a). Role-playing tests for assessing social skills: Are they valid? Are they useful? *Journal of Consulting and Clinical Psychology, 47,* 335–342.

Bellack, A. S., Hersen, M., & Turner, S. M. (1979b). Relationship of role-playing and knowledge of appropriate behavior to assertion in the natural environment. *Journal of Consulting and Clinical Psychology, 47,* 16–24.

Campbell, D. T., & Fiske, D. W. (1959). Convergent and discriminant validation by the multitrait-multimethod matrix. *Psychological Bulletin, 56,* 81–105.

Christensen, D. (1982). The relationship between self-consciousness and interpersonal effectiveness and a new scale to measure individual differences in self-consciousness. *Personality and Individual Differences, 3,* 177–188.

Curran, J. P., Corriveau, D. P., Monti, P. N., & Hagerman, S. B. (1980). Social skill and social anxiety. *Behavior Modification, 4,* 493–512.

Eisler, R. M., Hersen, M., Miller, P. M., & Blanchard, E. B. (1975). Situational determinants of assertive behaviors. *Journal of Consulting and Clinical Psychology, 43,* 330–340.

Exner, J. E. (1973). The Self Focus Sentence Completion Test: A study of egocentricity. *Journal of Personality Assessment, 37,* 437–455.

Fiske, D. W. (1971). *Measuring the concepts of personality.* Chicago: Aldine.

Hartman, L. M. (1983). A metacognitive model of social anxiety: Implications for treatment. *Clinical Psychology Review, 3,* 435–456.

Hartman, L. M. (1984). Cognitive components of social anxiety. *Journal of Clinical Psychology, 40,* 137–139.

Hartman, L. M. (1986). Social anxiety, problem drinking and self-awareness. In L. M. Hartman & K. R. Blankstein (Eds.), *Perception of self in emotional disorder and psychotherapy* (pp. 265–282). New York: Plenum Press.

Hartman, L. M., Krywonis, M., & Morrison, E. (1988). Psychological factors and health-related behaviour change: Preliminary findings from a controlled clinical trial. *Canadian Family Physician, 34,* 1045–1050.

Klajner, F., Hartman, L. M., & Sobell, M. B. (1984). Treatment of substance abuse by relaxation training. *Addictive Behaviors, 9,* 41–55.

Klein, D. F. (1970). Psychotropic drugs and the regulation of behavioral activation in psychiatric illness. In W. L. Smith (Ed.), *Drugs and cerebral function* (pp. 69–81). Springfield, IL: Thomas.

Lang, N. J. (1968). Fear reduction and fear behavior: Problems in treating a construct. In J. M. Shlien (Ed.), *Research in psychotherapy* (Vol. 3, pp. 90–102). Washington, DC: American Psychological Association.

McFall, R. N. (1982). A review and reformulation of the concept of social skills. *Journal of Behavioral Assessment, 4,* 1–33.

Meichenbaum, D. (1977). *Cognitive behavior modification: An integrative approach.* New York: Plenum Press.

Millon, T., & Millon, R. (1974). *Abnormal behavior and personality.* Philadelphia: Saunders.

Mischel, W. (1968). *Personality and assessment.* New York: Wiley.

Richardon, F. C., & Tasto, D. L. (1976). Development and factor analysis of a social anxiety inventory. *Behavior Therapy, 7,* 453–462.

Spielberger, C. D., Gorsuch, R. L., & Lushene, R. E. (1970) *The state–trait anxiety inventory: Test manual for Form X.* Palo Alto, CA: Consulting Psychologists Press.

Trower, P., Byrant, B., & Argyle, M. (1978). *Social skills and mental health.* Pittsburgh: University of Pittsburgh Press.

Turner, S. M., Beidel, P. C., Dancu, C. V., & Keys, D. J. (1986). Psychopathology of social phobia and comparison to avoidant personality disorder. *Journal of Abnormal Psychology, 95,* 389–394.

Watson, D., & Friend, R. (1969). Measurement of social-evaluative anxiety. *Journal of Consulting and Clinical Psychology, 33,* 448–457.

Wilson, G. T., Abrams, D. B., & Lipscomb, T. R. (1980). Effects of intoxication levels and drinking pattern on social anxiety in men. *Journal of Studies on Alcohol, 41,* 250–264.

Name index

Subject index

embarrassability, 3, 7, 26, 29, 30, 79, 92, 93, 112, 126, 190, 192, 201, 323
embarrassed smiling, 5, 6, 100–2, 113; *see also* smiling
embarrassment
  contagious, 30
  cross-cultural studies, 6, 88, 97, 190, 192, 206, 213, 219–26
  in different languages, 7, 183–4, 186, 230–1, 248
  empathic, 30
  vs. shame, 8, 40, 45, 47, 62, 63, 77, 183–9, 194, 195, 205, 206, 230, 248–9
  vs. shyness, 36, 39, 47, 54, 78–81, 93–4, 194, 198–9
  vicarious, 4, 30, 202
empathic embarrassment, 30
excuses, 31, 32, 35, 198, 293, 298, 302–4

facework, 31, 35, 36, 135, 187, 188, 200, 202, 207
facial expression, 38, 41, 87, 95, 108, 159, 163, 208, 209, 212, 260
  cross-cultural studies, 38, 90
facial feedback hypothesis, 208, 226
fear, 2, 37–44, 49, 63, 65, 67, 77, 90, 144, 148, 149, 152, 153, 170, 183, 203, 233, 242, 257, 261, 263, 264, 268, 269, 275, 278, 280, 323, 339
Fear of Negative Evaluation scale, 40, 108, 343–4, 347–8
fearful shyness, 42, 49, 78, 324–6
fluster, 4, 30, 187, 188, 192, 194
foolishness, 4, 37, 344

gaze avoidance, 5, 6, 37, 38, 88, 95–109, 113, 148, 194, 208, 210, 222, 225, 226, 239, 241, 243, 245, 246, 259
guilt, 2, 12, 37, 39–44, 51, 65, 70, 119, 124, 134, 135, 137, 138, 164, 184, 232, 240, 241

hedonic mode (of social behaviour), 9, 145, 147, 149, 150, 153, 158, 172
helping behaviour, 70, 121, 134–6, 159
humiliation, 2, 5, 39–44, 165, 169, 339, 353

ideal self, 11, 39, 121, 124, 162, 163, 164, 166
identity, 22, 29, 34, 52, 60, 72, 74, 162, 164, 165, 166, 201, 286, 294, 324, 340, 363
impression management, *see* self-presentation
indignation, 191
inferiority feelings, 164, 166, 167, 244, 245, 261, 353
inhibition, 3, 35, 59, 73, 90, 103, 119, 121,

138, 151, 258, 268, 274, 275, 280, 315, 317–22, 324
interaction anxiousness, 319
introversion, 19, 111, 323
irrational thought patterns, 258–60, 263, 268, 270, 271, 278, 281, 308, 327, 346, 349
iterated emotions, 200

labelling, 21, 39, 62, 70, 76, 80, 208, 209, 211, 264, 317
loneliness, 151, 318–19, 323, 328, 353

meta-cognition, 5, 12, 13, 328, 341–3, 351, 354
meta-communication, 273–5
meta-shame, 242
micro-teaching, 272, 275–7
misattribution, 111, 300
modesty, 6, 8, 14, 36, 157, 183, 188–91, 194–9, 202–4, 239, 247–9, 250, 257, 295
mortification, 2, 165

narcissism, 9, 34, 50, 52, 53, 163, 171, 319
nervousness, 33, 78, 79, 81–2, 208, 322

poise, 29, 30, 33, 34, 188, 191, 194, 307
private self, 11, 24, 52, 131, 162–9
private self-awareness, 11, 23, 67, 130
private self-consciousness, 34, 40, 125–6, 131, 323
Private Self-consciousness scale, 23, 125–6
private shyness, 20
protective self-presentation, 10, 34–5, 60, 73, 111, 287–91, 296, 299, 306, 308, 328
public self, 11, 24, 52, 131, 162, 164
public self-awareness, 11, 12, 14, 23, 24, 26, 27, 28, 97
public self-consciousness, 26, 34, 40, 49, 125–6, 130, 131, 132
Public Self-consciousness scale, 23, 26, 27, 125–6, 130, 131, 295
public shyness, 20
public speaking, 73, 161, 170

regret, 233, 247
reticence, 25, 35, 319

sadness, 41, 200
safety system, 145, 150, 153–5, 161, 168, 169
self, *see* ideal self; private self; public self
self-awareness, 3, 12, 23, 24, 51, 53, 67, 119–39, 144, 164, 201, 210, 212, 218, 239, 240, 329, 338, 341, 348, 350, 351